Collective Redress and EU Competition Law

Exploring obstacles to effective compensation of victims of competition infringements, this book categorises the types of victims harmed and the types of losses arising from these infringements to identify to what extent there is a need for enhanced private competition law enforcement in the European Union (EU) and the best way to address this need. It shows that there is a genuine need for facilitating consumer damages actions and that consumer claims are the only claims that can be pursued in a collective redress action. In order to compensate consumers and overcome barriers to effective enforcement of their right to damages, it structures a collective redress action for consumers by considering the following elements: *i.* the formation of the group, *ii.* the type of representative party, *iii.* funding mechanisms and *iv.* calculation and distribution of damages.

Dr Eda Şahin is a lecturer at the EU School of Law. She held business administration and law degrees from the University of Istanbul, Turkey. Eda was admitted to Istanbul Bar in 2007. She held an LLM in Competition Law and Policy from the University of East Anglia, Norwich, UK. Her LLM thesis analysed the passing-on defence in competition law in the EU, US and Turkey. She was awarded a Doctorate in Law from Queen Mary, University of London in 2016. After her PhD graduation, she returned to Turkey, and started working as a lecturer in law at a public university in order to serve her compulsory work in return for the-Turkish Ministry of National Education's scholarship she received to pursue her doctorate in the UK. In her current position as a lecturer, she is responsible for teaching Law of Obligations and Property Law at the undergraduate level and UK Contract Law and Family Law at the postgraduate level.

Routledge Research in Competition Law

Available titles in this series include:

The Internationalisation of Competition Rules
Brendan J. Sweeney

Antitrust Federalism in the EU and the US
Firat Cengiz

Competition and Regulation in the Airline Industry
Puppets in Chaos
Steven Truxal

Forthcoming titles in this series include:

Merger Control in Post-Communist Countries
EC Merger Regulation in Small Market Economies
Jurgita Malinauskaite

Merger Control in Europe
The Gap In The ECMR And National Merger Legislations
Ioannis Kokkoris

Harmonising Regulatory and Antitrust Regimes for International Air Transport
Jan Walulik

Collective Redress and EU Competition Law
Eda Şahin

Competition Policy and Network Industries
Structural Separation in the Telecommunications Sector
Pierluigi Congedo

Collective Redress and EU Competition Law

Eda Şahin

Routledge
Taylor & Francis Group
LONDON AND NEW YORK

First published 2019
by Routledge
2 Park Square, Milton Park, Abingdon, Oxon OX14 4RN

and by Routledge
605 Third Avenue, New York, NY 10017

First issued in paperback 2021

Routledge is an imprint of the Taylor & Francis Group, an informa business

Publisher's Note
The publisher has gone to great lengths to ensure the quality of this reprint but points out that some imperfections in the original copies may be apparent.

British Library Cataloguing-in-Publication Data
A catalogue record for this book is available from the British Library

Library of Congress Cataloging-in-Publication Data
Names: Sahin, Eda.
Title: Collective redress and EU competition law / Eda Sahin.
Description: Abingdon, Oxon ; New York, NY : Routledge, 2019. |
Series: Routledge research in competition law | Based on author's thesis (doctoral - Queen Mary University of London, 2016) issued under title: Collective redress mechanisms for consumer damages claims. |
Includes bibliographical references and index.
Identifiers: LCCN 2018035935 | ISBN 9781138478442 (hbk)
Subjects: LCSH: Antitrust law--European Union countries. | Class actions (Civil procedure)--European Union countries.
Classification: LCC KJE6530 .S24 2019 | DDC 343.2407/21--dc23
LC record available at https://lccn.loc.gov/2018035935

Typeset in Galliard
by Taylor & Francis Books

ISBN 13: 978-1-03-224167-8 (pbk)
ISBN 13: 978-1-138-47844-2 (hbk)

DOI: 10.4324/9781351068727

Contents

Preface

The introduction of a collective redress action was discussed as part of a reform process concerning enhancement of private competition law enforcement in the EU. The lack of a collective redress action was regarded as one of the obstacles that hampered the exercise of the right to damages and resulting in victims of competition infringements to rarely seek compensation. This procedural tool allows the bundling of the claims of similarly situated numerous persons to be dealt with in a single lawsuit, by design diverging from the traditional individualistic litigation and relying upon representation. The main question of this book concerns how to design a collective redress action for consumer damages claims arising from EU competition infringements. The issue has not to date been approached in a systematic and structured fashion that analyses the suitability of the damages claims of victims to resolution in a collective redress action and the design of each element of this action in this respect. To this end, this book demonstrates that both the purpose and working principle of a collective redress action are well suited to address consumer claims for which there is a need for such an action and, if designed appropriately, a collective action provides a realistic opportunity for consumers to exercise their right to damages and obtain redress. On this basis, it seeks to formulate a collective action with respect to *i.* the membership mechanism, *ii.* the type of representative, *iii.* funding mechanisms and *iv.* calculation and distribution of damages, and therefore aims to contribute to the body of knowledge and debate around collective redress, which have been, and are likely to continue to be, one of the most controversial issues in private competition law enforcement.

Acknowledgements

This book is a revised and updated version of my PhD thesis from Queen Mary, University of London, which was completed in January 2016. The completion of this work was made possible through the assistance and encouragement of many people, for which I am very grateful.

First of all, I would like to express my deepest gratitude to my primary supervisor, Professor Eyad Maher Dabbah, for all of his valuable and constructive suggestions and his useful critiques that helped shape my research. He was with me every step of the way and supported me throughout my PhD with his patience and knowledge. It was a great pleasure and privilege for me to have the opportunity to conclude this research under his supervision.

Secondly, I would like to express my very great appreciation to my secondary supervisor Dr Maksymilian Del Mar for his continuous support, guidance and encouragement throughout my research at Queen Mary, University of London and beyond. I was grateful to him for his feedbacks that led me to shape my thoughts.

I would also like to express my warmest thanks to my closest friends Dr Andriani Kalintiri and Dr Kadir Bas for their friendship and continuous support from the beginning of my research till the very end. I am grateful to all my friends and colleagues in London who made the difficult and stressful times bearable. I should also thank the PhD community at Nansen Village, London.

Finally, my family deserves my gratitude; both my mother Tuncay Cevik and my brother M. Yigit Sahin have been a constant support throughout. I must thank my husband, Eren Sengul. He was always there cheering me up and stood by me through the good times and bad times. I could never have accomplished this work without his love, support, and understanding.

This book is dedicated to the memories of my grandparents, Guzide Cevik and Ahmet Cevik.

List of abbreviations

ABA	American Bar Association
ADR	Alternative Dispute Resolution
AG	Advocate General
Ashurst Study	Ashurst Study on the Conditions of Claims for Damages in Case of Infringement of EC Competition Rules, Comparative Report
ATE	After-the-event
BEUC	The European Consumer Organisation
BIS	Department for Business, Innovation and Skills
CAT	Competition Appeal Tribunal
CDC	Cartel Damages Claims
CFA	Conditional fee agreement
CJEU	The Court of Justice of the European Union
CMA	Competition and Markets Authority
Commission	European Commission
Communication	Communication from the Commission to the European Parliament, the Council, the European Economic and Social Committee and the Committee of the Regions towards a European Horizontal Framework for Collective Redress
Directive	Directive 2014/104/EU of the European Parliament and of the Council of 26 November 2014 on Certain Rules Governing Actions for Damages under National Law for Infringements of the Competition Law Provisions of the Member States and of the European Union
EC	European Community
ECCG	European Consumer Consultative Group
ECN	European Competition Network
ECR	European Court Reports
ECtHR	European Court of Human Rights
EU	European Union
EU Courts	The General Court of the European Union and Court of Justice of the European Union

Evaluation Study	Evaluation of the Effectiveness and Efficiency of Collective Redress Mechanisms in the European Union, Final Report, Part I: Main Report
FCALA	Fairness in Class Action Litigation Act of 2017
FRCP	Federal Rules of Civil Procedure
General Court	The General Court of the European Union
GLO	Group Litigation Orders
Green Paper	Green Paper on Damages Actions for Breach of EC Antitrust Rules
Green Paper on Collective Redress	Green Paper on Consumer Collective Redress
Impact Assessment	Staff Working Document Accompanying Document to the White Paper on Damages Actions for Breach of the EC Antitrust Rules – Impact Assessment
OECD	The Organisation for Economic Co-operation and Development
OFT	Office of Fair Trading
OJ	Official Journal of the European Union
Practical Guide	Staff Working Document: Practical Guide Quantifying Harm in Actions for Damages Based on Breaches of Article 101 or 102 of the Treaty on the Functioning of the European Union Accompanying the Communication from the Commission on Quantifying Harm in Actions for Damages based on Breaches of Article 101 or 102 of the Treaty on the Functioning of the European Union
Public Consultation	Staff Working Document Public Consultation: Towards a Coherent European Approach to Collective Redress
Recommendation	Recommendation on Common Principles for Injunctive and Compensatory Collective Redress Mechanisms in the Member States Concerning Violations of Rights Granted under Union Law
Report on the Recommendation	Report from The Commission to The European Parliament, The Council and The European Economic and Social Committee on the implementation of the Commission Recommendation of 11 June 2013 on common principles for injunctive and compensatory collective redress mechanisms in the Member States concerning violations of rights granted under Union law
SWPGP	Staff Working Paper Annex to the Green Paper Damages Actions for Breach of the EC Antitrust Rules
SWPWP	Staff Working Paper Accompanying the White Paper on Damages Actions for Breach of the EC Antitrust Rules
TEU	Treaty on European Union
TFEU	Treaty on the Functioning of the European Union
TLF	Third-party litigation funding

UK	United Kingdom
US	United States
Welfare Impact Report	Report for the European Commission – Making Antitrust Damages Actions More Effective in the EU: Welfare Impact and Potential Scenarios
White Paper	White Paper on Damages Actions for Breach of the EC Antitrust Rules

Table of cases

European Union

C-6/90 and C-9/90 *Andrea Francovich and Danila Bonifaci and others v Italian Republic* [1991] ECR I-05357

Case C-177/16 *Autortiesību un komunicēšanās konsultāciju aģentūra/Latvijas Autoru apvienība' v Konkurences padome* [2017] ECLI:EU:C:2017:689

C-127/73 *Belgische Radio en Televisie and Societé Belge des Auteurs, Compositeurs et Editeurs de Musique v SV SABAM and NV Fonior* [1974] ECR 51

C-46/93 and C-48/93 *Brasserie Du Pecheur SA v Federal Republic of Germany and The Queen v Secretary of State for Transport, Ex Parte Factortame Ltd and Others* [1996] ECR I-1029, Opinion of AG Tesauro Delivered on 28 November 1995

226/84 *British Leyland Public Limited Company v Commission* [1986] ECR 3263

C-536/11 *Bundeswettbewerbsbehörde v Donau Chemie AG and Others* [2013] ECR I-0000, Opinion of AG Jääskinen delivered on 7 February 2013

45/76 *Comet v Produktschap voor Siergewassen* [1976] ECR 2043

C-453/99 *Courage Ltd. v Bernard Crehan* [2001] ECR I-6297, Opinion of AG Mischo delivered on 22 March 2001

C-385/07P *Der Grüne Punkt – DSD v Commission* [2009] ECR I-06155

6/72 *Europemballage Corporation and Continental Can Company Inc. v Commission* [1973] ECR 00215

C-199/11 *Europese Gemeenschap v Otis NV and Others* [2012] ECR I-0000

C-202/07 P *France Télécom SA v Commission* [2009] ECR I-02369

C-128/92 *H. J. Banks & Co. Ltd v British Coal Corporation* [1994] ECR 1994 I-01209

C-557/12 *Kone AG and Others v ÖBB-Infrastruktur AG* [2014] EU:C:2014:1317, Opinion of AG Kokott delivered on 30 January 2014

C-52/09 *Konkurrensverket v TeliaSonera Sverige AB* [2011] ECR I-527

C-271/91 *M. Helen Marshall v Southampton and South-West Hampshire Area Health Authority* [1993] ECR I-04367

26/62 *NV Algemene Transport – en Expeditie Onderneming van Gend & Loos v Netherlands Inland Revenue Administration* [1963] ECR-00001

C-360/09 *Pfleiderer AG v Bundeskartellamt* [2011] ECR I-000

C-5/94 *R v Ministry of Agriculture, Fisheries and Food, ex p Hedley Lomas* [1996] ECR I-02553

33/76 *Rewe v Landwirtschaftskammer fuer das Saarland* [1976] ECR 1989

27/76 *United Brands Company and United Brands Continental v Commission* [1978] ECR 207

C-295/04 and C-298/04 *Vincenzo Manfredi v Lloyd Adriatico Assicurazioni SpA* [2006] ECR I-06619, Opinion of AG Geelhoed delivered on 26 January 2006

Lithgow and others v The United Kingdom (App no 9006/80; 9262/81; 9263/81; 9265/81; 9266/81; 9313/81; 9405/81) (ECtHR, 1986)

Wendenburg and others v Germany (App no 71630/01) (ECtHR, 2003)

Commission decisions

2000/12/EC *1998 Football World Cup* (Case IV/36.888) [2000] OJ L 5/55

84/379/EEC *British Leyland* [1984] OJ L 207/11

76/353/EEC *Chiquita* [1976] OJ L 95/1

2001/892/EC *Deutsche Post AG – Interception of Cross-Border Mail* (COMP/C-1/36.915) [2001] OJ L 331/40

2001/463/EC *DSD (Duales System Deutschland)* (COMP D3/34493) [2001] OJ L 166/1

75/75/EEC *General Motors Continental* [1975] OJ L 29/14

1999/60/EC *Pre-Insulated Pipe Cartel* (Case IV/35.691/E-4) [1998] OJ L 24/1

United States

Supreme Court

Amchem Products., Inc.v Windsor, 521 US 591 (1997)

California v ARC America Corp., 490 US 93 (1989)

Comcast Corp. v Behrend, 569 US 27 (2013)

Eisen v Carlisle and Jacquelin, 417 US 156 (1974)

Hanover Shoe v United Shoe Machinery Corp., 392 US 481 (1968)

Hansberry v Lee, 311 US 32 (1940)

Illinois Brick Co v Illinois, 431 US 720 (1977)

Phillips Petroleum Co. v Shutts, 472 US 797 (1985)

Lower Courts

B.W.I. Custom Kitchen v Owens-Illinois, 235 Cal.Rptr. 228 (Cal. App. 1987)

Carrera v Bayer Corp, 727 F.3d 300 (3d Cir. 2013)

Cipro Cases I and II, Case nos J.C.C.P. 4154 and 4220 (Cal. Super. 2013)

Danvers Motor Co. v Ford Motor Co., 543 F.3d 141 (3d Cir. 2008)

Eisen v Carlisle and Jacquelin, 391 F.2d 555 (2d Cir. 1968)

In re Baby Products Antitrust Litigation, Case no WL 5996622013 (E.D. Pa 2011)

In re Baby Products Antitrust Litigation, 708 F.3d 163 (3rd Cir. 2013)

In re Bayer Corp. Combination Aspirin Products Marketing and Sales Practices Litigation, Case no 09-MD-2023 (BMC) (E.D.N.Y. 2013)
In re Buspirone Antirust Ligation, 185 F.Supp. 2d 363 (S.D.N.Y. 2002)
In re Cardizem CD Antitrust Litigation, 218 F.R.D. 508 (E.D. Mich. 2003)
In re Catfish Antitrust Litigation, 826 F. Supp. 1019 (N.D.Miss. 1993)
In re Cipro Cases I, II, 121 Cal.App.4th 402 (Cal. App. 2004)
In re Compact Disc Minimum Advertised Price Antitrust Litigation, MDL no 1361 (D. Me. 2001)
In re Delta/AirTran Baggage Fee Antitrust Litigation, 317 F.R.D. 675 (N.D. Ga. 2016)
In re Domestic Air Transportation Antitrust Litigation, 141 F.R.D. 534 (N.D. Ga. 1992)
In re Graphics Processing Units Antitrust Litigation, 253 F.R.D. 478 (N.D. Cal. 2008)
In re Hydrogen Peroxide Antitrust Litigation, 552 F.3d 305 (3d Cir. 2008)
In re Infant Formula Multidistrict Litigation, Case no 4:91-cv-00878-MP (N.D. Fla. 2005)
In re Lithium Ion Batteries Antitrust Litigation, Case no 13-MD-2420 YGR (N. D. Cal. 2018)
In re Methionine Antitrust Litigation, MDL no 00–1311 CRB (N.D. Cal. 2001)
In re Methionine Antitrust Litigation, MDL no 00–1311 (N.D. Cal. 2003)
In re Microsoft Corp. Antitrust Litigation, 127 F. Supp. 2d 702 (D. Md. 2001)
In re Minolta Camera Products Antitrust Litigation, 668 F.Supp. 456 (D.Md. 1987)
In re NASDAQ Market- Makers Antitrust Litigation, 169 F.R.D. 493 (S.D.N.Y. 1996)
In re Remeron End-Payor Antitrust Litigation, Case nos 02–2007 (FSH), 04–5126 (FSH), (D.N.J. 2005)
Jones v National Distillers, 56 F. Supp. 2d 355 (S.D.N.Y. 1999)
Mirfasihi v Fleet Mortg. Corp., 356 F.3d 781 (7th Cir. 2004)
Pickett v Iowa Beef Processors, 209 F.3d 1276 (11th Cir. 2000)
Schwartz v Dallas Cowboys Football Club, Ltd., 362 F. Supp. 2d 574 (E.D. Pa. 2005)
Somers v Apple Inc., Case nos C 07–06507 JW, C 05–00037 JW (N.D. Cal. 2009)
State of West Virginia v Chas. Pfizer & Co., 314 F. Supp. 710 (S.D.N.Y. 1970)
Sullivan v DB Investments, Case nos 04-CV-2819 (SRC), 01-CV-4463 (SRC), 04-CV-4098 (SRC), (D.N.J. 2008)
Valley Drug Co. v Geneva Pharmaceuticals, Inc., 350 F.3d 1181 (11th Cir. 2003)
Windham v American Brands, Inc., 565 F.2d 59 (4th Cir. 1977)

United Kingdom

Dorothy Gibson v Pride Mobility Products Limited [2016] (CAT Case no 1257/7/7/16)
Emerald Supplies Ltd and another v British Airways plc [2009] EWHC 741 (Ch), [2009] UKCLR 801

Emerald Supplies Ltd v British Airways Plc [2010] EWCA Civ 1284
The Consumers Association v JJB Sports PLC [2007] (CAT Case no 1078/7/9/07)
Walter Hugh Merricks v MasterCard Incorporated & Others [2017] (CAT Case no 1266/7/7/16)

Others

Sentenza del Giudice di Pace di Bitonto no 172/2003, *Manfredi Vincenzo c Lloyd Adriatico Assicurazioni*

Table of legislation

European Union

Treaties and regulations

Charter of Fundamental Rights of the European Union, (OJ C 364/1, 2000)
Consolidated Version of the Treaty on the Functioning of the European Union, (OJ C 83/47, 2010)
Consolidated Version of the Treaty on European Union, (OJ C 83/13, 2010)
Council Regulation (EC) No 1/2003 of 16 December 2002 on the Implementation of the Rules on Competition Laid down in Articles [101] and [102] of the Treaty, (OJ L 1/1, 2003)
Regulation (EC) No 861/2007 of the European Parliament and of the Council of 11 July 2007 establishing a European Small Claims Procedure, (OJ L 199/1, 2007)
Regulation (EU) No 524/2013 of the European Parliament and of the Council of 21 May 2013 on Online Dispute Resolution for Consumer Disputes and Amending Regulation (EC) No 2006/2004 and Directive 2009/22/EC, (OJ L 165/1, 2013)

Directives

Council Directive 93/13/EEC of 5 April 1993 on Unfair Terms in Consumer Contracts, (OJ L 095, 1993)
Directive 2005/29/EC of the European Parliament and of the Council of 11 May 2005 Concerning Unfair Business-to-Consumer Commercial Practices in the Internal Market and Amending Council Directive 84/450/EEC, Directives 97/7/EC, 98/27/EC and 2002/65/EC of the European Parliament and of the Council and Regulation (EC) No 2006/2004 of the European Parliament and of the Council, (OJ L 149/22, 2005)
Directive 2009/22/EC of the European Parliament and of the Council of 23 April 2009 on Injunctions for the Protection of Consumers' Interests (Codified Version), (OJ L 110/30, 2009)
Directive 2013/11/EU of the European Parliament and of the Council of 21 May 2013 on Alternative Dispute Resolution for Consumer Disputes and Amending

Regulation (EC) No 2006/2004 and Directive 2009/22/EC, (OJ L 165/63, 2013)

Directive 2014/104/EU of the European Parliament and of the Council of 26 November 2014 on Certain Rules Governing Actions for Damages under National Law for Infringements of the Competition Law Provisions of the Member States and of the European Union, (OJ L 349/1, 2014)

Notices and guidelines

Commission Notice on Cooperation between National Courts and the Commission in Applying Articles [101 and 102 of the Treaty], (OJ C 39/6–12, 1993)

Commission Guidelines on the Method of Setting Fines pursuant to Article 23(2)(a) of Regulation No 1/2003, (OJ C 210/02, 2006)

Commission Guidelines on the Application of Article [101](3) of the Treaty, (OJ C 101/97, 2004)

Commission Guidelines on the Effect on Trade Concept Contained in Articles [101] and [102] of the Treaty, (OJ C 101/81, 2004)

Commission Guidance on the Commission's Enforcement Priorities in Applying Article [102 TFEU] to Abusive Exclusionary Conduct by Dominant Undertakings, (OJ C 45/7, 2009)

Commission Guidelines on Vertical Restraints, (OJ C 130/1, 2010)

United Kingdom

Competition Act, 1998

Civil Procedure Rules, 1998

Competition Appeal Tribunal Rules, no 1372, 2003

Competition Appeal Tribunal Guide to Proceedings, 2005

Conditional Fee Agreements Order, no 689, 2013

Collective Proceedings and Collective Settlements in the Competition Appeal Tribunal: Draft Tribunal Rules, 2014

Consumer Rights Act 2015 (c.15), 2015, sch 8

Competition Appeal Tribunal Rules, no 1648, 2015

United States

Federal Rules of Civil Procedure, 1966

Model Rules of Professional Conduct, 1983

Clayton Antitrust Act, 15 USC, 1914

Class Action Fairness Act, 28 USC, 2005

Sherman Act, 15 USC, 1890

The Fairness in Class Action Litigation Act of 2017, H.R. 985

Others

Australia, Federal Court of Australia Act, no 156, 1976
British Columbia, Class Proceedings Act, RSBC 1996
Ontario, Class Proceedings Act, 1992

1 Introduction

Background

Paucity of actions for damages for competition infringements

European Union (EU) competition law enforcement comprises elements both of a public and private nature. With regard to public enforcement, both national competition authorities and the European Commission (Commission) enforce Articles 101 and 102 of the Treaty on the Functioning of the European Union (TFEU).[1] In addition, private persons may enforce competition law before national courts. Both articles are directly applicable;[2] they confer rights on individuals that national courts must safeguard and enforce.[3] The *Courage* decision made clear that there is an EU right to damages.[4] Victims of competition infringements can seek compensation for harm suffered before national courts. A victim may bring a follow-on action after an infringement decision taken by a competition authority or by the Commission and rely on its findings. It is also possible to bring a stand-alone action where an infringement has not been prosecuted by the public enforcers.

While the existence of the EU right to damages is a matter of EU law, the exercise of that right is subject to national law.[5] Due to the principle of national procedural autonomy, in the absence of EU rules governing the subject, Member States determine the procedural framework for EU competition claims. However, this autonomy is subject to limitation; EU law limits this autonomy through the well-established principles of effectiveness and equivalence developed by the Court of Justice of the European Union (CJEU). National procedural rules governing

1 *Consolidated Version of the Treaty on the Functioning of the European Union* (OJ C 83/47, 2010).

2 See eg Case 26–62 *NV Algemene Transport- en Expeditie Onderneming van Gend & Loos v Netherlands Inland Revenue Administration*[1963] ECR-00001; Case C-127/73 *Belgische Radio en Televisie and Societé Belge des Auteurs, Compositeurs et Editeurs de Musique v SV SABAM and NV Fonior* [1974] ECR 51, para 16.

3 Case C-453/99 *Courage Ltd. v Bernard Crehan* [2001] ECR I-6297, para 23.

4 *Ibid* para 26.

5 W van Gerven, 'Of Rights, Remedies and Procedures', *Common Market Law Review*, 37 (2000), 501–536, 503–504.

claims based on EU law, according to the effectiveness principle, must not render the exercise of directly effective EU rights virtually impossible or overly difficult, and, according to the equivalence principle, must not be less favourable than those governing similar domestic claims.[6]

That said, victims of competition infringements in the EU rarely seek compensation for their loss in courts, despite the existence of the EU right to damages. This is especially the case for consumers due to the way in which they are harmed by competition infringements and due to the type of loss they suffered. As a result, the right to damages is not exercised in an effective way and victims do not usually obtain compensation for the harm incurred. While public enforcement has always had a significant role,[7] private enforcement through damages actions is still at a developmental stage,[8] despite the fact that the Commission highlighted the importance of increased private enforcement more than 30 years ago.[9]

Indeed, private enforcement compensates victims,[10] and leads to an increase in the total amount of enforcement,[11] thereby contributing to compliance with the law, which is expressed as 'better respect of the law', and to enhanced deterrence.[12] It also complements public enforcement efforts in cases where public enforcement has limited resources, has priorities,[13] or is controlled by interest groups.[14] Private enforcement lessens the burdens and risks on public enforcers by

6 See eg Case 33/76 *Rewe v Landwirtschaftskammer fuer das Saarland* [1976] ECR 1989; Case 45/76 *Comet v Produktschap voor Siergewassen* [1976] ECR 2043; *Courage* (fn 3) para 29.

7 See eg DJ Gerber, 'Private enforcement of competition law: a comparative perspective', in *The Enforcement of Competition Law in Europe*, ed. by TMJ Möllers and A Heinemann, 1st edn (Cambridge: Cambridge University Press, 2007), 431–452, 431; R Whish and D Bailey, *Competition Law*, 7th edn (Oxford: Oxford University Press, 2012), 295.

8 R Nazzini and A Nikpay, 'Private Actions in EC Competition Law', *Competition Policy International*, 4(2) (2008), 107–141, 119; AP Komninos, 'Civil Antitrust Remedies between Community and National Law', in *The Outer Limits of European Union Law*, ed. by C Barnard and O Odudu (Oxford and Portland, Oregon: Hart Publishing, 2009), 363–400, 363.

9 Commission, *Thirteenth Report on Competition Policy (published in conjunction with the 'Seventeenth General Report on the Activities of the European Communities 1983')*, 1984, paras 217–218.

10 See eg A Ezrachi, *EU Competition Law: An Analytical Guide to the Leading Cases*, 4th edn (Oxford and Portland, Oregon: Hart Publishing, 2014), 545.

11 Commission, *Staff Working Paper Annex to the Green Paper Damages actions for breach of the EC antitrust rules* (SEC(2005)1732, Brussels, 2005), (SWPGP), para 5.

12 E Paulis, 'Policy Issues in the Private Enforcement of EC Competition Law', in *Private Enforcement of EC Competition Law*, ed. by J Basedow (The Netherlands: Kluwer Law International, 2007), 7–16, 16.

13 *Ibid* 8. Walle states that it is not easy to increase public enforcement and public penalties, because budgetary constraints bar the former and political and legal reasons bar the latter. SV Walle, *Private Antitrust Litigation in the European Union and Japan – A Comparative Perspective* (Antwerpen-Apeldoorn: Maklu, 2013), 253.

14 C Hodges, 'Competition Enforcement, Regulation and Civil Justice: What Is the Case?', *Common Law Market Review*, 43 (2006), 1381–1407, 1395.

shifting them onto private litigants.[15] In addition, private enforcement furthers the clarity and development of the content of competition infringements,[16] thereby raising the legitimacy and awareness of competition law.[17] Judicial independence of courts also makes private enforcement independent *vis-à-vis* public enforcement.[18] However, currently none of these objectives can be performed by private enforcement through damages actions because victims rarely seek redress when they are harmed by competition infringements across the EU.

The main issues that contribute to the paucity of actions for damages in competition cases have been identified as difficulties in obtaining access to evidence, short limitation periods, high litigation costs, lack of effective collective redress actions and the uncertainty of a number of important legal issues. These issues are the passing-on defence, the binding effect of national competition authorities' decisions, fault requirement, and the calculation and allocation of damages. In order to remedy this situation, the Commission had put forward proposals including collective redress until the Directive and the Directive has addressed most of these issues excluding collective redress.[19]

The need for collective redress in competition law enforcement

Collective redress actions had been part of ongoing work in private competition law enforcement in the EU in the last decade. In a traditional two-party lawsuit, a single plaintiff sues a single defendant. However, when a breach of law, like a competition infringement, causes widespread harm, a collective redress action – as a procedural tool – enables the resolution of the dispute between parties where one of the parties consists of a large number of persons.

The central tenet of this book is how to formulate a collective redress action to assist consumers in obtaining compensation for the loss suffered due to EU competition infringements. The structure and methodology are prescribed by two factors, namely the need for a collective redress action and the design framework for such an action. The first part focuses on the need in this area and the characteristics of damages claims of victims which fit the purpose and practical

15 See private enforcement in the US achieves this goal, CA Jones, 'Deterrence and Compensation in New Competition Regimes: The Role of Private Enforcement', in *New Competition Jurisdictions: Shaping Policies and Building Institutions*, ed. by R Whish and C Townley (Cheltenham UK: Edward Elgar Publishing, 2012), 167–182, 173.

16 WPJ Wils, 'The Relationship between Public Antitrust Enforcement and Private Actions for Damages', *World Competition*, 32 (2009), 1–32, 6.

17 Walle (fn 13) 238.

18 AP Komninos, *EC Private Antitrust Enforcement: Decentralised Application of EC Competition Law by National Courts* (Oxford and Portland, Oregon: Hart Publishing, 2008), 15.

19 *Directive 2014/104/EU of the European Parliament and of the Council of 26 November 2014 on Certain Rules Governing Actions for Damages under National Law for Infringements of the Competition Law Provisions of the Member States and of the European Union* (OJ L 349/1, 2014) (Directive).

functioning of a collective redress action. To this end, it discusses the purpose and working principle of such an action as well as the reason that it has been created in the first place. This discussion leads to the question of whether a need for collective redress exists only for certain victims, analysing both the nature of their losses and distinctive characteristics of competition law that give rise to the paucity of damages claims. It also deals with the objective(s) a collective redress action should pursue in order to satisfy this need. Although there are various other factors that would shape an EU-wide collective redress action, this book focuses on the compensation and deterrence objectives of actions for damages to formulate a collective redress action.

After the first part has justified not only the need for a collective redress action for consumers, but also the better suitability of consumer claims for collective redress actions, the second part moves on to design such an action to address the grievances of consumers in EU competition cases. It analyses: *i.* the formation of group membership, *ii.* the standing to bring a collective action on behalf of affected consumers, *iii.* funding of such actions and *iv.* calculation and distribution of a damages award. By examining these issues, each element of this action is designed to address the distinctive nature of the claims of the victims identified as the beneficiaries of the collective action in light of the submitted objective(s).

Reflection on the term 'collective redress'

Unsurprisingly, the introduction of a collective redress action is no simple task; it touches upon political considerations in both purpose and implementation and there are various factors that can be taken into account in its formulation which might dictate a different design framework for this action.

A wide variety of terms are used to refer to collective redress actions. These include 'collective actions'[20] and 'group actions'[21] in some civil law jurisdictions and 'class actions' in the United States (US), Australia and Canada.[22] This book also uses the term 'class action' when analysing US procedure in order to avoid confusion between EU and US mechanisms. The terms 'collective litigation' and 'group litigation' are used to describe the whole procedure, ie the notion of litigative representation.[23] This notion applies to a situation where a group of people

20 See eg Brazil, France, Italy, and Spain, A Gidi, 'Class Actions in Brazil – A Model for Civil Law Countries', *American Journal of Comparative Law*, 51 (2013), 311–408, 335–336.

21 See eg Sweden, PH Lindblom, 'Individual Litigation and Mass Justice: A Swedish Perspective and Proposal on Group Actions in Civil Procedure', *The American Journal of Comparative Law*, 45(4) (1997), 805–831.

22 See R Mulheron, *The Class Action in Common Law Legal Systems: A Comparative Perspective* (Oxford and Portland, Oregon: Hart Publishing, 2004) 5.

23 SC Yeazell, 'From Group Litigation to Class Action Part II: Interest, Class, and Representation', *UCLA Law Review*, 27 (1980), 1067–1121, 1069.

qualifies as a party, whereas collective actions and group actions refer to the character of the suit and the rights that arise therefrom.[24]

It is important to note that the EU has arrived at the term 'collective redress mechanisms' – chosen for the political considerations triggered by the sensitivity of the issue and opposition shown by some Member States.[25] Over the course of the European initiative toward collective redress, the mechanism has taken several names. The Ashurst study used the term 'class actions' for opt-out systems and 'collective claims' for the representation of identified or identifiable persons.[26] Subsequently, the Green Paper referred to such a mechanism as 'collective actions'[27] and therefore here a shift in terminology is observed from 'class actions' to 'collective actions'.[28] The White Paper used 'collective actions' and 'collective redress mechanisms' interchangeably.[29] The recent horizontal approach that proposes a mechanism to address all breaches of EU law (horizontal approach) also prefers the term 'collective redress mechanisms'.[30]

The reason behind underlying the first change in terminology was to distance the European approach from that used in the US.[31] The motive of the second

24 Gidi (fn 20) 335–336.

25 Especially from Germany and France, C Hodges, 'Current discussions on consumer redress: collective redress and ADR', *ERA Forum*, 13 (2012), 11–33, 16–17. Similarly see AP Komninos, 'Private Enforcement in the EU with Emphasis on Damages Actions', in *Handbook on European Competition Law – Enforcement and Procedure*, ed. by I Lianos and D Geradin (Cheltenham UK: Edward Elgar Publishing, 2013), vol.II, 228–272, 263.

26 D Waelbroeck, D Slater and G Even-Shoshan, *Ashurst Study on the Conditions of Claims for Damages in Case of Infringement of EC Competition Rules, Comparative Report* (Brussels, 2004), (Ashurst Study) 43–44.

27 Commission, *Green Paper on Damages Actions for Breach of EC Antitrust Rules* (COM(2005) 672 final, Brussels, 2005), (Green Paper) para 2.5.

28 See Hodges, Current discussions (fn 25) 15.

29 Commission, *White Paper on Damages Actions for Breach of the EC Antitrust Rules* (COM(2008) 165 final, Brussels, 2008), (White Paper) para 2.1; Commission, *Staff Working Paper Accompanying the White Paper on Damages actions for Breach of the EC Antitrust Rules* (SEC(2008) 404, Brussels, 2008), (SWPWP) paras 3, 7.

30 The term 'collective redress actions' is also used in the horizontal approach. Commission, *Staff Working Document Public Consultation: 'Towards a Coherent European Approach to Collective Redress'* (SEC(2011)173 final, Brussels, 2011) (Public consultation); *Recommendation on Common Principles for Injunctive and Compensatory Collective Redress Mechanisms in the Member States Concerning Violations of Rights Granted Under Union Law* (Strasbourg, C(2013) 3539/3, 2013), (Recommendation); *Communication from the Commission to the European Parliament, the Council, the European Economic and Social Committee and the Committee of the Regions 'Towards a European Horizontal Framework for Collective Redress'* (COM(2013) 401/2, Brussels, 2013), (Communication). See Chapter 3 for further analysis.

31 Hodges, Current discussions (fn 25) 15. See according to the Welfare impact report, the terms 'collective actions' and 'class actions' are synonyms. Centre for European Policy Studies (CEPS), Erasmus University Rotterdam (EUR) and Luiss Guido Carli (LUISS), *Report for the European Commission 'Making Antitrust Damages Actions More Effective in the EU: Welfare Impact and Potential Scenarios', Final Report*, 2007, (Welfare impact report) 276, fn 443.

change from 'collective actions' to 'collective redress mechanisms' begins with a shift in the collective redress proposal specific to competition law to a proposal applicable to all EU law breaches. When the collective redress debate was limited to competition law, the focus was on a judicial procedure that could deliver compensation to the victims. The horizontal approach, on the other hand, broadens the collective redress concept embracing judicial and non-judicial mechanisms for injunctions and damages.[32]

This book uses the terms 'collective redress actions' and 'collective actions' interchangeably throughout to refer to the judicial procedure for damages. In that regard, it defines a collective redress action as a court-based mechanism that allows one or more persons as representatives of the group (the representative party) to sue on behalf of similarly situated persons who are harmed by the same or a similar wrong (the group) and therefore share the same or similar issues of fact or law (shared issues).[33] Through representation, the group becomes 'a single litigative entity'[34] and their claims are determined in a single lawsuit. Group members are bound by the decision given on the shared issues by the court[35] and in the event of success, the remedy is applicable to all even if they have not actively taken part in the suit.[36]

Issues relating to the design of a collective redress action

There are two main issues to consider in respect of collective redress. The first arises when choosing between judicial and non-judicial means by which to deliver compensation to victims. The second concerns whether a (judicial) collective redress action can make the exercise of the right to damages a reality in practice and result in the victims seeking damages, thereby delivering compensation to those harmed by competition infringements. This book refers to these two issues before justifying its focus on judicial collective redress actions.

Judicial v non-judicial means of collective redress

Non-judicial means encompass regulatory and voluntary mechanisms. 'Regulatory' describes public compensation, for instance, authorising the Commission or national competition authorities to order infringers to pay compensation alongside fines at the end of an investigation.[37] 'Voluntary' describes alternative out-of-court

32 Public consultation (fn 30) paras 7, 15; Recommendation (fn 30) para 14.
33 See Mulheron, Class action (fn 22) 3.
34 SC Yeazell, *From Medieval Group Litigation to the Modern Class Action* (New Haven and London: Yale University Press, 1987), 1–2.
35 Mulheron, Class action (fn 22) 3.
36 Yeazell (fn 34) 1.
37 It can also be part of settlement or commitment procedure. See further A Ezrachi and M Ioannidou, 'Public Compensation as a Complementary Mechanism to Damages Actions: From Policy Justifications to Formal Implementation', *Journal of European Competition Law & Practice*, 3(6) (2012), 536–544, 543.

mechanisms such as mediation, arbitration, alternative dispute resolution (ADR) systems and collective out-of-court settlements. The debate here focuses on whether judicial or non-judicial means of collective redress work better to assist victims of competition infringements in obtaining redress. The issue can be approached by considering several factors: which mechanism produces the fairest and morally appropriate results, which is most time and cost efficient, which best advances a compensation and/or deterrence objective, which increases legal certainty and procedural fairness for both parties and which encourages greater compliance with law.[38]

In regulatory mechanisms, the right to seek damages in court remains[39] and the Commission would simply order the infringers to pay compensation along with fines.[40] DG COMP once argued that its resources are not enough to deal with the compensation of victims as part of its enforcement activities[41] and also that compensation is outside the field of its competence.[42] This attitude is not surprising as the motive behind the introduction of a collective redress action is the relative scarcity of private competition law enforcement through damages actions. Similarly, commentators, who propose public compensation, emphasise that they only suggest this option in the absence of a collective redress action.[43]

With respect to voluntary mechanisms, it has been argued that these mechanisms not only increase access to justice[44] but also involve potentially less cost and

38 See further C Hodges, *The Reform of Class and Representative Actions in European Legal Systems: A New Framework for Collective Redress in Europe* (Oxford and Portland, Oregon: Hart Publishing, 2008), 3.

39 Ezrachi and Ioannidou (fn 37) 543.

40 *Ibid* 542.

41 Hodges, 'Collective Redress: A Breakthrough or a Damp Sqibb?', *Journal of Consumer Policy*, 37(1) (2014), 67–89,74. During the reform process of private enforcement in the UK, the proposal with respect to delivering compensation through public enforcement was rejected on the grounds that it would bring cost burdens and undermine the leniency programme by casting doubts on whether the Office of Fair Trading [now the Competition and Markets Authority (CMA)] accepted the leniency application for the purposes of redress. BIS, *Private Actions in Competition Law: A Consultation on Options for Reform – Impact Assessment* (London, 2012), para 239. See also, it would be dependent upon the priorities and policies of the public enforcer, J C Alexander, 'An Introduction to Class Action Procedure in The United States' (presented at the Debates over Group Litigation in Comparative Perspective, Geneva, Switzerland, 2000), 1–26, 16 <http://law.duke.edu/grouplit/papers/classactionalexander.pdf> [accessed 27 January 2018].

42 Commission, *Proposal for a Directive of the European Parliament and of the Council on Certain Rules Governing Actions for Damages Under National Law for Infringements of the Competition Law Provisions of the Member States and of the European Union*, (2013/0185 (COD), COM(2013) 404 final, Strasbourg, 2013) (Directive proposal), explanatory memorandum, para 1.1. See, similarly, Commission, *Proposal for a Council Directive on Rules Governing Damages Actions for Infringements of Articles [101] and [102] of the Treaty*, 2009 (Withdrawn Directive), explanatory memorandum para 1.2. <http://allegati.unina.it/postlaurea/perf/Exclusiva_Juridico.pdf> [accessed 1 July 2018].

43 Ezrachi and Ioannidou (fn 37) 537–538.

44 J Stuyck, 'Setting the Scene', in *Cases, Materials and Text on Consumer Law*, ed. by H-W. Micklitz, J Stuyck, and E Terryn, Ius Commune Casebooks for a Common Law of Europe (Oxford and Portland, Oregon: Hart Publishing, 2010), 1–69, 6.

burden as compared with judicial proceedings.[45] However, in practice, there are some drawbacks. For instance, a settlement is reached through mediation mostly after a successful court case, or parties are not bound by collective out-of-court settlements unless there is a previous court decision as in the Netherlands,[46] or external pressures are needed in order for an ADR system to work effectively, such as risk of a serious and/or ongoing loss of reputation or threat of regulatory action.[47] One can infer from this, *inter alia*, that alternative mechanisms work well in cases where it is easy to prove the infringement/damage or the infringement/damage is already proven. This does not fit in with the particular complexities of competition claims where the proof of infringement and damage is already difficult. Indeed, the success rate of competition cases are low.[48] When this is the case, one can question why an infringer wishes to agree to pay damages knowing that victims encounter difficulties in proving the infringement as well as their loss.

Nonetheless, the availability of alternative mechanisms contributes to the enforcement of rights,[49] allowing victims to select the most appropriate one for their case.[50] This said, they do not substitute legal procedures.[51]According to Hodges, judicial procedures should be applicable as a last resort[52] because a judicial collective action is an old-fashioned technique.[53] However, the European Parliament is of the view that '[t]hese mechanisms should remain, as the name indicates, merely an alternative to judicial redress, not a precondition therefore'.[54] Indeed, if alternative means of collective redress were to be made mandatory,

45 SWPWP (fn 29) para 41.
46 Commission – DG SANCO, *Summary of the Leuven Brainstorming Event on Collective Redress: Collecting Thoughts and Experiences on Collective Redress*, 2007, 1–5,3 <http://ec.europa.eu/consumers/redress_cons/docs/summary_leuven_event.pdf> [accessed 19 June 2013].
47 Hodges, The Reform (fn 38) 233.
48 C Brown and D Ryan, 'The Judicial Application of European Competition Law' (presented at the Fide Congress Madrid, 2010) para 1.3 <http://webcache.googleusercontent.com/search?q=cache:lGlqcMBbbMgJ:www.matrixlaw.co.uk/wp-content/uploads/2016/03/21_04_2010_10_30_47_FIDE_-_UK_report_-_Judicial_application_of_Euopean_competition_law_FINAL_261009-SW9-Redline.doc+&cd=38&hl=en&ct=clnk&gl=tr&client=safari> [accessed 1 July 2018].
49 D-P L Tzakas, 'Effective Collective Redress in Antitrust and Consumer Protection Matters: A Panacea or a Chimera?', *Common Market Law Review*, 48 (2011), 1125–1174, 1134.
50 H-W Micklitz and A Stadler, 'The Development of Collective Legal Actions in Europe, Especially in German Civil Procedure', *European Business Law Review*, 17(5) (2006), 1473–1503, 1498.
51 See D Fairgrieve and G Howells, 'Collective Redress Procedures – European Debates', *International & Comparative Law Quarterly*, 58(2) (2009), 379–409, 404.
52 C Hodges, 'Collective Redress in Europe: The New Model', *Civil Justice Quarterly*, 29(3) (2010), 370–395, 375.
53 Hodges, Current discussions (fn 25) 20.
54 European Parliament, *Motion for a European Parliament Resolution on 'Towards a Coherent European Approach to Collective Redress'* (2011/2089(INI), 2012), para 25 <http://www.europarl.europa.eu/sides/getDoc.do?type=REPORT&language=EN&reference=A7-0012/2012#title1> [accessed 1 July 2018].

plaintiffs would be obligated to have recourse to them first before initiating legal proceedings and this might impair their fundamental legal rights to bring a case to courts.[55] In addition, out-of-court mechanisms, which are dependent upon the infringer's willingness to cooperate, require victims to have a realistic possibility of enforcing their claims for damages before courts.[56] Otherwise, although a court action remains an option, infringers would not have any motivation to agree to pay damages. There is also the risk that infringers might abuse preconditioned alternative mechanisms through lengthy proceedings and delays or they might give lesser damages to the victims concerned.[57]

All in all, alternative methods can perfectly be in place alongside a judicial procedure. This said, it seems reasonable to have a judicial collective redress action in place to make the enforcement of victims' right to damages effective in the EU.[58] The existence of such an action not only paves the way for other alternative mechanisms to be introduced but also is necessary for other mechanisms to work in practice as a judicial mechanism provides a strong incentive for parties to agree out of court.[59] Indeed, judicial collective actions help '[r]educe the inequality between the victims (often the weaker party) and the infringers (often the financially stronger party) in out-of-court/settlement discussions'.[60] In this respect, the next section sheds light on the debate about a judicial collective redress action and key elements of its design.

Elements of collective redress actions

In relation to a judicial collective redress action, first, there has been a debate about where need lies in the field of private enforcement. In other words, it asks to what extent there is a need for a collective redress action for all victims or only for certain victims. A second and pertinent debate concerns which factor(s) and objectives would play a role in designing a collective action to meet this need. Each element of a collective redress action changes with respect to the chosen factor or objective and therefore has different capacities in meeting this need. Subsequently, debates concentrate on how to design such an action to address the claims of victims considering the submitted need and/or objective(s). In this respect, four key elements are discussed:[61] grouping damages claims of victims, choosing the representative to bring an action on their behalf, providing

55 See, inter alia, BIS, *Private Actions in Competition Law: A Consultation on Options for Reform – Government Response* (London, 2013), para 3.9.
56 European Parliament, Motion (fn 54) para 25. Similarly, Commission, *Staff Working Document Accompanying Document to the White Paper on Damages Actions for Breach of the EC Antitrust Rules – Impact Assessment* (SEC(2008) 405, Brussels, 2008), (Impact assessment), para 36; SWPWP (fn 29) para 41.
57 Tzakas (fn 49) 1134.
58 SWPWP (fn 29) para 42; Tzakas (fn 49) 1134.
59 Public consultation (fn 30) para 20.
60 SWPWP (fn 29) para 41.
61 Both this book and the EU efforts focus on these elements. *Ibid*, para 44. See further Chapter 3.

appropriate funding mechanisms and calculating and apportioning damages award. Indeed, in a collective action, the fact that there is a large group on the one side of the suit, rather than a single plaintiff as per the traditional model of litigation, entails constructing some procedural aspects of the litigation differently.[62]

The first element is determining the group membership, which can be either left to the courts to decide or enacted by law.[63] There are three ways to establish eligibility for the represented group: opt-in, opt-out and mandatory systems. Opt-in requires the identification of all members of the group by taking their consent to be part of the action. Opt-out automatically encompasses those harmed who satisfy the group definition, but grants members the right to be excluded from the group. Opt-in actions are brought on behalf of individually identified group members, whereas opt-out actions are brought on behalf of identifiable members. In mandatory systems, those harmed are automatically included and have no right of exclusion from the described group.

Theoretically, none of those systems make members party to the litigation.[64] The operation of a collective action suggests the representation of the members of the group without making them parties to the action.[65] The party to the action is the representative who brings the case on behalf of the group. This representative party can be one of the members of the group (lead plaintiff) who is affected by the same wrong, or an ideological claimant,[66] such as a consumer association or trade organisation, or a public body, such as an ombudsman. Collective actions that allow an ideological claimant to represent a group are also called 'representative actions'.[67]

Another key element is the financing of such an action in respect of who is liable for the litigation costs and to what extent. There exist various systems in different legal regimes that address the liability for costs and they can be applied alone or in combination. First, under the loser-pays rule – also called the English rule,[68] costs-shifting,[69] or the two-way costs rule[70] – the expenses of the successful party are recovered by the party who loses the litigation. In one-way costs-shifting,

62 JA Campion and VA Stewart, 'Class Actions: Procedure and Strategy', *Advocates' Quarterly*, 19 (1997), 20–66, 24.
63 Mulheron, Class action (fn 22) 31–34.
64 See Gidi (fn 20) 339. However, the US opt-in rule in 1938 made group members parties to the lawsuit, see further Chapter 6.
65 Mulheron, Class action (fn 22) 30.
66 R Mulheron, *Costs and Funding of Collective Actions: Realities and Possibilities*, A Research Paper for Submission to the European Consumers' Organisation (BEUC) (Brussels, 2011), 1–133, 5 <http://www.law.qmul.ac.uk/docs/staff/department/71112.pdf> [accessed 31 July 2015].
67 Recommendation (fn 30) para II/3(d).
68 PH Lindblom, 'National Report: Group Litigation in Sweden' (presented at the Globalisation of Class Actions, Oxford, 2007), 1–47, 16 <http://globalclassactions.stanford.edu/sites/default/files/documents/Sweden_National_Report.pdf> [accessed 31 July 2015].
69 Mulheron, Costs and funding (fn 66) 11.
70 Mulheron, Class action (fn 22) 437.

the representative party or the group can recover its costs from the defendants in the event of success, but the defendants cannot recover their costs from the opponent in a winning case.[71] The 'no-way' costs rule, or 'American rule', makes both parties responsible for their own costs irrespective of the outcome of the case.[72]

Collective actions can be funded by group members or their representative. Other options involve public or private funds, insurance companies, legal aid mechanisms, third-party litigation funders, and lawyers working under contingency fee arrangements.[73] The representative party, be it a lead plaintiff or ideological claimant, hires a lawyer and agrees on some kind of remuneration scheme. This may be an hourly fee agreement whereby the lawyer is paid for her time irrespective of the result of the case.[74] The hourly fee may also be decided by the court on a case-by-case assessment. This is called the lodestar method:[75] the court first multiplies the hourly fee of the lawyer by the hours worked on the case, then adjusts this amount according to certain criteria. Alternatively, the arrangement can be on the basis of conditional or contingency fee agreements.[76] Conditional fee agreements (CFAs) can also be designed as 'no win no fee', as per contingency fee arrangements. In 'no win no fee' arrangements, the lawyer finances the action and receives payment in the event of success.[77]

The final issues to be addressed in collective actions seeking damages are the calculation and distribution of monetary relief. Damages might be determined by the court on an individual basis or measured as a whole for the group (aggregate damages assessment).[78] After damages are awarded, an appropriate way to apportion it amongst group members would subsequently be found. Depending on the case at hand, the options are to distribute to each and every member of the group to the greatest extent possible or to use it for related purposes, cy-près. If a sum is left undistributed, there are also means by which to address this issue, such as distributing it to the identified group members on a pro-rata basis, assigning it to the defendant, a governmental body, the ideological claimant or any other organisation, or cy-près methods.

The aforementioned concerns call for a new and critical assessment of shaping an EU collective redress action in the field of private competition law enforcement. To date, the formulation of a collective redress action has not been analysed in a systematic and comprehensive way in competition law, taking into account the

71 DN Dewees, JRS Prichard and MJ Trebilcock, 'An Economic Analysis of Cost and Fee Rules for Class Actions', *The Journal of Legal Studies*, 10(1) (1981), 155–185, 164. See *Clayton Antitrust Act*, 15 USC, 1914, sec 4.
72 Mulheron, Class action (fn 22) 436.
73 SWPWP (fn 29) para 45.
74 SE Keske, *Group Litigation in European Competition Law: A Law and Economics Perspective* (Antwerp-Oxford-Portland: Intersentia, 2010) 46.
75 TS Ulen, 'An Introduction to the Law and Economics of Class Action Litigation', *European Journal of Law and Economics*, 32 (2011), 185–203, 192.
76 Keske (fn 74) 46–47.
77 *Ibid* 47.
78 Mulheron, Class action (fn 22) 407.

need in this field and characteristics of the damages claims of the victims of competition infringements that fit the working principle and purpose of such an action. The importance of this analysis cannot be overstressed in order to offer a solution to the current situation in the EU and provide a realistic means for the victims to obtain redress in practice.

Methodology

The issue of design and introduction of a collective redress action is highly topical due to ongoing and upcoming consultations at the EU and national levels and the recent adoption of such an action in the United Kingdom (UK). Yet, a comprehensive study on the way in which a collective redress action operates in practice and addresses consumer damages claims is missing from the legal scholarship on private EU competition law enforcement. With this in mind, this book focuses on the structure of a collective redress action for consumers in EU competition cases and relies on four groups of resources to make its analysis.

This book firstly examines reported judicial decisions within the EU in the field of private competition law enforcement. The aim is to analyse these decisions in order to draw its arguments from the EU courts'[79] stance towards actions for damages, objectives of actions for damages and the right to damages for competition infringements. Moreover, over the years, the Commission has published various papers explaining its position on collective redress and other related issues. Therefore, the book investigates and evaluates the wording of the relevant provisions of the Directive on damages actions, the Commission's studies, working papers and documents, reports and recommendations on private enforcement and on collective redress actions both in the context of competition law and the horizontal approach.

That said, private enforcement encompasses several remedies: damages awards and other civil sanctions. These other sanctions include injunctions, restitution claims and nullity of a contractual obligation. However, this book concentrates on devising a collective action for damages in the EU and, in this respect, does not examine other remedies. The reason for this is that empirical evidence shows that there is no need to facilitate claims for these remedies because these remedies have already been sought by plaintiffs, ie by businesses.[80]

Where relevant and appropriate this book benefits from US examples which offer both positive and negative lessons for formulating collective redress actions in the EU. US competition law[81] regime has over a century of tradition in private

79 According to the article 19 of *Consolidated Version of the Treaty on European Union* (TEU), the Court of Justice of the European Union encompasses, *inter alia*, the Court of Justice and the General Court. This Book refers to the EU Courts as comprising both the Court of Justice of the European Union (CJEU) and the General Court of the European Union (General Court).

80 See Chapter 2.

81 Competition law is primarily referred to as antitrust law in the US. However, for coherency purposes, this book uses the term 'competition', instead of 'antitrust' for all competition law issues in the EU and US.

enforcement.[82] The US class action regime is not only part of this tradition[83] but is also considered as one of the well-developed, well-established and longstanding regimes in the world.[84] Its examples are followed by many jurisdictions globally.[85] The US regime provides specific examples of which claims may be grouped together to be determined in a class action, how class actions are formulated to address a substantial number of damages claims and how class actions work in practice and, in this respect, may provide significant grounds upon which to build a European approach and make recommendations. Therefore, the analysis takes into account US legislation, particularly the Federal Rules of Civil Procedure (FRCP) rule 23 and reported judicial decisions in the field of private enforcement, including class actions. This book includes an evaluation of various court decisions and uses them to further its own arguments and recommendations.

However, it is important to note that this book examines the class action certification criteria of the US regime only to reveal the utility of these actions. It does not provide a detailed analysis of how those criteria should be met for the commencement of the action but gives a brief overview of their functioning, to the extent that this helps identify the type of claims that aim to be addressed by the class action procedure. This book also aims to study the class action practice under US federal competition law in courts and does not intend to study such actions under state competition laws. However, an exception is made where the book refers to some case examples to show the application of class actions for indirect purchaser consumers as these have no standing under federal law but the majority of states have recognised their standing to sue.

This book focuses on the formulation of a collective redress action and does not intend to answer questions regarding the practicalities of its implementation in the EU, including the competence of the EU in this field, respecting the principles of proportionality and subsidiary, and the appropriate legislative tool for regulating this field or the most suitable Treaty provision for any legislative act. Therefore, this book does not consider issues surrounding a potential harmonisation of national procedural rules. Nevertheless, because its aim is to provide an analysis of collective redress actions in EU competition law, this book explains the arguments for and against binding EU rules and reasons for the efforts of the Commission in relation to collective redress for completeness purposes.

It is beyond the scope of this book to examine questions from an economics perspective, such as human decision making (behavioural economics), societal welfare and deterrence.[86] Neither does it discuss any of the issues from a cost-

82 See F Cengiz, 'Antitrust Damages Actions: Lessons from American Indirect Purchasers' Litigation', *International and Comparative Law Quarterly*, 59 (2010), 39–63, 41.

83 MM Dabbah, *International and Comparative Competition Law* (Cambridge: Cambridge University Press, 2010) 257.

84 Mulheron, Class action (fn 22) 16.

85 See eg Canada and Australia, *ibid.*

86 Economics also concerns the potential cost of collective actions for damages *vis-à-vis* the social harm caused by competition infringement. See further M Hviid and S Peyer,

efficiency perspective, including error costs, harmonisation costs, costs for possible increased litigation nor implementation costs of collective redress. However, it refers to the ways of computing competition damages.

The book does not address the private international law aspect of EU competition law disputes and collective actions, such as cross-border issues concerning the functioning of such actions and relevant jurisdictional rules because this aspect does not have an effect on the design of a collective action. Neither does it examine collective redress actions of national laws in the EU or the ways in which they are applied by national courts. The reason for this is that the findings of the studies conducted by the Commission and the external contractors point out the lack of effective collective redress action in Member States. These studies concluded that the existing national collective redress actions do not produce satisfactory results nor constitute a solution to the problem in the EU. Therefore, the analysis here uses these already available findings to show the need for structuring a collective action that overcomes the barriers to effective redress.

Structure

The focus of this book is on structuring a judicial collective redress action. In this respect, the second chapter explores the concept of collective redress action and the need for it in the field of private EU competition law enforcement in order to set the grounds for the analyses, discussions and proposals for the following chapters. The chapter provides a history of the creation and establishment of the procedure. It also explains its purpose and functioning, identifies the problem in the EU in general and with respect to consumers, and discusses the role of such an action in overcoming this problem based on the submitted need for consumers. It establishes that the purpose and practical functioning of a collective redress action show that such an action could be a means by which to increase the consumers' chances to seek compensation.

The third chapter scrutinises collective redress initiative in competition law, in consumer law and in the horizontal approach respectively. The motivation for collective redress proposals are explained as two distinct initiatives in competition and consumer law and the Commission's proposals in competition law are critically appraised. It then analyses the prevailing horizontal approach and how this addresses the issue. This chapter infers the necessity of a distinctive approach to competition claims, based on the particular characteristics of competition law alongside the particular characteristics of consumer damages as a result of competition infringements. Accordingly, it suggests that these characteristics need to be reflected in the formulation of a collective redress action to deliver real benefits to affected consumers.

'Response to EC Consultation 'Towards a Coherent European Approach to Collective Redress', 2011, 1–7, 2. <http://ec.europa.eu/competition/consultations/2011_collective_redress/hviid_peyer_en.pdf> [accessed 31 July 2015]; BJ Rodger, 'Why Not Court? A Study of Follow-on Actions in the UK', *Journal of Antitrust Enforcement*, 1 (1) (2013), 104–131, 130 fn 178.

The fourth chapter explores the objective(s) of collective redress actions in EU competition cases. The discussion in this chapter informs the formulation of such an action in the sixth, seventh and eighth chapters. This chapter focuses on the objectives of compensation and deterrence. It first explains the EU institutions' stance towards the objectives of actions for damages in order to pave the way for the analysis in the context of collective redress. It also examines the primary objective of collective redress actions and how this contributes to the achievement of other objective(s) and beneficial effects. Lastly, it discusses whether a collective redress action for consumers need to pursue a different objective due to the particular characteristics of these claims. It argues that the whole point of the debate around the introduction of a collective action is to provide victims who are not otherwise able to do so with a realistic means to seek redress. It then concludes that compensation ought to be the main objective when designing a collective redress action.

The fifth chapter aims to present a complete picture of adverse effects upon consumers when Articles 101 and 102 TFEU are infringed in order to identify the characteristics of their damages claims. It explains competition infringements, the different categories of victims that they may harm, focusing on competitors, intermediaries and consumers, and the types of damages that arise. The analysis then gives examples of the types of competition infringements that cause harm to consumers by means of high prices, employing case studies to show how and the extent. It finally identifies the different ways in which consumers incur damages. At the end of this analysis, the chapter submits that the characteristics of consumer claims fit the purpose of collective redress action.

The preliminary conclusion drawn from these chapters is that consumer claims are well suited to be determined by a collective redress action. This book then moves on to structure a collective redress action, an area that the majority of the literature has negative views about and an area that is considered as one of the most topical and controversial topics in the field of private competition law enforcement.

In that regard, the sixth chapter formulates a collective redress action with respect to the systems for establishing the group membership and forming the group. The book acknowledges the fact that the introduction of an EU-wide collective action for consumer damages claims arising from competition infringements is a sensitive issue and therefore any proposal needs to represent an acceptable option for interested stakeholders. The chapter starts by describing possible membership mechanisms and the way in which they operate, and assesses their ability to deliver redress to affected consumers. It concludes that both opt-in and opt-out collective actions should be made available to affected consumers and the discretion to choose between them should be left to courts. The chapter then examines the definition of the group, the types of claims best suited to be determined in a single lawsuit, and different groups of consumers in forming a group. It submits that the group should be defined in a way which only consists of direct and indirect consumers harmed by competition infringements.

The seventh chapter continues to design a collective redress action with respect to the types of representative parties and funding options. It discusses who ought to be allowed to represent a group of affected consumers in a collective action and what kind of funding mechanisms should be made available to a representative party who brings the collective action on behalf of consumers. It is argued that the standing to bring actions on behalf of affected consumers should be granted to consumer associations who would work with lawyers in collective actions and various means of funding mechanisms should be made available to the representative party, including contingency fee arrangements so that these organisations would bring these cases to the courts in practice.

The eighth chapter is also devoted to the formulation of the collective action for consumer damages claims in respect of the calculation of overcharge damages as a group and distribution of the damages award. It first discusses the ways to calculate the damages of the group and the overcharge harm of consumers per product. The chapter then analyses the ways to directly compensate the group of consumers for their harm and ways to deal with undistributed damages. At the end of the analysis, this chapter proposes aggregate damages assessment for the calculation of damages of the group of consumers to avoid individual assessments and submission of individual proof. Following this, it suggests ways to distribute the damages award to the group members to the greatest possible extent. Where applicable, direct reimbursement to the victims via electronic methods should be preferred, and as an alternative way, the group members could be asked to submit evidence of purchase to obtain their shares. In the event of undistributed damages, part of the sum could be allocated to the representative party who brings the collective action and part could be given to the special fund which provides financing for collective actions. Overall, this book shows that if such an action is implemented, it would increase consumer chances to exercise their right to damages and obtain compensation.

2 The notion of and need for collective redress actions

Introduction

This chapter introduces the purpose and development of a collective redress action in order to show the conditions and types of claims that give rise to the need for such an action. To this end, the second section of the chapter explores the steps by which such an action has evolved in order to provide a better understanding of why it has been created and how it functions. Benefiting from US procedure, it describes the policy rationale behind its introduction into law. This analysis helps to demonstrate the type of claims a collective action aims to assist in reaching court. The third section of the chapter, firstly, explains the background to the EU collective redress initiative by addressing the relatively low level of damages actions. Secondly, it analyses the shortcomings that give rise to this level of actions. Thirdly, it elucidates the paucity of damages actions with respect to the types of claimants, the nature of consumer claims and consumer difficulties when seeking damages through individual actions and through existing aggregation mechanisms. These explanations make clear the need for such an action for consumers. Then, the chapter focuses on how a collective action can address consumer claims and overcome the difficulties they encountered in obtaining compensation.

The concept and function of collective redress procedures

A short summary of evolution and policy rationale

Historically, the form of the collective redress action passed through three phases.[1] In seventeenth century England,[2] this device was created as an exception to individual litigation in order to avoid repetitive litigation.[3] It differed vastly from

1 SC Yeazell, 'Group Litigation and Social Context: Toward A History of the Class Action', *Columbia Law Review*, 77(6) (1977), 866–896, 867, 871.

2 However, its roots went back to the 12th century, SC Yeazell, 'The Past and Future of Defendant and Settlement Classes in Collective Litigation', *Arizona Law Review*, 39 (1997), 687–704, 688; R Mulheron, *The Class Action in Common Law Legal Systems: A Comparative Perspective* (Oxford and Portland, Oregon: Hart Publishing, 2004), 9, fn 52.

3 See further Yeazell, Group litigation (fn 1) 866, 868–871.

modern collective litigation. First, the group members were already part of a social group in the community. They did have a leader who had to have been specifically authorised to represent them in court.[4] Secondly, this device was used not to protect the legal rights of aggregated persons, but rather used to set the rules for customary law that governs relationships in rural agricultural communities, thereby shaping future behaviour.[5] Judgments had the character of administrative rulings binding all individuals who had not been parties to the suit.[6] Declaratory judgments were issued and no aggregate damage awards were observed.[7] Hence, it is not possible to regard these cases as involving law or litigation in the modern sense.[8]

The second phase was during the late eighteenth and early nineteenth centuries. In that time, the first US collective action was observed in 1820;[9] it is not certain whether the US system derived from the English.[10] Evolution of legal and political thought in this second phase directed courts in both England and the US to reinterpret existing case law. The groups they confronted had no more cohesion but they did have 'abstractly defined' shared interests[11] due to a transition from agricultural community to a market economy.[12] This transition eventually resulted in the third phase beginning in the mid-twentieth century. With the arrival of a mass-production economy, of the industrial age, an individualised system of litigation had little role to play in reducing the discrepancy between the individuals and infringers.[13] The group structure had changed; this was no longer a social organism but shared an economic interest, who sought a different remedy.[14] This phase necessitated the redesign of the procedure and constitutes the base of modern collective litigation procedure.[15]

In England since 1850 collective litigation has been eroded[16] by the concepts of individual rights and remedies which prevail in the English civil justice system.[17] However, the US has incorporated a class action procedure into law. This procedure was adopted in the FRCP in 1938, before it adopted its current form in

4 *Ibid* 877–878.
5 *Ibid* 871.
6 *Ibid* 892.
7 *Ibid* 888.
8 *Ibid* 871.
9 SC Yeazell, *From Medieval Group Litigation to the Modern Class Action* (New Haven and London: Yale University Press, 1987), 213.
10 *Ibid* 220. See on the contrary, the US imported this procedure from England, A Homburger, 'Private Suits in the Public Interest in the United States of America', *Buffalo Law Review*, 23 (1974), 343–410, 347.
11 Yeazell, From medieval group litigation (fn 9) 160–161.
12 SC Yeazell, 'From Group Litigation to Class Action Part I: Interest, Class, and Representation', *UCLA Law Review*, 27 (1980), 514–564, 562.
13 See *ibid.*
14 Yeazell, From medieval group litigation (fn 9) 165.
15 Yeazell, Group litigation (fn 1) 867.
16 Yeazell, From medieval group litigation (fn 9) 211–212.
17 DR Hensler and others, *Class Action Dilemmas: Pursuing Public Goals for Private Gain* (Arlington: RAND, 2000), 10.

1966.[18] Therefore, the US is seen as a 'hometown of class actions'[19] and this feature entails a brief examination on the rationales which shape its current form.

In the US, three types of harm induced the development of class actions: harm to consumers, harm to the environment and harm to individuals due to racial treatment.[20] Although all three notions affected the way in which class actions were formed more or less similarly, for the purposes of this book, only 'harm to consumers' is considered. Many consumers were affected by the same defendant's wrong. Therefore, *i.* they all shared a common or general interest and *ii.* it was impractical to bring all victims before courts due to the size of the group.[21] Besides, it was unlikely they were going to pursue individual litigation as their injuries were of a small value for a single claimant. However, consumer losses were large in aggregate. The power of the group relative to the individual had constituted the main motive for the introduction of this procedure;[22] when individual redress was unlikely, aggregate losses can be remedied.[23]

From this standpoint, class actions were created as a procedural tool to help remedy the situation through courts.[24] They have a dual mandate: *i.* '[r]educ[ing] units of litigation by bringing under one umbrella what might otherwise be many separate but duplicating actions', *ii.* '[p]rovid[ing] means of vindicating the rights of groups of people who individually would be without effective strength to bring their opponents into court at all'.[25] Therefore, a class action is defined as an action that is brought by a representative party for the '[p]rotection of a right that belongs to a group of people (object of the suit), [and the] judgment will bind the group as a whole (*res judicata*)'.[26]

In this way, claims of numerous victims can be determined in one single suit that is brought by the representative party.[27] There are actually two parties to the action: *i.* the plaintiff representing all the members of the group and *ii.* the

18 Mulheron, Class action (fn 2) 9. See it was first adopted in 1842 in Federal Equity Rules, rule 48, ST Spence, 'Looking Back … In a Collective Way: A Short History of Class Action Law', *Business Law Today*, 11(6) (2002), 21–24, 23.

19 Mulheron (fn 2) 9.

20 Yeazell, From medieval group litigation (fn 9) 244.

21 SN Berk, 'In the Wake of *Concepcion* and *Dukes*, Consumer Class Action Lawyers must Soldier Forward by Leveraging Their Rich History and Taking Some Clues from the Whistleblower Bar', *The Corporate Observer – Consumer Protection*, 2012, 1–10, 9 <http://www.thecorporateobserver.com/uploads/file/120111%20Qui%20Tam%20Class%20Action%20Article_FINAL.pdf> [accessed 18 October 2013].

22 Yeazell, From medieval group litigation (fn 9) 244.

23 *Ibid.* Similarly, L Nader, 'Disputing without the Force of Law', *Yale Law Journal*, 88 (1979), 998–1021, 1021.

24 Yeazell (fn 9) 244.

25 B Kaplan, 'A Prefatory Note', *Boston College Law Review*, 10(3) (1969), 497–500, 497. See advisory committee also referred to small claimants, Homburger (fn 10) 361.

26 A Gidi, 'Class Actions in Brazil – A Model for Civil Law Countries', *American Journal of Comparative Law*, 51 (2013), 311–408, 334.

27 See Mulheron, Class action (fn 2) 5. It could also be on the defendants' side, but this book only considers the plaintiff group.

defendant(s).[28] The class action procedure is characterised as an anomaly because of its representative character.[29] It challenges the individual autonomy by binding all members to the outcome of the decision where the representative acts on their behalf in court.[30] In the traditional model of adjudication the plaintiff actively participates in the lawsuit while an agent acts on her behalf within the knowledge of the client; the judge is a neutral arbiter of issues subject to dispute.[31] However, the class action procedure, which is more than simply a suit with many claims,[32] diverges from traditional litigation. It makes it possible to determine the claims of the group of plaintiffs who are represented and that their representative has the power both to control all the parameters of the suit and to take important decisions.[33]

Therefore, there are disparate views in the literature around class actions. Some describe them as 'legalised blackmail'[34] or a 'Frankenstein's Monster';[35] others see them as 'the most socially useful remedy in history'[36] or a 'social mission'[37] or a 'most powerful legal tool',[38] or 'the wisest and most efficient way of promoting individual justice'.[39] In light of these contradictions, the next section discusses the purpose and functioning of the procedure in order to understand its utility and ability when addressing the grievances of large numbers of victims.

The purpose of the procedure

The representative nature of the procedure is considered as an extension of the individual litigation that is so impractical in situations where there are many

28 A Stadler, 'Collective Action as an Efficient Means for the Enforcement of European Competition Law', in *Private Enforcement of EC Competition Law*, ed. by J Basedow (The Netherlands: International Competition Law Series, volume 25, Kluwer Law International, 2007), 195–213, 210.

29 Yeazell, From medieval group litigation (fn 9) 8.

30 *Ibid* 13–14.

31 A Lahav, 'Fundamental Principles for Class Action Governance', *Indiana Law Review*, 37 (2004), 65–140, 75.

32 *Ibid* 75.

33 The lawyer of the group in the US, *ibid* 75–76.

34 M Handler, 'The Shift from Substantive to Procedural Innovation in Antitrust Suits – The Twenty-Third Annual Antitrust Review', *Columbia Law Review*, 71(1) (1971), 1–36, 9.

35 Dissenting in *Eisen v Carlisle and Jacquelin*, 391 F.2d 555 (2d Cir. 1968) para 572.

36 AL Pomerantz, 'New Developments in Class Actions – Has Their Death Knell Been Sounded', *Business Lawyer*, 25(3) (1970), 1259–1266, 1259.

37 J Kalajdzic, 'Access to a Just Result: Revisiting Settlement Standards and Cy-Pres Distributions', *Canadian Class Action Review*, 6(1) (2010), 215–251, 217.

38 JC Alexander, 'An Introduction to Class Action Procedure in The United States' (presented at the Debates over Group Litigation in Comparative Perspective, Geneva, Switzerland, 2000), 1–26,1 <http://law.duke.edu/grouplit/papers/classactionalexander.pdf> [accessed 1 July 2018].

39 DL Shapiro, 'Class Actions: The Class as Party and Client', *Notre Dame Law Review*, 73(4) (1998), 913–961, 916.

victims with identical or similar claims.[40] In reality, victims, even if aware of others similarly situated, do not usually come together as a group to pursue their claims by hiring a lawyer and by sharing the litigation costs, risks and burden of providing data. Particularly when the value of their loss is not significant, there is no motive for them to do so.[41] The representative nature of this procedure becomes of great importance when traditional litigation falls short of a realistic option for the claimants to have recourse to courts.[42] The resources of the victims and the value of their loss may make it unfeasible to pursue an individual lawsuit and, if this is the only available option, they would remain uncompensated.[43] On this basis, the very objective of a class action is to give recourse to those harmed to obtain damages through an action brought on their behalf where it would not otherwise be likely.[44]

This is confirmed by the certification criteria of class actions in the US: numerosity, commonality, typicality and adequacy.[45] Two additional criteria are set out for actions seeking damages: *i.* common issues to the class must predominate over individual issues (predominance) and *ii.* class action must be a superior tool *vis-à-vis* other available methods for fair and efficient adjudication of the dispute (superiority).[46] These criteria demonstrate why such a procedure exists and what kind of claims are best suited to be determined in a single lawsuit.

Due to the numerosity test, the size of the group matters.[47] Notably, for instance, the Australian regime advocates the numerosity criterion not only for the avoidance of the filing of many individual actions that can otherwise undermine efficiency but also for enhancing access to justice for victims with small value losses.[48] The US regime specifically requires that a group should involve a number of individuals[49] which would render the participation of all group members in the action extremely difficult or inconvenient[50] and therefore makes the class action a practical and convenient means to solve the dispute.[51]

40 Yeazell, From medieval group litigation (fn 9) 13–14.
41 *Ibid* 10.
42 Homburger (fn 10) 347; F Valdes, 'Procedure, Policy and Power: Class Actions and Social Justice in Historical and Comparative Perspective', *Georgia State University Law Review*, 24(3) (2007), 627–661, 636.
43 See AD Lahav, 'Symmetry and Class Action Litigation', *UCLA Law Review*, 60 (2013), 1494–1522, 1517.
44 Mulheron, Class action (fn 2) 248.
45 FRCP rule 23(a).
46 See the further criteria assessing these, FRCP rule 23(b)(3).
47 Mulheron, Class action (fn 2) 115.
48 *Ibid.* See also *Federal Court of Australia Act*, no 156, 1976, sec 33C(1).
49 Mulheron, Class action (fn 2) 123.
50 *Ibid* 121.
51 It is difficult to give an exact number; it could be a very small group or large, see Mulheron, Class action (fn 2) 124. See eg a group of 1.5 million individuals was certified, W Hubbard, 'Optimal Class Size, Dukes, and the Funny Thing about Shady Grove', *DePaul Law Review*, 62 (2013), 693–709, 693. See also in a price-fixing class action case, the Court certified a class of 28 million passengers who were alleged to suffer harm as a result of the collusion between two airline companies over a first-

The size of the group, *inter alia*, determines the impracticability of joinder requirement.[52]

After establishing that a group would consist of a large of number of individuals, the tests of the adequacy of the representative and the typicality of claims determine which claims need to be grouped to be dealt with in a single proceeding. These two tests overlap in the sense that both entail there should be no adverse interest between the representative and group members.[53] It is obviously important for a procedure that is built upon representation that the representative should '[f]airly and adequately protect the interests of the [group]'.[54] The typicality test also aims to form a group that consists of individuals who have same or similar grievances[55] and who are affected by the same course of conduct.[56]

The commonality test, supplemented by the predominance test in class actions seeking damages, aims to bring together the claims that have questions substantially relating to the resolution of the dispute.[57] The predominance test concerns consolidating claims with common issues that prevail over individual issues. In order to give the certification decision, the judge examines to what extent individual issues need to be addressed to solve the controversy,[58] ie whether it is possible to establish the infringement on a group-wide basis, that it imposed harm on the group members, and damage estimation.[59] It is therefore clear that the issue of alikeness makes such an action suitable for dealing with myriad damages claims.[60]

In class actions seeking damages, it is not enough to satisfy the tests above to justify the class action treatment if another more practical means of handling the dispute is available.[61] The superiority test is thus closely linked to the aforementioned requirements. The typicality requirement groups the claims that have

checked baggage fee, *In re Delta/AirTran Baggage Fee Antitrust Litigation*, 317 F.R. D. 675 (N.D. Ga. 2016).

52 A Andreangeli, *Private Enforcement of Antitrust: Regulating Corporate Behaviour through Collective Claims in the EU and US* (Cheltenham UK: Edward Elgar Publishing, 2014), 103.

53 *In re Catfish Antitrust Litigation* 826 F. Supp. 1019 (N.D.Miss. 1993) para 1037.

54 FRCP, rule 23(a)(4); Mulheron, Class action (fn 2) 276.

55 Andreangeli (fn 52) 109.

56 *In re Catfish* (fn 53) para 1036.

57 Andreangeli (fn 52) 105.

58 Federal Judicial Center, '*Manual for Complex Litigation* (fourth)' (2004), (MCL) 262 <http://www.fjc.gov/public/pdf.nsf/lookup/MCL40000.pdf/$file/MCL40000.pdf> [accessed 1 July 2018].

59 DM Allen and CS Coutroulis, 'Back to the Future: Toward A More Rigorous Analysis of Antitrust Class Actions', *Antitrust Bulletin*, 48 (2003), 463–503, 473–475; JP Davis and EL Cramer, 'Antitrust, Class Certification, and the Politics of Procedure', *George Mason Law Review*, 17(4) (2010), 969–1033, 971.

60 A Erbsen, 'From "Predominance" to "Resolvability": A New Approach to Regulating Class Actions', *Vanderbilt Law Review*, 58(4) (2005), 995–1088, 998.

61 See 'Notes of Advisory Committee on Rules—1966 Amendment to Rule 23(b)(3)', 1996 <http://www.law.cornell.edu/rules/frcp/rule_23> [accessed 1 July 2018].

sufficient similarity,[62] the commonality and predominance requirements ensure that common issues are significant enough and will not leave an array of issues for individual treatment.[63] In this way, the action achieves judicial economy, '[e] conomies of time, effort, and expense [...]'[64] and renders the class action a superior tool.[65] The numerosity requirement has a similar effect, the larger the group the fewer the options for adjudicating the dispute.[66]

The superiority test is generally satisfied if the value of the members' claims is an obstacle to individual proceedings,[67] meaning there are no other available methods and the class action is the only option for litigation.[68] For instance, a court concluded – in a case where the claim value for each member was $70 – that economic reality dictates the only means for the claimants to get compensation in a complex competition case is a class action.[69] If the pursuit of individual litigation is economically feasible, then plaintiffs may wish to do so to control their own cases, rather than be represented in a class action that is essentially a departure from traditional procedure.[70] In the US, there are judgments that denied certification on the grounds that the group members have high value claims.[71]

Consequently, although its scope is wider than for that for which it was created, when taken together these requirements reveal the purpose of this procedure: to make the litigation a viable option for a large group of individuals with small and sufficiently homogenous[72] claims. Indeed, class action functions much better for these types of losses than its reputation in the EU suggests.[73] The next section explains the efforts of the Commission towards a collective redress action in order to establish the link between the purpose of and the need for such an action.

62 Mulheron, Class action (fn 2) 313.
63 *Ibid* 209.
64 Notes of advisory committee (fn 61).
65 Mulheron, Class action (fn 2) 313.
66 *Ibid* 259.
67 S Calkins, 'An Enforcement Official's Reflections on Antitrust Class Actions', *Arizona Law Review*, 39 (1997), 413–451, 439. See the fact that the defendants were sophisticated, influential or wealthy plays a role in the court's assessment of the superiority of the class action, Mulheron, Class action (fn 2) 237.
68 See eg *Phillips Petroleum Co. v Shutts*, 472 US 797 (1985) para 809.
69 *Eisen v Carlisle and Jacquelin* 417 US 156 (1974) para 161.
70 Mulheron, Class action (fn 2) 229–230.
71 *Ibid.*
72 S Harnay and A Marciano, 'Seeking Rents through Class Actions and Legislative Lobbying: A Comparison', *European Journal of Law and Economics*, 32(2) (2011), 293–304, 298. Similarly, NERA Economic Consulting, 'Memo: Comments in Relation to the White Paper on Damages Actions for Breach of the EC Antitrust Rules', 2008, para 15 <http://ec.europa.eu/competition/antitrust/actionsdamages/white_paper_comments/nera_en.pdf> [accessed 1 July 2018].
73 G Wagner, 'Collective Redress – Categories of Loss and Legislative Options', *Law Quarterly Review*, 127 (2011), 55–82, 72.

Setting the scene for EU collective redress actions

The recognition and exercise of the right to damages

In the context of EU competition law enforcement, public and private enforcement are regarded as mutually complementary[74] and reinforcing one another.[75] In practice actions for damages are rarely brought before national courts and victims of competition infringements are generally uncompensated for loss suffered. In the last decade, the Commission's efforts have been concentrated on changing this private enforcement landscape. Indeed, the rationale behind the modernisation and decentralisation of competition enforcement between the years of 1999–2004[76] was the Commission's desire to share its enforcement tasks with national competition authorities and courts,[77] particularly in an enlarged EU.[78] An increased use of private enforcement is regarded as a support for the Commission's own enforcement efforts,[79] to which the CJEU has also contributed with its landmark judgments.

The CJEU in *Francovich*, a state liability case, announced an EU right to damages.[80] Following the decision, it was emphasised that this right should not

74 See eg Commission, *Proposal for a Directive of the European Parliament and of the Council on Certain Rules Governing Actions for Damages under National Law for Infringements of the Competition Law Provisions of the Member States and of the European Union*, (2013/0185 (COD), COM(2013) 404 final, Strasbourg, 2013) (Directive proposal) para 1.2. See also eg RJ van den Bergh and PD Camesasca, *European Competition Law and Economics: A Comparative Perspective*, 2nd edn (London: Sweet & Maxwell, 2006), 330; E Paulis, 'Policy Issues in the Private Enforcement of EC Competition Law', in *Private Enforcement of EC Competition Law*, ed. by J Basedow (The Netherlands: Kluwer Law International, 2007), 7–16, 9; AP Komninos, *EC Private Antitrust Enforcement: Decentralised Application of EC Competition Law by National Courts* (Oxford and Portland, Oregon: Hart Publishing, 2008), xiv, 15.

75 Commission, *Communication from the Commission on Quantifying Harm in Actions for Damages Based on Breaches of Article 101 or 102 of the Treaty on the Functioning of the European Union* (OJ C 167/19, 2013), paras 1–2; N Dunne, 'The Role of Private Enforcement within EU Competition Law', in *Cambridge Yearbook of European Legal Studies*, ed. by A Albors-Llorens, KA Armstrong, and MW Gehring, vol.16 (Oxford and Portland, Oregon: Hart Publishing, 2014), 143–187, 145.

76 Commission, '*White Paper on Modernisation of the Rules Implementing Articles [101] and [102] of the EC Treaty' Commission Programme No 99/027* (COM(1999) 101 final, Brussels, 1999). For more information on the Commission's initiatives in the 1990s, see Komninos, EC private antitrust enforcement (fn 74) 45 et seq.

77 *Council Regulation (EC) No 1/2003 of 16 December 2002 on the Implementation of the Rules on Competition Laid down in Articles [101] and [102] of the Treaty*, (OJ L 1/1, 2003), recitals 3, 7; R Whish and D Bailey, *Competition Law*, 7th edn (Oxford: Oxford University Press, 2012), 296.

78 Commission, *Staff Working Document Public Consultation: Towards a Coherent European Approach to Collective Redress* (SEC(2011)173 final, 2011), para 3; SV Walle, *Private Antitrust Litigation in the European Union and Japan – A Comparative Perspective* (Antwerpen-Apeldoorn: Maklu, 2013), 160.

79 See eg C Hodges, 'Competition Enforcement, Regulation and Civil Justice: What Is the Case?' *Common Law Market Review*, 43 (2006), 1381–1407, 1382.

80 Joined cases C-6/90 and C-9/90 *Andrea Francovich and Danila Bonifaci and others v Italian Republic* [1991] ECR I-05357 para 33.

change depending on the perpetrator, whether state or individual, because its basis is the principle of effectiveness of EU law.[81] Although the Courts' previous rulings indicated the possibility,[82] there was no clarity regarding the availability of an action for damages in competition law until 2001. Then, for the first time, the Court in *Courage* dealt with the question of whether Member States were obliged to secure a damages remedy for the harm arising from EU competition infringements and answered in the affirmative.[83] Five years later, *Manfredi* reiterated the same view.[84] Those decisions have drastically changed the status quo[85] and led the Commission to take active steps to enhance private enforcement through damages actions as the 'Guardian of the Treaty'.[86]

In 2004, the Ashurst study examined the obstacles to successful damages claims in the then 25 Member States. It established that there was a 'total underdevelopment' and 'astonishing diversity' between the national laws and their attitudes.[87] It found 60 judged damages actions[88] on the basis of either EU or national competition law, out of which only 28 resulted in a damages award.[89] The number of cases presented in the Ashurst study has been criticised due to the data collection method[90] that left out settlements[91] and cases resolved by arbitration.[92] It is also true that some Member States do not

81 Komninos, EC private antitrust enforcement (fn 74) 166.
82 See eg Opinion of Advocate General (AG) van Gerven delivered on 27 October 1993 in Case C-128/92 *H. J. Banks & Co. Ltd v British Coal Corporation* [1994] ECR 1994 I-01209, para 37; Case C-5/94 *R v Ministry of Agriculture, Fisheries and Food, ex p Hedley Lomas* [1996] ECR I-02553, paras 31–32.
83 Case C-453/99 *Courage Ltd. v Bernard Crehan* [2001] ECR I-6297, paras 25–26.
84 Joined Cases C-295/04 and C-298/04 *Vincenzo Manfredi v Lloyd Adriatico Assicurazioni SpA* [2006] ECR I-06619, paras 60–61.
85 See it is open to debate whether the Commission would have been able to propose such measures in its papers without *Courage*, Komninos EC private antitrust enforcement (fn 74) 162.
86 V Milutinovic, *The 'Right to Damages' under EU Competition Law: From Courage v. Crehan to the White Paper and Beyond* (The Netherlands: Kluwer Law International, 2010), 29.
87 D Waelbroeck, D Slater and G Even-Shoshan, *Ashurst Study on the Conditions of Claims for Damages in Case of Infringement of EC Competition Rules, Comparative Report* (Brussels, 2004), 1.
88 See two cases that were discovered after the publication of the study, J Lawrence, 'Seeking the Perfect Balance: Some Reflections on the Commission Green Paper on Damages Actions for Breach of the EC Antitrust Rules', in *European Competition Law Annual 2006: Enforcement of Prohibition of Cartels*, ed. by CD Ehlermann and I Atanasiu (Oxford and Portland, Oregon: Hart Publishing, 2006), 457–476, 458, fn 4.
89 See only eight of these cases based on EU competition law alone, Ashurst study (fn 87) 1.
90 S Peyer, 'Private Enforcement of Competition Law – A Case Study from Germany', *University of East Anglia, CCP Working Paper no 10–12*, 2010, 1–74, 7 <http://competitionpolicy.ac.uk/documents/8158338/8256105/CCP+Working+Paper+10-12.pdf/fedbb885-d48d-4506-86e6-42dba23b8980> [accessed 1 July 2018].
91 Whish and Bailey (fn 77) 296.
92 D Waelbroeck and D Slater, 'The Commission's Green Paper on Private Enforcement: "Americanization" of EC Competition Law Enforcement?', in *European Competition*

publish all cases.[93] Nonetheless, the study revealed a relatively low number of damages actions and the reasons for this.[94]

Subsequently, the welfare impact report analysed the level of private enforcement through damages actions in the then 27 Member States from 2004 to 2007[95] and found a slight and fragmented development that was still not far from Ashurst's 'total underdevelopment'.[96] It observed damages actions in only ten Member States with a total of 96 cases slightly higher than the number identified by the Ashurst study.[97] Moreover, although the majority of these were follow-on cases,[98] only 18 cases led to an award at final judgment.[99]

In the study for a directive in 2013, the Commission reiterated that the situation had not changed much since *Courage*; 12 years later many victims were still unable to file damages claims and obtain compensation through individual or collective actions.[100] The great majority of actions for damages were observed in the UK, Germany and the Netherlands,[101] and only 28% of the Commission infringement decisions between the years of 2006 and 2012 resulted in actions for damages which were brought mostly by large businesses.[102] No actions following a Commission decision were reported in 20 Member States.[103] It then stated that

93 Komninos, EC private antitrust enforcement (fn 74) 179, fn 231.

94 See Whish and Bailey (fn 77) 296.

95 Centre for European Policy Studies (CEPS), Erasmus University Rotterdam (EUR) and Luiss Guido Carli (LUISS), *Report for the European Commission 'Making Antitrust Damages Actions More Effective in the EU: Welfare Impact and Potential Scenarios', Final Report*, 2007 (Welfare impact report) 39.

96 *Ibid* 551.

97 *Ibid* 39–40.

98 *Ibid* 40.

99 *Ibid* 42.

100 Commission, *Executive Summary of the Impact Assessment – Damages Actions for Breach of the EU Antitrust Rules, Accompanying the Proposal for a Directive of the European Parliament and of the Council on Certain Rules Governing Actions for Damages under National Law for Infringements of the Competition Law Provisions of the Member States and of the European Union* (SWD(2013) 204 final, Strasbourg, 2013), para 1.

101 Commission, *Staff Working Document – Impact Assessment Report – Damages Actions for Breach of the EU Antitrust Rules Accompanying the Proposal for a Directive of the European Parliament and of the Council on Certain Rules Governing Actions for Damages under National Law for Infringements of the Competition Law Provisions of the Member States and of the European Union* (SWD(2013) 203 final, Strasbourg, 2013), (SWD-IAR) para 52.

102 15 out of 54 cases, *ibid* paras 52–53. See it has been stated as 25% in Commission, *Press Release on Antitrust: Commission Proposes Legislation to Facilitate Damage Claims by Victims of Antitrust Violations* (IP/13/525, Brussels, 2013), 1–3, 1 <http://europa.eu/rapid/press-release_IP-13-525_en.htm> [accessed 1 July 2018].

103 SWD-IAR (fn 101) para 52. See in Member States there are also very few follow-on actions following national competition authorities' decisions and stand-alone actions almost have no share, D Calisti and L Haasbeek, 'The Proposal for a Directive on Antitrust Damages Actions: The European Commission Sets the Stage for Private Enforcement in the European Union', *CPI Antitrust Chronicle*, 8(1) 2013, 1–9, 1 <https://www.competitionpolicyinternational.com/the-proposal-for-a-directive-on-a

victims of competition infringements each year approximately forego between €5.7 billion and €23.3 billion in the EU.[104]

The right to damages has long been established but, as seen above, victims of competition infringements do not exercise this right effectively. Since 2005, the Commission has identified barriers to a more effective enforcement of right to damages. One of these barriers is the difficulty in obtaining the relevant evidence to prove the infringement, damage and the causal link between the infringement and the damage suffered. Competition cases are not only fact sensitive but also subject to information asymmetry.[105] The problem of information asymmetry in competition cases refers to the fact that the relevant evidence of the alleged infringement is in the hands of the infringer or of third parties[106] and that claimants face difficulties in having access to the evidence possessed by infringers or third parties.[107] It is especially the case in stand-alone actions, but there is another problem in follow-on action,[108] which is the absence of a clear probative value of the decisions of national competition authorities.[109]

Another barrier is high costs and risks associated with competition litigation that discourage victims from suing the infringers for damages.[110] The complex nature of proof and quantification of competition damages also makes the competition litigation risky for claimants, but, in addition to this, there are uncertainties as regards the appropriate scope of damages that victims of competition infringements should be entitled to.[111] According to the Commission, the uncertainties do not end there because the absence of clear rules on the standing of indirect purchasers and on the passing-on defence constitutes another barrier for victims to obtain compensation. These uncertainties are such as whether victims can sue, how they prove the pass-on and their case and how their damage is calculated.[112] Lastly, the lack of effective collective redress actions, especially for small claimants, is considered as another barrier to the effective enforcement of the right to damages.[113]

ntitrust-damages-actions-the-european-commission-sets-the-stage-for-private-enforcement-in-the-european-union/> [accessed 1 July 2018].

104 Welfare impact report (fn 95) 157–158; SWD-IAR (fn 101) para 67.

105 Commission, *Staff Working Paper Accompanying the White Paper on Damages Actions for Breach of the EC Antitrust Rules* (SEC(2008) 404, Brussels, 2008), (SWPWP) paras 65–66.

106 *Ibid*; Directive proposal (fn 74) explanatory memorandum para 4.2.

107 Directive proposal (fn 74) explanatory memorandum para 4.2.

108 See Chapter 1 for the definitions of stand-alone and follow-on actions.

109 Directive proposal (fn 74) explanatory memorandum para 1.2. See further Chapter 6.

110 Commission, *Staff Working Paper Annex to the Green Paper Damages Actions for Breach of the EC Antitrust Rules* (SEC(2005)1732, Brussels, 2005), (SWPGP), para 10; SWPWP (fn 105) para 22.

111 SWPWP (fn 105) para 180.

112 SWPGP (fn 110) paras 38–39; *ibid* para 27; Directive proposal (fn 74) explanatory memorandum para 1.2. See the detailed analysis on passing-on in Chapter 5.

113 SWPWP (fn 105) para 24; Directive proposal (fn 74) explanatory memorandum para 1.2.

In light of this, the proposal for introducing a collective redress action is presented as one of the ways to increase the number of actions for damages. Competition infringements impose harm on diverse stakeholders, such as competitors, suppliers, direct and indirect purchasers. However, the situation is not the same for all claimants. The most recent study for the Directive highlighted that it is mainly large companies that bring actions for damages. Although the above studies have drawn attention to the general paucity of actions for damages, the Commission has put emphasis on the necessity of having such an action for claims that are uneconomical to litigate individually.[114] This is in line with the previously submitted purpose of a collective action. In this respect, the following section refers to other studies that establish the need in this area in respect of the type of the claimant. By so doing, it also aims to identify the claims that fit the purpose of a collective redress action.

The need for collective redress actions for consumers

Barriers to the effective compensation of consumers

Danov notes that large companies currently pursue damages claims in the EU.[115] Walle finds that in the EU actions for damages have primarily been brought by businesses and have led to major awards.[116] He shows that while competitors and companies who are direct purchasers from the defendant have recovered significant damages due to the significant value of their damages claims, consumers have rarely filed a claim.[117] A study on private enforcement of any remedy in Spain identifies one consumer-initiated case out of 323.[118] Another study observes that the level of competition litigation is high in Germany[119] but identifies only one consumer and indirect purchaser claim.[120] In Rodger's study on EU private enforcement, all competition-related cases are analysed in the period of 1999–2012.[121] The study shows that the paucity of private enforcement is mainly

114 SWPGP (fn 110) para 188; Commission, *White Paper on Damages Actions for Breach of the EC Antitrust Rules* (COM(2008) 165 final, Brussels, 2008) (White Paper) para 2.1.

115 See the cases in M Danov, 'Collective Redress and Competition Law Claims: Some Specific Issues', in *Collective Redress in Europe – Why and How?*, ed. by E Lein and others (London: The British Institute of International and Comparative Law, 2015), 337–355, 341.

116 Walle (fn 78) 241.

117 *Ibid* 232.

118 F Marcos, 'Competition Law Private Litigation in the Spanish Courts (1999–2012)', *IE Law School Working Paper no AJ8–202*, 1–111, 12 <http://ssrn.com/abstract=2351770> [accessed 1 July 2018].

119 The study involves all remedies. S Peyer, 'Private Antitrust Litigation in Germany from 2005 to 2007: Empirical Evidence', *Journal of Competition Law and Economics*, 8(2) (2012), 331–359, 338.

120 *Ibid* 345.

121 These cases include injunctions, declarations, defence, pre-action disclosure, nullity and damages. BJ Rodger, 'The Empirical Data Part 2: Provisions Relied Upon, Remedies and Success', in *Competition Law Comparative Private Enforcement and*

limited to damages actions – only 17.1% of all cases.[122] Unsurprisingly perhaps, it finds only 41 individual consumer cases out of all the case law, 1263 cases.[123]

It is therefore possible to argue that any private enforcement initiative should be concentrated on enabling consumers to obtain compensation.[124] The fact that consumers are less likely to bring individual actions for damages is related to the type of the loss they suffer. On this basis, it is sensible to draw a distinction between consumer and business losses. Within the application of the Articles 101 and 102 TFEU, the concept of 'consumers' encompasses both customers and consumers,[125] but they need to be distinguished from one another for the sake of collective redress. The Commission seems to apply this distinction to collective redress considering that once it suggested different designs for other purchasers and consumers[126] and referred to those claimants separately.[127]

Customers can be defined as any intermediary further down in the supply chain who purchase directly/indirectly from the infringers and who act in the pursuit of trade.[128] Consumers are the persons who make a purchase for purposes outside trade or business, ie end-users.[129] The way in which infringement causes harm and the kind of loss suffered likely differs between these two groups. Consumers are at the bottom of the distribution chain, purchase for personal use and sustain damages related to price enhancement. Their losses tend to be individually smaller, similar and widespread *vis-à-vis* commercial entities.[130]

Collective Redress across the EU, ed. by BJ Rodger (The Netherlands: Kluwer Law International, 2014), 121–156, 124.

122 *Ibid.*

123 BJ Rodger, 'Collective Redress Mechanisms and Consumer Case-Law' in *Competition Law Comparative Private Enforcement and Collective Redress across the EU*, ed. by BJ Rodger (The Netherlands: Kluwer Law International, 2014), 157–192, 162.

124 Walle (fn 78) 241.

125 See eg Commission, *Guidelines on the Application of Article [101](3) of the Treaty* (OJ C 101/97, 2004), para 84; Commission, *Guidance on the Commission's Enforcement Priorities in Applying Article [102 TFEU] to Abusive Exclusionary Conduct by Dominant Undertakings* (OJ C 45/7, 2009), para 19, fn 15.

126 Commission, *Green Paper on Damages Actions for Breach of EC Antitrust Rules* (COM(2005) 672 final, Brussels, 2005), (Green Paper) option 26.

127 *Ibid.* Similarly, the White Paper mentioned consumers and small and medium-sized businesses (SMEs), White Paper (fn 114) para 2.1.

128 In the context of this book, see further Chapter 5.

129 The definition of consumer is the same in consumer law. See *Council Directive 93/13/EEC of 5 April 1993 on Unfair Terms in Consumer Contracts*, (OJ L 095, 1993), art. 2(b); *Directive 2005/29/EC of the European Parliament and of the Council of 11 May 2005 Concerning Unfair Business-to-Consumer Commercial Practices in the Internal Market and Amending Council Directive 84/450/EEC, Directives 97/7/EC, 98/27/EC and 2002/65/EC of the European Parliament and of the Council and Regulation (EC) No 2006/2004 of the European Parliament and of the Council*, (OJ L 149/22, 2005), art. 2(a). See also economics adopts the same definition, P Akman, '"Consumer" versus "Customer": The Devil in the Detail', *Journal of Law and Society*, 37(2) (2010), 315–344, 317.

130 See further Chapter 5.

With this in mind, it is difficult for consumers to pursue individual actions for the following reasons. First, competition infringements entail the investigation of a broad set of facts[131] containing complex as well as economic analysis.[132] However, consumers as end-users *i.* are not in a position to know the market conditions, *ii.* may lack sufficient understanding of competition law and how to suspect an infringement, *iii.* may not be aware that competition infringement inflicts harm on them. Indeed, consumers suffer from informational disadvantage against the infringer. As mentioned, there exists information asymmetry between the defendant and claimants in competition cases but its degree differs from victim to victim. The relevant evidence on the facts of anticompetitive behaviour is held and concealed by the infringer or by third parties; this is neither known nor easily attainable by consumers.[133] Furthermore, administrative burdens, costs and risks of bringing an action deter consumers from suing,[134] especially due to the small value of their losses. The outcome of a competition case is too uncertain.[135] Litigation costs can be high because cases tend to take a long time. For instance, competition cases take the longest time – 48 months – before the General Court.[136] Hence, courts and lawyers need to exert more effort in these cases. Consumers' financial positions also prevent them suing and the loss at stake does not provide enough incentive to pursue such a complex litigation individually.

Inadequacy of existing aggregation mechanisms

Given that consumers generally eschew bringing an individual action, the existing aggregation mechanisms[137] also do not assist them in claiming damages. Almost all national legal systems have some form of aggregation mechanism to deal with large

131 Green Paper (fn 126) para 2.1.

132 Commission, *Staff Working Document Accompanying Document to the White Paper on Damages Actions for Breach of the EC Antitrust Rules – Impact Assessment* (SEC (2008) 405, Brussels, 2008), (Impact assessment) para 31; SWPWP (fn 105) para 314; SM Colino, *Competition Law of the EU and UK*, 7th edn (Oxford: Oxford University Press, 2011), 2. Robertson states that the exercise carried out by judges in competition litigation is more complex than any exercise done in commercial litigation. A Robertson, 'UK competition litigation: from Cinderella to Goldilocks?', *Competition Law Journal*, 9(2) (2010), 275–294, 282.

133 See Green Paper (fn 126) para 2.1; White Paper (fn 114) para 2.2.

134 SWPWP (fn 105) para 50.

135 C Leskinen, 'Collective Actions: Rethinking Funding and National Cost Rules', *Competition Law Review*, 8(1) (2011), 87–121, 111.

136 M van der Woude, 'The General Court: The Need and Opportunity for Reform' (King's College, London, 2013) <http://www.kcl.ac.uk/law/research/centres/european/KCL-Marc-van-der-Woude-GC-Reform-08-03-13.pdf> [accessed 29 January 2015].

137 The term is defined as any procedural tool designed to decide a number of matters together. S Rodrigue and L Plumpton, 'The Globalisation of Anti-Trust: How the Internationalisation of Collective Redress is Changing the Game', *Class and Group Actions 2014*, 2013, 31–39, 32 <http://www.torys.com/Publications/Documents/Publication%20PDFs/CA2013-4.pdf> [accessed 1 July 2018].

numbers of plaintiffs when a wrong causes the same, or similar, damages.[138] Although it differs from legal system to legal system and there exists no standard categorisation,[139] it is useful to organise these aggregation mechanisms to explain their inadequacy compared with a collective redress action with respect to consumer claims.[140] These are consolidation of cases, joinder actions, test cases and claim assignment.

The procedure of consolidation of cases allows the judge to combine several lawsuits before the court into one if they raise common questions.[141] In joinder actions[142] several plaintiffs pursue their claims together against the same defendant or the judge can decide to join the claims in one suit due to some commonality shared between them.[143] These two procedures achieve some degree of procedural efficiency as similar or related claims are heard in a single forum. When combined, the costs and risks of the litigation are to an extent reduced for claimants, but only for those who have already brought their own actions to courts.[144] However, both procedures resemble the traditional two-party litigation, because the judges must apply all the procedures on an individual basis for each plaintiff.[145] The plaintiffs' claims and damages awards are determined separately.[146] Therefore, these procedures neither deal with the claims in a cost and time efficient manner nor work when the court needs to combine the cases brought by a significant number of plaintiffs into one action with individual rulings.[147]

Test cases are available when filed claims have common factual and legal issues. In this scenario, the court rules on one of the claims; the others are suspended until the test case is decided.[148] Although the test case is an individual action on one filed claim, it affects other plaintiffs' interests.[149] This procedure suffers

138 JA Jolowicz, 'Group Litigation, Damages, and Judicial Control by Civil Courts', in *Judicial Review in International Perspective*, ed. by M Andenas and D Fairgrieve (The Netherlands: Kluwer Law International, 2000), vol.II, 481–491, 482.

139 See ZS Tang, 'Consumer Collective Redress in European Private International Law', *Journal of Private International Law*, 7(1) (2011), 101–147, 103. The number of procedures discussed here is not exhaustive, rather is illustrative.

140 European Parliament states that small claims procedure shows a similar pattern. European Parliament, *Resolution on 'Towards a Coherent European Approach to Collective Redress'* (2011/2089(INI), 2012) para 10 <http://www.europarl.europa.eu/sides/getDoc.do?pubRef=-//EP//TEXT+TA+P7-TA-2012-0021+0+DOC+XML+V0//EN> [accessed 1 July 2018]. See also *Regulation (EC) No 861/2007 of the European Parliament and of the Council of 11 July 2007 establishing a European Small Claims Procedure*, (OJ L 199/1, 2007).

141 SE Keske, *Group Litigation in European Competition Law: A Law and Economics Perspective* (Antwerp-Oxford-Portland: Intersentia, 2010) 194.

142 It is also named joint actions. See eg Ashurst study (fn 87) 43; Stadler (fn 28) 201.

143 Stadler (fn 28) 201.

144 *Ibid* 202.

145 Keske (fn 141) 40.

146 Stadler (fn 28) 202.

147 H-W Micklitz and A Stadler, 'The Development of Collective Legal Actions in Europe, Especially in German Civil Procedure', *European Business Law Review*, 17(5) (2006), 1473–1503, 1476–1477; Wagner (fn 73) 66.

148 G Barling, 'Collective Redress for Breach of Competition Law – A Case for Reform', *Competition Law Journal*, 2011, 5–20, 11.

149 See in the context of Germany, Stadler (fn 28) 202–203.

inadequacies similar to joinder actions.[150] Furthermore, the outcome of the test case does not resolve other similar legal actions, it merely serves as a precedent.[151] It has thus been criticised for being unduly costly, causing procedural inefficiencies and creating unnecessary duplication.[152]

It is established that consolidation of cases, joinder actions and test cases operate as the traditional two-party litigation and therefore do not assist in the determination of the claims of myriad number of plaintiffs. Moreover, they require that individuals have already filed their claims.[153] However, currently the problem in the EU is consumers do not bring an action in the first place.[154]

Another aggregation mechanism is Group Litigation Orders (GLO).[155] This procedure aims to enable a single court to deal with multiple individual claims having common or related issues of law.[156] It is a case management tool rather than a collective action.[157] The claimants register their names on the listing created for the case at hand and in this way the ruling of the court on common or related issues proceeded as a test case[158] becomes binding on the others in this list.[159] It makes the registered claimants both parties to the case and members of the group.[160] Consequently, it is no different from individual litigation.[161]

There is also a new strategy for aggregating individual claims into one lawsuit: claim assignment.[162] The Cartel Damage Claims SA (CDC), as the best known example, simply buys the damages claims from victims to bundle them into a lawsuit in its own name and on its own account, thereby solely undertaking costs and risks in and out of the court proceedings.[163] To date, five cases have been

150 See Keske (fn 141) 41.

151 Micklitz and Stadler (fn 147) 1479; Tang (fn 139) 103; Barling (fn 148) 11.

152 J Blennerhassett, 'Is It Time to Get the Multi-Party Started? Exploring the Spectrum of Mass Harm Redress in Ireland', *Supreme Court Law Review (2d)*, 53 (2011), 347–383, 373.

153 Welfare impact report (fn 95) 269.

154 Stadler (fn 28) 202.

155 It is introduced in 2000 in the UK. *Civil Procedure Rules* (CPR), 1998, part 19, sec III. Note that this book refers to England and Wales as the UK.

156 *Ibid* part 19.10.

157 Walle (fn 78) 179.

158 N Andrews, 'Multi-Party Actions and Complex Litigation in England', *European Business Law Review*, 23(1) (2012), 1–24, 19.

159 C Bernard and S Bourjade, 'Economic Incentives in Class Actions: An Analysis through the US/EU Examples', *Global Competition Litigation Review*, 6(1) (2013), 12–17, 14; *ibid* 20.

160 Andrews (fn 158) 19.

161 R Mulheron, 'Some Difficulties with Group Litigation Orders – And Why a Class Action Is Superior', *Civil Justice Quarterly*, 24 (2005), 40–68, 47.

162 Impact assessment (fn 132) para 53.

163 See CDC, 'Comments on the UK Government's Proposals on Private Actions in Competition Law: A Consultation on Options for Reform Published in April 2012', 2012, 1 <http://www.carteldamageclaims.com/CDC%20Comments_UK%20Proposals%20Private%20Actions%20in%20Competition%20Law_2012.pdf> [accessed 24 January 2013].

brought using this mechanism.[164] Claim assignment cannot actually be qualified as an action built upon representation because the CDC owns the claims.[165] Additionally, it can only operate effectively where the number of plaintiffs is small and their individual damages are significant.[166] In other words, this mechanism would not work in cases where a large number of individuals are harmed[167] because in practice it would be nearly impossible to get in touch with each to purchase their claims. It also might not be worth the effort if damages claims are not of substantial value.

All this suggests that there is a need for an EU collective redress action. It should also be noted that the issue is not that consumers do not want to seek redress. On the contrary, they do not have the appropriate procedural tool at their disposal. The Euro-barometer survey shows that 79% of consumers would be more likely to defend their rights if collective redress actions were made available so that they could do so with other affected consumers.[168]

However, another set of problems arises from existing collective redress actions of Member States. There are countries that have no such action,[169] amidst which some have no intention of adopting one at all.[170] Collective redress actions also vary widely from Member State to Member State.[171] Although almost all Member States assert that they have some form of collective redress action,[172] only a very few have and operate this system in real terms[173] and those are rarely used.[174] The diverse scope and procedural characteristics of national collective redress actions present inequalities between Member States[175] and therefore the exercise of the right to damages through

164 CDC, 'Cases' <http://www.carteldamageclaims.com> [accessed 1 July 2018].

165 ELI, 'Statement of the European Law Institute on Collective Redress and Competition Damages Claims', 2014, 1–81, 56 <http://www.europeanlawinstitute.eu/fileadmin/user_upload/p_eli/Projects/S-5-2014_Statement_on_Collective_Redress_and_Competition_Damages_Claims.pdf> [accessed 1 July 2018].

166 Wagner (fn 73) 75.

167 E Kocher, 'Collective Rights and Collective Goods: Enforcement as Collective Interest', in *Mass Justice: Challenges of Representation and Distribution*, ed. by J Steele and W H Van Boom (Cheltenham UK: Edward Elgar Publishing, 2011), 118–135, 122; *ibid.*

168 Commission, *Consumer Attitudes towards Cross-Border Trade and Consumer Protection: Analytical Report*, 2011, 56 <http://ec.europa.eu/consumers/strategy/docs/consumer_eurobarometer_2011_en.pdf> [accessed 1 July 2018].

169 See these eight countries in P Buccirossi and M Carpagnano, 'Is It Time for the European Union to Legislate in the Field of Collective Redress in Antitrust (and How)?', *Journal of European Competition Law and Practice*, 4(1) (2013), 3–15, 4.

170 JG Delatre, 'Beyond the White Paper: Rethinking the Commission's Proposal on Private Antitrust Litigation', *Competition Law Review*, 8(1) (2011), 29–58, 37.

171 See eg Commission, *Recommendation on Common Principles for Injunctive and Compensatory Collective Redress Mechanisms in the Member States Concerning Violations of Rights Granted under Union Law* (2013/396/EU, OJ L 201/60, 2013), preamble 9.

172 Ashurst study (fn 87) 2.

173 *Ibid* 42–47.

174 *Ibid* 105.

175 Directorate-General for Internal Policies, *Collective Redress in Antitrust* (IP/A/ECON/ST/2011-PE 475.120, 2012), para 2.2.1.

such actions differs from one country to another.[176] The overall performance of the existing actions is also unsatisfactory.[177] Rodger's study on private competition law enforcement observes only five collective actions on behalf of consumers across Europe between 1999–2012.[178]

The role of collective redress actions

The concept of access to courts[179] or access to justice[180] can be an issue in situations where numerous victims are harmed by the same or similar wrong, particularly where small losses make individual litigation unviable[181] even if claims are strong.[182] Collective actions enhance their litigation possibilities *vis-à-vis* the traditional individualistic procedures.[183]

First, a collective redress action reduces costs to reasonable levels per case. In individual litigation, even if all evidence collected in the initial trial is available and used in any subsequent cases, each lawsuit necessitates time and resources outlaid on lawyers and courts.[184] Through a collective redress action, claims arising from similar facts are addressed in a single lawsuit. This avoids repetition[185] and prevents each individual from expending effort and costs on a lawsuit against the same defendant for the same conduct.[186] For instance, when an Austrian consumer association initiated a lawsuit on behalf of 16 consumers, it did cost in total

176 See eg The Law Society of England and Wales, 'Response to Towards a Coherent European Approach to Collective Redress', 2011, point 6 <http://ec.europa.eu/competition/consultations/2011_collective_redress/law_society_of_england_and_wales_en.pdf> [accessed 1 July 2018].
177 Ashurst study (fn 87) 105.
178 Rodger, Collective redress mechanisms (fn 123) 162.
179 See eg A Ezrachi, 'From Courage v Crehan to the White Paper – The Changing Landscape of European Private Enforcement and the Possible Implications for Article 82 EC Litigation', in *Abuse of Dominant Position: New Interpretation, New Enforcement Mechanisms?*, ed. by M-O Mackenrodt, BC Gallego, and S Enchelmaier (Berlin: Springer, 2010), 117–135, 130.
180 See eg SWPWP (fn 105) para 40.
181 See Commission, *Communication from the Commission to the European Parliament, the Council, the European Economic and Social Committee and the Committee of the Regions 'Towards a European Horizontal Framework for Collective Redress'* (COM (2013) 401 final, Strasbourg, 2013), art. 1.2.
182 See R Nordh, 'Group Actions in Sweden: Reflections on the Purpose of Civil Litigation, the Need for Reform and a Forthcoming Proposal', *Duke Journal of Comparative and International Law*, 11 (2001), 381–404, 388; R Nazzini, 'The Objective of Private Remedies in EU Competition Law', *Global Competition Litigation Review*, 4 (2011), 131–146, 141.
183 PH Lindblom, 'Individual Litigation and Mass Justice: A Swedish Perspective and Proposal on Group Actions in Civil Procedure', *The American Journal of Comparative Law*, 45(4) (1997), 805–831, 817–819.
184 Keske (fn 141) 74.
185 E Elhauge and D Geradin, *Global Competition Law and Economics*, 2nd edn (New York, USA: Thomson Reuters/Foundation Press, 2011), 31.
186 Keske (fn 141) 74.

65.000 Euros, but 16 individual cases would have cost 176.000 Euros.[187] Also, theoretically, defendants have to only prepare one defence against the group in a collective action rather than numerous defences in the instance that several individual cases are brought.[188] In this way, collective actions realise economies of scale to litigants.[189] As a consequence, group members may take advantage of lower costs per individual, and depending on the formulation of the action, the members may not bear any risk associated with losing the case or litigation costs.[190]

Secondly, consumers who are unaware of the infringement and the resulting loss are included in or join the collective action filed by the representative party and thereby gain the chance to obtain redress. The representative party pursues competition infringements and brings a collective action on their behalf. Additionally, the group members have shared issues that require the use of the same body of evidence.[191] For instance, market definition, market power, market shares, whether conduct is anticompetitive, whether it caused harm to consumers are common to the group in question.[192] This has the benefit of procedural efficiency and also a few members of the group or the representative party can bring evidence from which all members would benefit.[193]

Lastly, under the current private enforcement system, victims can of course claim their damages through individual actions. However, in cases where the competition infringement causes widespread harm, were thousands of victims to decide to file individual cases, courts would be clogged.[194] This in turn could result in a failure to manage these claims and thereby a loss of public confidence in the judicial system.[195] Indeed, Member States have adopted collective redress actions when judges have encountered the difficulty of dealing with large numbers of similar claims.[196] Determining these claims in a single lawsuit using a collective

187 Commission, *Consultation Paper for Discussion on the Follow-up to the Green Paper on Consumer Collective Redress*, 2009, para 24 <http://ec.europa.eu/consumers/redress_cons/docs/consultation_paper2009.pdf> [accessed 1 July 2018].

188 D Rosenberg, 'Mass Tort Class Actions: What Defendants Have and Plaintiffs Don't', *Harvard Journal on Legislation*, 37 (2000), 393–431, 393–394; R Michaels, 'European Class Actions and Applicable Law', in *Cross-Border Class Actions: The European Way*, ed. by A Nuyts and NE Hatzimihail (Munich: Sellier European Law Publishers, 2014), 111–141, 117. See it might be different in opt-in actions, Chapter 6.

189 TS Ulen, 'An introduction to the law and economics of class action litigation', *European Journal of Law and Economics*, 32 (2011), 185–203, 187.

190 See further Chapter 6.

191 Collective redress in antitrust (fn 175) para 4.2.

192 Elhauge and Geradin (fn 185) 31.

193 See Mulheron, Class action (fn 2) 50.

194 J Almunia, 'Common Standards for Group Claims across the EU' (University of Valladolid, School of Law, 2010), 1–7, 4 <http://europa.eu/rapid/pressReleasesAction.do?reference=SPEECH/10/554&format=HTML&aged=0&language=EN&guiLanguage=en> [accessed 1 July 2018].

195 C Hodges, 'From Class Actions to Collective Redress: A Revolution in Approach to Compensation', *Civil Justice Quarterly*, 28(1) (2009), 41–66, 43.

196 C Hodges, 'Collective Redress: A Breakthrough or a Damp Sqibb?', *Journal of Consumer Policy*, 37(1) (2014), 67–89, 82.

redress action achieves procedural efficiency, ie economies of scale to the judiciary.[197] Such an action allows the courts to manage the case within reasonable delay and costs.[198] It also avoids conflicting judgments[199] so that similar recoveries are given to similarly situated claimants.[200] This benefits the defendant in terms of proportionality and fairness;[201] a collective redress action promotes uniformity of decisions, and defendants are not exposed to inconsistent judgments delivered by different courts on the same matter.[202]

Concluding remarks

This chapter examined the reason for the creation and adoption of a collective redress action in historical and modern contexts in order to demonstrate the purpose and functioning of collective redress actions which would inform its suitability to the need for such an action in private competition law enforcement in the EU. Collective redress actions enable the representative party to bring an action on behalf of similarly situated victims. These actions are built upon representation – an exception to individual litigation for two main purposes: procedural efficiency and making it more likely to deliver redress in situations where a wrong harms numerous persons with the same or similar and small damages. It would be impractical to bring all the claimants in court and pursue multiple similar actions; courts would be unable to manage these claims in an efficient and timely manner. Through such actions the claims of a significant number of individuals can be determined in a single lawsuit. Where these numerous victims have losses that do not allow them to file an individual action most victims eschew suing the infringer(s) in the face of the risks, costs and burden of the litigation. The design of collective redress actions enables either the group members to share the risks, costs and burdens of litigation or the representative party to endure these.

In the EU, the debate on collective redress actions has arisen from the rarity of victims of competition infringements seeking redress. It is especially the case for victims whose losses do not economically motivate them to pursue such a complex and lengthy litigation. Indeed, studies demonstrate how very rare consumers ask for damages through individual actions and existing aggregation mechanisms. These aggregation mechanisms in the Member States have features akin to traditional two-party litigation and are not designed to resolve the dispute between a group encompassing a myriad of individuals and the defendant(s). Consumers, who are at the end of the distribution chain, do not do business in the market and purchase an overcharged product for their own use. The value of their damages, their financial situation and their knowledge of competition infringements are obstacles to filing an individual action. Similarly, existing collective redress actions

197 SWPWP (fn 105) para 39. In the same vein, see Michaels (fn 188) 117.
198 Public consultation (fn 78) para 5.
199 Nazzini (fn 182) 141.
200 Mulheron, Class action (fn 2) 49.
201 Nazzini (fn 182) 141.
202 See Mulheron, Class action (fn 2) 49.

of Member States have been unsuccessful in offering a real opportunity for consumers to obtain compensation; only five collective actions have been brought on behalf of consumers across Europe. This makes clear the need for a collective redress action for consumers.

An EU-wide collective redress action, if designed properly, could be a means by which to increase the consumers' chances to seek compensation. Such an action would result in lower litigation costs *vis-à-vis* multiple individual actions and achieves procedural efficiency by preventing duplication of sources and efforts. It enables courts to deal with and rule on a large number of claims. This procedural device would make it possible for a judge to give a decision binding all group members and award damages to the group as a whole. It provides a realistic means for consumers to recover the losses arising from competition infringements because they can join or be included in an action filed by a representative party and benefit from evidence gathered to establish the infringement and harm. Consumers also share litigation costs and risks of losing the case, in fact, depending on the design, they might not endure these at all. A collective redress action therefore can constitute a solution for consumer damages claims. Later chapters will analyse the design framework of an EU-wide procedure, starting with the next chapter on the collective redress proposals of the Commission.

3 Commission initiatives on collective redress actions

Introduction

This chapter explores the Commission's efforts towards developing a structure for collective redress actions in order to provide a better understanding of the motive for these efforts and collective redress proposals. It is important to note that, until 2011, collective redress proposals came under two distinct initiatives for competition and consumer law in the EU. After that point, a horizontal approach merging these initiatives has become prevalent in order to avoid fragmentation of the law.

In respect of this, the chapter first examines the collective redress proposals under those distinct initiatives, offering an analysis on the Commission's efforts to establish a collective redress action and the proposed measures in each area. Secondly, it explains the horizontal approach toward collective redress actions and its aim to address claims arising from breach of any EU law. It also looks at the recent assessment on the impact of horizontal approach on collective redress in the EU. Thirdly, the chapter discusses a distinctive approach to competition damages claims, exploring the need in this area, its specific features and implications for the design of a collective redress action.

Two distinct initiatives in competition and consumer law

Commission efforts in competition law

The Green Paper

The *Courage* judgment and the Ashurst Study's findings led to the Commission's issuance of the Green Paper in 2005.[1] Its main aim was to make recommendations to overcome identified obstacles to damages actions for competition infringements, and by so doing *i.* render the recovery of losses easier for victims and *ii.* strengthen competition law enforcement.[2] A collective redress action was one

1 Commission, *Staff Working Paper Annex to the Green Paper Damages Actions for Breach of the EC Antitrust Rules* (SEC(2005)1732, Brussels, 2005), (SWPGP) paras 22, 28–29.

2 Commission, *Green Paper on Damages Actions for Breach of EC Antitrust Rules* (COM(2005) 672 final, Brussels, 2005), (Green Paper) 3.

of the proposals, and was primarily considered to enable consumers and small claimants to sue for damages.[3]

The Green Paper adopted two distinct definitions for collective redress actions. First, in a representative action, the representative party, such as a consumer association brings the action on behalf of a group of identified individuals who are generally its members. Second, a collective action is an action filed on behalf of identified or identifiable individuals.[4] The Commission however clearly stated that its collective action definition differed from an opt-out action as the latter is brought on behalf of unidentified persons.[5]

The paper then recommended the adoption of two different actions for consumers and for other purchasers.[6] For consumers, consumer associations or other qualified entities would bring a collective or representative action.[7] In this way, it permitted the group to consist of either identified or identifiable consumers. Regarding the distribution of damages, the Green Paper opened discussion as to whether damages should be given to the representative party or to the members. If it was awarded to the association, damages would be calculated based on illicit profit of the defendant. However, if it was awarded to group members, this calculation would be based on individual loss.[8] For purchasers other than final consumers, the Green Paper suggested an opt-in collective action and found that the existing aggregation mechanisms are to some extent adequate to address their claims.[9]

The Green Paper attracted a great deal of attention from interested stakeholders[10] and created greater awareness[11] of both the right to damages and the difficulties inherent when attempting to enforce this right.[12] However, the situation had not changed much in the EU. The Commission argued that consumers were still far from fully exercising their right to damages and preparation was made for an ensuing paper to include, *inter alia*, a proposal for the introduction of a collective redress action to empower consumers to seek redress.[13] Taking into account the *Manfredi* judgment and comments submitted to the Commission in

3 *Ibid* para 2.5.
4 SWPGP (fn 1) para 192.
5 *Ibid* para 192, fn 122.
6 Green Paper (fn 2) para 2.5.
7 SWPGP (fn 1) paras 198–199.
8 Green Paper (fn 2) 2.5.
9 SWPGP (fn 1) para 201.
10 Commission, *Staff Working Document Accompanying Document to the White Paper on Damages Actions for Breach of the EC Antitrust Rules – Impact Assessment* (SEC (2008) 405, Brussels, 2008), (Impact assessment) para 9.
11 *Ibid* para 53.
12 R Becker, N Bessot and E De Smijter, 'The White Paper on Damages Actions for Breach of the EC Antitrust Rules', *Competition Policy Newsletter*, 2 (2008), 4–11, 4.
13 N Kroes, 'Making Consumers' Right to Damages a Reality: The Case for Collective Redress Mechanisms in Antitrust Claims' (presented at the Conference on collective redress for European consumers, Lisbon, 2007), 1–5, 3–4 <http://europa.eu/rapid/press-release_SPEECH-07-698_en.htm?locale=en> [accessed 1 July 2018].

response to the Green Paper, the Commission published the White Paper in 2008[14] with the purpose of proposing '[b]alanced measures that are rooted in European legal culture and traditions'.[15]

The White Paper

In the White Paper, the Commission took a different approach although it expressed the clear need for adopting such an action for consumers. The approach of the Green Paper had been merely to favour consumers' interests above others and to propose a particular collective redress action accordingly. The White Paper put forward a complementary combination of representative and opt-in actions without differentiating between the claims of consumers and of (small) businesses. The Commission stated that qualified entities might be unwilling or unable to pursue every claim, to which end an opt-in action should also be made available to take the place of a representative action.[16]

Again, two distinct definitions were adopted. An opt-in action is brought by one of the victims on behalf of identified persons.[17] This time a representative action is defined as an action brought on behalf of identified or, in rather restricted cases, identifiable persons.[18] The representative party is no longer limited to consumer associations, but included state bodies and trade associations.[19] Regarding the distribution of damages, the Commission permitted the damages to be awarded to the representative party who should preferably directly reimburse those harmed but exceptionally use it for related purposes or allocate it to related entities.[20]

As opposed to the Green Paper, the White Paper precisely rejected the introduction of an opt-out action[21] yet its suggestion for representative actions recalls an opt-out action.[22] A representative party can sue on behalf of identifiable

14 Becker, Bessot and De Smijter (fn 12) 4.

15 Commission, *White Paper on Damages Actions for Breach of the EC Antitrust Rules* (COM(2008) 165 final, Brussels, 2008) para 1.2. On the contrary, Lundgren asserts that there is no European legal culture. N Lundgren, *White Paper on Damages Actions for Breach of the EC Antitrust Rules*, Debates of the European Parliament, 2009, 1–135, 133 <http://www.europarl.europa.eu/sides/getDoc.do?pubRef=-//EP//NONSGML+CRE+20090325+SIT+DOC+PDF+V0//EN&language=EN> [accessed 1 July 2018].

16 White Paper (fn 15) para 2.1.

17 Commission, *Staff Working Paper Accompanying the White Paper on Damages actions for Breach of the EC Antitrust Rules* (SEC(2008) 404, Brussels, 2008), (SWPWP) paras 57–58.

18 *Ibid* para 52.

19 White Paper (fn 15) para 2.1.

20 SWPWP (fn 17) para 56.

21 *Ibid* para 58.

22 R Mulheron, 'The Case for an Opt-out Class Action for European Member States: A Legal and Empirical Analysis', *Columbia Journal of European Law*, 15 (2009), 409–453, 451. Similarly, European Parliament, ECON, *Draft Report on the White Paper on Damages Actions for Breach of the EC Antitrust Rules* (2008/2154(INI), 2008), (Draft report) 8 <http://www.europarl.europa.eu/sides/getDoc.do?pubRef=

victims, in restricted cases, but there is no clarity as to the nature of those cases. Additionally, in actions on behalf of identifiable victims, it is also possible, albeit exceptionally, that the damages awards could be used by the related entities or for related purposes, like cy-près distribution.[23] Arguably, in order to avoid opposition to the recommendation of an opt-out action, the Commission attempted to differentiate its proposal again by defining the opt-out action as an action brought on behalf of unidentified individuals.[24]

Compared with the Green Paper, the White Paper has been criticised for its conservative approach[25] as the Green Paper had proposals on multiple damages, cost protection for claimants, damages recovery based on defendant's illegal gain and opt-out actions were neither recognised nor rejected. As a result, the White Paper's proposals did not fulfil expectations of an action that would progress previous efforts.[26] In terms of collective redress, the White Paper to some extent follows the Green Paper,[27] although regrettably makes no distinction between consumer and business claims.[28]

Withdrawn Directive in 2009

Subsequently to the White Paper, the Commission launched a proposal for a council Directive on damages actions.[29] This Directive stated that competition infringements often create scattered damages, especially for small claimants

-//EP//NONSGML+COMPARL+PE-412.315+01+DOC+PDF+V0//EN&langua ge=EN> [accessed 1 July 2018]; D-PL Tzakas, 'Effective Collective Redress in Antitrust and Consumer Protection Matters: A Panacea or a Chimera?', *Common Market Law Review*, 48 (2011), 1125–1174, 1138–1139.

23 SWPWP (fn 17) para 52, fn 30. See Chapter 8.

24 *Ibid* para 58.

25 See eg, J Pheasant and A Bicarregui, 'Striking the Right Balance Towards a "Competition Culture" Not a "Litigation Culture"? Comment on the European Commission's White Paper on Damages Actions for Breach of EC Antitrust Rules', *Global Competition Litigation Review*, 1(2) (2008), 98–106, 99; JS Kortmann and CRA Swaak, 'The EC White Paper on Antitrust Damage Actions: Why the Member States Are (Right to Be) Less Than Enthusiastic', *European Competition Law Review*, 30(7) (2009), 340–351, 341; J Goyder and A Albors-Llorens, *Goyder's EC Competition Law*, 5th edn (Oxford University Press, UK, 2009), 649; HKS Schmidt, 'Private Enforcement – Is Article 82 EC Special?', in *Abuse of Dominant Position: New Interpretation, New Enforcement Mechanisms?*, ed. by M-O Mackenrodt, B C Gallego, and S Enchelmaier (Berlin: Springer, 2010), 137–163, 163.

26 Editorial Comments, 'A Little More Action Please! – The White Paper on Damages Actions for Breach of EC Antitrust Rules', *Common Market Law Review*, 45(3) (2008), 609–615, 615.

27 R Mulheron, 'Antitrust Litigation: A White Paper Tinged with Green?', *Brussels Agenda, the Viewpoint Contribution*, 2008 <http://www.hadjimichalis.gr/keimena/Brussels_Agenda/Brussels_Agenda_2008_05.pdf> [accessed 1 July 2018].

28 M Ioannidou, 'Enhancing the Consumers' Role in EU Private Competition Law Enforcement: A Normative and Practical Approach', *Competition Law Review*, 8(1) (2011), 59–85, 76.

29 This was a different proposal on damages actions from the Directive enacted in 2014.

including consumers. Therefore, the availability of a collective redress action was found crucial for them in order to recover their losses.[30] The Directive then put forward two types of collective redress action: a representative and a group action. The latter was defined as an action jointly brought by two or more harmed individuals[31] in which other victims of the same infringement would be allowed to join the action after the court has been seized of group action.[32] The design of this group action appears to qualify as a joinder rather than an opt-in action.[33]

Even though the withdrawn Directive pointed out that the respondents to the Green Paper and White Paper had welcomed the suggestions of these papers because neither paper provided for an opt-out action,[34] it suggested an opt-out action in the form of a representative action, without explicit articulation. According to this proposal, in representative actions qualified entities that satisfy the criteria laid down therein to become entitled to be the representative party[35] could sue on behalf of those harmed who are defined as a group but need not be all individually identified.[36] The individuals who satisfy the group definition have the right to choose not to be represented by these entities but if they acquiesce, they are bound by the decision adopted at the end of the litigation.[37] The withdrawn Directive proposed that damages awards should be distributed to group members to the greatest possible extent and a portion of the damages award could be allocated to the representative party to cover litigation expenses.[38]

This Directive proposal was withdrawn in October 2009. One reason for withdrawal was timing; publication was viewed politically inappropriate at the very end of the then Commissioner's mandate,[39] but this is not the only explanation. Opposition to the introduction of opt-out actions,[40] harmonised rules in private enforcement and an emerging desire to adopt a collective redress action applicable not just to competition infringements but to all EU law infringements contributed to its withdrawal.[41] Consequently, the withdrawn Directive is the last work of the Commission on collective redress in the field of competition law. In these three papers, the Commission proved a desire to establish a collective redress action but did not put forward clear and consistent proposals, particularly as regards opt-out

30 Commission, *Proposal for a Council Directive on Rules Governing Damages Actions for Infringements of Articles [101] and [102] of the Treaty*, 2009 (Withdrawn Directive), explanatory memorandum para 4.2 <http://allegati.unina.it/postlaurea/perf/Esclusiva_Juridico.pdf> [accessed 1 July 2018].
31 *Ibid* art. 4.1.
32 *Ibid* art. 4.3.
33 Ioannidou (fn 28) 75, fn 88. See further Chapter 2.
34 Withdrawn Directive (fn 30) explanatory memorandum para 2.1.
35 See *ibid* art. 6.
36 *Ibid* art. 5(2).
37 *Ibid* art. 5(4).
38 *Ibid* art. 5(5).
39 F Rizzuto, 'The Private Enforcement of European Union Competition Law: What Next?', *Global Competition Litigation Review*, 3(2) (2010), 57–68, 58–59.
40 Ioannidou (fn 28) 78.
41 Rizzuto (fn 39) 58–59.

actions. The next section gives a brief analysis of the Commission's proposals in consumer law before turning to the horizontal approach.

Commission efforts in consumer law

It was unclear in the beginning whether collective redress in consumer law was intended to be approached as distinct from competition law. EU Consumer Policy Strategy 2007–2013 explicitly announced that collective redress actions were to be considered for both areas of law.[42] However, a year later, the Green Paper on collective redress in consumer law, with reference to the White Paper's suggestions, drew attention to the need for a distinct approach in competition law due to its specific nature and because the victims it aimed to address do not only encompass consumers.[43] Thus, a distinctive approach for each area was adopted.

In consumer law, two studies on collective redress actions by external contractors were concluded before the publication of the consultation paper. First, a study which identified the obstacles encountered by consumers in claiming redress found that consumers rarely brought an action against the infringements that cause widespread and low- or medium-value damages.[44] Secondly, an evaluation study, which analysed 13 Member States for over a period of ten years, compared consumer benefit in Member States that have a collective redress action with the consumer detriment in Member States that do not.[45] It concluded that a collective redress action is likely to benefit consumers, but its absence has little negative economic impact.[46] Based on the findings of this study, Hodges argued that it is not established in consumer law that the problem and the solution require such a judicial mechanism.[47] It should not be overlooked that national laws might have some kind of collective redress action that nevertheless provides no realistic means to consumers,[48] and thus the detriment of its absence was found modest. However, the studies could have demonstrated a clear need for collective redress, which in turn would guide the adoption of an appropriate mechanism.

42 Commission – Communication from the Commission to the Council, the European Parliament and the EESC, *EU Consumer Policy Strategy 2007–2013: Empowering Consumers, Enhancing Their Welfare, Effectively Protecting Them* (COM(2007) 99 final, Brussels, 2007), para 5.3.

43 Commission, *Green Paper on Consumer Collective Redress* (COM(2008) 794 final, Brussels, 2008), (Green Paper on collective redress) para 1.5.

44 Civic Consulting of the Consumer Policy Evaluation Consortium, *Commission – DG SANCO, Study Regarding the Problems Faced by Consumers in Obtaining Redress for Infringements of Consumer Protection Legislation, and the Economic Consequences of Such Problems, Final Report, Part I: Main Report* (Brussels, 2008), 4–5.

45 Civic Consulting (Lead) and Oxford Economics, *Commission – DG SANCO, Evaluation of the Effectiveness and Efficiency of Collective Redress Mechanisms in the European Union, Final Report, Part I: Main Report* (SANCO/2007/B4/004, Brussels, 2008), (Evaluation study), 4.

46 *Ibid* 5.

47 C Hodges, 'Current Discussions on Consumer Redress: Collective Redress and ADR', *ERA Forum*, 13 (2012), 11–33, 18.

48 Similarly, Evaluation study (fn 45) 5.

In light of the foregoing, the Green Paper on consumer law avoided suggesting a design for a collective redress action as opposed to competition law[49] and discussed four possible options, ranging from no action to the launch of an EU judicial collective redress action.[50] The last option put forward various funding possibilities, favoured the standing of consumer associations or ombudsmen, and did not dismiss opt-out actions.[51]

Combining the two: a horizontal approach toward collective redress actions

Overview of the reasons leading to horizontal approach

The absence of some sort of collective redress is seen as a missing piece of European architecture.[52] Following publication of the papers and studies for collective redress actions consonant with the distinct initiatives, interested stakeholders requested a horizontal approach establishing common rules that would apply to a collective action for any breach across the EU in order to eliminate the inconsistency between different proposals.[53] In other words, the stakeholders called for a horizontal approach in order to avoid a fragmented and vertical approach to collective redress.[54] By so doing, even though the enforcement frameworks and damages claims arising from consumer law breaches and competition infringements are completely separate, they are linked in the political arena.[55]

With respect to the White Paper, the European Parliament recognised the existence of this problem for the victims of competition infringements when obtaining compensation in the case of widespread loss, but remarked that the same is valid for other areas of law,[56] such as consumer and environment

49 Ioannidou (fn 28) 60.
50 Green Paper on collective redress (fn 43) paras 19–60. In 2009, a fifth option was introduced: 'an EU-wide judicial collective redress mechanism including collective ADR'. Commission, *Consultation Paper for Discussion on the Follow-up to the Green Paper on Consumer Collective Redress*, 2009, para 3.2.5 <http://ec.europa.eu/consumers/redress_cons/docs/consultation_paper2009.pdf> [accessed 1 July 2018].
51 Green Paper on collective redress (fn 43) paras 48–57.
52 D Wallis, 'EU Initiatives in the Area of Collective Redress – Which Options?' (presented at the Righting Private Wrongs: Competition Law, Investor Claims and Mass Litigation in the EU, London: BIICL, 2013).
53 Commission, *Staff Working Document Public Consultation: Towards a Coherent European Approach to Collective Redress* (SEC(2011)173 final, 2011), (Public consultation) para 11; Commission, *Communication from the Commission to the European Parliament, the Council, the European Economic and Social Committee and the Committee of the Regions 'Towards a European Horizontal Framework for Collective Redress'* (COM(2013) 401 final, 2013), (Communication), para 1.3.
54 L Athanassiou, 'Collective Redress and Competition Policy' in *Cross-Border Class Actions: The European Way*, ed. by A Nuyts and NE Hatzimihail (Munich: Sellier European Law Publishers, 2014), 145–171, 146.
55 See Hodges, Current discussions (fn 47) 16.
56 European Parliament, Draft report (fn 22) para 3.

law.[57] In its resolution on the White Paper the Parliament acknowledged that the call for a consistent approach does not necessarily mean the introduction of a single horizontal instrument to address all areas and implementing the necessary measures in competition law should not therefore be delayed.[58]

In 2010, the Commission changed its work-programme in a way directly contrary to work-programmes of the previous three years.[59] The initiative change was added to the work programme at the last moment.[60] The new strategy was to determine common legal principles for collective redress.[61] In view of that, the next step was announced to place emphasis on reinforcement of the private enforcement of EU law in general, not specifically in competition law[62] and enhancing collective redress actions, again not just in competition law.[63]

This new consensus deviated from the Commission's original initiative, namely forming a distinctive approach to competition claims to lay the ground for a more complicated reform effort,[64] ie the adoption of a general framework. It clearly had a political side as the reporter stated that the reason why the European Parliament was advocating a horizontal approach was a political choice in order to be involved in the process as a legislator.[65] With this horizontal approach, the debate shifted from how to design a collective redress action for competition cases to whether

57 Commission, *Executive Summary of the Impact Assessment – Damages Actions for Breach of the EU Antitrust Rules* (SWD(2013) 204 final, Strasbourg, 2013), 1–10, 9.

58 European Parliament, *European Parliament Resolution of 26 March 2009 on the White Paper on Damages Actions for Breach of the EC Antitrust Rules* (2008/2154(INI), Strasbourg, 2009), paras 5–6 <http://www.europarl.europa.eu/sides/getDoc.do?pubRef=-//EP//NONSGML+TA+P6-TA-2009-0187+0+DOC+PDF+V0//EN> [accessed 1 July 2018].

59 See eg Commission, *Communication on the Commission Legislative and Work Programme 2009: Acting now for a better Europe* (COM(2008) 712 final, vol.1, Brussels, 2008), Annex 1, 6.

60 Rizzuto (fn 39) 59.

61 Commission, *Communication on the Commission Work Programme 2010: Time to Act* (COM(2010) 135 final, vol.1, Brussels, 2010), para 3.1. Similarly, see the work programmes from 2011 to 2015, Commission, 'Commission Work Programmes', *European Commission at Work* <http://ec.europa.eu/atwork/key-documents/index_en.htm> [accessed 1 July 2018]. Same approach towards a horizontal framework on collective redress is also found in Commission, *Towards a Coherent European Approach to Collective Redress: Next Steps – Joint Information Note by Vice-President Viviane Reding, Vice-President Joaquín Almunia and Commissioner John Dalli* (SEC (2010) 1192 OJ 1932, Brussels, 2010) <http://kartellblog.de/wordpress/wp-content/uploads/Kommission-2010-information-Towards-European-Collective-Redress> [accessed 1 July 2018].

62 R Whish and D Bailey, *Competition Law*, 7th edn (Oxford: Oxford University Press, 2012), 328.

63 J Almunia, 'Common Standards for Group Claims across the EU' (University of Valladolid, School of Law, 2010), 1–7, 2 <http://europa.eu/rapid/pressReleasesAction.do?reference=SPEECH/10/554&format=HTML&aged=0&language=EN&guiLanguage=en> [accessed 1 July 2018].

64 Goyder and Albors-Llorens (fn 25) 649.

65 K-H Lehne, *Report on the White Paper on Damages Actions for Breach of the EC Antitrust Rules,* Debates of the European Parliament, 2009, 1–135, 134 <http://

there should be a single horizontal instrument and what common rules would apply to all areas.

The proposals under the horizontal approach

Public consultation

In 2011, a public consultation on collective redress was published by the competition, consumer and justice directorates with the main aim of determining a general EU legal framework for citizens and businesses,[66] and in particular for small claimants,[67] without limitation to any type of claim.[68] This framework was intended to fit with existing EU legal tradition[69] and the legal orders of the then 27 Member States.[70] Despite suggesting a design framework for collective redress, common core principles were established to constitute a base for further legislative initiatives in any area of law. As such were:[71]

> (1) the need for effectiveness and efficiency of redress; (2) the importance of information and of the role of representative bodies; (3) the need to take account of collective consensual resolution as a means of alternative dispute resolution; (4) the need for strong safeguards to avoid abusive litigation; (5) availability of appropriate financing mechanisms, notably for citizens and SMEs; (6) the importance of effective enforcement across the EU.

It seems that these principles were drafted in generalities and not specifically related to the formulation of a collective redress action. It is debatable how they can be reflected in a formulation of the action when their content and meaning are not clearly stated.[72] Moreover, the involvement of the multiple Directorates of the Commission, rather than just that of competition, was criticised for increasing the number of political interests, making the outcome difficult to predict.[73] Accordingly, two years after the public consultation, another work on collective redress

www.europarl.europa.eu/sides/getDoc.do?pubRef=-//EP//NONSGML+CRE+20090325+SIT+DOC+PDF+V0//EN&language=EN> [accessed 1 July 2018].

66 Public consultation (fn 53) para 10.

67 *Ibid* para 4.

68 This was going to be supported by European Parliament, *Motion for a European Parliament Resolution on 'Towards a Coherent European Approach to Collective Redress'* (2011/2089(INI), 2012), para 1 <http://www.europarl.europa.eu/sides/getDoc.do?type=REPORT&language=EN&reference=A7-0012/2012#title1> [accessed 1 July 2018].

69 Public consultation (fn 53) para 10.

70 *Ibid* para 12.

71 *Ibid* para 15.

72 Ioannidou (fn 28) 61.

73 AA Foer and EP Schultz, 'Will Two Roads Still Diverge? Private Enforcement of Antitrust Law Is Getting Harder in the United States. But Europe May Be Making It Easier', *Global Competition Litigation Review*, 3 (2011), 107–112, 112.

has been issued by the Commission, which again pursues a horizontal approach but with the distinction of more concrete suggestions.

Recommendation and communication

A directive proposal on actions for damages in competition law, which was then signed into law,[74] was launched alongside the Recommendation[75] and Communication on collective redress.[76] The Directive aims to achieve effective enforcement of EU competition rules by structuring the coordination between public and private enforcement and by enabling victims to obtain full compensation for the harm suffered.[77] It is applicable to damages actions if they are available in Member States either individual or collective without requiring the introduction of the latter.[78] It expressed that because individual damages actions are available in all Member States, it did not intend to put countries under any obligation to implement a collective redress action into their legal systems in order to realise the submitted aims.[79]

This would seem yet a contradictory statement from the Commission, since one of those submitted aims is to enable the victims to recover full compensation. The Commission has stated repeatedly that the victims of competition infringements rarely seek redress through individual damages actions. It is the reason that the introduction of an EU collective redress action is discussed in the first place.[80] If the availability of individual damages actions suffices, in other words, if the availability of individual damages actions ensures victims receive compensation for their loss, then the debate on collective redress need not have occurred at any length. The reason given to exclude a collective redress action from the material scope of the Directive does not match the Commission's previous declarations.

74 *Directive 2014/104/EU of the European Parliament and of the Council of 26 November 2014 on Certain Rules Governing Actions for Damages under National Law for Infringements of the Competition Law Provisions of the Member States and of the European Union*, (OJ L 349/1, 2014) (Directive).

75 Commission, *Recommendation on Common Principles for Injunctive and Compensatory Collective Redress Mechanisms in the Member States Concerning Violations of Rights Granted under Union Law* (2013/396/EU, OJ L 201/60, 2013) (Recommendation).

76 Communication (fn 53).

77 Commission, *Proposal for a Directive of the European Parliament and of the Council on Certain Rules Governing Actions for Damages Under National Law for Infringements of the Competition Law Provisions of the Member States and of the European Union*, (2013/0185 (COD), COM(2013) 404 final, Strasbourg, 2013) (Directive proposal), explanatory memorandum, para 1.2.

78 Commission, *Frequently Asked Questions: Commission Proposes Legislation to Facilitate Damage Claims by Victims of Antitrust Violations* (MEMO/13/531, Brussels, 2013), 1–4, 3 <http://europa.eu/rapid/press-release_MEMO-13-531_en.htm> [accessed 1 July 2018].

79 *Ibid.*

80 See Chapter 2.

In fact, some amendments suggested for the Directive in the European Parliament included specific provisions for collective redress but they were not accepted, after debate.[81] As a result, the Directive gives no place to collective redress. As of the Ashurst study in 2004, the Commission had been working on collective redress for over a decade and yet chose not to adopt a legislative proposal as a way forward and did not even clarify the initiatives in competition law. The Directive only refers to the respective treatment in the Recommendation and Communication that apply to all areas of EU law.[82]

A Recommendation led by the Justice Commissioner was issued in June 2013 to set non-binding rules for collective redress actions throughout the EU and calling upon Member States to have such an action applicable to all areas.[83] It intended to enhance access to justice, stop illegal behaviour, avoid abusive litigation and assist victims in obtaining redress for the loss caused by violations of rights granted under EU law.[84] It did not state any specific need for such an action for consumers nor did it contain provisions specific to any area of law. Instead, it presented common principles with regard to the character of the representative party and of the notice they should issue,[85] the need for preserving the loser pays rule,[86] general principles for funding,[87] when a follow-on collective action should start[88] and the need for judicial control to prevent unmeritorious cases.[89] Moreover, it stated that, contingency fees can exceptionally be allowed provided that there are national rules to regulate them;[90] punitive damages should be prohibited;[91] forming the group (except in certain situations requiring an opt-out solution) should be based on the opt-in principle;[92] and, finally, judicial mechanisms ought to be accompanied by ADR.[93]

In addition, a Communication accompanying the Recommendation provided an overview of the main views expressed in public consultation and of the position

81 European Parliament, *Opinion of the Committee on the Internal Market and Consumer Protection for the Committee on Economic and Monetary Affairs on the Proposal for a Directive of the European Parliament and of the Council on Certain Rules Governing Actions for Damages under National Law for Infringements of the Competition Law Provisions of the Member States and of the European Union* (COM(2013)0404 – C7–0170/2013–2013/0185(COD), 2014) amendments 1, 2, 5, 15, 20, 21 <http://www.europarl.europa.eu/sides/getDoc.do?type=REPORT&reference=A7-2014-0089&format=XML&language=EN#top> [accessed 1 July 2018].

82 Directive proposal (fn 77) explanatory memorandum para 2.1.

83 Communication (fn 53) para 1.1; C Hodges, 'Collective Redress: A Breakthrough or a Damp Sqibb?', *Journal of Consumer Policy*, 37(1) (2014), 67–89, 85.

84 Including injunctions, Recommendation (fn 75) para I.1.

85 *Ibid* paras III/4–7, III/10–12.

86 *Ibid* para III/13.

87 *Ibid* paras III/14–16.

88 *Ibid* paras V/33–34.

89 *Ibid* paras III/8–9.

90 *Ibid* paras V/29–30.

91 *Ibid* para V/31.

92 *Ibid* paras V/21–24.

93 *Ibid* paras V/25–28.

of the Commission on some central issues with respect to collective redress.[94] It reiterated the principles established by the Recommendation and identified central tenets that any European approach should respect. A collective redress action should:[95]

- be capable of effectively resolving a large number of individual claims for compensation of damage, thereby promoting procedural economy;
- be capable of delivering legally certain and fair outcomes within a reasonable timeframe, while respecting the rights of all parties involved;
- provide for robust safeguards against abusive litigation; and
- avoid any economic incentives to bring speculative claims.

It has been argued that the expected action has a general remit encompassing all types of cases, making Member States less willing to take a step that has an impact on the entire enforcement system.[96] Nonetheless, the Recommendation, as a non-binding document, required that Member States adopt a collective redress action based on the established principles by July 2015. Two years after that the Commission was expected to evaluate the practical impact of the Recommendation on the submitted aims in order to decide whether further measures are needed.[97]

Impact of the horizontal approach on collective redress

In January 2018, the report on the implementation of the Recommendation was published by the Commission.[98] The report assesses the legal developments regarding collective redress in Member States and identifies the number of actions brought using the rules on collective redress four years after the adoption of the Recommendation. The report also discusses whether the Recommendation has facilitated access to justice and prevented abusive litigation. At the end, the report concludes on whether there is a need for further action concerning collective redress in the EU.[99]

The findings of the report are not surprising.[100] In spite of the Recommendation, nine Member States have not adopted any form of collective action to allow

94 Communication (fn 53) para 1.1.
95 *Ibid* para 3.
96 Hodges, Collective redress (fn 83) 85–86.
97 Recommendation (fn 75) paras VII/38–41.
98 Commission, *Report from The Commission to The European Parliament, The Council and The European Economic and Social Committee on the Implementation of the Commission Recommendation of 11 June 2013 on Common Principles for Injunctive and Compensatory Collective Redress Mechanisms in the Member States Concerning Violations of Rights Granted under Union Law*, (COM(2018) 40 final, Brussels, 2018) (Report on the Recommendation), 1.
99 *Ibid* 1.
100 As expected by many, A Biard, 'Collective Redress in the EU: A Rainbow Behind the Clouds?', *ERA Forum*, (2018), 1–16, 1 <https://www.researchgate.net/publication/325207411_Collective_redress_in_the_EU_a_rainbow_behind_the_clouds> [accessed 3 July 2018].

victims to obtain compensation.[101] Only seven Member States have implemented legislation on collective redress after the adoption of the Recommendation and their collective redress design diverges from the principles established by the Recommendation.[102] In total 19 Member States have a compensatory collective redress action in place and more than half of these states make such actions available in specific sectors, generally for consumer claims.[103] All these mean that they do not follow the horizontal approach, diverging from the proposals of the Recommendation. Moreover, despite the availability of collective redress actions, in some Member States practice shows that victims do not recourse to these actions when suffered a loss as national legislation sets out rigid conditions and the procedure is lengthy and costly, overweighing the benefits of using collective actions.[104]

The report concludes that there is still a great divergence between the Member States in terms of the availability as well as the nature of collective redress actions and the implementation of safeguards against the potential abusive litigation.[105] Since the follow-up of the Recommendation is rather limited, the report states that the main aim of facilitating access to justice for the benefit of the functioning of the single market is still far from being realised.[106] The Recommendation is found successful only in inspiring discussions on facilitation of access to justice and in drawing attention to prevention of abusive litigation across the EU.[107]

At the end of the report, the Commission sets out its roadmap for collective redress. According to this, the Commission aims to further promote the principles established in the Recommendation to improve access to justice, to prevent abuses and to ensure safe use of collective redress.[108] The Commission also refers to its work programme for 2018[109] and its initiative on 'New Deal for Consumers',[110] stating that its efforts would focus on strengthening redress in EU consumer law.[111] In April 2018 the Commission published a

101 Report on the Recommendation (fn 98) 3.
102 *Ibid* 2.
103 *Ibid* 3. See further for country reports, Commission, *Study on the State of Collective Redress in the EU in the Context of the Implementation of the Commission Recommendation* prepared by the British Institute of International and Comparative Law (JUST/2016/JCOO/FW/CIVI/0099, 2017).
104 Report on the Recommendation (fn 98) 20.
105 *Ibid* 4, 20.
106 *Ibid* 20.
107 *Ibid* 19.
108 *Ibid* 20.
109 Commission, *Press Release on Commission Work Programme 2018: An Agenda for a More United, Stronger and More Democratic Europe* (IP/17/4002, Strasbourg, 2017) <http://europa.eu/rapid/press-release_IP-17-4002_en.htm> [accessed 1 July 2018].
110 Commission, *Communication from the Commission to the European Parliament, The Council, The European Economic and Social Committee and the Committee of the Regions – Commission Work Programme 2018* (COM(2017) 650 final, Strasbourg, 2017) 7.
111 Report on the Recommendation (fn 98) 21.

proposal for a directive in consumer law.[112] In the context of 'New Deal for Consumers', the Commission in its Inception Impact Assessment discusses further procedural redress opportunities for consumers in mass harm situations where qualified entities will be able to ask courts and/or administrative authorities to stop the breach and ensure redress for the affected consumers.[113] It seems the future of collective redress is now more unclear than ever as there is no certain step determined to be taken by the Commission to make the compensation of victims a reality in competition law.

Distinctive approach toward collective redress actions

The focus of this book is upon shaping collective redress actions for consumer damages claims arising from competition infringements. However, the Commission's horizontal approach to such actions necessitates a brief examination of the different features of laws that might not fit into the introduction of a 'one-size-fits-all' action. The aim of the horizontal approach is to expand the scope of the proposals for collective redress by merging the two initiatives of competition and consumer law and to propose a collective action to address claims arising from any breach of EU law. It is, however, important to assess the demand for such an action in any particular area. Thus, this demand determines the existence and extent of the problem, whether such an action provides a solution, how this action would be designed to address this problem and what aim(s) it would serve.

Potential shortcomings of the horizontal approach

In consumer law, the possibility of introducing a collective redress action to enhance consumer redress was mentioned several times in the past.[114] Hodges

112 Commission, *Proposal for a Directive of the European Parliament and of the Council amending Council Directive 93/13/EEC of 5 April 1993, Directive 98/6/EC of the European Parliament and of the Council, Directive 2005/29/EC of the European Parliament and of the Council and Directive 2011/83/EU of the European Parliament and of the Council as Regards Better Enforcement and Modernisation of EU Consumer Protection Rules* (COM(2018) 185 final, 2018/0090(COD), Brussels, 2018).

113 Commission, *Inception Impact Assessment: A New Deal for Consumers — Revision of the Injunctions Directive*, (Ares (2017)5324969, 2017), 4 <www.ec.europa.eu/info/law/better-regulation/initiatives/ares-2017-5324969_en> [accessed 3 July 2018].

114 Commission, *Consumer Redress – Commission Memorandum to the Council* (COM (84) 692, Luxembourg, 1984), 10 <http://aei.pitt.edu/1597/1/1597.pdf> [accessed 1 July 2018]; *Three Year Action Plan of Consumer Policy in the EEC (1990–1992)* (COM(90) 98 final, Brussels, 1990), para 4.iv <http://aei.pitt.edu/3712/> [accessed 1 July 2018]; *Internal Market After 1992: Meeting the Challenge (the Sutherland Report)* (SEC(92) 2044, 1992), 10–13 <http://aei.pitt.edu/1025/1/Market_post_1992_Sutherland_1.pdf> [accessed 1 July 2018]; *Action Plan on Consumer Access to Justice and the Settlement of Consumer Disputes in the Internal Market* (COM(96) 13 final, Brussels, 1996), 17 <http://eur-lex.europa.eu/LexUriServ/LexUriServ.do?uri=COM:1996:0013:FIN:EN:PDF> [accessed 1 July 2018]; *Consumer Strategy 2007–2013* (fn 42) para 5.3.

stated that mass consumer problems have awaited a solution since 1960s.[115] Still, the studies have not resulted in specific solutions *vis-à-vis* competition law.[116] In fact, the first detailed efforts to establish a judicial collective redress action for damages were made in this area[117] after studies in the competition field recognised the extent of the problem for consumers.

In addition to the criticism that a need for a judicial mechanism has not been clearly established,[118] the rationale for the development of consumer law is to protect the weak[119] from an imbalance of economic power between consumer and supplier.[120] The protection is generally provided *ex ante* through mandatory prohibition of trade practices detrimental to consumers.[121] Some posit, therefore, that consumer law is more effective in protecting consumers through preventive rather than remedial means.[122] It is also the case that there are already means available to address the redress problem in consumer law, such as injunctions[123] and ADR[124] directives.[125] For instance, the Portuguese opt-out actions have been rarely used in consumer law due to, *inter alia*, the existence of the non-judicial and conciliatory mechanisms.[126] This suggests that further efforts focus on assessing need in order to determine an appropriate mechanism accordingly.

115 Hodges, Current discussions (fn 47) 16.
116 Tzakas (fn 22) 1128. Similarly, C Hodges, 'Collective Redress in Europe: The New Model', *Civil Justice Quarterly*, 29(3) (2010), 370–395, 394.
117 See the regulatory measures only enable seeking injunctions, C Hodges, *The Reform of Class and Representative Actions in European Legal Systems: A New Framework for Collective Redress in Europe* (Oxford and Portland, Oregon: Hart Publishing, 2008), 104.
118 See *supra* section 'Commission efforts in consumer law'.
119 KJ Cseres, 'Consumer Protection in the European Union', in *Regulation and Economics*, ed. by RJ Van Den Bergh and AM Pacces, 2nd edn (Cheltenham: Edward Elgar Publishing, 2012), 163–228, 163. Similarly, T Bourgoignie, 'Characteristics of Consumer Law', *Journal of Consumer Policy*, 14(3) (1991), 293–315, 301.
120 GG Howells and S Weatherill, *Consumer Protection Law*, 2nd edn (England: Ashgate Publishing, Ltd., 2005), 6.
121 KJ Cseres, 'The Controversies of the Consumer Welfare Standard', *Competition Law Review*, 3(2) (2006), 121–173, 130.
122 J Goldring, 'Consumer Law and Legal Theory: Reflections of a Common Lawyer', *Journal of Consumer Policy*, 13(2) (1990), 113–132, 124; *ibid.* See also the Green Paper on collective redress aimed collective redress actions to improve deterrence in consumer law, Green Paper on collective redress (fn 43) para 7; G Wagner, 'Collective Redress – Categories of Loss and Legislative Options', *Law Quarterly Review*, 127 (2011), 55–82, 58.
123 *Directive 2009/22/EC of the European Parliament and of the Council of 23 April 2009 on Injunctions for the Protection of Consumers' Interests (Codified Version)*, (OJ L 110/30, 2009) (Injunctions directive).
124 *Directive 2013/11/EU of the European Parliament and of the Council of 21 May 2013 on Alternative Dispute Resolution for Consumer Disputes and Amending Regulation (EC) No 2006/2004 and Directive 2009/22/EC*, (OJ L 165/63, 2013). See also *Regulation (EU) No 524/2013 of the European Parliament and of the Council of 21 May 2013 on Online Dispute Resolution for Consumer Disputes and Amending Regulation (EC) No 2006/2004 and Directive 2009/22/EC*, (OJ L 165/1, 2013).
125 Tzakas (fn 22) 1128–1129; Hodges, Collective redress (fn 83) 76.
126 L Tortell, *Evaluation of the Effectiveness and Efficiency of Collective Redress Mechanisms in the European Union – Country Report Portugal*, 2008, 1–33, 2 <http://ec.europa.

Moreover, consumer law operates under a fragmented approach where competition law does not necessitate one.[127] This would affect not only the structure of a collective action but also its workability in consumer law. For instance, in misleading advertising cases the evidence is in the public domain and accessible by anyone. Representative parties and consumers would be aware of the breach and that the breach caused harm. One can argue that alternative mechanisms would work better in these cases as it would be easier to prove the breach and harm.[128] If a judicial collective redress action is designed for claims arising from misleading advertising, contrary to competition claims, there would be no need to implement measures to overcome unawareness, barriers to access to evidence and the cost of searching for infringements and collecting evidence.[129] In misleading advertising cases, a collective redress action does not require the presence of elements that are necessary for its working in competition law.

Another implication of this fragmented approach can be observed in product liability cases. These cases give rise to damages to property or personal injury. It means that in order to calculate damages the court needs to make individual damage assessments.[130] This makes these cases unsuitable to be determined in a single proceeding as there is a large group of persons on one side in a collective action and it is beyond the capacity of any court to perform numerous individualised factual inquiries and legal analyses in order to establish causation and calculate the amount of loss suffered on an individual basis.[131] As a result, a collective redress action in consumer law not only requires a different formulation depending on the type of the breach but also does not work in every case.

Furthermore, litigation in the public interest varies greatly from litigation in an economic field. In respect of this, it is difficult to strike the right balance with a horizontal approach to collective redress action. It has indeed been argued that different collective actions ought to be provided for torts endangering health, such as pollution.[132] Some of these are observed in environmental law.[133] Environmental goods of common interest, such as the air, the climate and the sea, are not

eu/consumers/archive/redress_cons/pt-country-report-final.pdf> [accessed 1 July 2018].

127 Ioannidou (fn 28) 62.

128 See the argument that alternative mechanisms are better suited to claims that are easy to prove or that are already proven, Chapter 1.

129 See further Chapter 6.

130 GO Robinson and KS Abraham 'Collective Justice in Tort Law', *Virginia Law Review*, 78(7) (1992), 1481–1519, 1486; A Erbsen, 'From "Predominance" to "Resolvability": A New Approach to Regulating Class Actions', *Vanderbilt Law Review*, 58(4) (2005), 995–1088, 999.

131 See how this affects grouping of claims in a collective redress action in Chapter 6.

132 They must be more powerful, A Layton, 'Collective Redress: Policy Objectives and Practical Problems', in *Extraterritoriality and Collective Redress*, ed. by D Fairgrieve and E Lein (Oxford: Oxford University Press, 2012), 93–104, 95.

133 Wagner (fn 122) 61.

subject to any property rights that give ownership.[134] The damage to these is impersonal, but the public suffers all.[135] For instance, everybody is affected by such as impairment of natural resources or extinction of endangered species.[136] Designing a collective redress action for such damages claims requires taking different considerations into account in order to formulate a workable mechanism.

One concern is whether the opt-in system that has been advocated by the horizontal approach throughout the collective redress debate is suitable. Another relates to the preservation of loser-pays rule. It is debatable whether a system should encourage representative parties to claim damages by sparing them from incurring the risk of the opponent's costs when environmental matters are at stake.[137] The further concern relates to the objective(s) of a collective redress action, in this situation the primary objective might not be compensation, as suggested by the Recommendation.[138]

It would also be sensible to consider that these claims are different from competition claims and suggest different collective redress actions. The calculation and distribution of damages in both cannot be the same. These environmental law claims can involve damages to common goods[139] as opposed to the economic loss of competition claims. The distribution of damages would differ greatly because the former causes no direct individual harm.[140] Similarly, the appropriate representative party could be different for both.

All in all, particular characteristics of different areas of law suggest different considerations when formulating a collective redress action. It is doubtful to what extent the proposals in the horizontal approach operate to assist all types of claims. It is not possible for such an approach to consider the features of all EU law areas in structuring collective redress actions and an overall assessment could fail to include considerations specific to some areas, including competition law.[141] It is obvious from the report on the Recommendation that Member States disagree

134 *Ibid*; M Hinteregger, 'Reconciling Multilayer Interests in Environmental Law – Access to Justice in Environmental Matters in the European Union and the United States', in *Collective Actions: Enhancing Access to Justice and Reconciling Multilayer Interests?*, ed. by S Wrbka, S Van Uytsel and M Siems (Cambridge: Cambridge University Press, 2012), 143–166, 146–147.

135 Wagner (fn 122) 62.

136 *Ibid.* In addition, some environmental breaches cause harm to individuals. In that case, tort liability arises and damages can be claimed for personal injury or death, Hinteregger (fn 134) 166. This obviously requires different damage calculation methods compared with competition claims. Claims for damages for personal injury or death necessitate individual determinations of causal link and damages calculation. See further for how these individual determinations affect the grouping of claims for collective redress purposes in Chapter 6.

137 See Public consultation (fn 53) 10, fn 15.

138 Communication (fn 53) para 3.1.

139 Wagner (fn 122) 62.

140 *Ibid.*

141 See similarly in respect to the reform process of collective actions in the UK, Ministry of Justice, *The Government's Response to the Civil Justice Council's Report: 'Improving Access to Justice through Collective Actions'*, 2009, para 13 <http://collections.europa

with the horizontal approach as only six of them allow collective redress actions across all areas of law.[142] While a general collective redress framework could be a means to provide redress in some areas of law, this might not be the case for others. Although not all types of EU law infringements can be analysed here, it is sufficient to say that different areas might require different rules and a common ground might not address the specificities and specific need of each area. With this in mind, the next section analyses a competition-specific initiative for collective redress actions.

The case for a distinctive competition law approach

Competition law calls for such an action to be established. A single breach could inflict harm on a great number of persons,[143] yet the number of individual damages actions is historically low and consumers particularly almost never sue for damages. This is due to the specificities of competition damages litigation[144] and the characteristics of consumer losses arising from competition infringements. This has triggered efforts to introduce a collective redress action in order to increase the chances of victims to obtain compensation.[145] Redress problems might exist in other areas, but the Commission pointed out that in this area '[t]he size of the uncompensated harm and the problems encountered are particularly big'.[146] In its reply to the public consultation, the UK government similarly stressed the importance of considering any likely negative and positive impacts, economic and otherwise, before introducing such an action to an area of law[147] and stated that a collective action ought to be adopted only for competition law where there is a robust assessment of need.[148]

The horizontal approach has not conducted a detailed analysis of the categories of loss and victim in order to structure a collective redress action accordingly. This raises a question as to what extent its common rules satisfy the need in competition law. Indeed, it has been suggested that distinctive approaches, such as regarding competition law,[149] could be attached to the general umbrella of the horizontal approach.[150]

rchive.org/tna/20100208150045/http:/www.justice.gov.uk/about/docs/government-response-cjc-collective-actions.pdf> [accessed 1 July 2018].

142 Report on the Recommendation (fn 98) 3.

143 BIS, *Private Actions in Competition Law – A Consultation on Options for Reform* (London, 2012), para 5.1.

144 Impact assessment (fn 10) para 31.

145 See further Chapter 2. See also, where available, the practical experience gathered from the Member States shows that collective actions are mostly used in competition law, especially in the form of follow-on actions, Report on the Recommendation (fn 98) 4.

146 Impact assessment (fn 10) para 31.

147 UK Government, 'UK Response to EU Consultation on Collective Redress', 2011, paras 4, 8 <http://ec.europa.eu/competition/consultations/2011_collective_redress/uk_en.pdf> [accessed 1 July 2018].

148 *Ibid* para 3.

149 Wallis (fn 52).

150 V Smith, 'European Commission Public Consultation "Towards a Coherent European Approach to Collective Redress"', 2011, 1–17, 5 <http://ec.europa.eu/competition/consultations/2011_collective_redress/smith_vincent_en.pdf> [accessed 1 July 2018]; Athanassiou (fn 54) 170.

With this in mind, a study analysing the collective redress action in competition law by the Directorate-General for Internal Policies concluded that, in the event of adopting a horizontal collective redress action there would be a need for further interventions in competition cases due to the particular characteristics of this area of law.[151] While defining the area covered by the Recommendation, the Communication also refers to these characteristics of competition law, and states that they are addressed in the Directive,[152] although the Directive comprises no rules with respect to collective redress. In one of the accompanying documents to the Directive, the Commission acknowledges that the specificities of competition law pose the possibility of specific rules for collective redress but it opts for a horizontal approach.[153] The Commission further states that specific provisions could be established in a separate chapter of the horizontal instrument or in subsequent separate legal instruments.[154] This is in line with the view of the European Parliament after the public consultation. The European Parliament favoured a legally binding horizontal framework alongside a limited number of rules for specific areas, such as competition law, in separate chapters or in separate legal instruments.[155]

It seems even with the horizontal approach, there would be distinct rules through distinctive approaches in some areas, such as competition law, and this eventually results in a different formula. The aim is not to create fragmentation of the law, but this would occur, even using the horizontal approach. Moreover, the horizontal approach makes little contribution to the ongoing situation for damages actions for competition infringements as the Recommendation has a non-binding character[156] and the suggested proposals are a step backwards when considering the previous studies in competition law. These may form the reasons to suggest a distinctive approach to competition claims.

It should also be noted that it is neither unusual nor impractical that such actions are restricted to specific areas, as demonstrated in some Member States.[157] For instance, Germany provides a collective action that applies only to capital market claims.[158] In Belgium, collective redress legislation applies only to consumer rights.[159] In the UK, a collective action can be brought for competition

151 European Parliament, Directorate-General for Internal Policies, *Collective Redress in Antitrust* (IP/A/Econ/ST/2011–19, 2012), para 3.4.
152 Communication (fn 53) para 1.1.
153 Executive summary of the impact assessment (fn 56) para 16.
154 *Ibid* para 22.
155 European Parliament, Motion (fn 68) para 17.
156 See the Commission favoured the adoption of a directive in competition law, Almunia (fn 63) 7.
157 Hodges, Collective redress (fn 83) 85.
158 A Halfmeier, 'The Revised German KapMuG' (presented at the Righting Private Wrongs: Competition Law, Investor Claims and Mass Litigation in the EU, London: BIICL, 2013). See other sectoral approaches to collective redress in Germany, E Lein, 'Germany', *Focus on Collective Redress* <http://www.collectiveredress.org/collective-redress/reports/germany/overview> [accessed 1 July 2018].
159 Report on the Recommendation (fn 98) 3.

claims. During the discussions of collective redress, the UK government favoured a competition-specific solution which was believed to not only produce a better outcome but also be more attainable.[160] The legislation that changes the collective redress action for competition claims was adopted in 2015.[161]

Finally, there is also a discussion of the suitable legislative act for an EU collective redress action. It is not easy to conclude on EU intervention in procedures, as there is an extensive and diverse literature on the matter.[162] With respect to this, there are arguments for and against binding rules of collective redress actions in competition law. One of the arguments favouring binding rules is based on the principle of effectiveness.[163] In the absence of EU rules on the matter, principles of equivalence and effectiveness limit national procedural autonomy that determines remedies and procedural rules for the exercise of the rights conferred by EU law.[164] In the directive proposal, the Commission sees the absence of effective collective redress actions as an obstacle in national laws, making the exercise of the right to damages impossible and overly difficult in practice. It further states despite slight improvements, the situation has not changed in most Member States since the Green Paper was published in 2005.[165] It has also been observed that among national systems that have such an action, nearly all have designed it differently.[166] Therefore, they have different degrees of effectiveness, which not only presents uneven enforcement of the right to damages[167] but also gives rise to the risk of forum-shopping outside and within the EU,[168] thereby undermining the level playing field.[169]

In light of this, it has been argued that there ought to be a competition-specific approach for collective redress because this would *i.* lead to the adoption of a coherent and consistent action across the EU *ii.* promote uniformity in the application of EU competition provisions *iii.* contribute to the creation of level playing field and *iv.* limit the risk of forum shopping.[170] There are also economic arguments favouring binding EU rules, such as these rules can lead to efficiencies and reduced transactions costs.[171]

160 Ministry of Justice (fn 141) para 9. The Civil Justice Council (CJC) that proposed to adopt a generic collective action in the UK argued that their aim was not to implement a 'one-size-fits-all' model but instead attach specific regimes for some areas to the generic model, such as competition and employment law. R Mulheron, 'Recent Milestones in Class Actions Reform in England: A Critique and a Proposal', *Law Quarterly Review*, 127 (2011), 288–315, 294–295.
161 *Consumer Rights* Act 2015 (c.15), 2015, sch 8. See further Chapter 6.
162 P Craig, *EU Administrative Law*, 2nd edn (Oxford: Oxford University Press, 2012), 725.
163 Collective redress in antitrust (fn 151) para 2.2.1.
164 Case C-453/99 *Courage Ltd. v Bernard Crehan* [2001] ECR I-6297, para 29.
165 Directive proposal (fn 77) para 1.2. See further Chapter 4.
166 Joint information note (fn 61) para 10.
167 *Ibid.*
168 Almunia (fn 63) 6.
169 Joint information note (fn 166) para 10.
170 Collective redress in antitrust (fn 151) para 3.6.
171 C Cauffman and N Philipsen, 'Who Does What in Competition Law: Harmonizing the Rules on Damages for Infringements of the EU Competition Rules?', *Maastricht*

On the other hand, an argument against binding rules is that Member States should be able to decide the rules that are best for their citizens and should therefore be able to experiment with different regimes in order to achieve that most desirable.[172] Indeed, experimentation could serve as an example for other Member States, demonstrating the strong and weak points of a practised action.[173] However, the Commission declares that Member States have made little progress in this field over a decade and it is still difficult or nearly impossible for victims to exercise their right to damages.[174] This makes further wait unpromising.

It has also been asserted that – due to the diversity between existing collective redress mechanisms – implementation of binding EU rules is impossible without considerably changing national systems.[175] This might bring untoward procedural values to bear upon national laws,[176] because each Member State has a different procedural law shaped by its own distinctive cultural heritage.[177] However, it should be noted that membership of the EU naturally affects national laws.[178] For instance, the CJEU holds that umbrella victims are entitled to sue for damages where Austrian courts have denied them damages.[179] The Directive also introduces some new rules in national laws, such as the rebuttable presumptions that cartels cause harm[180] and that the overcharge harm is passed on to indirect purchasers.[181]

Finally, it has been argued that EU law does not pursue the primary goal of a unified system of remedies and procedural rules; rather it acknowledges national fragmentation. Therefore, binding EU rules would be justifiable only when limited to certain sectors.[182] This again supports a distinctive approach to competition law.

Another side to the matter concerns obtaining political support. When the EU level efforts were limited to competition claims, the Commission planned to adopt binding measures.[183] On top of that, at the time the Commission was in the view that non-binding documents result in further fragmentation of national laws.[184]

European Private Law Institute, Working Paper no 2014/19, 2014, 1–43, 15–20 <http://awards.concurrences.com/IMG/pdf/who.pdf> [accessed 1 July 2018].

172 Hodges, The reform of class and representative actions (fn 117) 181; Cauffman and Philipsen (fn 171) 14.

173 See Cauffman and Philipsen (fn 171) 14.

174 See *supra* fn 165.

175 Hodges, The reform of class and representative actions (fn 117) 181.

176 Craig (fn 162) 726.

177 C Harlow, 'A Common European Law of Remedies?', in *The Future of Remedies in Europe*, ed. by T Novitz, C Kilpatrick and P Skidmore (Oxford and Portland, Oregon: Hart Publishing, 2000), 69–83, 83.

178 Craig (fn 162) 726.

179 Case C-557/12 *Kone AG and Others v ÖBB-Infrastruktur AG* [2014] EU: C:2014:1317, paras 11, 33–34.

180 Directive (fn 74) art. 17(2).

181 *Ibid* art. 14(2).

182 M Dougan, *National Remedies Before the Court of Justice: Issues of Harmonisation and Differentiation* (Oxford and Portland, Oregon: Hart Publishing, 2004), 201–202.

183 See *supra* fn 156.

184 Impact assessment (fn 10) para 147.

However, as part of the horizontal approach, the Recommendation follows non-binding measures. It has been stated that a lack of political support leads to the instigation of a non-binding Recommendation.[185] The exclusion of collective redress from the Directive would seem to indicate the same. Disagreement between Member States leads to the omission of collective redress,[186] whereby the Directive stands a much better chance of convincing the European Parliament and Member States.[187]

The adoption of the Directive on damages actions demonstrates that there is political support for enhancement of the exercise of individual right to damages and for removal of the diversity of national laws that give rise to inequality and uncertainty as regards the conditions under which individual damages actions are filed.[188] Collective redress actions can be considered in a similar context; if political support is obtained, which may happen after the effectiveness assessment of the Commission regarding the Recommendation, binding EU rules on collective redress in competition law might once again become a possibility.[189]

Indeed, consumers supported binding collective redress measures whereas the majority of businesses opposed.[190] According to Article 288 TFEU, these binding rules can be a regulation or directive. Where Member States are not required to take any action to implement the former, they are free to choose the appropriate tools to transpose the latter into national laws. For this reason, the preference should be given to a directive to introduce a collective action to competition law.[191]

185 Wallis (fn 52); J Drexl, 'Consumer Actions After the Adoption of the EU Directive on Damage Claims for Competition Law Infringements', *Max Planck Institute for Innovation and Competition Research Paper no 15–10*, 2015, 1–34, 25 <http://papers.ssrn.com/sol3/papers.cfm?abstract_id=2689521> [accessed 1 July 2018].

186 L Amos and others, 'EU Update', *Computer Law and Security Review*, 29 (2013), 616–620, 619.

187 J Zöttl, S Clerckx and F Amato, 'Antitrust Alert: EU Commission Proposes New Measures to Foster Damages Litigation', 2013 <http://m.jonesday.com/antitrust-alert–eu-commission-proposes-new-measures-to-foster-damages-litigation-06-20-2013/> [accessed 1 July 2018].

188 Directive (fn 74) preamble paras 4, 7–8.

189 See some stakeholders are in the view of introducing binding EU rules for such an action in competition law, Communication (fn 53) para 2.1.

190 Commission, *Staff Working Document – Impact Assessment Report – Damages Actions for Breach of the EU Antitrust Rules* (SWD(2013) 203 final, Strasbourg, 2013) para 20. See business organisations are concerned with the proportionality and subsidiarity of an EU-wide collective redress action for consumers, Report on the Recommendation (fn 98) 20.

191 See eg C Leskinen, 'Collective Actions: Rethinking Funding and National Cost Rules', *Competition Law Review*, 8(1) (2011), 87–121, 115; Z Juska, 'Obstacles in European Competition Law Enforcement: A Potential Solution from Collective Redress', *European Journal of Legal Studies*, 7(1) (2014), 125–153, 147. Similarly, see directives are generally the chosen tools, K Davies, *Understanding European Union Law*, 4th edn (Oxford: Routledge, 2011), 58.

Concluding remarks

This chapter analysed the collective redress proposals in the EU in order to present the reasons why the introduction of a collective redress action is discussed and the proposals in this respect. This analysis provides the basis for the assessment of the proposals in competition law when formulating the action in later chapters.

Originally, the Commission pursued its work on collective redress in the fields of competition and consumer law as distinct initiatives. The efforts in these areas led to different outcomes for collective redress. In competition law, the fact that victims of competition infringements, especially consumers, only rarely obtain compensation for their loss induced the Commission to propose the introduction of a collective redress action. However, more consistent and clear collective redress proposals could have been made.

In this respect, where the Green Paper considered such an action a necessary tool to provide a realistic possibility for consumers to reach court, the White Paper took a different approach. Despite acknowledging the clear need for such an action for consumers, it drew no distinction between consumer and business claims. In addition, the Commission adopted two distinct definitions and design frameworks for representative and collective actions within these two papers. The Green Paper provided for an opt-in representative and collective action for consumers, albeit with the possibility that collective actions could be brought on behalf of identifiable members. The White Paper suggested an opt-in collective action and, tacitly, an opt-out representative action. That said, the two most recent works in this area, ie the White Paper and the withdrawn Directive, seem to settle on an opt-out nature for representative actions although the White Paper suggested that it be used in restricted cases. The Commission avoided articulating an opt-out proposal explicitly due to fear of opposition. Nonetheless, the Commission's wish to introduce such an action can be seen in concrete proposals in two papers and a directive proposal.

In consumer law, the studies do not clearly establish need, which resulted in the Commission bringing forward options rather than submitting a collective redress proposal. After separate considerations of a collective redress action in these two fields, an approach to introduce such an action for claims arising from any EU law breach has prevailed in order to avoid fragmentation of the law. On this basis, first, a public consultation was published to determine common principles that would guide any collective redress action adopted in any area of EU law. The rather vague wording of these principles raises concerns regarding their ability to guide any design framework. Subsequently, the Recommendation was published which called for the implementation of a horizontal collective redress action in national laws. It would seem that a lack of political support gave rise to this non-binding horizontal document. However, the extent to which all areas of EU law are compatible with this common approach is still an open question. In other words, it does not reflect the need and the specificities of laws in the formulation of the action, and it might fall short when assisting victims in seeking redress in some areas of law. As expected, a few Member States follow the horizontal approach when adopting a legislation on collective redress.

It appears that the Commission no longer considers collective redress actions solely for competition claims. The Directive does not include any provisions for collective redress and only refers to the Recommendation in this respect. To this end, the European Parliament, the Commission and interested stakeholders have acknowledged that competition claims are likely to require specific provisions for collective redress, but this can be achieved in a separate legal instrument attached to the horizontal document. This said, providing unique rules for competition claims in a separate legal instrument disregards the main purpose of the horizontal approach, giving rise to fragmentation of the law.

Establishing the need for the introduction of a collective action in a specific area is important; it identifies the extent of the problem, determines whether such an action would constitute a solution, and, if affirmative, how to formulate the action accordingly. In this context, a distinctive approach to competition cases makes more sense; the problem and the demand for such an action are identified, and by reflecting the need and the particular characteristics of competition law, a design specific to assist consumer damages claims in obtaining redress could prove to be beneficial. The next chapter analyses the objectives that a collective redress action would pursue in competition cases.

4 Objectives of collective redress actions in EU competition enforcement

Introduction

The objectives pursued by private enforcement have some important consequences in relation to the design framework for collective redress. Therefore, this chapter seeks to identify the primary objective of a collective redress action and provides a basis for the formulation of this action in the following chapters. The chapter begins with a brief overview of the current debate around the objectives of actions for damages and clarifies the scope and meaning of compensation and deterrence objectives. The third section of the chapter explains the approach of the EU courts and of the Commission toward the objectives of damages actions. Then, the fourth section of the chapter assesses the objective(s) pursued by collective redress actions, discussing the goal of EU competition law enforcement and how it gives rise to the need for such an action. Building on this discussion, the chapter answers the question of the extent to which a collective redress action realises the compensation and deterrence objectives by establishing the relationship between them. Lastly, it reflects on whether the objective sought by a collective redress action ought to be different if it is formulated for consumer damages claims.

Determining the objectives and their significance

The Commission's efforts in private competition law enforcement are spurred by the fact that the victims of competition infringements rarely bring an action and obtain compensation, despite having the right to damages. In light of this, measures proposed are intended to enhance the exercise of the right to damages. Important, therefore, is identification of the primary objective of private competition law enforcement through actions for damages, an objective that would serve the need in this area and that would be reflected and advanced by any adopted measures.[1] As one of these measures, a collective redress action enabling

1 See M Ioannidou, 'Enhancing the Consumers' Role in EU Private Competition Law Enforcement: A Normative and Practical Approach', *Competition Law Review*, 8(1) (2011), 59–85, 62–63. See also AG Tesauro states with respect to the Member States' autonomy that '[j]udicial remedies for the infringement of rights conferred by [EU law] is firmly tied to the result sought by [it]'. Opinion of AG Tesauro Delivered on

individuals to pursue their damages claims collectively in a single lawsuit would accordingly be designed to advance that objective.

Much of the discussion has revolved around two principal objectives:[2] *i.* to compensate victims for their losses and *ii.* to deter market actors from engaging in an infringement. In the literature, these objectives are widely recognised as the objectives of damages actions for competition infringements.[3] Some commentators prioritise deterrence,[4] others compensation,[5] and some both.[6] These two objectives are put forward by EU courts in the recognition of the right to damages for competition infringements. Furthermore, both objectives are identified and discussed by the Commission in its papers in order to be used as a base for proposed measures for enhancing damages actions, including the collective redress action.[7]

28 November 1995 in Joined Cases C-46/93 and C-48/93 *Brasserie Du Pecheur SA v Federal Republic of Germany and The Queen v Secretary of State for Transport, Ex Parte Factortame Ltd and Others* [1996] ECR I-1029, para 47.

2 SV Walle, *Private Antitrust Litigation in the European Union and Japan – A Comparative Perspective* (Antwerpen-Apeldoorn: Maklu, 2013), 238.

3 See eg C Diemer, 'The Green Paper on Damages Actions for Breach of the EC Antitrust Rules', *European Competition Law Review*, 27(6) (2006), 309–316, 310–311; RJ Van den Bergh and PD Camesasca, *European Competition Law and Economics: A Comparative Perspective*, 2nd edn (London: Sweet&Maxwell, 2006), 332–333; J Basedow, 'Introduction', in *Private Enforcement of EC Competition Law*, ed. by J Basedow (The Netherlands: Kluwer Law International, 2007), 1–5, 2; A Ezrachi, *EU Competition Law: An Analytical Guide to the Leading Cases*, 4th edn (Oxford and Portland, Oregon: Hart Publishing, 2014), 545; T Eger and P Weise, 'Some Limits to the Private Enforcement of Antitrust Law: A Grumbler's View on Harm and Damages in Hardcore Price Cartel Cases', *Global Competition Litigation Review*, 3(4) (2010), 152–160, 154; Brick Court Chambers, *Competition Litigation: UK Practice and Procedure*, ed. by M Brealey and N Green (Oxford: Oxford University Press, 2010), 453; S Bourjade, 'The Role of Private Litigation in Antitrust Enforcement', *Global Competition Litigation Review*, 3(3) (2010), 118–123, 119; A Jones and B Sufrin, *EU Competition Law: Text, Cases & Materials*, 5th edn (Oxford: Oxford University Press, 2014), 1087.

4 F Hoseinian, 'Passing-on Damages and Community Antitrust Policy – An Economic Background', *World Competition*, 28(1) (2005), 3–23, 5 SE Keske, *Group Litigation in European Competition Law: A Law and Economics Perspective* (Antwerp-Oxford-Portland: Intersentia, 2010) 58.

5 D Waelbroeck and D Slater, 'The Commission's Green Paper on Private Enforcement: "Americanization" of EC Competition Law Enforcement?', in *European Competition Law Annual 2006: Enforcement of Prohibition of Cartels*, ed. by C-D Ehlermann and I Atanasiu (Oxford and Portland, Oregon: Hart Publishing, 2006), 425–455, 427; P Nebbia, 'Damages Actions for the Infringement of EC Competition Law: Compensation or Deterrence?', *European Law Review*, 33(1) (2008), 23–43, 36; R Nazzini, 'The Objective of Private Remedies in EU Competition Law', *Global Competition Litigation Review*, 4 (2011), 131–146, 138.

6 Diemer (fn 3) 310–311; A Ezrachi and M Ioannidou, 'Public Compensation as a Complementary Mechanism to Damages Actions: From Policy Justifications to Formal Implementation', *Journal of European Competition Law and Practice*, 3(6) (2012), 536–544, 538.

7 See *infra* section 'The approach of the Commission'.

The compensatory function of damages actions ensures that victims obtain compensation for their losses.[8] It aims to restore victims to the position in which they would have been but for infringement.[9] This is the *ex post* correction of the consequences arising from competition infringements;[10] the wrong or the injury is corrected by the damages award.[11] A monetary payment of compensation is related to the magnitude of the harm inflicted.[12] The compensation objective thus entails the infringing undertaking to be held liable for the loss occasioned by its action; no more and no less.[13] For these reasons, this objective is usually ascribed to corrective justice[14] which '[e]nsure[s] that all harms are compensated notwithstanding the effects and costs this may have'.[15] As a result, corrective justice is attained by making good the loss incurred by those harmed to the greatest possible extent[16] and in requiring the defendant to fully compensate the harm caused.[17]

The deterrence objective, on the other hand, aims to prevent competition infringements[18] by punishing the infringing undertaking so that it refrains from committing future violations and/or by deterring other actors from entering into

8 Commission, *Staff Working Paper Annex to the Green Paper Damages Actions for Breach of the EC Antitrust Rules* (SEC(2005)1732, Brussels, 2005), (SWPGP) para 147; AP Komninos, 'Relationship between Public and Private Enforcement: *Quod Dei Deo, Quod Caesaris Caesari*' (presented at the 16th Annual EU Competition Law and Policy Workshop – Integrating Public and Private Enforcement of Competition Law: Implications for Courts and Agencies, Florence, 2011) 1–26, 3 <http://ssrn.com/abstract=1870723> [accessed 1 July 2018].

9 Centre for European Policy Studies (CEPS), Erasmus University Rotterdam (EUR) and Luiss Guido Carli (LUISS), *Report for the European Commission 'Making Antitrust Damages Actions More Effective in the EU: Welfare Impact and Potential Scenarios', Final Report*, 2007, 59.

10 WPJ Wils, 'Should Private Antitrust Enforcement be Encouraged in Europe?', *World Competition*, 26(3) (2003), 1–21, 10.

11 CT Galligan, 'Disaggregating More-Than-Whole Damages in Personal Injury Law: Deterrence and Punishment', *Tennessee Law Review*, 71 (2003), 117–154, 119. According to Varuhas, a damage remedy is second-alternative to actual compliance, as a claimant clearly prefers to never incur injury in the first place. JNE Varuhas, *Damages and Human Rights* (Oxford and Portland, Oregon: Hart Publishing, 2016), 21.

12 See Welfare impact report (fn 9) 77.

13 G Wagner, 'Collective Redress – Categories of Loss and Legislative Options', *Law Quarterly Review*, 127 (2011), 55–82, 67.

14 Galligan (fn 11) 119; Van den Bergh and Camesasca (fn 3) 332–333; Jones and Sufrin (fn 3) 1087. See corrective justice pertains to not only compensatory justice but also restitutionary and retributive justice, P Cane, 'Distributive Justice and Tort Law', *New Zealand Law Review*, 4 (2001), 401–420, 406–407; K Horsey and E Rackley, *Tort Law*, 3rd edn (Oxford: Oxford University Press, 2013), 11.

15 J Kloub, 'White Paper on Damage Actions for Breach of the EC Antitrust Rules: Plea for a More Holistic Approach to Antitrust Enforcement', *European Competition Journal*, 5(2) (2009), 515–547, 520.

16 *Ibid.*

17 Wagner (fn 13) 59; Horsey and Rackley (fn 14) 11.

18 Wils, Should private antitrust enforcement be encouraged (fn 10) 9.

or continuing to adopt anticompetitive conducts.[19] Whilst people do not always act rationally,[20] do not always have the full information,[21] or hold different degrees of risk averseness,[22] this objective is based on the assumption that the potential infringer considers the probable gain, the probability of detection and punishment, and the level of fine and compensation to be paid when deciding whether to infringe the law.[23] An action for damages would create additional cost and risks[24] and increase any potential monetary sanction in the form of damages.

It has been argued that these objectives are in conflict, that policymakers must therefore decide which to prioritise,[25] and that this choice yields different preferences.[26] The compensation objective requires a correlation between loss and damage, and in this way links the parties to each other as wrongdoer and sufferer.[27] The deterrence objective, on the other hand, is unconcerned with who recovers damages and to what level; it is concerned with rather that *i.* the infringer pays damages and so does not gain advantage from the wrongdoing and *ii.* making the infringer pay should be at minimum cost.[28] Deterrence embraces the possibility of dealing with the infringer's action independent to the victim's loss,[29] which supports the concept of awarding 'more-than-whole damages',[30] ie punitive damages that aim to punish and/or deter the wrongdoer,[31] but this contradicts the compensation objective.[32] Before searching for the possible interaction

19 The former is called as 'specific deterrence', while the latter is 'general deterrence'. AP Komninos, 'Private Enforcement in the EU with Emphasis on Damages Actions', in *Handbook on European Competition Law – Enforcement and Procedure*, ed. by I Lianos and D Geradin (Cheltenham UK: Edward Elgar Publishing, 2013), vol.II, 228–272, 231–232.

20 See eg ME Wheeler, 'Antitrust Treble-Damage Actions: Do They Work?', *California Law Review*, 61(6) (1973), 1319–1352, 1321.

21 See eg JE Stiglitz, 'Information and the Change in the Paradigm in Economics', *American Economic Review*, 92(3) (2002), 460–501, 461.

22 AM Polinsky and S Shavell, 'The Economic Theory of Public Enforcement of Law', *Journal of Economic Literature*, 38(1) (2000), 45–76, 50.

23 See WPJ Wils, 'Optimal Antitrust Fines: Theory and Practice', *World Competition*, 29 (2) (2006), 183–208, 193.

24 Komninos, Private enforcement in the EU (fn 19) 232.

25 Nebbia (fn 5) 36; Ioannidou (fn 1) 70; Walle (fn 2) 239.

26 See Nebbia (fn 5) 36.

27 EJ Weinrib, 'Deterrence and Corrective Justice', *UCLA Law Review*, 50 (2002), 621–640, 624.

28 Keske (fn 4) 87. The approach that sees deterrence superior generally explains the reasons within the framework of economics, see eg GT Schwartz, 'Mixed Theories of Tort Law: Affirming Both Deterrence and Corrective Justice', *Texas Law Review*, 75 (1997), 1801–1834, 1801; V Smith, 'Publication Review', *European Law Review*, 37 (3) (2012), 353–355, 354 (reviewing SE Keske, *Group Litigation in European Competition Law: A Law and Economics Perspective* (Antwerp-Oxford-Portland: Intersentia, 2010)).

29 Weinrib (fn 27) 628.

30 Galligan (fn 11) 117.

31 SWPGP (fn 8) para 116.

32 R Van Den Bergh, 'Private Enforcement of European Competition Law and the Persisting Collective Action Problem', *Maastricht Journal*, 1 (2013), 12–34, 16.

between these two objectives in the context of collective redress procedures, the following section examines the EU institutions' view on the objectives of actions for damages.

Objectives of actions for damages

The approach of the EU courts

As recognised by the EU courts, victims of competition infringements have the right to damages. The courts see this right as part of individuals' legal assets[33] and attach considerable importance to the compensatory and deterrence functions of actions for damages. The *Courage* [34] and *Manfredi* [35] judgments made it clear that if claiming damages were not open to any individual for the loss arisen from a contract or conduct liable to restrict or distort competition, the full effectiveness of the Treaty and, in particular, the practical effect of the prohibition laid down would be at risk.[36] By so saying, the Court submitted a compensatory function of damages actions.[37] These judgments also expressed a deterrence function[38] by establishing that the existence of the right to damages reinforces the function of EU competition rules and discourages competition infringements, thereby making a significant contribution to the maintenance of effective competition in the EU.[39] In this way, the right to damages has been established to serve the effective enforcement of EU competition rules.[40]

33 See eg Case C-453/99 *Courage Ltd. v Bernard Crehan* [2001] ECR I-6297, para 19; Case C-536/11 *Bundeswettbewerbsbehörde v Donau Chemie AG and Others* [2013] ECR I-0000, para 20.

34 *Courage* (fn 33) para 26.

35 Joined Cases C-295/04 and C-298/04 *Vincenzo Manfredi v Lloyd Adriatico Assicurazioni SpA* [2006] ECR I-06619, para 90.

36 Similarly, Case C-199/11 *Europese Gemeenschap v Otis NV and Others* [2012] ECR I-0000, para 41; *Donau Chemie* (fn 33) para 21; Case C-557/12 *Kone AG and Others v ÖBB-Infrastruktur AG* [2014] EU:C:2014:1317, para 21.

37 CA Jones and D Beard, 'Case Comment "Co-Contractors, Damages and Article 81: ECJ Finally Speaks"', *European Competition Law Review*, 23 (2002), 246–256, 253.

38 *Ibid;* Nazzini (fn 5) 142.

39 *Courage* (fn 33) para 27; Opinion of AG Mischo delivered on 22 March 2001 in *Courage*, para 57; *Manfredi* (fn 35) para 91. See also Case C-360/09 *Pfleiderer AG v Bundeskartellamt* [2011] ECR I-000, para 29; *Otis* (fn 36) para 42; *Donau Chemie* (fn 33) para 23; *Kone* (fn 36) para 23.

40 For *Courage,* see Jones and Beard (fn 37) 253; AP Komninos, 'New Prospects for Private Enforcement of EC Competition Law: *Courage v. Crehan* and the Community Right to Damages', *Common Market Law Review*, 39(3) (2002), 447–487, 468–469. For *Courage* and *Manfredi*, Nazzini (fn 5) 140; D Leczykiewicz, 'Enforcement or Compensation? Damages Actions in EU Law after the Draft Common Frame of Reference', *Oxford Legal Studies Research Paper no 59/2012*, 2012, 1–18, 5 <http://papers.ssrn.com/sol3/papers.cfm?abstract_id=2159722> [accessed 1 July 2018]. See Nebbia argues that the enforcement rationale was mentioned by the Court just to reinforce the basis of liability not to establish it, Nebbia (fn 5) 35.

The Court in *Manfredi* was additionally asked whether Article 101 TFEU requires national courts to award punitive damages and provide greater gain than the loss incurred in order to deter infringements.[41] First, the Advocate General (AG) in *Manfredi* mentioned that the potential for actions for damages contributes to deterrence[42] and, if unavailable in Member States, there is no need to award punitive damages to ensure the useful effect of Article 101 TFEU.[43] Similarly, the Court, after acknowledging the deterrence function of damages actions,[44] held that Member States are not required to award punitive damages unless awarding these kinds of damages is possible in similar domestic actions.[45]

The Court in *Manfredi* also stated that the principle of effectiveness and the right to seek damages suggest that victims recover full compensation, ie not only the overcharge harm but also loss of profits and interest.[46] In referring to *Marshall*, [47] the Court added that the award of interest constitutes an essential component of compensation.[48] According to the *Marshall* case, in situations where real equality of opportunity is denied, appropriate measures must be taken to restore such equality. Such measures must guarantee real and effective judicial protection and have a real deterrent effect on the defendant.[49] Full compensation is the measure[50] by which those aims are pursued, comprising not only damages sustained as a result of unlawful act but also the award of interest.[51] In this respect, full compensation indicates that *i.* individuals would be fully compensated and *ii.* the defendant would be at risk of responsibility for the whole loss caused.[52] This is in accordance with the rationale adopted by *Courage* and *Manfredi* that stressed a dual function.[53] From this perspective, the objective of full compensation, with the right to damages and enforcement, serves not only the compensation objective but also that of the deterrence.[54] This is why it is necessary to establish the link between these two objectives.

The approach of the Commission

Triggered by the case law, the Commission focuses on enhancing damages actions, and identifies the objectives that the proposed measures aim to serve. The

41 *Manfredi* (fn 35) para 83.
42 Opinion of AG Geelhoed delivered on 26 January 2006 in *Manfredi*, para 65.
43 *Ibid* para 70.
44 *Manfredi* (fn 35) para 91.
45 *Ibid* paras 92–93.
46 *Ibid* para 95; *Donau Chemie* (fn 33) para 24.
47 Case C-271/91 *M. Helen Marshall v Southampton and South-West Hampshire Area Health Authority* [1993] ECR I-04367.
48 *Manfredi* (fn 35) para 97.
49 *Marshall* (fn 47) para 24.
50 *Ibid* para 26.
51 *Ibid* paras 29–31.
52 Nazzini (fn 5) 142.
53 *Ibid.*
54 See *ibid.*

Green Paper acknowledged that damages actions pursue the compensation and deterrence objectives equally,[55] and, alongside public enforcement, contribute to creating and sustaining a competitive economy.[56] In order to incentivise individuals to bring their claims in court it proposed to award double damages in cartel cases.[57] The Green Paper was criticised for emphasising that damages actions were capable of concurrently achieving two aims,[58] and for opening a discussion around multiplier of damages which was reminiscent of the US style private actions for treble damages.[59]

Those criticisms seem to be taken into account in subsequent papers.[60] Since 2008 the Commission has recognised compensation as the primary objective. The proposals in the White Paper,[61] the withdrawn Directive[62] and the Directive[63] intend to fully compensate victims for the loss suffered.[64] As the Commission states, the principle of full compensation provides neither under- nor over-

55 Commission, *Green Paper on Damages Actions for Breach of EC Antitrust Rules* (COM(2005) 672 final, Brussels, 2005), (Green Paper) para 1.1; SWPGP (fn 8) paras 4–6. See the former Notice saying that the application of EU competition law by national courts pursues both objectives, Commission, *Notice on Cooperation between National Courts and the Commission in Applying Articles [101 and 102 of the Treaty]* (OJ C 39/6–12, 1993), para 16.

56 Green Paper (fn 55) para 1.1.

57 SWPGP (fn 8) para 150. Similarly, E Paulis, 'Policy Issues in the Private Enforcement of EC Competition Law', in *Private Enforcement of EC Competition Law*, ed. by J Basedow (The Netherlands: Kluwer Law International, 2007), 7–16, 13.

58 Waelbroeck and Slater (fn 5) 2. Similarly, eg, ICC, '*ICC Comments on the Commission's Green Paper on Damages Actions for Breach of the EC Antitrust Rules*', 2006, 1–12, 1 <http://ec.europa.eu/competition/antitrust/actionsdamages/files_green_paper_comments/icc.pdf> [accessed 1 July 2018]; CBI, 'EC Commission Green Paper on Damages Actions – CBI Response', 2006, 1–10, 1 <http://ec.europa.eu/competition/antitrust/actionsdamages/files_green_paper_comments/cbi.pdf> [accessed 1 July 2018].

59 See eg Wagner (fn 13) 56.

60 M Hazelhorst, 'Private Enforcement of EU Competition Law: Why Punitive Damages Are a Step Too Far', *European Review of Private Law*, 18(4) (2010), 757–772, 757; A Aresu, 'Optimal Contract Reformation as a New Approach to Private Antitrust Damages in Cartel Cases', *European Law Review*, 35(3) (2010), 349–369, 350.

61 Commission, *White Paper on Damages Actions for Breach of the EC Antitrust Rules* (COM(2008) 165 final, Brussels, 2008), (White Paper) para 1.2.

62 Commission, *Proposal for a Council Directive on Rules Governing Damages Actions for Infringements of Articles [101] and [102] of the Treaty*, 2009, (Withdrawn Directive) explanatory memorandum, paras 1.1–1.2 <http://allegati.unina.it/postlaurea/perf/Exclusiva_Juridico.pdf> [accessed 1 July 2018].

63 *Directive 2014/104/EU of the European Parliament and of the Council of 26 November 2014 on Certain Rules Governing Actions for Damages under National Law for Infringements of the Competition Law Provisions of the Member States and of the European Union*, (OJ L 349/1, 2014), art. 3.

64 It is overcharge and/or lost profits plus interest for the period between the injury occurred and the damages award paid. Commission, *Staff Working Paper Accompanying the White Paper on Damages Actions for Breach of the EC Antitrust Rules* (SEC(2008) 404, Brussels, 2008), para 310; Withdrawn Directive (fn 62) art. 1(2); Directive (fn 63) art. 3(2).

compensation[65] and therefore requires national legal systems to refrain from setting a ceiling on the compensation recoverable by plaintiffs.[66] The deterrence function of damages actions is, however, acknowledged. It has been noted that the mechanisms that ensure 'full compensation' would inherently deter;[67] by paying compensation the infringers bear the cost of their actions[68] which would, in turn, enhance compliance with competition law.[69]

The Commission submits that the main purpose of their efforts is to achieve effective enforcement of competition law. It has been stated that the proposals contained in the White Paper and in the withdrawn Directive are intended to enhance effective enforcement.[70] The Directive seeks to serve the same aim by, *inter alia*, enabling the victims of competition infringements to obtain full compensation for the loss sustained.[71]

The foregoing indicates that actions for damages cater to a compensation objective, which is consistent with the need in this area.[72] Such actions, by pursuing a main objective of compensation, contribute to the enforcement of competition rules and to deterrence. However, a consistent approach toward objectives would lead to the adoption of a definite policy in this area. The inconsistencies between and within the Commission's papers prevent the introduction of measures capable of advancing the identified objective and put the success of any effort at risk.

Indeed, the question of punitive damages can be given as an example that shows an inconsistency. While the Green Paper proposed double damages, the White Paper stated that punitive damages can be reconsidered if an incentive is needed to encourage plaintiffs to file damages actions, in light of the imbalance between the risks of litigation and the expected reward.[73] It further stated that the

65 Commission, *Staff Working Document Accompanying Document to the White Paper on Damages Actions for Breach of the EC Antitrust Rules – Impact Assessment* (SEC (2008) 405, Brussels, 2008), para 95.
66 SWPWP (fn 64) para 310.
67 White Paper (fn 61) para 1.2; Commission, *Communication from the Commission on Quantifying Harm in Actions for Damages Based on Breaches of Article 101 or 102 of the Treaty on the Functioning of the European Union* (OJ C 167/19, 2013), art. 2.
68 White Paper (fn 61) para 1.2; Commission, *Proposal for a Directive of the European Parliament and of the Council on Certain Rules Governing Actions for Damages Under National Law for Infringements of the Competition Law Provisions of the Member States and of the European Union*, (2013/0185 (COD), COM(2013) 404 final, Strasbourg, 2013), (Directive proposal) explanatory memorandum para 1.2.
69 Directive proposal (fn 68) explanatory memorandum para 1.2.
70 White Paper (fn 61) paras 1.2; SWPWP (fn 64) para 318; Withdrawn Directive (fn 62) paras 1.1, 3.1.
71 Directive proposal (fn 68) explanatory memorandum para 1.2.
72 See Chapter 2. See also that victims of competition infringements find claims for damages more attractive than claims for injunctions as the latter does not provide any financial benefits to the victims, Z Juska, 'The Effectiveness of Antitrust Collective Litigation in the European Union: A Study of the Principle of Full Compensation', *International Review of Intellectual Property and Competition Law*, 49(1) (2018), 63–93, 67.
73 SWPWP (fn 64) para 195.

principle of full compensation does not prevent Member States from awarding such damages to victims if they find it appropriate.[74] The recently adopted Directive, however, states that full compensation principle should not result in overcompensation, including by means of punitive damages[75] and making the award of punitive damages irreconcilable with it.[76]

It should also be noted that some proposals contained in the White Paper and the Directive are not in line with the submitted principal objective of compensation. In addition to its approach toward punitive damages, the White Paper proposed a rebuttable presumption on passing-on – that the entire overcharge was passed on to consumers.[77] However, this could lead to overcompensation of those who were not affected by paying the entire overcharge.[78] In addition, one of the suggestions in the directive proposal stated that if it is legally impossible for indirect purchasers to claim compensation due to evidential complexities, such as remoteness or causation,[79] the defendant should not be allowed to evoke the passing-on defence[80] as it should not be allowed to get away with the illegal gain.[81] This could deny real victims recovery as, even if the harm is properly quantified, Member States, in accordance with their tort law rules, can refrain from awarding damages to indirect purchasers.[82] This could also compensate direct purchasers for a loss they have not actually suffered.[83] This proposal was not

74 *Ibid* para 194.
75 Directive (fn 63) art. 3(3). Similarly, eg Commission, *Communication from the Commission to the European Parliament, the Council, the European Economic and Social Committee and the Committee of the Regions 'Towards a European Horizontal Framework for Collective Redress'* (COM(2013) 401 final, 2013), paras 2.3, 3.1; European Parliament, *Motion for a European Parliament Resolution on 'Towards a Coherent European Approach to Collective Redress'* (2011/2089(INI), 2012) para 20 <http://www.europarl.europa.eu/sides/getDoc.do?type=REPORT&language=EN&reference=A7-0012/2012#title1> [accessed 1 July 2018]; J Almunia, 'Common Standards for Group Claims across the EU' (University of Valladolid, School of Law, 2010), 1–7, 6 <http://europa.eu/rapid/pressReleasesAction.do?reference=SPEECH/10/554&format=HTML&aged=0&language=EN&guiLanguage=en> [accessed 1 July 2018].
76 C Cauffman and N Philipsen, 'Who Does What in Competition Law: Harmonizing the Rules on Damages for Infringements of the EU Competition Rules?', *Maastricht European Private Law Institute, Working Paper no 2014/19*, 2014, 1–43, 6 <http://awards.concurrences.com/IMG/pdf/who.pdf> [accessed 1 July 2018].
77 White Paper (fn 61) para 2.6.
78 See Chapter 8.
79 Similarly, SWPWP (fn 64) para 205.
80 Directive proposal (fn 63) art. 12(2).
81 *Ibid* explanatory memorandum, para 4.4.
82 F Maier-Rigaud, 'Towards a European Directive on Damages Actions', *IESEG School of Management Working Paper no 2013-ECO-16*, 2013, 1–19, 14 <http://lem.cnrs.fr/LinkClick.aspx?fileticket=ujRpEFT6XrY%3D&tabid=1198&language=fr-FR> [accessed 1 July 2018].
83 European Parliament, *Opinion of the Committee on the Internal Market and Consumer Protection for the Committee on Economic and Monetary Affairs on the Proposal for a Directive of the European Parliament and of the Council on Certain Rules Governing Actions for Damages under National Law for Infringements of the Competition Law Provisions of the Member States and of the European Union* (COM(2013)0404 – C7–

accepted by the European Parliament as it was found at odds with the case law that establishes any individual can claim damages. Moreover, the term 'legal impossibility' was deemed too vague and likely to lead overcompensation.[84]

The next sections seek to analyse these objectives and the link between them in order to identify the primary objective of a collective redress action. The decision of the objective(s) such an action pursues affects both its design[85] and its ability to serve the need in the field of private competition law enforcement.

Compensation and deterrence objectives for collective redress actions

The unique competition law enforcement goal and its implications for collective redress actions

Shaping an EU-wide collective redress action for competition claims entails considering the specific policy objectives in this area of law.[86] EU competition law is enforced in the context of internal market integration.[87] In other words, EU competition provisions aim to establish and maintain undistorted competition in the internal market[88] and therefore both public and private enforcement serve this albeit with different tools.[89] While public enforcement uses punitive means,[90] private enforcement through damages actions relies on the availability of the right of individuals to sue for damages before national courts. As the case law clearly submits, there must be an EU right to damages not only because it allows the victims to seek compensation but also because it leads to a strengthened enforcement and deterrence of competition infringements, thereby better working of the internal market.[91] Indeed, EU right to damages is provided to the victims on the basis of the enforcement rationale.[92]

This reveals the role of Member State courts in the enforcement of that right through the distinction between the existence and exercise of the right to

0170/2013–2013/0185(COD), 2014), amendment 40 <http://www.europarl.europa.eu/sides/getDoc.do?type=REPORT&reference=A7-2014-0089&format=XML&language=EN#top> [accessed 1 July 2018].

84 *Ibid.*

85 A Erbsen, 'From "Predominance" to "Resolvability": A New Approach to Regulating Class Actions', *Vanderbilt Law Review*, 58(4) (2005), 995–1088, 1087.

86 D-PL Tzakas, 'Effective Collective Redress in Antitrust and Consumer Protection Matters: A Panacea or a Chimera?', *Common Market Law Review*, 48 (2011), 1125–1174, 1127.

87 MM Dabbah, *International and Comparative Competition Law* (Cambridge: Cambridge University Press, 2010), 164.

88 See eg *Courage* (fn 33) para 20; Case C-52/09 *Konkurrensverket v TeliaSonera Sverige AB* [2011] ECR I-527, paras 20–21; Opinion of AG Kokott delivered on 30 January 2014 in *Kone*, para 56.

89 Opinion of AG Kokott in *Kone* (fn 88) para 56.

90 *Ibid* para 59.

91 See N Bucan Gutta, *The Enforcement of EU Competition Rules by Civil Law* (Antwerpen-Apeldoorn: Maklu, 2014), 40.

92 Nazzini (fn 5) 139; Leczykiewicz (fn 40) 5.

damages.[93] With respect to the former, the *Courage* and *Manfredi* decisions clarify that as a matter of EU law there must be a right to damages before national courts irrespective of the position in national law.[94] On the other hand, the exercise of the right to damages is within the legal power of the national courts of each Member State in the absence of EU measures on the matter provided that the principles of equivalence and effectiveness are respected.[95] In the context of collective redress, since the principle of equivalence provides that the collective redress action available to national competition infringements should apply to EU competition infringements as well, a problem arises mainly in respect of the effectiveness principle. This principle requires national procedural rules not to render the exercise of the right to damages practically impossible or overly difficult.

In citing *Van Gen den Loos,* [96] first *Francovich,* [97] then *Courage,* [98] mention with similar wording that the Treaty imposes burdens and rights on individuals. *Francovich*'s influence on *Courage* is not limited to that. Both cases and later *Manfredi* establish that national courts must ensure that EU provisions take full effect and must protect the individual rights emanating therefrom.[99] This is in accordance with the doctrine of direct effect and the principle of effectiveness.[100] In light of this, the principle of effectiveness as a general EU law principle[101] comprises the principles of both full effectiveness of EU law and effective judicial protection of individual's rights.[102] The former principle refers to the enforcement of EU law in the general interest[103] and sees the individual right to damages as instrumental to the achievement of the objectives of the EU.[104] The latter principle concerns the exercise of the right to damages.[105]

It should be noted with respect to the principle of effective judicial protection that TEU provides that 'Member States shall provide remedies sufficient to ensure

93 *Courage* (fn 33) para 29; *Manfredi* (fn 35) para 64. Similarly, SWPWP (fn 64) paras 308–309.
94 Jones and Sufrin (fn 3) 1104.
95 *Manfredi* (fn 35) para 64.
96 Case 26/62 *NV Algemene Transport – en Expeditie Onderneming van Gend & Loos v Netherlands Inland Revenue Administration* [1963] ECR-00001, para II.B.
97 Joined cases C-6/90 and C-9/90 *Andrea Francovich and Danila Bonifaci and others v Italian Republic* [1991] ECR I-05357, para 31.
98 *Courage* (fn 33) para 19.
99 *Francovich* (fn 97) para 32; *ibid* para 25; *Manfredi* (fn 35) para 89.
100 Nebbia (fn 5) 28.
101 T Tridimas, *The General Principles of EU Law*, 2nd edn, (Oxford: Oxford University Press, 2006), 418.
102 M Dougan, *National Remedies Before the Court of Justice: Issues of Harmonisation and Differentiation* (Oxford and Portland, Oregon: Hart Publishing, 2004), 26–27; *ibid* 418; S Prechel, 'Protection of Rights: How Far?', in *The Coherence of EU Law: The Search for Unity in Divergent Concepts*, ed. by S Prechal and B van Roermund (Oxford: Oxford University Press, 2008), 155–182, 156; Nazzini (fn 5) 137; Ioannidou (fn 1) 63.
103 Dougan (fn 102) 38.
104 Nazzini (fn 5) 137.
105 *Ibid.*

effective legal protection in the fields covered by Union law'.[106] With the TEU's primary law status, Craig argues that the EU courts will be more willing to make sure that national laws do not undermine the protection of the EU rights.[107] Similarly, Arnull posits that the principle of effective judicial protection is now superior to national procedural autonomy.[108] The AG in *Donau Chemie* suggests that this provision requires national remedies to be '[a]ccessible, prompt, and reasonably cost effective'.[109]

Competition infringements might impose harm on a great number of consumers in a similar way, but these mostly remain uncompensated for their loss as they are discouraged from bringing individual action against infringements due to the burdens, costs and risks associated with competition litigation. In the absence of a collective redress action, affected consumers rarely obtain compensation for harm suffered and that infringers mostly benefit from their wrongdoing.[110] Moreover, this absence undermines the effectiveness of EU law as the rights are not fully respected and individuals do not enjoy their rights granted by EU law. Indeed, the *Francovich* decision stated that if individuals were unable to obtain redress when the rights emanating from EU law were violated, the full effectiveness of EU rules and the protection of the rights granted therefrom would be impaired.[111]

In light of this, it does not suffice that there is a theoretical possibility to bring an action in courts which respects the principle of equivalence.[112] According to the principle of full effectiveness, Member States need to have the mechanism that enables individuals who are harmed by competition infringements to effectively exercise their right to damages, even where these are many in number with losses that do not justify the filing of an action in practice.[113] Similarly, the Commission states that the full effectiveness principle requires Member States to provide a realistic means for every individual to obtain compensation for the loss resulting from the practices that restrict or distort competition.[114] In this context, this is also reflected in the principle of effective judicial protection which concerns access to courts.[115] This principle is interpreted as enabling individuals

106 TEU, (OJ C 83/13, 2010), art. 19(1).
107 P Craig, *EU Administrative Law*, 2nd edn, (Oxford: Oxford University Press, 2012) 726.
108 A Arnull, 'The Principle of Effective Judicial Protection in EU Law: An Unruly Horse?', *European Law Review*, 36(1) (2011), 51–70, 68.
109 Opinion of AG Jääskinen delivered on 7 February 2013 in *Donau Chemie,* para 47. See also *Charter of Fundamental Rights of the European Union*, (OJ C 364/1, 2000), art. 47(1).
110 See Nazzini (fn 5) 141.
111 *Francovich* (fn 97) para 33.
112 Nazzini (fn 5) 141; N Dunne, 'The Role of Private Enforcement within EU Competition Law', in *Cambridge Yearbook of European Legal Studies,* ed. by A Albors-Llorens, KA Armstrong and MW Gehring, vol.16 (Oxford and Portland, Oregon: Hart Publishing, 2014), 143–187, 182.
113 Nazzini (fn 5) 141.
114 Impact assessment (fn 65) para 30.
115 See AP Komninos, *EC Private Antitrust Enforcement: Decentralised Application of EC Competition Law by National Courts* (Oxford and Portland, Oregon: Hart Publishing, 2008), 145.

to obtain redress for harm suffered through the infringement of their rights by a breach of EU law.[116]

As previously showed, despite individual actions, existing aggregation mechanisms and collective actions, consumers almost never exercise their right to damages.[117] Thus, a collective redress action, if designed properly, renders the exercise of the right to damages more likely for those harmed and especially for those who would not otherwise have filed a damages claim.

Objectives of collective redress actions

It has been argued that a collective redress action can advance both compensation and deterrence objectives which are generally claimed to be the main goals of civil procedure[118] and are also regarded as justifications for the introduction of such an action.[119] This entails identifying the primary objective of a collective redress action and establishing the link between the objectives of compensation and deterrence because the objective pursued determines the final shape of the action.

The compensatory objective

A collective redress action makes the exercise of the right to damages more likely in practice rather than merely a theoretical possibility. In so doing, it increases the chances for individuals to recover damages.[120] Therefore, the immediate effect of a collective redress action is to compensate victims and, on this basis, the compensatory function qualifies as the primary objective. Given the fact that the action is capable of delivering compensation to great numbers of consumers, the more the number of victims compensated for their loss the more the compensatory objective is fulfilled.

Serving a primary objective of compensation automatically brings beneficial effects, but it does not change the fact that the rationale behind a collective action is to give compensation to the victims of competition infringements. In restoring a large number of individuals to the position they would have been in had an infringement not occurred by way of compensation, such an action provides an *ex-post* correction of the negative consequences of competition infringements on the victims[121] and '[r]estore[s] the market to its normal balance, of being a level playing field with strong competition'.[122]

116 Nebbia (fn 5) 30.
117 See Chapter 2.
118 PH Lindblom, 'Individual Litigation and Mass Justice: A Swedish Perspective and Proposal on Group Actions in Civil Procedure', *The American Journal of Comparative Law*, 45(4) (1997), 805–831, 809.
119 A Lahav, 'Fundamental Principles for Class Action Governance', *Indiana Law Review*, 37 (2004), 65–140, 70.
120 SWPWP (fn 64) para 40.
121 See similarly, with respect to the obligation to provide compensation to the victims of competition infringements, Opinion of AG Kokott in *Kone* (fn 88) para 57.
122 See C Hodges, 'European Competition Enforcement Policy: Integrating Restitution and Behaviour Control an Integrated Enforcement Policy, Involving Public and Private Enforcement with ADR', *World Competition*, 34(3) (2011), 383–396, 384.

The case law in the field of competition law considers the right to damages necessary for victims to obtain compensation for their loss, to strengthen the working of EU competition rules and to discourage anticompetitive behaviour, thereby contributing significantly to the maintenance of effective competition in the EU.[123] Collective actions can compensate more victims compared with individual actions. To the extent that as many consumers as possible recover damages, there is a risk that defendants could be held liable for the entire loss. The more victims of competition law infringements exercise their right to damages and obtain compensation, the more it serves to the achievement of the effective enforcement of EU competition law.[124] The next section shows how the pursuit of compensation objective promotes deterrence.

The deterrence objective

Deterrence aims that competition provisions are not infringed and that the anticompetitive effects that competition provisions seek to avoid do not occur.[125] In light of this, it refers to '[i]nfluenc[ing] the future behaviour of all market actors to comply with the law and act virtuously'.[126] A credible threat of monetary payment which diminishes the prospective utility of the infringement alters the cost-benefit calculation in the minds of would-be infringers and discourages them from infringing the law.[127] Public enforcement through fines and actions for damages through compensation impose monetary burden on infringers, making infringement less profitable.[128]

One can argue that public enforcement is the main enactor of deterrence.[129] Firstly, the remedies imposed by the Commission intend to suppress illegal conduct and prevent repetition;[130] fines are the main instrument available to the Commission for these purposes.[131] It has specifically been stated that fines aim to deter.[132] Fines are also accepted to '[n]ormally have disgorgement of the unjust enrichment as one of their effects [although] the proceeds of fines normally go

123 See *supra* 'The approach of the EU courts'.
124 See the full compensation of all victims results in effective enforcement, Nazzini (fn 5) 141.
125 Wils, Should private antitrust enforcement be encouraged (fn 10) 9.
126 Hodges, European competition enforcement policy (fn 122) 384.
127 Wils, Should private antitrust enforcement be encouraged (fn 10) 9; Keske (fn 4) 67–68. Similarly, Varuhas (fn 11) 21.
128 See A Stadler, 'Collective Action as an Efficient Means for the Enforcement of European Competition Law', in *Private Enforcement of EC Competition Law*, ed. by J Basedow (The Netherlands: International Competition Law Series, volume 25, Kluwer Law International, 2007), 195–213, 200.
129 Similarly, Nazzini (fn 5) 138.
130 Case 41–69 *ACF Chemiefarma NV v Commission* [1970] ECR 661 preamble para 10.
131 C Hodges, 'A Market-Based Competition Enforcement Policy', *European Business Law Review*, 22 (2011), 261–291, 262.
132 Commission, *Guidelines on the Method of Setting Fines pursuant to Article 23(2)(a) of Regulation No 1/2003* (OJ C 210/02, 2006), paras 4, 30–31.

into the public budget rather than to the victims [...]'.[133] Secondly, through public enforcement actual infringements are brought to an end.[134] Thirdly, the Commission's resources, experience and wide-ranging investigative powers can be used throughout the EU to uncover competition infringements.[135] Private competition law enforcement, although not mature enough at present to detect infringements and/or make the infringer responsible for the full loss caused, contributes to the deterrence objective through compensation if enhanced.

A collective redress action which incurs a real risk of infringers being taken to court and paying higher damages compared to the non-availability of such an action[136] would further deterrence. The collective action is capable of amplifying the defendant's responsibility by making them pay compensation to a large number of victims. To illustrate this, a study examining 64 cartel decisions of the Commission in the period of 1975 and 2009 concludes that even though fines imposed are increasing, they fall short of the illicit profit generated by cartel members. It finds that only in half of cases fines correspond to the amount of illicit profit.[137] In this context, the payment of compensation would supplement fines and add to the defendant's monetary responsibility, limiting any competitive advantage of infringement.[138] It also increases the cost of infringement.[139] The avoidance of this liability may result in decreased likelihood of engagement in anticompetitive conduct[140] and the cessation of actual engagement in anticompetitive conduct.[141] Consequently, a collective redress action would improve compliance with competition law.

Moreover, due to the low levels of actions for damages in the EU, undertakings only consider fines as a monetary sanction at the infringement decision stage. This

133 Wils, Optimal antitrust fines (fn 23) 190.

134 When the Commission finds an infringement, it implements appropriate measures to terminate it. Article 105 TFEU; Council Regulation (EC) No 1/2003 of 16 December 2002 on the Implementation of the Rules on Competition Laid down in Articles [101] and [102] of the Treaty, (OJ L 1/1, 2003) (Regulation 1/2003), art. 7. Note actions for injunctions also operate in this respect.

135 R Whish and D Bailey, *Competition Law*, 7th edn (Oxford: Oxford University Press, 2012), 305.

136 Welfare impact report (fn 9) 302.

137 E Combe and C Monnier, 'Fines against Hard Core Cartels in Europe: The Myth of Overenforcement', *Antitrust Bulletin*, 56(2) (2011), 235–275, 237, 267.

138 DR Hensler and others, *Class Action Dilemmas: Pursuing Public Goals for Private Gain* (Arlington: RAND, 2000), 421.

139 BIS, *Impact Assessment, Private Actions in Competition Law – A Consultation on Options for Reform* (London, 2012), para 147.

140 See eg C Smithka, 'From Budapest to Berlin: How Implementing Class Action Lawsuits in the European Union Would Increase Competition and Strengthen Consumer Confidence', *Wisconsin International Law Journal*, 27 (2009), 173–193, 177; LS Simard, 'Fees, Incentives and Deterrence: A Reply to Professor Fitzpatrick', *Suffolk University Law School Research Paper no 11–22*, 2011, 1–9, 4–5 <http://ssrn.com/abstract=1832828> [accessed 1 July 2018].

141 Similarly, EM Iacobucci, 'Cartel Class Actions and Immunity Programmes', *Journal of Antitrust Enforcement*, 1(2) (2013), 272–295, 281–283.

is especially the case where those harmed by the infringement are consumers.[142] Absent collective actions, those claims for damages would be either not brought at all[143] or brought only in rare instances.[144] However, collective redress actions make it more likely for them to recover damages.[145] Therefore, the availability of these actions presents a credible threat of litigation to the defendant where individual litigation is not a realistic possibility.[146]

As a result, a collective redress action, when designed appropriately, ensures the exercise of the right to damages and realises the compensation objective. This, in turn, advances deterrence. The more victims obtain compensation through a collective redress action the more the defendants are at risk of liability for the full harm caused. The next section reflects on whether the objectives pursued differ if the action is designed for consumers.[147]

Collective redress actions for consumers: do the objectives pursued differ?

When the Green Paper stressed the necessity of having a collective action for consumers, it stated that fostering consumer claims using this action would contribute to the objectives of both compensation and deterrence and further the development of a competition culture.[148] The White Paper, by acknowledging this necessity for consumers,[149] made it clear that compensation is the sole objective. However, in the literature it has been argued that collective redress actions for consumers who incur widely dispersed, similar and small losses[150] should pursue a deterrence objective[151] – the fact that these consumers

142 See CR Leslie, 'The Significance of Silence: Collective Action Problems and Class Action Settlements', *Florida Law Review*, 59 (2007), 71–134, 75.

143 SD Susman, 'Prosecuting the Antitrust Class Action', *Antitrust Law Journal*, 49 (1980), 1513–1527, 1515–1516; JA Jolowicz, 'Group Litigation, Damages, and Judicial Control by Civil Courts', in *Judicial Review in International Perspective*, ed. by M Andenas and D Fairgrieve (The Netherlands: Kluwer Law International, 2000), vol.II, 481–491, 483.

144 Wagner (fn 13) 67. See Chapter 2.

145 This is Duval's finding according to the data he collected from the class action suits in Northern District of Illinois between 1966–1973. BS Duval, 'The Class Action as an Antitrust Enforcement Device: The Chicago Experience (II)', *American Bar Foundation Research Journal*, 1(4) (1976), 1273–1358, 1346.

146 Simard (fn 140) 4–5.

147 This discussion relates to consumers in competition law, see the definition of consumer in Chapter 2.

148 SWPGP (fn 8) para 188.

149 See Chapter 3.

150 See further Chapter 5.

151 KW Dam, 'Class Actions: Efficiency, Compensation, Deterrence, and Conflict of Interest', *The Journal of Legal Studies*, 4(1) (1975), 47–73, 60; M Handler and MD Blechman, 'Antitrust and the Consumer Interest: The Fallacy of Parens Patriae and A Suggested New Approach', *The Yale Law Journal*, 85(5) (1976), 626–676, 670; DL Shapiro, 'Class Actions: The Class as Party and Client', *Notre Dame Law Review*, 73 (4) (1998), 913–961, 924; M Gilles and G Friedman, 'Exploding the Class Action Agency Costs Myth: The Social Utility of Entrepreneurial Lawyers', *University of*

do not receive much compensation legitimises the concern of making the defendant liable for the harm done.[152]

In shaping collective redress actions pursuing either compensation or deterrence objectives results in different formulations. In theory, the compensation objective aims to provide compensation to the victims irrespective of the amount of loss suffered whereas the deterrence objective does not concern the distribution of damages or compensating the real victims so long as the defendant pays. In other words, if a collective redress action were designed based on the deterrence objective, there would be no need to calculate the damages of the victims or distribute these damages to the victims, it rather would aim that the defendant does not benefit from its actions. To illustrate this, Germany, for instance, has a skimming-off action for claims arising from unfair competition. According to such an action, an association sues for skimming off excess profits on behalf of consumers in order to deprive the defendants of their illegal gain. At the end of litigation, the award goes to the state budget; victims do not get any compensation for their losses.[153]

As a result, formulating a collective redress action to promote deterrence does not deliver any direct benefits to those harmed. Pursuing a deterrence objective moves this action away from the main reason for debate over the introduction of such an action, that is, compensation of victims. If the collective action is designed to deter infringers, with or without the action of this kind consumers will remain uncompensated for their losses. Therefore, a collective redress action ought to rather be designed to compensate consumers to the greatest possible extent.[154] In other words, each element of a collective redress action should be formulated to pursue the objective of compensation, ie to deliver compensation to the affected consumers.

Concluding remarks

This chapter analysed the primary objective of a collective redress action in order to formulate it accordingly in later chapters. Identifying the primary objective

Pennsylvania Law Review, 155 (2006), 103–164, 105; S Issacharoff and GP Miller, 'Will Aggregate Litigation Come to Europe?', *Vanderbilt Law Review*, 62(1) (2008), 179–210, 187.

152 Gilles and Friedman (fn 151) 105; Wagner (fn 13) 63; Ioannidou (fn 1) 69, E Kocher, 'Collective Rights and Collective Goods: Enforcement as Collective Interest', in *Mass Justice: Challenges of Representation and Distribution*, ed. by J Steele and WH van Boom (Cheltenham, UK: Edward Elgar Publishing Limited, 2011), 118–135, 122.

153 H-W Micklitz and A Stadler, 'The Development of Collective Legal Actions in Europe, Especially in German Civil Procedure', *European Business Law Review*, 17 (2006), 1473–1503, 1482–1483.

154 D Marcus, 'Attorneys' Fees and the Social Legitimacy of Class Actions', *University of Pennsylvania PeNNumbra*, 159 (2010), 157–166, 166. Similarly, in the US context, Silver argues that it is courts' responsibility that those harmed are compensated even if their losses are small. C Silver, '"We Are Scared to Death": Class Certification and Blackmail', *New York University Law Review*, 78, 1357–1430, 1368.

pursued by private competition law enforcement through damages actions paves the way for procedural tools that are designed to follow and advance the same objective in order to satisfy the need in this field. This identification is significant because pursuing either a compensation or deterrence objective gives rise to different outcomes. The compensation objective seeks to provide redress to the victims of competition infringements through damages paid by the defendant, whereas deterrence seeks to avoid adoption of anticompetitive practices. A deterrence objective has no interest in recouping the victims' losses and restoring them to their rightful position, rather it is interested in making infringement unprofitable for current and prospective infringers at the lowest possible cost. Thus, the choice of compensation or deterrence as primary objective would influence the design of a collective redress action.

The EU institutions find appropriate either the pursuit of both objectives or a compensation objective alone. In acknowledging the existence of the EU right to damages for victims of competition infringements, the case law recognises both the compensation and deterrence objectives. According to the CJEU, the existence of such a right makes possible for aggrieved parties to obtain full compensation and strengthens the working of the EU competition rules, discouraging infringements and therefore contributing significantly to the maintenance of effective competition. In this way, the Court establishes the enforcement rationale. Owing to a low level of damages actions, the Commission – with reference to the relevant EU jurisprudence – proposed measures to enhance the exercise of this right. In line with the Court's approach, the Green Paper embraced both objectives as equally promoted by actions for damages. Beginning with the White Paper, the Commission stresses that any measure aiming to shape actions for damages should respect and advance compensation only. However, this identification is not truly reflected in the Commission's suggestions in the White Paper and in the directive proposal. This again shows the significance of determining a primary objective and consistently promoting and advancing it through adopted measures.

Private enforcement through damages actions relies on the existence and exercise of the right to damages for competition infringements. When the existence of the right is a matter of EU law, procedures for the exercise of this right are determined by the Member States in the absence of EU rules on the matter. The Member States are bound not to discriminate between the procedural rules that are available to similar domestic actions from those applicable to EU competition cases and not to render the exercise of this right overly difficult or impossible. However, neither the availability of individual actions nor the existing aggregation mechanisms and collective actions in Member States suffice to deliver redress to consumers. If designed properly, a collective redress action makes the exercise of the right to damages more likely for those who are unlikely to file an action in practice. Since a collective action provides a real opportunity for those harmed to seek compensation before courts, it pursues a primary objective of compensation that in turn contributes to deterrence.

A collective redress action not only increases individuals' chances of obtaining compensation but also is capable of addressing the grievances of a great number of persons *vis-à-vis* individual actions. It is thus capable of being a credible threat to the defendant of being taken to court and held accountable for the harm caused. This, however, does not change the fact that primary objective of a collective redress action is compensation. The pursuit of compensation at the same time furthers a deterrence objective because, with a low number of actions for damages, current and prospective infringers in the EU only take into account the fine they would pay if infringement is discovered. They do not consider the risk of being sued and becoming liable for the award of compensation. This is especially the case when they impose harm on consumers.

This said, designing a collective action for consumer damage claims does not necessitate pursuing a different objective. According to some commentators, as competition infringements cause widespread losses to consumers, the objective of such an action should not aim to compensate small injuries but rather to deter infringers by making them liable for the full harm inflicted. However, the entire point of the discussion around the introduction of such an action is to provide victims who are not otherwise able to do so with a realistic means to seek redress. By this reasoning, it should serve a compensation objective. Submitting deterrence as a primary objective contradicts this reasoning and leaves the affected consumers uncompensated irrespective of the availability of such an action. As long as the damages award can be distributed among consumers even if the individual losses are small, the action seeks to fully compensate the harmed consumers. To this end, the following chapter intends to identify the ways in which consumers are affected by competition infringements in order to present the characteristics of consumer damages claims that are subject to be dealt with in a collective action.

5 Consumer damages claims in EU competition cases

Introduction

This chapter analyses the way in which competition infringements cause harm to consumers in order to show the characteristics of their damages claims and different groups of harmed consumers. This analysis forms a basis for the formulation of a collective redress action for consumer damages claims in the following chapters. The chapter is formed of three substantive sections. The second section begins with an overview of competition infringements and their possible harmful effects on the situation of the claimant. It then examines the two principal categories of harm that are subject to damages actions, ie overcharge and loss of profits caused by infringements upon different categories of injured parties. This examination helps to identify the characteristics of the claims of consumers and other stakeholders.

The third section of the chapter addresses consumer damages claims. In order to present a complete picture of how competition infringements harm consumers by means of high prices, it considers the types of infringements of Articles 101 and 102 TFEU that lead to overcharge. It also carries out case studies to illustrate the means and extent of the harm caused to consumers. Finally, since consumers can be injured in different ways, the fourth section of the chapter scrutinises the ways in which consumers are harmed as a result of competition infringements.

Damages caused by competition infringements

The types of competition infringements

Infringements of Articles 101 and 102 TFEU give rise to actions for damages before national courts if they cause harm to claimants. Article 101 TFEU comprises three paragraphs: the first embodies the prohibition, the second is the sanction of nullity and the third provides a legal exception. The collusive practices prohibited by this provision enable firms to jointly enjoy market power they would not otherwise have and, in this way, restrict competition, reduce quantities and/or increase prices.[1] Both horizontal and vertical agreements[2] are dealt with under this provision if they affect trade between Member States[3] and have as their object or effect to prevent, restrict or distort competition in the internal market.[4]

Horizontal agreements that are made between otherwise competing firms,[5] such as horizontal price-fixing, horizontal market sharing, collusive tendering and information exchange agreements, might result in a claim for damages. For instance, in *Manfredi,* the plaintiff, although unusual, was a consumer who purchased insurance from cartel members. Through exchange of information, cartel members (insurance companies) managed to coordinate and fix prices in the insurance sector.[6] The plaintiff claimed damages for the overcharge resulting from the unlawful increase in premiums[7] and recovered €889.10, double the amount of the loss he incurred.[8]

Vertical agreements are concluded between parties trading at different levels of the production or distribution chain,[9] such as imposing maximum or minimum resale prices and quantity fixing.[10] For instance, in *Courage*, [11] the plaintiff who was a party to a vertical agreement and one of the tied tenants brought an action for damages.[12] Under the lease agreement between the parties, the plaintiff was obliged to purchase a fixed minimum quantity of specified beers from the defendant at the price set by the defendant.[13] The plaintiff claimed that this beer tie was a breach of Article 101 TFEU and sought damages suffered due to excessive prices

1 M Motta, 'Cartels in the European Union: Economics, Law, Practice' (presented at the Fifty Years of the Treaty: Assessment and Perspectives of Competition Policy in Europe, IESE Business School, Barcelona, 2007), 1–32, 1 <http://www.barcelonagse.eu/tmp/pdf/motta_cartelseulaw.pdf> [accessed 1 July 2018].
2 The term agreement comprises decisions of associations of undertakings and concerted practices.
3 See further Commission, *Guidelines on the Effect on Trade Concept contained in Articles [101] and [102] of the Treaty* (OJ C 101/81, 2004).
4 See the illustrative list of practices in Article 101(1) TFEU.
5 BJ Rodger and A MacCulloch, *Competition Law and Policy in the EU and UK*, 5th edn (Oxford: Routledge, 2015), 161.
6 Joined Cases C-295/04 and C-298/04 *Vincenzo Manfredi v Lloyd Adriatico Assicurazioni SpA* [2006] ECR I-06619, paras 2, 11.
7 *Ibid* para 2.
8 P Nebbia, '... So What Happened to Mr. Manfredi? The Italian Decision Following the Ruling of the European Court of Justice', *European Competition Law Review*, 28 (11) (2007), 591–596, 591, 595.
9 Commission, *Guidelines on Vertical Restraints* (OJ C 130/1, 2010), para 2.1.
10 M Motta, *Competition Policy: Theory and Practice* (USA: Cambridge University Press, 2009) 303–304. See further J Goyder, 'Cet Obscur Objet: Object Restrictions in Vertical Agreements' *Journal of European Competition Law and Practice,* 2(4) (2011), 327–339, 333.
11 Case C-453/99 *Courage Ltd. v Bernard Crehan* [2001] ECR I-6297.
12 R Whish and D Bailey, *Competition Law*, 7th edn (Oxford: Oxford University Press, 2012), 298.
13 *Courage* (fn 11) para 5.

charged by the defendant who aimed to drive the tied tenants including the plaintiff, out of business.[14]

In addition, unilateral conduct can cause harm to claimants and give rise to a claim for damages. In this respect, Article 102 TFEU seeks to curtail abusive behaviour of dominant undertaking. This article prohibits the abusive conduct of one or more undertakings of a dominant position within the internal market, or in a substantial part of it, if the abuse affects trade between the Member States. The provision, which provides a non-exhaustive list of abuses,[15] is applicable to both exclusionary and exploitative abuses.[16] The latter is conduct of a dominant undertaking which directly imposes harm on its customers[17] by exploiting the strength of its position in the market.[18] An exclusionary abuse is conduct of the dominant undertaking which aims to exclude competitor(s) from the market or harm their competitive position[19] and/or prevents or limits the entry of potential competitors.[20] Although some abuses can be either or both, such as discriminatory practices[21] and tying,[22] excessive prices and unfair trading conditions can be given as examples of exploitative abuses[23] and predatory pricing, refusal to supply, rebates, margin squeezing and exclusive dealing agreements as examples of exclusionary abuses.[24]

14 *Ibid* paras 6–7. Ironically, the plaintiff was not awarded any damages after 13 years of litigation, but contributed significantly to the development of private competition law enforcement. Whish and Bailey (fn 12) 299.
15 P Akman, 'The European Commission's Guidance on Article 102TFEU: From *Inferno* to *Paradiso*?', *Modern Law Review*, 73(4) (2010), 605–630, 606.
16 See eg Case 6/72 *Europemballage Corporation and Continental Can Company Inc. v Commission* [1973] ECR 00215, para 26. See there might be another type of abuse, single market abuses, Whish and Bailey (fn 12) 202.
17 P Akman, 'Exploitative Abuse in Article 82EC: Back to Basics?', *University of East Anglia, CCP Working Paper no 09–1*, 2008, 1–37, 8 <http://www.uea.ac.uk/polopoly_fs/1.105848!ccp09-1.pdf> [accessed 1 July 2018].
18 *Ibid* 3–4; HKS Schmidt, 'Private Enforcement – Is Article 82 EC special?', in *Abuse of Dominant Position: New Interpretation, New Enforcement Mechanisms?*, ed. by M-O Mackenrodt, BC Gallego and S Enchelmaier (Berlin: Springer, 2010), 137–164, 151.
19 Akman, Exploitative abuse (fn 17) 4.
20 Oxera, A Komninos and others, *Quantifying Antitrust Damages – Towards Non-Binding Guidance for Courts*, Study Prepared for the Commission (Luxembourg, 2009), iii. These effects on competitors are mainly labelled as foreclosure, Commission, *Staff Working Document: Practical Guide Quantifying Harm in Actions for Damages Based on Breaches of Article 101 or 102 of the Treaty on the Functioning of the European Union* Accompanying *the Communication from the Commission on Quantifying Harm in Actions for Damages Based on Breaches of Article 101 or 102 of the Treaty on the Functioning of the European Union* (SWD(2013) 205, Strasbourg, 2013), (Practical guide) para 180.
21 R O'Donoghue and AJ Padilla, *The Law and Economics of Article 102 TFEU*, 2nd edn (Oxford and Portland, Oregon: Hart Publishing, 2013), 237.
22 See the text accompanying *infra* fn 31.
23 Whish and Bailey (fn 12) 202.
24 *Ibid* 210.

As a result, broadly, through infringements of Articles 101 and 102 TFEU, infringers seek to increase their profits by softening competition in the market.[25] In order for those harmed to seek damages, they must have suffered loss by these infringements. The next section therefore explores the possible adverse effects of competition infringements on the situation of the claimants.

The types of harm resulting from competition infringements

Competition infringements mainly result in overcharge, loss of profits and reduction of choice, quality or innovation.[26] Through anticompetitive practices, infringers may be able to charge higher prices and/or offer reduced quality products,[27] meaning purchasers can receive poor quality products for the same or higher price.[28] In addition, infringer(s) may restrict output, enabling them to increase prices and reduce consumer choice.[29] Limitation of choice can stem from higher prices, reduction in variety, or innovation or quality of products.[30] For instance, tying, that makes consumer's purchase conditional on the purchase of another product, restricts their options and freedom of action as a means of reducing choice.[31] Furthermore, reduction of innovation may result from competition infringement[32] as impairing or eliminating competition in the market may reduce incentive to innovate.[33]

These are the possible harmful effects of competition infringements, and, in principle, one can argue that all should be compensated. However, competition litigation focuses on two categories of harm: overcharge and lost profits. This is the case in the US[34] and the Directive[35] and the papers published by the

25 F Maier-Rigaud and U Schwalbe, 'Quantification of Antitrust Damages', in *Competition Damages Actions in the EU: Law and Practice*, ed. by D Ashton and D Henry (Cheltenham UK: Edward Elgar Publishing, 2013), 210–261, 213.
26 Oxera (fn 20) iii, 15. Similarly, Guidelines on vertical restraints (fn 9) para 101.
27 See WH van Boom, 'The Law of Damages and Competition Law: Bien Étonnés de Se Trouver Ensemble?', in *Competition of Private Losses – The Evolution of Torts in European Business Law*, ed. by R Schulze (Munich: Sellier, 2011), 165–178, 165.
28 EL Cramer and DC Simons, 'Parties Entitled to Pursue a Claim', in *Private Enforcement of Antitrust Law in the United States: A Handbook*, ed. by AA Foer and RM Stutz (Cheltenham UK: Edward Elgar Publishing, 2012), 64–94, 79–80.
29 *Ibid* 79.
30 RH Lande and NW Averitt, 'Using the Consumer Choice Approach to Antitrust Law', *Antitrust Law Journal*, 74 (2007) 175–264, 175.
31 Akman, Exploitative abuse (fn 17) 27–28.
32 Another effect might be '[a] slowing-down in the rate at which improvements in efficiency are achieved, or at which inefficient firms exit the market'. Oxera (fn 20) 15.
33 Maier-Rigaud and Schwalbe (fn 25) 218.
34 CM Korenblit, 'Quantifying Antitrust Damages – Convergence of Methods Recognized by U.S. Courts and the European Commission', *Competition Policy International – Antitrust Chronicle*, 1 (2012), 1–9, 3.
35 *Directive 2014/104/EU of the European Parliament and of the Council of 26 November 2014 on Certain Rules Governing Actions for Damages under National Law for Infringements of the Competition Law Provisions of the Member States and of the European Union*, (OJ L 349/1, 2014), art. 2(2).

Commission to provide guidance on the quantification of harm follow the same route.[36] It has been found hard to prove that there is a causal link between an infringement and these other harmful effects.[37]

Moreover, quantifying reduction of choice or quality requires a more complex analysis than that employed for overcharge and lost profits.[38] In the attempt, the results might be unreliable as economic models to compute these losses are underdeveloped.[39] For instance, it has been suggested that surveys can be conducted to measure '[c]onsumers' willingness to pay for product attributes, such as enhanced features or quality of service that may have been affected by an infringement'.[40]

In respect of reduction in innovation, consumers are harmed because they are '[d]eprived of the higher utility of more innovative products'.[41] However, it is difficult to prove that restricting innovation is anticompetitive.[42] Since these innovations never occurred, or the innovative products never reached market, identifying these victims is unfeasible,[43] assessing their individual damages is incommensurable,[44] and the demonstration of a causal link between the infringement and reduced innovation is problematic.[45] In the US, a few claimants have claimed damages for this kind of harm, but courts generally reject them on the grounds of either standing or causation.[46] For instance, a class action for damages on behalf of consumers who claimed to be harmed due to Microsoft's conduct, which stifled innovation of competitors, was declined by the court[47] since their injuries were found '[e]ntirely speculative and beyond the competence of a judicial proceeding to create in hindsight a technological universe that never came into existence'.[48]

36 Commission, *Draft Guidance Paper: Quantifying Harm in Actions for Damages Based on Breaches of Article 101 or 102 of the Treaty on the Functioning of the European Union – Public Consultation* (Brussels, 2011), para 19; Practical guide (fn 20) para 21.
37 Maier-Rigaud and Schwalbe (fn 25) 236, fn 53.
38 Oxera (fn 20) 45.
39 *Ibid.*
40 *Ibid.*
41 M-O Mackenrodt, 'Private Incentive, Optimal Deterrence and Damage Claims for Abuses of Dominant Positions – The Interaction between the Economic Review of the Prohibition of Abuses of Dominant Positions and Private Enforcement', in *Abuse of Dominant Position: New Interpretation, New Enforcement Mechanisms?*, ed. by M-O Mackenrodt, BC Gallego and S Enchelmaier (Berlin: Springer, 2010), 165–189, 188.
42 H Hovenkamp, 'Restraints on Innovation', *Cardozo Law Review*, 29(1) (2007), 247–260, 253.
43 Mackenrodt (fn 41) 188.
44 *Ibid*; DA Crane, *The Institutional Structure of Antitrust Enforcement* (Oxford: Oxford University Press, 2011), 173. Similarly, PE Areeda, H Hovenkamp, RD Blair and CP Durrance, *Antitrust Law: An Analysis of Antitrust Principles and Their Application*, 3rd edn (New York: Aspen Publishers, 2006), vol.IIA, 145.
45 See Oxera (fn 20) 16.
46 Areeda and others (fn 44) 142–143.
47 Hovenkamp, Restraints on innovation (fn 42) 258.
48 *In re Microsoft Corp. Antitrust Litigation*, 127 F. Supp. 2d 702 (D. Md. 2001), para 711.

It therefore appears that actions for competition damages primarily concentrates on the overcharge harm and/or lost profits of those harmed. For this reason, the rest of the chapter focuses on overcharge and lost profits. The next section studies different groups of victims who suffer either or both lost profits and overcharge damages in order to search for the characteristics of the damages claims of victims of competition infringements.[49]

Potential damages of competition infringements

Competition infringements resulting in an anticompetitive price increase, ie pricing above competitive levels causes overcharge harm.[50] Overcharge is any positive difference between the price actually paid and the price that would have prevailed in a 'but-for' world in which the infringement had not occurred,[51] ie the counterfactual price.[52] Purchasers of infringing undertakings suffer overcharge harm and, in fact, a large number of individuals can be affected if the overcharge is passed along the distribution chain.[53]

Loss of profits is the difference between the profits[54] the plaintiff would have earned in the absence of the anticompetitive act and the profits the plaintiff earned in actuality.[55] Intermediate sellers[56] can incur both loss of profits and the overcharge harm, whereas competitors can only incur the former. Indeed, competitors may profit when an infringement gives rise to a price increase or reduced output, as per cartels or exploitative abuses, by raising their own prices and/or output.[57] However, exclusionary abuses directly impose harm on competitors by way of

49 The discussion relates to competitors, intermediaries and consumers. See further groups that can be affected by competition infringements, such as suppliers, creditors, employees, producers of the complements to the overcharged product, eg T Calvani, 'Cartel Penalties and Damages in Ireland: Criminalization and the Case for Custodial Sentences', in *Criminalization of Competition Law Enforcement: Economic and Legal Implications for the EU Member States*, ed. by KJ Cseres, MP Schinkel, and FOW Vogelaar (Cheltenham UK: Edward Elgar Publishing, 2006), 270–289, 279; Mackenrodt (fn 41) 186; S Van Uytsel, 'Collective Actions in a Competition Law Context – Reconciling Multilayer Interests to Enhance Access to Justice', in *Collective Actions: Enhancing Access to Justice and Reconciling Multilayer Interests?*, ed. by S Wrbka, S Van Uytsel and M Siems (Cambridge: Cambridge University Press, 2012), 57–92, 69.

50 RG Harris and LA Sullivan, 'Passing on the Monopoly Overcharge: A Comprehensive Policy Analysis', *University of Pennsylvania Law Review*, 128(2) (1979), 269–360, 269.

51 Directive (fn 35) art. 4.

52 CR Leslie, 'Antitrust Damages and Deadweight Loss', *Antitrust Bulletin*, 51(3) (2006), 521–567, 529–30.

53 Mackenrodt (fn 41) 178.

54 'Profits are simply the difference between revenues [a]nd expenses (the expenditures required to manufacture and sell the firm's products).' WH Page, *Proving Antitrust Damages: Legal and Economic Issues*, 2nd edn (USA: ABA Section of Antitrust Law, 2010), 89.

55 *Ibid*; Practical guide (fn 20) para 183.

56 These being producers, distributors or retailers. Oxera (fn 20) 26.

57 N Wahl, 'Damages for Infringement of Competition Law', *Scandinavian Studies in Law*, 41 (2001), 553–564, 561; Areeda and others (fn 44) 203.

reduced revenues and/or increased costs.[58] In a broad sense, loss of profits can encompass lost growth and development opportunities,[59] future profits foregone after the infringement ends,[60] lost investment[61] and loss of reputation.[62] Considering the number of harmed competitors and the way they are harmed, their injuries tend to be concentrated[63] and of large value.[64]

Intermediate sellers who use an overcharged product as an input or who resell it on the market[65] are harmed in two ways by competition infringements leading to a price increase. First, if they bear the entire or a proportion of overcharge, they incur overcharge harm as a result of purchasing the product at an artificially enhanced price. Secondly, if they transfer the overcharge partially or entirely downwards in the form of an increase in prices in compliance with the illegal overcharge, their overcharge harm is reduced by the extent of the amount passed on.[66] This might result in a decrease in the quantity of goods sold,[67] depending on the elasticity of a firm's demand to price increases. For instance, if the demand is perfectly inelastic the full amount of the overcharge can be passed on to the customers by raising prices without incurring any lost profits.[68]

If an increase in prices leads to a loss of sales volumes, it is referred to as 'volume effect'.[69] As the practice has so far shown, national courts have not included the volume effect when quantifying damages stemming from pass-on.[70] However, this effect occurs when raising prices leads to a decrease in demand and therefore fewer sales.[71] For these reasons, the overcharge harm to an intermediate seller is inextricably linked to volume effect. Full absorption of overcharge indicates no reduction in volume; if a loss of profits arises from volume effect, this implies that the intermediary has passed some of the overcharge down the supply chain to its customers.[72] Despite this link, lost sales and overcharge harm can be claimed separately.[73]

58 Oxera (fn 20) 22.
59 Calculating damages based on this kind of harm can be too speculative. Page, Proving antitrust damages (fn 54) 95.
60 Where the foreclosed competitor could not either re-enter the market or regain its previous market share. Practical guide (fn 20) para 206.
61 H Hovenkamp, 'Antitrust's Protected Classes', *Michigan Law Review*, 88(1) (1989), 1–48, 11.
62 Practical guide (fn 20) para 183.
63 H Hovenkamp, *Federal Antitrust Policy: Law of Competition and Its Practice*, 4th edn (USA: West, 2011), 669; Crane (fn 44) 171.
64 Areeda and others (fn 44) 202.
65 See Practical guide (fn 20) para 161.
66 See further *infra* section 'Indirect consumers'.
67 See Mackenrodt (fn 41) 172.
68 Areeda and others (fn 44) 382.
69 Oxera (fn 20) xi; Practical guide (fn 20) para 162.
70 RBB Economics and Cuatrecasas, Gonçalves Pereira, *Study on the Passing-on of Overcharges*, Study Prepared for the Commission (Brussels, 2016) ii.
71 Practical guide (fn 20) para 162.
72 *Ibid* paras 175–176.
73 Oxera (fn 20) xi.

The damages claim of any intermediate seller would have individual characteristics. Each likely suffers different levels of overcharge damages. The amount of overcharge passed downwards could vary in each layer of the supply chain. This means intermediate sellers at different layers might be subject to different amounts. In addition, each seller would decide, according to its own conditions, how much overcharge it would absorb and how much to pass on. In light of this, and the unique conditions in which every business operates, the lost profits damages of intermediate sellers can vary greatly.[74]

Consumers cannot suffer lost profits; they are harmed by way of paying higher prices. All direct consumers bear the whole overcharge and all indirect consumers bear the amount of overcharge passed on to them.[75] Their claims are similar because the distribution chain ends at the consumer level. This means there can be no further pass-on[76] and consumers have no choice but to pay the overcharge. Additionally, consumer losses are smaller than that of businesses. It has been argued that this is because the amount of overcharge naturally falls as the overcharged product moves down the supply chain.[77] While this may be true, even if the whole overcharge is passed along consumer losses tend to be smaller because they do not purchase for the purposes of trade but for individual consumption. Finally, the increase in prices harms many consumers because there are a substantial number of individuals at the consumer level.

It is therefore possible to submit that the characteristics of consumer damages claims fit the characteristics of claims suited to a collective redress action. Such are numerous similar claims with a value that makes them not viable to be pursued in individual proceedings.[78] Arguably, the Commission itself in a way establishes a direct link between consumer damages and the need for a collective redress action. The Green Paper submitted that because individual consumer damages are low a collective redress action would provide an efficient form of redress.[79] The White Paper stated that there was a clear need for collective redress actions for small claimants, including consumers, whose damages are scattered and relatively low value.[80]

With the aim of to providing examples that harm consumers, the next section discusses the types of infringements that give rise to an increase in prices. It also uses case studies in order to demonstrate both how consumers are affected by these infringements and the characteristics of their damages claims.

74 See further Chapter 6.
75 Oxera (fn 20) 26. See *infra* section 'Indirect consumers'. This book uses the term 'direct consumers' to refer to the consumers who purchase from the infringer(s) and uses the term 'indirect consumers' to refer to the consumers who purchase from intermediaries.
76 Oxera (fn 20) 28.
77 Areeda and others (fn 44) 412.
78 See Chapter 2.
79 Commission, *Staff Working Paper Annex to the Green Paper Damages Actions for Breach of the EC Antitrust Rules* (SEC(2005)1732, Brussels, 2005), para 180.
80 Commission, *White Paper on Damages Actions for Breach of the EC Antitrust Rules* (COM(2008) 165 final, Brussels, 2008), (White Paper) para 2.1.

The overcharge as a measure of damages in consumer cases

Overcharge in collusion cases

Practices giving rise to overcharge

As previously mentioned, Article 101 TFEU applies to both vertical and horizontal agreements. Possible negative effects of vertical agreements,[81] ie foreclosure, softening of competition and collusion up- or downstream, might lead to an increase in prices and therefore harm consumers.[82] The welfare impact report finds that private litigation against such practices is already common in the EU. There were 61 cases out of 96 dealing with vertical agreements before national courts between 2004 and 2007.[83] However, no damages have yet been awarded in these cases.[84] It has been further stated that these victims are companies, such as direct competitors at an upstream or downstream level,[85] and therefore they are likely to bring cases to the courts.[86] In the US, the Georgetown study, which gathered data on all private competition cases filed in five federal districts between the years of 1973 and 1983,[87] found that consumers initiated almost no such cases. Indeed, consumers brought 268 cases in total, of which only four were vertical price-fixing cases.[88] On this basis, it appears that the typical claimant in these cases is not a consumer. However, the situation is different in cartel cases, for instance, in the US, the Georgetown study found that consumers brought individual horizontal price-fixing cases with the highest ratio of 36%.[89]

Cartels are the infringements most often associated with damages to consumers.[90] As a collusion between competitors, they either considerably reduce or fully eliminate the intensity of competition between competitors.[91] In this way, cartel members manage to increase prices by engaging in price fixing, limiting

81 See the possible positive effects of vertical restraints, Guidelines on vertical restraints (fn 9) paras 106–107.

82 *Ibid* para 101.

83 Centre for European Policy Studies (CEPS), Erasmus University Rotterdam (EUR) and Luiss Guido Carli (LUISS), *Report for the European Commission 'Making Antitrust Damages Actions More Effective in the EU: Welfare Impact and Potential Scenarios', Final Report*, 2007, (Welfare impact report) 40.

84 *Ibid* 42.

85 *Ibid* 77.

86 *Ibid* 319.

87 SC Salop and LJ White, 'Economic Analysis of Private Antitrust Litigation', *Georgetown Law Journal*, 74 (1986), 1001–1064, 1002.

88 *Ibid* 1008. Note that the figures here are different from that of the welfare impact report, because, although the report refers to the same source, the figures of the original study do not correspond to the figures in the report. See the figures of Welfare impact report (fn 83) 118.

89 Salop and White (fn 87) 1008.

90 Welfare impact report (fn 83) 35.

91 Maier-Rigaud and Schwalbe (fn 25) 213.

output, dividing/sharing markets, and allocating customers or territories,[92] and thereby resulting in damages to consumers through overcharge.[93] It is possible for cartels to implement high price increases soon after beginning to operate. For instance, the Commission found an EU-wide cartel involving, *inter alia*, price fixing, market sharing and bid-rigging of district heating pipes. The decision revealed, whilst the plan was to raise prices by 30–35% over two years, they succeeded in increasing them by 15–20% in the first year of operation.[94] The practical guide notes that 93% of past cartels resulted in an overcharge, averaging about 20%.[95]

In order to assist victims in quantifying and claiming damages, the Directive provides for a rebuttable presumption that cartels cause harm through price increases[96] by, *inter alia*, stating that it is very exceptional that a cartel does not have this effect.[97] This was also proposed during the UK private enforcement reform, but subsequently rejected by the government, as rebutting such a presumption was found difficult in cases with multiple levels of purchasers.[98] The main difference between these two is that there is no fixed amount of overcharge mentioned in the EU, whereas the UK recommended 20%, a figure established by relevant economics literature.[99]

A cartel's effect on prices, when taken in combination with duration, demonstrates the extent of harm caused. A cartel operates in the EU for eight years on average,[100] and the longer the operation the higher the damages

92 Practical guide (fn 20) para 127.

93 JM Connor and RH Lande, 'Optimal Cartel Deterrence: An Empirical Comparison of Sanctions to Overcharges', *American Antitrust Institute Working Paper no 11–08*, 2011, 1–62, 1 <http://works.bepress.com/cgi/viewcontent.cgi?article=1006&context=robert_lande> [accessed 1 July 2018].

94 Commission Decision, *1999/60/EC Pre-Insulated Pipe Cartel* (Case IV/35.691/E-4) [1998] OJ L 24/1, para 126.

95 Based on 114 cartels, Practical guide (fn 20) paras 142–143. See further for the sample and the empirical data, Oxera (fn 20) 88–92. Note that there are other figures cited in the literature, such as cartels give rise to higher prices of 28–54% within the EU. BIS, *Private Actions in Competition Law: A Consultation on Options for Reform – Impact Assessment* (London, 2012), para 9.

96 Directive (fn 35) art. 17(2).

97 It is also because the fact that cartels are secret in nature makes it very difficult for the victims to access relevant documents to prove their cases but cartel members already have these documents to rebut the presumption. Commission, *Proposal for a Directive of the European Parliament and of the Council on Certain Rules Governing Actions for Damages Under National Law for Infringements of the Competition Law Provisions of the Member States and of the European Union*, (2013/0185 (COD), COM(2013) 404 final, Strasbourg, 2013), para 4.5.

98 BIS, *Private Actions in Competition Law: A Consultation on Options for Reform – Government Response* (London, 2013), paras 4.36–4.37.

99 BIS, *Private Actions in Competition Law – A Consultation on Options for Reform* (London, 2012), para 4.40.

100 The study examined 110 cartels between 1990–2008 and found 8.08 years of duration. O De, 'Analysis of Cartel Duration: Evidence from EC Prosecuted Cartels', *International Journal of the Economics of Business*, 17(1) (2010), 33–65, 42, 44. See it is 8.8 years in the US, MC Levenstein and VY Suslow, 'Breaking up Is Hard to Do:

caused.[101] The welfare impact report estimated the annual negative effects of EU-wide cartels and found that these would create €1.2 billion deadweight loss and impose €12.2 billion overcharge on consumers.[102] In another example given by the Commission, the annual direct cost of hard-core cartels[103] to consumers and other victims across the EU is between €13 billion and over €37 billion.[104]

In this respect, the following hypothetical case studies intend to demonstrate how a cartel may affect numerous consumers and give rise to damages actions. In this respect, the following hypothetical case studies intend to demonstrate how a cartel may affect numerous consumers and give rise to damages actions.

Case studies

CASE STUDY 1

Consider two travel companies, Bus A and Bus B, each providing passenger coach services on the same and most popular routes: London to Brussels (route 1) and London to Paris (route 2). Although the journey time in both directions is similar, the fares of Bus B are higher than those of Bus A. For the sake of simplicity, assume that there are no other players in the market, meaning consumers had no adequate alternatives. Under these circumstances, the managers of Bus A and B met in 2006 to come to an agreement that Bus A would cede route 2 in exchange for exclusive operation on route 1. Consequently, they form a market-sharing cartel which operates for eight years.

This collusion not only reduces competition between two firms but also allows them to raise prices while keeping market shares at stable levels due to the absence of competition. Accordingly, during eight years of cartel operation, they manage

Determinants of Cartel Duration', *University of Michigan, Ross School of Business, Working Paper no 1150*, 2010, 1–50, 16 <http://www-personal.umich.edu/~maggiel/Duration.pdf> [accessed 1 July 2017].

101 A Mazurkeviciute, 'Determinants of the European Price-Fixing Cartels' Duration: Focus on Internal Cartel Organization' (presented at the X Workshop SIEPI, Perugia: IEL, Collegio Carlo Alberto, 2012), 1–53, 1 <http://www.siepi.univpm.it/sites/www.siepi.univpm.it/files/siepi/SIEPI%202012/papers/MAZURKEVICIUTE.pdf> [accessed 18 July 2013].

102 Welfare impact report (fn 83) 107.

103 They are defined as anticompetitive practices of competitors '[t]o fix prices, make rigged bids (collusive tenders), establish output restrictions or quotas, or share or divide markets by allocating customers, suppliers, territories, or lines of commerce'. OECD, *Recommendation of the Council Concerning Effective Action Against Hard Core Cartels* (C(98)35/FINAL, 1998), 1–4, 3 <http://www.oecd.org/daf/competition/2350130.pdf> [accessed 1 July 2018].

104 Commission, *Staff Working Document – Impact Assessment Report – Damages Actions for Breach of the EU Antitrust Rules Accompanying the Proposal for a Directive of the European Parliament and of the Council on Certain Rules Governing Actions for Damages under National Law for Infringements of the Competition Law Provisions of the Member States and of the European Union* (SWD(2013) 203 final, Strasbourg, 2013), (SWD-IAR) para 64.

Table 5.1 Overcharge harm incurred by consumers

Prices per return ticket Companies	*Counterfactual prices*		*Cartel prices*	
	Route 1	*Route 2*	*Route 1*	*Route 2*
Bus A	€73	€76	€90	No service
Bus B	€77	€84	No service	€100
% of cartel overcharge		20%[105]	25%[106]	

to gradually increase prices to a level whereby consumers are paying substantially more on return tickets for the routes concerned. Table 5.1 illustrates the extent of the overcharge harm incurred by consumers travelling on these routes during the period in which the cartel operated.

On route 1, consumers pay 20% more per ticket compared to the situation without infringement; that figure is 25% for route 2 consumers. That hundreds of consumers might be travelling on these routes in one day, and that each has to endure these higher prices for eight years, reveals the magnitude of damages suffered by consumers.

CASE STUDY 2

Another hypothetical case example concerns a price-fixing cartel. Assume that three telephone operators with aggregate market share of about 70% of the telecoms market in the EU agreed to fix prices for calls across Europe in 2010 and that this cartel is only uncovered in 2014. In order to maximise their profits, the operators conspired not only on prices at which the product should be sold to consumers but also on the discounts provided. By virtue of this agreement, each operator easily applied identical rates and policies to their customers without experiencing any drop in sales during the four years of their operation as a cartel. As a result, these firms eliminated competition between them, restricting competition in the internal market. Table 5.2 illustrates how consumers were harmed by paying higher prices in this price-fixing conspiracy. For the amount of damages per consumer, it is useful to consider, firstly, the information that cartel, in this hypothetical scenario, operated for four years, and secondly, the findings of a 2011 study that indicated that a European consumer makes, on average, 144 minutes of outgoing mobile calls per month.[107] Applying this data to the example presented here shows that a

105 Average counterfactual price for route 1: (73+77)/2= €75. % of cartel overcharge: 90–75=15, 15/75=20%.

106 Average counterfactual price for route 2: (76+84)/2=€80. % of cartel overcharge: 100–80=20, 20/80=25%.

107 GSMA, *European Mobile Industry Observatory 2011* (London, 2011), 1–74, 4 <http://www.gsma.com/publicpolicy/wp-content/uploads/2012/04/emofullwebfinal.pdf> [accessed 1 July 2018].

Table 5.2 Prices paid by consumers as a result of price fixing

Companies	*Prices per minute*		*Average*
	Counterfactual prices	*Cartel prices*	*% of cartel overcharge*
Operator A	€0.13	€0.21	40%[108]
Operator B	€0.14	€0.21	
Operator C	€0.18	€0.21	

consumer of these operators paid, respectively, €553, €484 and €207 extra during these four years.[109] Moreover, this infringement is highly likely to create widespread damage considering the number of consumers who use mobile phones. In fact, in a similar French case, a cartel affected 20 million mobile phone subscribers and caused around between €295 and €590 million damages in total to consumers in only two years.[110]

Overcharge in abuse of dominance cases

Practices giving rise to overcharge

An abuse of market power can also cause overcharge harm. The main feature of an exploitative abuse is its ability to directly and immediately harm consumers,[111] such as through excessive prices.[112] Excessive prices result in consumers paying more and therefore a wealth transfer occurs from purchasers to the dominant undertaking.[113] In light of this, a study concludes that national competition authorities of the new and candidate Member States extensively sanction dominant firms for charging excessive prices due to its effect on a large number of consumers.[114] An exclusionary abuse, on the other hand, directly harms

108 Average counterfactual price: (0.13+0.14+0.18)/3= €0.15. % of cartel overcharge: 0.21–0.15 = 0.6, 0.6/0.15 = 40%.

109 Loss per month for a consumer of operator A: 144 minutes x €0.08 = €11.52. Loss at the end of four years: €11.52 x 48 months= €552.96.

110 Commission, *Staff Working Document Accompanying Document to the White Paper on Damages Actions for Breach of the EC Antitrust Rules – Impact Assessment* (SEC (2008) 405, Brussels, 2008), para 32.

111 B Lyons, 'The Paradox of the Exclusion of Exploitative Abuse', *University of East Anglia, CCP Working Paper no 08–1*, 2007, 1–20, 2 <http://competitionpolicy.ac.uk/documents/107435/107587/ccp08-1.pdf> [accessed 1 July 2018]; Akman, Exploitative abuse (fn 17) 8.

112 Practical guide (fn 20) para 172.

113 Maier-Rigaud and Schwalbe (fn 25) 234; OECD, *Quantification of Harm to Competition by National Courts and Competition Agencies* (DAF/COMP(2011)25, 2011), 22 <http://www.oecd.org/daf/competition/QuantificationofHarmtoCompetition2011.pdf> [accessed 1 July 2018].

114 A Svetlicinii and M Botta, 'Article 102 TFEU as a Tool for Market Regulation: "Excessive Enforcement" Against "Excessive Prices" in the New EU Member States

competitors. However, consumers may be harmed by way of increased prices after the successful foreclosure of competitors from the market.[115]

It is apparent, for instance, in predatory pricing cases, where the dominant undertaking by cutting the prices to a loss[116] directly and immediately causes harm to its competitors while consumers enjoy lower prices during the predation period. Once an existing competitor has been controlled or a new entrant has been dismissed from the market,[117] the dominant undertaking can restrict output and raise prices in order to recoup losses incurred in this period.[118] Consumers are harmed afterwards by way of higher prices.[119] Therefore, recoupment is not required to establish the infringement,[120] but it is necessary to establish harm to consumers.[121]

Price discrimination abuses can also lead to excessive prices for those who are subject to higher price.[122] In other words, due to these abuses, the group of consumers who pay higher prices can suffer overcharge harm.[123] For instance, in *Deutsche Post AG* the Commission concluded that the conduct of the undertaking led to higher prices for the group of consumers who are the senders of the disputed mailings.[124] The discriminatory practice of *Deutsche Post AG* was to charge different prices for equivalent transactions by applying different tariffs,[125] significantly delaying the mail of the consumers in dispute.[126] As a result, these consumers paid higher prices for these services than others.[127] In the US, the

and Candidate Countries', *European Competition Journal*, 8(3) (2012), 473–496, 484.

115 Practical guide (fn 20) para 21b.

116 Whish and Bailey (fn 12) 739.

117 *Ibid.*

118 Welfare impact report (fn 83) 437.

119 *Ibid.*

120 See eg Case C-202/07 P *France Télécom SA v Commission* [2009] ECR I-02369, paras 110, 112.

121 Draft guidance paper (fn 36) para 191; Practical guide (fn 20) para 211.

122 O'Donoghue and Padilla (fn 21) 732.

123 See discrimination between consumers can constitute an abuse under Article 102 TFEU, P Akman, 'To Abuse, or Not to Abuse: Discrimination between Consumers', *European Law Review*, 32(4) (2007), 492–512, 499. See it is only if it is exclusionary or exploitative, R Nazzini, *The Foundations of European Union Competition Law: The Objective and Principles of Article 102* (Oxford: Oxford University Press, 2011), 249. See it is exploitation, DMB Gerard, 'Price Discrimination under Article 82 (2) (C) EC: Clearing up the Ambiguities', *Global Competition Law Centre Research Paper on the Modernisation of Article 82 EC*, 2005, 1–29, 18, fn 68 <http://ssrn.com/abstract=1113354> [accessed 1 July 2018]. See also in *1998 Football World Cup* decision the Commission found that the French organiser CFO discriminated between consumers who provided an address in France and those who did not. Commission Decision, 2000/12/EC *1998 Football World Cup* (Case IV/36.888) [2000] OJ/L 5/55, para 91.

124 Commission Decision, 2001/892/EC *Deutsche Post AG – Interception of Cross-Border Mail* (COMP/C-1/36.915) [2001] OJ L 331/40, paras 133.

125 *Ibid* para 127.

126 *Ibid* para 128.

127 *Ibid* para 133.

Georgetown study found that the ratio of price discrimination cases filed by consumers was 10.8%.[128]

Against this background, although abuse of dominance can cause harm to consumers, the number of actions for damages brought against it would still be low. In that regard, it should firstly be noted that there has been considerable debate over what constitutes an abuse of dominant position.[129] In other words, 'abuse' is not purely defined and the provision only sets out the examples of conducts that can be abusive.[130] The kinds of behaviour the dominant undertakings engage in might be welfare-enhancing.[131] However, distinguishing between pro- and anticompetitive conducts of dominant undertakings is not an easy exercise[132] because, unlike cartels, economics literature dealing with unilateral conduct is still developing and does not provide robust results.[133] All these create ambiguity and legal uncertainty for claimants.[134]

Additionally, the commitment procedure is heavily used in Article 102 TFEU cases.[135] As figures show, between May 2004 and December 2013 the Commission closed 77% of abuse of dominance proceedings by a commitment decision, and years 2008, 2010, 2012 and 2013 had the rate of 100%.[136] However, the commitment procedure would reduce victims' chances of bringing an action and obtaining compensation because this procedure allows the Commission to accept the commitments offered by the undertakings aiming to allay the competition concerns over their conduct and therefore to issue a commitment decision that does not contain a finding of an infringement.[137]

Indeed, the Regulation 1/2003 states that 'Commitment decisions should find that there are no longer grounds for action by the Commission without concluding whether or not there has been or still is an infringement'.[138] Having said that, in a recent judgment, Paris Commercial Court treated a commitment decision as the finding of wrongdoing since the undertakings agreed to commitments to

128 Salop and White (fn 87) 1008.

129 Whish and Bailey (fn 12) 192.

130 P Akman, *The Concept of Abuse in EU Competition Law: Law and Economic Approaches* (Oxford and Portland, Oregon: Hart Publishing, 2012), 1–2.

131 D Meyer, 'Panel Discussion – A Reformed Approach to Article 82 and the US Practice: An Overall Appreciation', in *European Competition Law Annual 2007: A Reformed Approach to Article 82 EC*, ed. by C-D Ehlermann and M Marquis (Oxford and Portland, Oregon: Hart Publishing, 2008), 193–196, 194.

132 *Ibid;* Whish and Bailey (fn 12) 193.

133 Akman, The concept of abuse (fn 130) 2.

134 *Ibid.*

135 EB de La Serre, 'Will the European Commission Reduce Use of the Commitment Procedure in Dominance Cases?', 2015 <http://www.mondaq.com/unitedstates/x/395022/Antitrust+Competition/Will+the+European+Commission+Reduce+Use+of+the+Commitment+Procedure+in+Dominance+Cases> [accessed 1 July 2018].

136 *Ibid.*

137 Council Regulation (EC) No 1/2003 of 16 December 2002 on the Implementation of the Rules on Competition Laid down in Articles [101] and [102] of the Treaty, (OJ L 1/1, 2003), art.9.

138 *Ibid* recital 13.

address competition concerns; the Court then awarded damages to the claimant on that basis.[139] This judgment shows that commitment decisions can signal for a competition infringement. However, it would be rare that a court finds the undertakings guilty of competition infringement because they provided commitments. The rule is, as expressed, commitment decisions do not contain a finding of an infringement.

In exclusionary abuse cases, there is usually an indirect link between an infringement and overcharge harm suffered by consumers. This means consumers might have difficulty identifying harm[140] and proving causation between the exclusionary conduct and the harm suffered as the conduct produces negative effects for consumers after first affecting competitors.[141] In addition to this, the kind of harm that an exclusionary abuse imposes on consumers would not be computed; for instance, tying causes a reduction of choice.[142] To date, almost all damages actions for exclusionary practices in the EU have been filed by competitors.[143] The situation is similar in the US. The Georgetown study found that 13% of consumer cases were tying/exclusive dealing cases and 9% were refusal to deal.[144]

In exploitative abuse cases, there is a direct link between harm suffered by consumers and excessive prices. However, there are only a handful of cases on excessive pricing.[145] Between 1980 and 2010 there were 11 exploitative and 40 exclusionary abuse decisions given by the Commission.[146] It has been argued that there is rarity of excessive pricing cases because it is hard to distinguish excessive *versus* competitive prices or submit whether these excessive prices are welfare-

139 A Duron, 'Private Damages Actions in the Wake of a Commitment Decision: New Risks after the Judgment of the Paris Commercial Court in Eco-Emballages', *Journal of European Competition Law and Practice*, (2015), 1–5, 4.

140 Oxera (fn 20) iii.

141 See P Buccirossi, 'Quantification of Damages in Exclusionary Practice Cases', *Journal of European Competition Law and Practice*, 1(3) (2010), 252–256, 253.

142 Note that in the US, tying cases are generally not subject to class actions because proof of coercion into buying the tied product is seen as an individual issue. ABA, Section of Antitrust Law, *Antitrust Class Actions Handbook* (USA: American Bar Association, 2010), 71. See also that tying can result in an increase in prices, Commission, *Guidance on the Commission's Enforcement Priorities in Applying Article [102 TFEU] to Abusive Exclusionary Conduct by Dominant Undertakings* (OJ C 45/7, 2009), paras 55–57.

143 Oxera (fn 20) iii.

144 Salop and White (fn 87) 1008.

145 See Commission Decision, 75/75/EEC *General Motors Continental* [1975] OJ L 29/14, para 8; Commission Decision, 76/353/EEC *Chiquita* [1976] OJ L 95/1, para 8; Commission Decision 84/379/EEC *British Leyland* [1984] OJ L 207/11 para 26; Case 226/84 *British Leyland Public Limited Company v Commission* [1986] ECR 3263; Commission Decision, *Deutsche Post AG* (fn 124) paras 166–167; Commission Decision, 2001/463/EC *DSD* (Duales System Deutschland) (COMP D3/34493) [2001] OJ L 166/1, paras 111–113; Case C-385/07P *Der Grüne Punkt – DSD v Commission* [2009] ECR I-06155, paras 92–93.

146 P Hubert and M-L Combet, 'Exploitative Abuse: The End of the Paradox?', *Concurrences Doctrines*, I(1) (2011), 44–51, 45.

enhancing, encouraging investment and innovation, or whether the market is capable of self-correcting in due course.[147]

These explanations do not imply that consumers who suffer an overcharge through abuse of dominance would not benefit from a collective redress action. The characteristics of consumer damages arising from the infringement of Article 102 TFEU fit the characteristics of the claims that a collective redress action aim to address and therefore such an action would assist these consumers in obtaining damages as well. When the ambiguities surrounding the concept of abuse in the meaning of Article 102 TFEU are overcome and the type of loss caused by Article 102 TFEU infringements can be calculated, ie reduction of choice, a collective redress action will increase the consumer chances of getting compensated. However, one might currently expect cartel cases to be more frequent than abuse of dominance cases. This can also be deduced from the number of cases that have been tackled by national competition authorities as Article 101 TFEU cases are considerably more than Article 102 TFEU cases.[148] With this in mind, the case studies below provide some insight into how abusive behaviour causes harm to consumers.

Case studies

CASE STUDY 1

Assume that company A is exclusively selling a rare and special kind of diamond, pink diamond, across the EU, which is used to produce various items such as watches, jewellery and clothes. Assume further, there are significant barriers to entry in the market because newcomers incur high sunk costs and require a large-scale entry due to economies of scale. This would give the incumbent advantage in marketing and maximising profit. Under these circumstances, A charged excessive prices that were approximately 30% more than the benchmark determined by comparing actual prices and costs and the price of common diamond. Since A holds monopoly in the upstream market, all intermediate sellers bought the product from A and paid higher prices, but, accordingly, were able to transfer the whole overcharge to consumers.

147 O'Donoghue and Padilla (fn 21) 734. See further the assessment of arguments against the prohibition and the difficulties the Commission and national competition authorities face in condemning excessive prices, eg, Whish and Bailey (fn 12) 718–720; Svetlicinii and Botta (fn 114) 478–480. See the CJEU's recent case on excessive pricing that provides guidance on how to define and determine excessive prices, Case C-177/16 *Autortiesību un komunicēšanās konsultāciju a⊠entūra/Latvijas Autoru apvienība' v Konkurences padome* [2017] ECLI:EU:C:2017:689.

148 The ratio of Article 101 TFEU cases are 55%, whereas the ratio of Article 102 TFEU cases are 33.75%. Cases including both were 10% of all. Commission, 'European Competition Network (ECN) Statistics', 2017 <http://ec.europa.eu/competition/ecn/statistics.html#3> [accessed 1 July 2018].

As a result of this infringement, each consumer had to pay 30% more for any product containing pink diamond. Considering the product range, there were numerous diamond-accented goods in the market that reached consumers. This means that a great number of consumers suffer an overcharge through the purchase of different kinds of products.

CASE STUDY 2

Consider company X, it has a 40% market share in the notebook market in the EU. Anti-virus programs and notebooks are two distinct products that are sold and purchased separately, but X bundles these items in order to offer notebook buyers a discount when they purchase its anti-virus program. Assume that if notebook and anti-virus program are bought separately from X, their prices are respectively €430 and €40, but if bought as a package their prices are €450, meaning if a consumer takes advantage of the bundling, she would pay €450 in total for both rather than €470.

Assume that company Y, which does not operate in the notebook market, sells an anti-virus program at the price of €40. In light of X's pricing policy, if Y wishes to continue trading in the anti-virus program market, it needs to sell the product at €20, because when a consumer is willing to pay €430 for X's notebook, the anti-virus program is then available at a price of €20. In order to persuade its consumers to buy its anti-virus program, Y reduces its prices to €20, but could not survive this pricing scheme and has to leave the market. Once X has driven Y out of the market, it seizes the opportunity to remove its pricing policy and charges €50 for the anti-virus program. Consumers are now worse off by paying more for the anti-virus program every time they buy from X, and a large number of consumers are likely to be affected.

These case studies were intended to demonstrate how and to what extent competition infringements leading to an anticompetitive price increase could adversely affect consumers. The next section explores the ways in which consumers are harmed. This analysis will provide a basis for how consumers can be grouped for the purposes of collective redress in the following chapter.

The ways in which consumers are harmed

Direct consumers

This first group purchases the product directly from the defendant.[149] If direct purchasers are intermediate sellers who sell on an overcharged product to their customers or use it when producing their own product for sale, they might be able to pass the entire or part of the overcharge along to their customers in the form of higher prices.[150] In this case, the damages direct purchasers can recover depend

149 Mackenrodt (fn 41) 172.
150 *Ibid* 172–173.

on how much of overcharge has been passed on.[151] This is, however, no concern for consumers, as the final users of the product, they do not perform any of these actions. As a result, if direct purchasers are consumers, they would be entitled to the whole overcharge.[152]

Indirect consumers

Where an infringement imposes a price increase, it is possible that intermediaries pass unlawful overcharge down the distribution chain by raising their prices. In this case, the infringement causes harm to another group. Indirect consumers buy the product in question from intermediaries who pass on this overcharge either partially or entirely.

Standing of indirect purchasers is one of the topical subjects in the field of private competition law enforcement. The fact that they do not have any direct relationship with the infringer[153] and therefore the way in which they are harmed by the infringement give rise to issues that influence policy choices regarding their standing to sue. Such issues include whether it is too complex to calculate their damages,[154] whether it is difficult for them to prove the harm suffered, and whether to favour the compensation or deterrence objective in the election to allow them to sue.

In the EU, the decision of *Courage* for the first time held that 'any individual' can claim damages for the loss caused by competition infringements.[155] At the time, this raised the question of whether the case law required that indirect purchasers should be able to sue for damages.[156] Building on the Court's statement, the Commission answered this question in the affirmative.[157] According to the Green Paper, the case law does not accept any restriction on the standing of those harmed[158] but a trade-off between the principle of full compensation of all victims and efficiency might be needed considering the complexities indirect purchasers encounter in claiming damages.[159] In light of this, four different policy combinations were offered with respect to indirect purchaser standing and passing-on defence.[160] The Green Paper then pointed out that in the event an option were to

151 *Ibid.*
152 AI Gavil, 'Thinking Outside the Illinois Brick Box: A Proposal for Reform', *Antitrust Law Journal*, 76 (2009), 167–203, 195.
153 White Paper (fn 80) para 2.1. See further Figure 5.1 'Indirect consumers flowchart' for the passing on of the overcharge to consumers.
154 See further Chapter 8.
155 See further Chapter 4.
156 See eg F Cengiz, 'Passing-On Defence and Indirect Purchaser Standing in Actions for Damages Against the Violations of Competition Law: What Can the EC Learn from the US?', *University of East Anglia, CCP Working Paper no 07–21*, 2007, 1–42, 29 <http://competitionpolicy.ac.uk/documents/107435/107587/ccp07-21.pdf> [accessed 1 July 2018].
157 SWPGP (fn 79) para 177.
158 *Ibid.*
159 *Ibid* paras 178–179.
160 Commission, *Green Paper on Damages Actions for Breach of EC Antitrust Rules* (COM(2005) 672 final, Brussels, 2005), options 21–24.

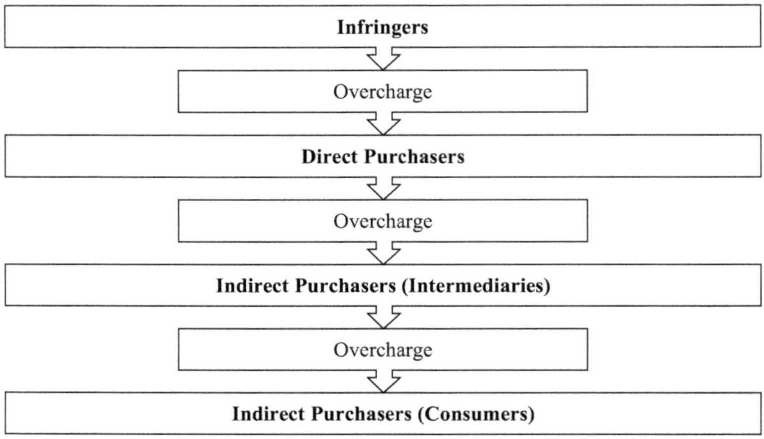

Figure 5.1 Indirect consumers flowchart

be chosen that did not permit a passing-on defence and standing of indirect purchasers, it should still be possible for consumers who are harmed by an infringement to obtain damages and a collective redress action should be introduced to allow this.[161]

Since that point, the Commission has been clear that the right to claim damages should be open to indirect purchasers,[162] which has been found in accordance with the principles of effectiveness[163] and full compensation.[164] According to the Directive, all those harmed should be entitled to compensation and this should not differ for direct or indirect purchasers.[165] Considering the difficulties proving and quantifying harm suffered by indirect purchasers, the Commission suggests a rebuttable presumption in their favour in the White Paper[166] and in the

161 SWPGP (fn 79) para 184. See against this exception, V Milutinovic, 'Private Enforcement Upcomig Issues', in *EC Competition Law: A Critical Assessment*, ed. by G Amato, C-D Ehlermann and A Komninos (Oxford and Portland, Oregon: Hart Publishing, 2007), 725–758, 746.

162 White Paper (fn 80) para 2.1; Welfare impact report (fn 83) 462; Commission, *Proposal for a Council Directive on Rules Governing Damages Actions for Infringements of Articles [101] and [102] of the Treaty*, 2009, art. 10 <http://allegati.unina.it/postlaurea/perf/Exclusiva_Juridico.pdf> [accessed 1 July 2018].

163 Welfare impact report (fn 83) 460.

164 White Paper (fn 80) paras 1.2, 2.1.

165 Directive (fn 35) art. 12(1). See that in some Member States in order for indirect purchasers to claim damages they have to fall under the protective scope of competition law, M Ioannidou, *Consumer Involvement in Private EU Competition Law Enforcement* (Oxford: Oxford University Press, 2015), 83.

166 White Paper (fn 80) para 2.6. Lande finds this presumption useful but argues that significant litigation over rebutting the presumption can be wasteful and lengthy; therefore, it should be conclusive. RH Lande, 'New Options for State Indirect Purchaser Legislation: Protecting the Real Victims of Antitrust Violations', *Alabama Law*

Directive.[167] The latter further explains it is only fair to put the burden of proof on the infringer where establishing the passing-on of overcharge is difficult for both parties.[168]

The US takes a different stance on the standing of indirect purchasers. This stance has been questioned, and moreover an amendment has been suggested at the federal level[169] and the majority of the states do not follow it. Indeed, more than 35 states permit indirect standing,[170] which is due to the fact that the Supreme Court approves of the recognition of indirect purchaser standing at state laws on the grounds that those laws were not pre-empted by federal law.[171] On the other hand, the same Supreme Court bars indirect purchasers from suing at the federal level despite Section 4 of the Clayton Act[172] which states 'any person' can claim damages.[173] The decisions of *Hanover Shoe* [174] and *Illinois Brick* [175] – the main precedents – preferred to sacrifice indirect purchaser standing for the considerations of effectiveness (in other words, deterrence)[176] and efficiency (ie evading litigation complexity).[177] The last one refers to judicial economy which should be promoted without placing an overwhelming burden on courts to make economic and factual assessment.[178]

The question of passing-on defence was raised for the first time in *Hanover Shoe*. The Court first held that it is insuperable to establish whether the infringer increased its prices on account of the overcharge due to the numerous factors that can influence pricing policies of a company in the real economic world.[179]

Review, 61(3) (2010), 447–492, 476. Indeed, proving the overcharge is passed on to indirect purchasers in the distribution chain is not an easy task to complete. In the US, for instance, California Federal Court rejected certification for the class of indirect purchasers as the burden to demonstrate pass-through rate is on them but indirect purchasers and their experts had failed to do so. *In re Lithium Ion Batteries Antitrust Litigation*, Case no 13-MD-2420 YGR (N.D. Cal. 2018).

167 Directive (fn 35) art. 14(2). See a similar presumption proposed in Withdrawn Directive (fn 162) art. 10(2). See further for the presumption, Chapter 8.

168 SWD-IAR (fn 104) para 156.

169 Antitrust Modernization Commission, *Report and Recommendations*, 2007, 1–449, 268–270 (AMC report) <http://govinfo.library.unt.edu/amc/report_recommendation/amc_final_report.pdf> [accessed 1 July 2018].

170 *Ibid* 269.

171 *California v ARC America Corp.*, 490 US 93 (1989), paras 100–106.

172 Clayton Antitrust Act, 15 USC, 1914.

173 Milutinovic, Private enforcement (fn 161) 736.

174 *Hanover Shoe v United Shoe Machinery Corp.*, 392 US 481 (1968).

175 *Illinois Brick Co v Illinois*, 431 US 720 (1977).

176 *Hanover Shoe* (fn 174) para 494; *ibid* para 735; BD Richman and CR Murray, 'Rebuilding Illinois Brick: A Functionalist Approach to the Indirect Purchaser Rule', *Southern California Law Review*, 81 (2007), 69–110, 74; F Cengiz, 'Antitrust Damages Actions: Lessons from American Indirect Purchasers' Litigation', *International and Comparative Law Quarterly*, 59 (2010), 39–63, 43.

177 *Hanover Shoe* (fn 174) para 493; *Illinois Brick* (fn 175) para 745; Richman and Murray (fn 176) 74.

178 Cengiz (fn 176) 43–44.

179 *Hanover Shoe* (fn 174) paras 492–493.

Secondly, it held that if passing-on defence were accepted, this would not only reduce direct purchasers' willingness to pursue a claim but also entitle consumers to sue for damages. According to the Court, consumers have small loss in the case at hand and correspondingly little interest in filling a class action. Hence, they would likely not bring a claim, allowing the defendants to keep their illegal gain, resulting in a reduction of the effectiveness of treble damages actions for competition infringements.[180]

After the rejection of the passing-on defence, the *Illinois Brick* decision precluded indirect purchaser standing for three reasons.[181] First, allowing indirect purchasers to sue would create duplicative recovery since the defendant cannot assert a passing-on defence due to *Hanover Shoe.* [182] Secondly, identifying, calculating and distributing the overcharge through each layer in the distribution chain would be complicated and require massive evidence.[183] Finally, performing such complex practices would result in an increase in both litigation costs and uncertainty, reducing direct purchasers' incentive to go to court. If direct purchasers decided not to sue, competition law enforcement would be compromised,[184] because indirect purchasers, especially consumers, are unlikely to bring damages actions as they are remote from the infringement[185] and generally have small value claims.[186] The Court submitted that in order to encourage private competition law enforcement, direct purchasers should be free of passing-on analysis and recover the full overcharge even if they wholly or partially passed it along.[187] The Court also acknowledged that this policy choice serves the deterrence objective but decided not to pursue the compensation objective for small claims of indirect purchasers.[188] This is a statement deliberately made by the Court so they avoided saying that they sacrificed compensation for the sake of deterrence. The wording of the Court's discussion was changed before publication and the argument with respect to sacrificing the objective of compensating victims for their losses to reach deterrence was removed.[189] It was a tough decision for the Court as the

180 *Ibid* para 494.
181 Calvani (fn 49) 278.
182 *Illinois Brick* (fn 175) paras 728–729, 735.
183 *Ibid* para 742.
184 *Ibid* para 745.
185 *Ibid* para 741.
186 *Ibid* para 745.
187 *Ibid* para 746. There are three exceptions under which indirect purchasers can sue for damages under federal law: if the infringer owns or controls the direct purchaser, or the direct purchaser is involved in the infringement, or customer and manufacturer are working under a 'cost-plus' exception rule that makes the customer purchase a fixed quantity of product irrespective of the increase in price. *Hanover Shoe* (fn 174) para 494; A Hamilton and D Henry, 'Bricks, Beer and Shoes: Indirect Purchaser Standing in the European Union and the United States', *Global Competition Litigation Review*, 5(3) (2012), 111–117, 115.
188 *Illinois Brick* (fn 175) paras 746–747.
189 AI Gavil, 'Antitrust Remedy Wars Episode I: Illinois Brick from Inside the Supreme Court', *St. John's Law Review*, 79(3) (2005), 553–624, 609–610.

decision was made by majority votes – six to three – there were thus three dissenting opinions.

These decisions have ignited a debate on indirect purchaser standing. The commentators in favour of the rejection primarily assert that direct purchasers have more incentives to sue, which makes them the most efficient enforcers because *i.* they are in a better position in terms of access to relevant information,[190] and *ii.* their loss, and the expected damages award, is higher.[191] It has also been argued that indirect purchaser suits would result in high litigation costs because *i.* it is not an easy task to prove the passing-on of overcharges and quantify the damages suffered, *ii.* the damages award would need to be divided between direct and indirect buyers.[192] Based on the latter, it has been stated that allowing indirect purchasers to sue does not mean that total damages award is changed and therefore indirect purchaser standing does not contribute to deterrence.[193]

These considerations do not appear to be convincing. With respect to the difficulty of computation of damages of indirect purchasers,[194] it has been argued that first, this difficulty does not justify that the damages suffered by indirect victims should be equal to zero.[195] Secondly, all competition cases have more or less this kind of difficulty.[196] In fact, the courts have and already exercise the judicial capacity to handle the issues of computation and distribution of indirect purchaser damages.[197] These cases are 40 years old, which means the development in technology and in the field of econometric modelling provide new and sophisticated tools with which courts can deal with damages actions brought by indirect purchasers.[198]

With respect to granting standing only to direct purchasers, indirect purchaser suits could add to deterrence[199] as direct purchasers' incentives to sue are not as high as expected. Direct purchasers *i.* often suffer small or no overcharge harm as

190 WM Landes and RA Posner, 'Should Indirect Purchasers Have Standing to Sue Under the Antitrust Laws? An Economic Analysis of the Rule of Illinois Brick', *University of Chicago Law Review*, 46(3) (1979), 602–635, 609.

191 *Ibid* 612; M Schwartz and GJ Werden, 'Illinois Brick and the Deterrence of Antitrust Violations – An Economic Analysis', *Hastings Law Journal*, 35 (1984), 629–668, 663.

192 WH Page, 'Indirect Purchaser Suits Under the Class Action Fairness Act – Reconciling Multilayer Interests in Antitrust Litigation', in *Collective Actions: Enhancing Access to Justice and Reconciling Multilayer Interests?*, ed. by S Wrbka, S Van Uytsel and M Siems (Cambridge: Cambridge University Press, 2012), 275–298, 294.

193 Van Uytsel (fn 49) 84.

194 *Illinois Brick* (fn 175) para 735.

195 JA Brander and TW Ross, 'Estimating Damages from Price-Fixing', *Canadian Class Action Review*, 3 (2006), 335–369, 340–367; MM Duffy, 'Chipping Away at the Illinois Brick Wall: Expanding Exceptions to the Indirect Purchaser Rule', *Notre Dame Law Review*, 87 (2012), 1709–1748, 1727.

196 Dissenting, *Illinois Brick* (fn 175) paras 758–759.

197 Harris and Sullivan (fn 50) 340; Areeda and others (fn 44) 161; P Whelan, 'Something of a Burden: Is the Passing-On Defence Appropriate?', *Competition Law Insight*, 5 (2008), 5–7, 6. See further Chapter 8.

198 Whelan (fn 197) 6.

199 Harris and Sullivan (fn 50) 350.

a result of the passing-on,[200] *ii.* have an ongoing relationship with the defendant which they may not wish to disrupt[201] and *iii.* may worry about retaliation.[202] Indeed, when direct purchasers brought almost no follow-on damages actions after the *Illinois Brick* decision, it was pointed out that possibly they passed the entire overcharge downwards and suffered no loss, or were afraid of disrupting their business relations with the defendant and/or of retaliation.[203] The indirect cases before state courts also seem to support this. In the *Microsoft* case, for instance, direct purchasers who passed the overcharge down the chain and benefited from most of the actions of the defendant[204] avoided filing a lawsuit,[205] whereas indirect purchaser consumers brought 14 class actions in state courts, of which 11 were certified.[206] It should also be noted that the number of indirect purchaser suits is not at the low levels[207] as opposed to what *Hanover Shoe*[208] and *Illinois Brick*[209] decisions had anticipated. Therefore, deterrence might actually be reduced by making the infringers immune to indirect purchaser claims.[210]

Moreover, in the absence of indirect standing, the real victims of anticompetitive behaviour cannot be compensated[211] and direct purchasers obtain a windfall at their expense.[212] Those real victims could be consumers who have no choice but to suffer the overcharge passed on.[213] The legislative discussion of the Sherman Act[214] expressed that intermediaries who are not the ultimate victims of competition infringements would not bring damages actions but that consumers

200 *Ibid* 277.
201 *Ibid* 352.
202 J Cirace, 'Apportioning Damages between Direct and Indirect Purchasers in Consolidated Antitrust Suits: ARC America Unravels the Illinois Brick Rule', *Villanova Law Review*, 35 (1990), 283–332, 320.
203 *Ibid.*
204 H Hovenkamp, 'Book Review – The Rationalization of Antitrust', *Harvard Law Review*, 116 (2003), 917–944, 941 (reviewing RA Posner, *Antitrust Law*, 2nd edn (Chicago: The University of Chicago Press, 2001)).
205 Richman and Murray (fn 176) 94. See it may be because of fear of economic retribution, Duffy (fn 195) 1710.
206 Page, Indirect purchaser suits (fn 192) 281. See for the analysis of certification decisions of the state courts in *Microsoft* case, WH Page, 'Class Certification in the Microsoft Indirect Purchaser Litigation', *Journal of Competition Law and Economics*, 1 (2) (2005), 303–338.
207 AMC report (fn 169) 269.
208 *Hanover Shoe* (fn 174) para 494.
209 *Illinois Brick* (fn 175) para 747.
210 Cirace (fn 202) 320, 322. Similarly, Dissenting, *Illinois Brick* (fn 175) para 749.
211 Dissenting, *Illinois Brick* (fn 175) para 749.
212 Whelan (fn 197) 5; Crane (fn 44) 167. See also it is unfair to deny indirect purchasers recovery, J Rüggeberg and MP Schinkel, 'Consolidating Antitrust Damages in Europe: A Proposal for Standing in Line with Efficient Private Enforcement', *World Competition*, 29(3) (2006), 395–420, 402; Gavil, Thinking outside the Illinois Brick box (fn 152) 184.
213 S Calkins, 'An Enforcement Official's Reflections on Antitrust Class Actions', *Arizona Law Review*, 39 (1997), 413–451, 442–443.
214 *Sherman Act*, 15 USC, 1890.

would.[215] The rejection of indirect purchaser standing in the *Illinois Brick* case has thus been criticised for not protecting consumer interests,[216] especially when the foundation of the US competition law lies in '[t]he effect of 'trusts' on prices of goods paid by consumers [...]'.[217] It has been argued that Congress aimed to benefit all consumers, not just the direct ones.[218] On this basis, the rejection has been regarded as an anomaly; competition law is designed to protect consumers and yet consumers who suffer loss through competition infringements are denied recovery at the federal level.[219] The rejection has also been found against the statutory language of the Clayton Act.[220]

All in all, the EU approach seems to make more sense. In the US, indirect purchasers do not have standing before federal courts but the Antitrust Modernisation Commission report has suggested overruling landmark decisions in order to enable both direct and indirect purchasers to claim damages, and apportioning the award, which would be the initial overcharge (trebled) between them.[221] In accordance with the compensatory principle of actions for damages, the EU not only allows indirect purchasers to bring an action but also provides tools to help them prove their cases and recover their losses by way of the rebuttable presumption. As a result, a consumer who is harmed by purchasing an overcharged product from an intermediary can claim damages for the harm suffered. The following two sections move to a more complicated area, examining deadweight loss and umbrella consumers.

Deadweight loss consumers

In reducing output and raising prices, competition infringements generate a deadweight loss, an economic term referring to inefficiency,[222] ie welfare not produced due to the infringement.[223] Simply put, the infringement prevents the occurrence of some transactions.[224] In this respect, deadweight loss consumers refer to non-purchasers[225] who, in response to a price increase, do not purchase a product or service.[226]

215 Hovenkamp, Antitrust's protected classes (fn 61) 25.
216 WH Page and JE Lopatka, 'Indirect Purchaser Suits and the Consumer Interest', *Antitrust Bulletin*, 48 (2003), 531–570, 534.
217 CA Jones, *Private Enforcement of Antitrust Law in the EU, UK and USA* (Oxford: Oxford University Press, 1999), 180.
218 AD Neale and DG Goyder, *The Antitrust Laws of the United States of America: A Study of Competition Enforced by Law*, 3rd edn (Cambridge: Cambridge University Press, 1980), 427.
219 Page and Lopatka (fn 216) 533.
220 Areeda and others (fn 44) 161–162.
221 AMC report (fn 169) vi.
222 Leslie (fn 52) 521; V Milutinovic, *The 'Right to Damages' under EU Competition Law: from Courage v. Crehan to the White Paper and Beyond* (The Netherlands: Kluwer Law International, 2010), 119.
223 Practical guide (fn 20) para 132, fn 109.
224 Leslie (fn 52) 521.
225 See further Chapter 8.
226 Van Uytsel (fn 49) 80.

These non-purchasers are possible direct purchasers of the defendant(s), but they encounter difficulties in proving and quantifying their damages.[227] The first difficulty concerns the causal link between infringement and harm incurred. These consumers need to establish that the reason that they did not purchase the overcharged product is due to the infringement. They need to show that they would have purchased the product at the competitive price.[228] The second difficulty concerns measuring the individual harm arising from purchases that would have been but were not made.[229] These consumers are harmed by deprivation of the benefits they would otherwise have derived from the product.[230] The quantification of their damages has therefore been found speculative for three reasons.[231] First, it is related to the non-purchaser's valuation of the product they did not purchase due to anticompetitive prices.[232] Secondly, it necessitates proving how many products would have been purchased at the competitive price.[233] This requires estimating the demand curve, which is not fully reliable compared with the overcharge estimation.[234] Thirdly, it is hard to identify the real victims,[235] ie those who would have purchased the product had the price been lower.[236] As a result, it has been submitted that there is '[n]o practical way to measure theoretically accurate damages for the quantity not sold […]'.[237]

Although the existence of deadweight loss is acknowledged by a few courts in the US,[238] the standing of non-purchasers to sue is generally denied[239] and no case awarding damages for deadweight loss has been observed.[240] Similarly, in the EU, deadweight loss appears not to be included in the damage computation in overcharge cases before national courts.[241] On the other hand, the Commission

227 Mackenrodt (fn 41) 182; *ibid* 85.
228 Hovenkamp, Antitrust's protected classes (fn 61) 31.
229 Page, Proving antitrust damages (fn 54) 233.
230 Mackenrodt (fn 41) 182; Van Uytsel (fn 49) 69.
231 Leslie (fn 52) 556.
232 *Ibid* 558.
233 Hovenkamp, Antitrust's protected classes (fn 61) 31; *ibid* 557; P Møllgaard, 'Assessment of Damages in the District Heating Pipe Cartel', in *Cases in European Competition Policy: The Economic Analysis*, ed. by B Lyons (Cambridge: Cambridge University Press, 2009), 159–176, 164, fn 9.
234 Brander and Ross (fn 195) 340–341.
235 Jones, Private enforcement (fn 217) 180.
236 Leslie (fn 52) 559.
237 Page, Proving antitrust damages (fn 54) 235.
238 Leslie (fn 52) 527.
239 H Hovenkamp, 'Quantification of Harm in Private Antitrust Actions in the United States', *University of Iowa Legal Studies Research Paper*, 2011, 1–10, 4 <http://dx.doi.org/10.2139/ssrn.1758751> [accessed 1 July 2018]. Similarly, Welfare impact report (fn 83) 79.
240 JM Connor and RH Lande, 'How High Do Cartels Raise Prices? Implications for Reform of the Antitrust Sentencing Guidelines', *Tulane Law Review*, 80 (2005), 513–569, 517; Calvani (fn 49) 277; JP Davis and RH Lande, 'Defying Conventional Wisdom: The Case for Private Antitrust Enforcement', *Georgia Law Review*, 48(1) (2013), 1–82, 35, fn 154.
241 See eg a Danish cartel case and a French mobile phone cartel case, respectively, in Møllgaard (fn 233) 164, 168; Oxera (fn 20) 27, fn 49.

sees their standing to sue possible on the basis of *Courage* and *Manfredi* decisions, though applicable legal rules determine what portion of such harm should be compensated.[242] The Commission, however, submits that the success of their claims hinges on proof of a causal link.[243] Considering that proving causation, quantifying damages and identifying those harmed is difficult, it is unlikely that non-purchasers can bring (successful) damages actions.

Umbrella consumers

There is another group of consumers who suffer overcharge by means of buying the substitute product from non-infringing sellers.[244] They are called umbrella consumers. Competition infringements that cause an increase in prices can create a price umbrella in the relevant product market, upon which basis the non-infringing sellers are also able to raise product prices.[245] By the same token, the demand to the products of non-infringing sellers increases because of the anticompetitive effects of the infringement, ie lower output and unlawful overcharge.[246]

Consumers who make purchases from non-infringing sellers can thus be harmed by the infringement[247] and can claim damages from the infringers.[248] They cannot sue the non-infringing sellers because these sellers have raised their prices due to umbrella effects of infringements not because they have formed a collusion or have abused their dominance.[249] In other words, the reason that these sellers increase their prices is not that they infringe competition rules. Therefore, these sellers cannot be subject to a competition case.

That said, it has been argued that the recovery of umbrella damages is unfair and speculative. Unfair because wealth transfer occurs from purchasers to the non-infringing sellers, not to the infringers who do not profit by the purchases of umbrella consumers.[250] It has been found speculative in terms of the measure of the harm[251] and causation.[252] First, umbrella consumers are connected to the infringement remotely;[253] their damages do not stem from buying the product

242 Draft guidance paper (fn 36) para 114; Practical guide (fn 20) para 133.
243 Welfare impact report (fn 83) 79.
244 Mackenrodt (fn 41) 181.
245 K Kirwan, 'Debunking the "Umbrella Theory" of Antitrust Standing', 2012, 1–3, 1–2 <http://www.lexology.com/library/detail.aspx?g=47c9ad69-0334-4b02-a4bc-6f89746a5c71> [accessed 1 July 2018].
246 R Inderst, F Maier-Rigaud and U Schwalbe, 'Umbrella Effects', *IESEG School of Management Working Paper no 2013-ECO-17*, 2013, 1–22, 2 <http://www.ieseg.fr/wp-content/uploads/2013-ECO-17_Maier-Rigaud.pdf> [accessed 1 July 2018].
247 WH Page, 'The Scope of Liability for Antitrust Violations', *Stanford Law Review*, 37 (6) (1985), 1445–1512, 1465.
248 Hovenkamp, Federal antitrust policy (fn 63) 683.
249 Mackenrodt (fn 41) 182; Van Uytsel (fn 49) 85.
250 Areeda and others (fn 44) 200.
251 Hovenkamp, Federal antitrust policy (fn 63) 683–684; Kirwan (fn 245) 2.
252 Areeda and others (fn 44) 200.
253 Mackenrodt (fn 41) 181.

from the infringer(s) or intermediate sellers. Secondly, there are many reasons that affect a company's decision to increase price.[254] In order for umbrella claims to be dealt with under competition law, it needs to be demonstrated that these sellers have increased their prices due to the infringement and not for any other economic reason.[255] In some circumstances, it may not be possible to identify the substitute products whose prices are affected by the price umbrella created by an overcharged product.[256]

In the US, although the Supreme Court has yet to rule on the issue,[257] umbrella purchasers are denied recovery due to the problems associated with proving harm and causation.[258] On the contrary, in the EU, the Commission argued that umbrella consumers should be able to claim damages.[259] Subsequently, the CJEU in *Kone* rules that umbrella consumers have standing to sue before courts.[260] That judgment provides answers to the above points, except that argument relating to difficulties in determining substitutes.

It was first acknowledged that one of the possible consequences of a cartel is that it raises the price umbrella on an overcharged product, in turn enabling the non-infringing sellers to increase their prices.[261] It is only natural that the non-infringing sellers observe the market price when determining their own prices.[262] With respect to the causation, the Court points out that so long as it is established that the particular characteristics of the relevant market and of the conduct in question suggest the unlawful overcharge results in umbrella effects and that the infringer(s) could not ignore those characteristics, infringers would be liable for umbrella damages.[263] The Court also submits that there is no requirement that the amount of loss subject to compensation corresponds to the profit obtained by the infringer(s).[264] It is not important that the purchases of umbrella consumers are not the gains of the defendant(s), consumers can claim compensation for the harm incurred so long as it is demonstrated that the defendant's anticompetitive behaviour caused that harm.[265]

254 Areeda and others (fn 44) 200.
255 JM Lave, 'Umbrella Standing: The Trade-off between Plaintiff Suit and Speculative Claims', *Antitrust Bulletin*, 48 (2003), 223–269, 228, fn 18; *ibid*; Mackenrodt (fn 41) 181.
256 Areeda and others (fn 44) 200–201; Hovenkamp, Federal antitrust policy (fn 63) 684.
257 See Circuit and District court decisions on umbrella damages, Lave (fn 255) 234.
258 RH Lande, 'Are Antitrust "Treble" Damages Really Single Damages?', *Ohio State Law Journal*, 54 (1993), 115–174, 147; *ibid*. See it has been stated that these damages are never or virtually never recovered, Connor and Lande (fn 240) 518.
259 Draft guidance paper (fn 36) para 114; Practical guide (fn 20) para 133.
260 Case C-557/12 *Kone AG and Others v ÖBB-Infrastruktur AG* [2014] EU:C:2014:1317, para 32.
261 *Ibid* paras 28–29.
262 *Ibid* paras 29.
263 *Ibid* para 34. See it has been argued that by saying so the court established a rebuttable presumption of causation, M Veenbrink and CS Rusu, 'Case Comment – Case C-557/12 *Kone AG and Others v ÖBB Infrastruktur AG*', *Competition Law Review*, 10(1) (2014), 107–115, 108.
264 *Kone* (fn 260) para 35.
265 Opinion of AG Kokott delivered on 30 January 2014 in *Kone*, paras 76, 78.

The final point concerns how to define the market and identify the substitute products in order to trace the effect of unlawful overcharge on the prices of substitutes with adequate accuracy.[266] For instance, one can argue that it is difficult to show to what extent the price of a bottle of sparkling water increased by a cartel would affect the prices of other soft drinks.[267] In *Kone*, however, this was not a problem because the defendants formed a cartel to divide the elevator and escalator market,[268] and the umbrella customer claimed to be harmed by the cartel by having to purchase elevators and escalators from non-infringing sellers at an artificially higher price.[269] In light of this, it has been suggested that umbrella consumers should be able to claim damages if they purchase '[t]he self-same product the defendants sold in the same clearly defined geographical market'.[270]

In consequence of *Kone*, the *a priori* exclusion of the right to claim damages of umbrella consumers is not possible. The reason they pay overcharges is the infringement that gives rise to higher prices. Hence, these consumers have standing to sue before courts and obtain damages so long as they can prove causation and damages. Although not free of proof problems, umbrella damages can be recovered in the EU.

Concluding remarks

This chapter demonstrated both the characteristics of damages claims of consumers and the way in which they are affected by competition infringements in order to submit that the characteristics of consumer claims fit the purpose of collective redress action and also use them in the collective redress formulation in the following three chapters.

Competition infringements, if they adversely affect the situation of claimants, give rise to a claim for damages. In this respect, not only horizontal and vertical agreements but also abusive exclusionary and exploitative conduct of dominant undertaking can cause harm to claimants and be subject to damages actions. These infringements cause losses in the form of overcharge, loss of profits, reduction in quality, choice and innovation. However, competition litigation generally focuses on damages for overcharges and loss of profits, as it is difficult to prove and quantify loss of quality, choice and innovation.

Different groups of injured parties may suffer either or both of these damages. Competitors only incur loss of profits and their losses are almost always direct and large. Intermediaries, on the other hand, can incur both overcharge and loss of profits. If they pass the overcharge partially or entirely on to their customers in the form of higher prices, they might experience fewer sales and therefore suffer loss of profits as well as overcharge harm for that part they absorbed. If they absorb the

266 Areeda and others (fn 44) 201.
267 Ibid.
268 *Kone* (fn 260) para 5.
269 *Ibid* para 10.
270 Areeda and others (fn 44) 201.

whole overcharge, they do not incur loss of profits but only the overcharge harm. In this respect, their losses tend to be different from each other. The amount of overcharge at each layer of the distribution chain is likely to vary. Even if subject to the same amount of overcharge at the same level, firms still individually choose how much overcharge they absorb or transfer, considering the conditions of their own businesses, such as the extent to which they would expect a drop in sales if they passed on the entire overcharge to their customers. Lastly, the amount of overcharge passed on and the unique environment within which each business operates affects the measure of lost profits they experience.

Consumers can only suffer overcharge harm by purchasing the product in question at an anticompetitive price. The group of consumers affected by an infringement would be large due to the number of persons at the consumer level. These only purchase the product for personal use and have no choice but to absorb the consumer level overcharge. Their losses therefore tend to be similar and smaller than that of businesses. These are the characteristics of consumer damages claims that fit the purpose of a collective redress action; furthermore these characteristics are those that signal the need for such an action. Both horizontal and vertical agreements and exclusionary and exploitative abuses can lead to overcharge.

The typical plaintiffs in vertical restraint cases seem to be upstream and downstream competitors. However, consumers might be expected to bring actions for damages against cartels. Moreover, exploitative abuses directly harm consumers, although there have been few exploitative abuse cases decided to date, where exclusionary abuses create damages directly to competitors and, after the successful foreclosure of competitors from the market, may create damages to consumers. The link between an exclusionary abuse and damages suffered by consumers is indirect, which might make it difficult to establish harm and a causal relationship. This does not suggest that consumers who are affected by vertical restraints or abusive conducts do not benefit from a collective action. These cases may not be as numerous as those against cartels, but a collective redress action would also assist these consumers in claiming their overcharge damages.

Finally, consumers are affected by competition infringements in different ways. This analysis has presented different groups of consumers harmed by infringements which will aid determination of whether their claims can be grouped for pursuit in a collective action, addressed in the following chapter. Direct consumers, who purchase the overcharged product from the defendant(s), are entitled to the entire overcharge. Indirect consumers, on the other hand, purchase the product from intermediaries who resell an overcharged product or use it in a product sold to their own customers. If intermediaries have passed the entire or a part of the overcharge along, indirect consumers are entitled to the consumer level overcharge; this might be either the initial overcharge or part of the initial overcharge passed on to them. The indirect link between their damages and an infringement raises the question of their standing to sue before courts. When deciding whether to allow them to sue, consideration was given to whether it is possible to quantify and prove indirect purchaser losses and whether the compensation or deterrence objective is favoured. The results entail different policy choices.

Indeed, the EU and the US have different policies with respect to indirect purchasers. Where a grant of standing has been suggested in the US, the EU has almost always favoured indirect standing. In order to assist indirect purchasers in obtaining damages, the recent Directive, following in the footsteps of the White Paper, suggests a rebuttable presumption in their favour. In addition to direct and indirect consumers, a further group is harmed by competition infringements through not purchasing an overcharged product. If they can prove a causal link between infringement and their decision not to purchase, the Commission sees their standing possible due to the case law on actions for damages. However, it should be noted that proving causation, quantifying damages and identifying those harmed still do not seem to lead to (successful) damages actions. The final group are umbrella consumers who purchase the substitute product from sellers other than infringer(s). These sellers are able to raise prices as a result of the price umbrella created by the infringement. After the CJEU's *Kone* decision, there is no question that these consumers can bring their damages claims before national courts. Bearing this in mind, the next chapter will begin formulating the collective redress action to address consumer damages claims.

6 Grouping collective claims

Opt-in *v* opt-out

Introduction

The analysis so far has justified that there is a genuine need to facilitate consumer claims and that the purpose and practical functioning of collective redress actions are suited to address consumer damages claims and that a collective redress action should aim to advance the primary objective of compensation. In this regard, the present chapter starts to formulate a collective redress action for consumer damages claims in competition cases, benefiting from the US experience. The second section of the chapter deals with establishing group membership. There are three systems for composing a represented group: opt-in, mandatory and opt-out. Each system is assessed with regard to their ability to provide compensation to consumers to the greatest extent possible and to make the pursuit of their claims in court a reality in practice. In addition to this assessment, the section explains the UK's new collective redress regime and extensively discusses the class action procedure in the US before concluding that opt-out actions are better in providing redress to a large group of similarly suited persons. However, the section also draws attention to the fact that the political environment in the EU ought to be considered when suggesting a system for collective redress.

The third section of the chapter deals with the ways in which a group is described for collective redress purposes. The questions of who is part of the represented group and how that group is formed determine the extent to which their damages claims are suitable to be dealt with in a single proceeding for compensation and the practical functioning of the action. This chapter therefore demonstrates that consumer damage claims are best suited to be grouped together for collective redress purposes.

Establishing the group membership

Opt-in actions

An opt-in action necessitates clear identification of the group members. Claimants must explicitly state their wish to be included in the group during a specified timeframe. According to the European Parliament, this identification stage should take place before the claim is brought, but joining in the action should be possible until the commencement of the litigation.[1] Occasionally this is allowed later,[2] for instance individuals participate in the action after the group certification stage,[3] the Recommendation suggests that the claimants should join in the action or leave the action at any time before the judgment is delivered.[4] This is reasonable as the opt-in action preserves the litigant autonomy principle; claimants decide whether to participate in the action and be bound by the judgment.[5] Claimants have thus control over litigation. To this end, some opt-in systems make the group members party to the litigation and divert from representation.[6] As a result, an opt-in action has been found to be easily fit within the legal systems of Member States,[7] with a modest change of rules,[8] because it respects the right of access to the courts[9] and it is similar to traditional two-party litigation.[10]

Indeed, an opt-in action has been regarded as an expansion to the joinder of parties[11] because, upon notification, each claimant must file a consent to the court to be included in the action, accompanied in some systems by the relevant

1 European Parliament, ECON, *Draft Report on the White Paper on Damages Actions for Breach of the EC Antitrust Rules*, (2008/2154(INI), 2008), paras 7–8 <http://www.europarl.europa.eu/sides/getDoc.do?pubRef=-//EP//NONSGML+COMPARL+PE-412.315+01+DOC+PDF+V0//EN&language=EN> [accessed 1 July 2018].

2 Commission, *Towards a Coherent European Approach to Collective Redress: Next Steps – Joint Information Note by Vice-President Viviane Reding, Vice-President Joaquín Almunia and Commissioner John Dalli* (SEC(2010) 1192 OJ 1932, Brussels, 2010), (Joint information note) para 9 <http://kartellblog.de/wordpress/wp-content/uploads/Kommission-2010-information-Towards-European-Collective-Redress> [accessed 1 July 2018].

3 It is the case in Poland. M Tulibacka, 'Poland', *Focus on Collective Redress,* para 3(b) <http://www.collectiveredress.org/collective-redress/reports/poland/generalcollectiveredressmechanisms> [accessed 1 July 2018].

4 Commission, *Recommendation on Common Principles for Injunctive and Compensatory Collective Redress Mechanisms in the Member States Concerning Violations of Rights Granted Under Union Law* (Strasbourg, C(2013) 3539/3, 2013), para V/23.

5 LS Mullenix, 'Competing Values: Preserving Litigant Autonomy in an Age of Collective Redress', *University of Texas, Public Law and Legal Theory Research Paper Series no 533*, 2014, 1–34, 28 <http://papers.ssrn.com/sol3/papers.cfm?abstract_id=2426829> [accessed 1 July 2018].

6 See Chapter 1.

7 Commission, *Staff Working Paper Accompanying the White Paper on Damages Actions for Breach of the EC Antitrust Rules* (SEC(2008) 404, Brussels, 2008), para 58.

8 G Wagner, 'Collective Redress – Categories of Loss and Legislative Options', *Law Quarterly Review*, 127 (2011), 55–82, 77.

9 C Leskinen, 'Collective Antitrust Damages Actions in the EU: The Opt-in v. the Opt-out Model', *IE Law School Working Paper no 10–03*, 2010, 1–56, 26 <http://papers.ssrn.com/sol3/papers.cfm?abstract_id=1612731> [accessed 1 July 2018]. See *infra* section 3.3.2.

10 SWPWP (fn 7) para 58.

11 M Hviid and S Peyer, 'Response to EC Consultation "Towards a Coherent European Approach to Collective Redress"', 2011, 1–7, 5 <http://ec.europa.eu/competition/consultations/2011_collective_redress/hviid_peyer_en.pdf> [accessed 1 July 2018].

evidence.[12] In this way, members and their alleged harm are identified.[13] As the Commission states, this renders the litigation complex as the defendant can challenge the claim of each group member.[14] Dealing with numerous claims in a lawsuit remains difficult for courts, which can undermine the utility of collective actions.[15] Therefore, in addressing the grievances of a large group opt-in actions would be neither practical nor feasible.

In the event of a large group, the way in which an opt-in action operates has its drawbacks for the representative party who must identify and contact each member to take their individual consents[16] and who therefore might be unwilling to commit to the effort, or be unable to do so. For instance, in the UK opt-in representative actions for competition infringements under the former section 47B of the Competition Act 1998, all group members had to be identified at the time the representative action was brought.[17] In order to make a damages claim, the representative party, ie the consumer association, had to submit a claim form contains each consumer's name,[18] supplemented by each consumer's consent to the action.[19] The amount claimed in damages on the claim form must also be specified, showing the evidence and calculations leading to this amount.[20] Following the first and only representative action in the UK, the consumers' association declared that they would not be filing another action under an opt-in basis due to the unnecessary costs and complexity involved.[21]

Despite the control an opt-in action gives consumers over litigation, they might not find it appealing enough to join the group due to *i.* the need to consent to the action before knowing the outcome,[22] especially where they are unfamiliar with the procedure and have small damages,[23] and *ii.* the fear of incurring responsibility for costs and risks associated with the litigation[24] where their names are known, generally, since the commencement of the action. In fact, the participation rate of opt-in actions is, although variable, less than 1% in cases brought on behalf of

12 SE Keske, *Group Litigation in European Competition Law: A Law and Economics Perspective* (Antwerp-Oxford-Portland: Intersentia, 2010), 44.
13 SWPWP (fn 7) para 58.
14 *Ibid.*
15 See Chapter 2.
16 O Dayagi-Epstein, 'Representation of Consumer Interest by Consumer Associations – Salvation for the Masses?', *Competition Law Review*, 3(2) (2006), 209–249, 219.
17 Joint information note (fn 2) para 9.
18 The Competition Appeal Tribunal (CAT), *Guide to Proceedings*, 2005, para 6.77.
19 CAT, *Competition Appeal Tribunal Rules,* no 1372, 2003, rule 33(1)(c); *ibid.*
20 CAT, Guide to proceedings (fn 18) para 6.78.
21 BIS, *Private Actions in Competition Law: A Consultation on Options for Reform – Final Impact Assessment* (London, 2013), para 155.
22 BIS, *Private Actions in Competition Law: A Consultation on Options for Reform – Impact Assessment* (London, 2012), para 176.
23 *Phillips Petroleum Co. v Shutts*, 472 US 797 (1985) para 813.
24 See R Mulheron, *Reform of Collective Redress in England and Wales: A Perspective of Need* (CJC, 2008), 1–161, 34 <https://www.judiciary.gov.uk/wp-content/uploads/JCO/Documents/CJC/Publications/Other+papers/reform-of-collective-redress.pdf> [accessed 1 July 2018].

consumers.[25] For instance, a French telecom case brought by the consumer association against a cartel achieved 0.06% opt-in participation rate – 12,350 out of 20 million consumers – for the recovery of €60.[26] In the UK *JJB sports* case[27] only 130 out of 2 million consumers opted in to the representative damages action against a price-fixing cartel to obtain up to £20 damages.[28]

This limited participation reveals the inadequacy of opt-in actions in delivering redress to a large number of consumers. When the loss at stake is not perceived as worth the time and effort of joining, the number of opt-ins remains very low.[29] For instance, businesses with a significant amount of loss would opt in to an action.[30] However, the fact that consumers do not elect to join in the action does not mean that they pursue individual litigation.[31] This means they would go uncompensated by an opt-in action as well. Since the action only benefits a small number of victims it also lessens the incentive for a representative party to bring a collective action.[32] Moreover, an opt-in action becomes non-economic when comparing litigation costs to the potential recovery of a small group.[33]

The way in which an opt-in action functions, the need for individual consent to the action and how these work to affect the court process when dealing with the claims of group members make an opt-in action less equipped to provide resolution to numerous claims. However, it appears that an opt-in action would work

25 Regarding Europe only, European Consumer Consultative Group (ECCG), *Opinion on Private Damages Actions,* 2010, para 2.6 <http://ec.europa.eu/dgs/health_consumer/dgs_consultations/docs/eccg/eccg_opinion_on_actions_for_damages_18112010_en.pdf> [accessed 1 July 2018]. Mulheron finds the same for opt-in actions on behalf of victims in the US, Europe and England, *ibid* ix.

26 Directorate-General for Internal Policies, *Collective Redress in Antitrust* (IP/A/Econ/ST/2011–19, 2012), 36. The procedure requires consumers to give mandates to the consumer association, BEUC, *Group Action: The Missing Tool* (Brussels, 2008), 1–26, 5 <http://ec.europa.eu/consumers/archive/redress_cons/responses/BEUC_en.pdf> [accessed 1 July 2018].

27 *The Consumers Association v JJB Sports PLC* [2007] (CAT Case no 1078/7/9/07).

28 Leskinen (fn 9) 10. Hodges states the opt-in rate is 0.3%. C Hodges, 'From Class Actions to Collective Redress: A Revolution in Approach to Compensation', *Civil Justice Quarterly*, 28(1) (2009), 41–66, 49, fn 33. Rodger states that there are only 144 opt-ins, see BJ Rodger, 'United Kingdom: A Licence to Print (Monopoly) Money? Replica Football Kit and Toys and Games, Resale Price Maintenance and the Competition Act 1998', in *Landmark Cases in Competition Law: Around the World in Fourteen Stories*, ed. by BJ Rodger (The Netherlands: Kluwer Law International, 2013), 319–343, 340.

29 B Wardhaugh, 'Bogeymen, Lunatics and Fanatics: Collective Actions and the Private Enforcement of European Competition Law', *Legal Studies*, 34(1) (2014), 1–23, 22.

30 R Becker, N Bessot and E De Smijter, 'The White Paper on Damages Actions for Breach of the EC Antitrust Rules', *Competition Policy Newsletter*, 2 (2008), 4–11, 4.

31 See the very few number of actions brought by consumers in Chapter 2.

32 T Chieu, 'Class Actions in the European Union?: Importing Lessons Learned From the United States' Experience into European Community Competition Law', *Cardozo Journal of International and Comparative Law*, 18 (2010), 123–157, 150.

33 CA Jones, 'Foreword – Opting-in to Opting-out: Why Collective Redress in Europe Should Adopt the Opt-out Approach to Class Actions', *Concurrences Journal*, 2 (2012), 1–3, 2.

where there is a small group of harmed individuals who can be easily identified and whose losses are of high value.

Mandatory actions

One form of composing a group for collective redress purposes is mandatory membership. The court initiates the action on behalf of all harmed individuals and does not give them the right to exit the group.[34] It has hence been argued that a mandatory action achieves greater procedural efficiencies in solving the dispute for all victims.[35] No individual case can be brought on the same issues after the collective action and there is no need to endure the costs of notifying the group members since they are all automatically part of the group without the right to opt out.[36] It has also been argued that this advances a deterrence objective because a defendant would become liable for the entire loss it caused.[37]

However, in practice an opt-out action is almost no different from a mandatory action when it is brought on behalf of consumers.[38] When the represented group consists of consumers, as low opt-out rates shows, a great majority remain in the action.[39] Under these circumstances, it seems difficult to justify why victims need to be prevented from opting out and therefore to choose not to be bound by the judgment to achieve the same effects.

Opt-out actions

The functioning of opt-out actions

In an opt-out action, a group consists of identifiable rather than individually identified persons.[40] Group members do not need to take any active steps to be part of the action unless they wish to opt out and they are not parties to the case before the court. Since they are not parties to the action, no counterclaims can be asserted against group members and they are not exposed to the discovery in the same manner as a party.[41] In order to commence the action, only the proposed group on whose behalf the case is filed needs to be defined by the representative

34 D Rosenberg, 'Class Actions for Mass Torts: Doing Individual Justice by Collective Means', *Indiana Law Journal*, 62(3) (1987), 561–596, 570.
35 *Ibid.*
36 See Keske (fn 12) 82.
37 *Ibid* 80–81.
38 Except the notification requirement, see *infra* section 'Take-up rates'.
39 See *infra* section 'Participation rates'.
40 CAT, *Collective Proceedings and Collective Settlements in the Competition Appeal Tribunal: Draft Tribunal Rules*, 2014, para 7(1); M Fischer, 'Class Definition', in *A Practitioner's Guide to Class Actions*, ed. by M Greer (USA: American Bar Association, 2011), 47–56, 47.
41 RH Dreyfuss, 'Class Action Judgment Enforcement in Italy: Procedural Due Process Requirements', *Tulane Journal of International and Comparative Law*, 10 (2002), 5–36, 12.

party.[42] The US regime requires specifying neither the exact persons nor the precise number.[43] The UK has recently adopted a new collective redress action, making opt-out actions available.[44] The UK's new regime requires only the representative party to submit a claim form that contains, *inter alia,* the group definition, the estimated number of group members and the relief sought.[45] Hence, the time, resources and costs expended on bringing an opt-out action tend to be less than those in an opt-in action.[46]

Moreover, as the group automatically comprises all affected consumers who satisfy the group definition, the group is formed more quickly[47] and likely to be larger in number than an opt-in action and therefore the total value of damages is correspondingly larger.[48] The greater group size in opt-out actions is attributed to the fact that group members have an incentive to stay in the group[49] because they do not need to do anything to enjoy the judgment at the end of the trial.[50] These passive group members are bound nonetheless by the results of a lawsuit that prevents them from re-litigating the adjudicated issues.[51] This, a lack of explicit consent to be part of the represented group and the fact that the members are not parties to the litigation are reasons that opt-out actions have been found to counteract the right of access to the courts,[52] which is why the role of notice needs to be discussed and the nature of the collective redress action revisited.

The role of notice

The right of access to the courts, which is also called the litigant autonomy principle or adversary principle in the EU,[53] broadly, requires structuring proceedings

42 FRCP 23(c)(1)(B); CAT, *Competition Appeal Tribunal Rules,* no 1648, 2015 (CAT rules) para 75(3).
43 RL Marcus and EF Sherman, *Complex Litigation: Cases and Materials on Advanced Civil Procedure,* 1st edn (St. Paul, Minnesota: West, 1985) 243.
44 *Consumer Rights* Act 2015 (c.15), 2015, sch 8, sec 47B(11).
45 CAT rules (fn 42) para 75(3).
46 Mulheron, Reform of collective redress (fn 24) 31.
47 C Bernard and S Bourjade, 'Economic Incentives in Class Actions: An Analysis through the US/EU Examples', *Global Competition Litigation Review,* 6(1) (2013), 12–17, 13.
48 TL Russell, 'Exporting Class Actions to the European Union', *Boston University International Law Journal,* 28 (2010), 141–180, 160; Jones, Foreword (fn 33) 1–2.
49 See *infra* section 'Participation rates'.
50 *Phillips Petroleum* (fn 23) para 810.
51 Dreyfuss (fn 41) 12.
52 Mullenix (fn 5) 28. See the argument that opt-out actions could be contrary to the right to a fair trial in the context of European Convention on Human Rights (ECHR) art. 6, R Nazzini and A Nikpay, 'Private Actions in EC Competition Law', Competition Policy International, 4(2) (2008), 107–141, 124; ZS Tang, 'Consumer Collective Redress in European Private International Law', *Journal of Private International Law,* 7(1) (2011), 101–147, 138.
53 Mullenix (fn 5) 28. In the US, it is due process rule, SC Yeazell, *From Medieval Group Litigation to the Modern Class Action* (New Haven and London: Yale University Press, 1987), 13.

to provide a real opportunity for the parties to involve and advocate their respective positions.[54] By assuring the active participation of the parties in the litigation, this right grants them the power to influence the outcome of a case whose consequences they bear.[55]

Group members in opt-out actions do not *i.* pick their representatives, *ii.* describe the group, *iii.* manage the case, *iv.* take the necessary decisions for the resolution of the dispute or *v.* settle the action. Instead, their representative performs these on their behalf.[56]

On this basis, it has been argued that an opt-out action runs counter to the right of access to the courts,[57] raising constitutional[58] and human rights concerns.[59] An opt-out action has been found at odds with the European tradition for undermining the individual control over litigation.[60] The Communication states that opt-out actions should be avoided in the EU because it neither acknowledges individuals' right to decide whether to sue or join the action, nor respects the party autonomy[61] and because the judgment in an opt-out action binds persons who are not identified,[62] although previously mentioned, the White Paper and the withdrawn Directive were not against the idea of a representative party bringing a case on behalf of identifiable persons.[63]

As it is based on representation, a collective redress action is different from traditional litigation[64] and group members are not parties to the action but rather are represented.[65] With respect to concerns for human rights, it is seen in the case law of the European Court of Human Rights (ECtHR) that the Court acknowledges representation where similarly situated persons are bound by the outcome even if they do not actively participate in the action. Two examples can be given in due

54 Dreyfuss (fn 41) 19.
55 *Ibid.*
56 AD Lahav, 'Fundamental Principles for Class Action Governance', *Indiana Law Review*, 37 (2004), 65–140, 67–68.
57 A Nordh, 'Group Actions – The Swedish Experience' (presented at the Colloque actions collectives Cour de Cassation, France, 2005), 1–14, 2 <http://www.courdecassation.fr/IMG/File/judge_nordh.pdf> [accessed 1 July 2018]; R Van den Bergh, 'Private Enforcement of European Competition Law and the Persisting Collective Action Problem', *Maastricht Journal*, 1 (2013), 12–34, 21.
58 Opt-out actions are found unconstitutional by some Member States. Commission, *Communication from the Commission to the European Parliament, the Council, the European Economic and Social Committee and the Committee of the Regions 'Towards a European Horizontal Framework for Collective Redress'* (COM(2013) 401/2, Brussels, 2013), para 3.4.
59 Tang (fn 52) 138; GE Kodek, 'Class Actions – Some Reflections from a European Perspective', in *Collective Redress in Europe – Why and How?*, ed. by E Lein and others (London: The British Institute of International and Comparative Law, 2015), 117–132, 125.
60 Wardhaugh (fn 29) 3.
61 Communication (fn 58) para 3.4.
62 *Ibid.*
63 See Chapter 3.
64 See further Chapter 2.
65 *Hansberry v Lee*, 311 US 32 (1940) para 41.

respect. In the first case, the applicant asserted that, as the representative had no obligation to obtain the represented parties' consent to agree to compensation in negotiations or to refer it to arbitration,[66] his right to court in the determination of compensation was infringed.[67] The ECtHR considered the representation necessary to render negotiations and arbitration workable for handling a multiplicity of individual claims.[68] Despite accepting that individual access was barred, the Court found no violation given the specific circumstances of the case and submitted that the applicant's interest was safeguarded by the representative.[69] A second case was brought by several lawyers who claimed that their property and due process rights had been impaired because the German constitutional court where before they were not parties to the litigation had abolished exclusive rights of audience in higher courts.[70] The ECtHR held that although they were prevented from individually appearing before the court, no violation had occurred because the German court heard the associations that defend the interests of the lawyers on the matter and '[i]n proceedings involving a decision for a collective number of individuals, it is not always required or even possible that every individual concerned is heard before the court'.[71]

In theory, a collective redress action, designed on any membership system, departs from individual control over the litigation.[72] In an opt-out action, this makes it possible to process the claims of a large group of individuals and deliver compensation,[73] ie practical realities.[74] This enables consumers to pursue damages claims that would otherwise almost never be brought. However, members should receive adequate information about the proceedings, be given a chance to take part, to be heard in the action[75] and to exit.[76] An opt-out action becomes compatible with the right of access to the courts if a notice is issued to provide members a realistic opportunity to use these rights.[77]

The opt-out regimes of the Netherlands and Norway in fact overcome this problem by adopting notice requirements.[78] The new UK opt-out regime also requires a notice to be issued in clear language to explain the case and rights of

66 *Lithgow and others v The United Kingdom,* (App no 9006/80; 9262/81; 9263/81; 9265/81; 9266/81; 9313/81; 9405/81) (ECtHR, 1986) para 28.
67 *Ibid* para 193.
68 *Ibid* para 28.
69 *Ibid* para 196.
70 *Wendenburg and others v Germany,* (App no 71630/01) (ECtHR, 2003), 2.
71 *Ibid* 28.
72 Leskinen (fn 9) 45.
73 See A Homburger, 'Private Suits in the Public Interest in the United States of America', *Buffalo Law Review*, 23 (1974), 343–410, 362.
74 D Marcus, 'Attorneys' Fees and the Social Legitimacy of Class Actions', *University of Pennsylvania PeNNumbra*, 159 (2010), 157–166, 166.
75 Yeazell (fn 53) 13.
76 GC Lilly, 'Modeling Class Actions: The Representative Suit as an Analytic Tool', *Nebraska Law Review*, 81 (2003), 1008–1055, 1034.
77 Leskinen (fn 9) 45.
78 *Ibid* 43.

members.[79] The Recommendation asks Member States to ensure the representative party disseminates information about the alleged infringement and their intention to bring a collective action for damages.[80]

In the US, a notice is mandatory for class actions seeking damages,[81] and must be given when the action is certified or a settlement is provisionally approved.[82] Although a notice is sent at the time of the certification, the court can call for another notice after approving the settlement, which is called 'super opt-out rights'.[83] Any amendment of the certification of the action may require the issuance of another notice[84] and the court has the power to direct notification before certification or at any time in the action it finds necessary in order to safeguard the interests of the members.[85] The notice aims to inform members of the existence and scope of the action, of the extent to which it will affect their rights, of the relief sought and of the means by which they can preserve those rights or exclude themselves.[86] The notice must therefore be concise and easy to understand.[87] Upon notice, members can participate in the litigation and monitor the performance of the representative and lawyer.[88] In case of the settlement, upon the issue of notice members can object to this settlement, exit the group or attend the settlement hearing.[89]

Additionally, the notice ought to seek to reach all group members. If members can be identified individually through public records, defendants' records or any other accessible source, personal notices should be issued.[90] To supplement or substitute personal notices, alternative methods can be used,[91] such as setting up a dedicated website on which to post notices and all necessary and follow-up information. A website is inexpensive and tends to reach more members due to

79 CAT rules (fn 42) para 81.
80 Recommendation (fn 4) para III/10.
81 FRCP 23(c)(2)(B).
82 FRCP 23(e)(2); T Eisenberg and GP Miller, 'The Role of Opt-Outs and Objectors in Class Action Litigation: Theoretical and Empirical Issues', *Vanderbilt Law Review*, 57 (2004), 1529–1567, 1535.
83 *Ibid.*
84 B Anderson and A Trask, *The Class Action Playbook* (Oxford: Oxford University Press, 2010), 177.
85 FRCP 23(d)(B).
86 Federal Judicial Center, '*Manual for Complex Litigation* (fourth)' (2004), (MCL) 289 <http://www.fjc.gov/public/pdf.nsf/lookup/MCL40000.pdf/$file/MCL40000.pdf> [accessed 1 July 2018]; Anderson and Trask (fn 84) 177. See also FRCP 23(c)(2)(B).
87 FRCP 23(c)(2)(B). See further Federal Judicial Center, 'Judges' Class Action Notice and Claims Process Check List and Plain Language Guide', (2010), 1–10 <http://www.fjc.gov/public/pdf.nsf/lookup/NotCheck.pdf/$file/NotCheck.pdf> [accessed 1 July 2018].
88 MCL (fn 86) 285.
89 *Ibid* 294.
90 R Mulheron, *The Class Action in Common Law Legal Systems: A Comparative Perspective* (Oxford and Portland, Oregon: Hart Publishing, 2004), 348.
91 MCL (fn 86) 287.

extensive internet use.[92] The notice may also be placed on the Commission's website. The Commission effectively uses its website to inform consumers of their rights and of ongoing studies or new developments. It also maintains a dedicated page on the relationship between competition law and consumers which explains the importance and functioning of competition law.[93]

Notices can also be published in newspapers, magazines or journals[94] or advertised on local television,[95] placed in public areas that members are likely to see[96] or circulated via the defendant's mailing.[97] The Recommendation also provides for Member States to set up national online registries for collective actions that should be accessible free of charge by interested persons to publish all the necessary information on the available means of obtaining compensation.[98] Member States and the Commission are going to be responsible for the interoperability of those registries.[99] These national registries can also be considered means by which to inform group members.[100]

However, even when a notice is issued, some criticism persists in relation to member inaction.[101] It has been argued that inaction is a common response that can be attributed to '[n]ot receiving the [n]otice, receiving but not understanding [it], setting the notice aside and losing it, completing but then forgetting to mail, and [l]aziness, procrastination, [c]onfusion and lack of comprehension'.[102] Particularly in consumer cases, if the loss at stake is small, the rights stated in the notice may not be found worth exercising.[103]

92 *Ibid.* See the other benefits of using internet for notices, B Walters, '"Best Notice Practicable" in the Twenty-First Century', *UCLA Journal of Law and Technology*, 7 (1) (2003), 1–28.

93 Commission, 'Competition: Delivering for Consumers' <http://ec.europa.eu/competition/consumers/index_en.html> [accessed 1 July 2018].

94 MCL (fn 86) 287.

95 DR Hensler and others, *Class Action Dilemmas: Pursuing Public Goals for Private Gain* (Arlington: RAND, 2000), 448.

96 See eg notices were posted in travel agencies, *In re Domestic Air Transportation Antitrust Litigation*, 141 F.R.D. 534 (N.D. Ga. 1992) para 549.

97 MCL (fn 86) 292.

98 Recommendation (fn 4) paras VI/35–37.

99 *Ibid.*

100 However, the Report on the Recommendation found that so far Member States do not follow this principle in their collective action legislation. Commission, *Report from The Commission to The European Parliament, The Council and The European Economic and Social Committee on the Implementation of the Commission Recommendation of 11 June 2013 on Common Principles for Injunctive and Compensatory Collective Redress Mechanisms in the Member States Concerning Violations of Rights Granted under Union Law*, (COM(2018) 40 final, Brussels, 2018) (Report on the Recommendation), 19.

101 DL Basset, 'Just Go Away: Representation, Due Process, and Preclusion in Class Actions', *Brigham Young University Law Review*, 2009(5) (2009), 1079–1126, 1120.

102 DL Basset, 'U.S. Class Actions Go Global: Transnational Class Actions and Personal Jurisdiction', *Fordham Law Review*, 72(1) (2003), 41–92, 86.

103 M Gilles and G Friedman, 'Exploding the Class Action Agency Costs Myth: The Social Utility of Entrepreneurial Lawyers', *University of Pennsylvania Law Review*, 155

According to inertia bias, where a default option is available people are unlikely to take an active step to choose a different option.[104] Hence, inaction applies to opt-in actions as much as to opt-out actions. It is one of the reasons why the ultimate size of the group differs substantially depending on the regime. Upon notice, in an opt-in action, potential members must take affirmative action to be part of the group,[105] and the figures show that, generally, consumers do not. In an opt-out action, consumer group members tend not to act within the specified period of time, perhaps because staying in the action is in their financial interest.[106]

Take-up rates show that, in cases where the group members must come forward to claim their damages, opt-out actions achieve higher rates than opt-in actions.[107] So long as the notice is effective and provides the group members a realistic opportunity to opt out or to be heard, an opt-out action compensates a broader group of claimants without raising concerns over their right of access to the courts. Since, in this case, if they wish they can attend the hearing and if they do not opt out it would be their choice to be bound by the outcome.[108]

The compensation objective and opt-out actions

An opt-out action by nature leads to a large group size. Participation and take-up rates can be considered as the indicators of the extent to which these actions are successful in providing compensation to affected consumers. The participation rates of opt-out actions show the number of members who stayed in the action. Take-up rates relate to how many members assert their right to recovery post-award.[109] The next sections consider the ability of an opt-out action to deliver compensation to consumers.

PARTICIPATION RATES

Participation rates of opt-out actions, where evidence is available, are generally very high, varying from at least 60% to over 99%.[110] In the EU, among the Member States with an opt-out action, the participation rate in the Netherlands is

(2006), 103–164, 132, 134. Similarly, DL Shapiro, 'Class Actions: The Class as Party and Client', *Notre Dame Law Review*, 73(4) (1998), 913–961, 936–937.

104 ELI, 'Statement of the European Law Institute on Collective Redress and Competition Damages Claims', 2014, 1–81, 43 <http://www.europeanlawinstitute.eu/fileadmin/user_upload/p_eli/Projects/S-5-2014_Statement_on_Collective_Redress_and_Competition_Damages_Claims.pdf> [accessed 1 July 2018].

105 Basset, Just go away (fn 101) 1119.

106 Jones, Foreword (fn 33) 2. See further *infra* section 'Participation rates'.

107 See further *infra* section 'Take-up rates'.

108 For the latter argument, Nazzini and Nikpay (fn 52) 124.

109 M Herron, 'The Proposed UK Competition Law Class Action and Treatment of Unclaimed Sums: A Policy and Practical Perspective', *Competition Law Journal*, 2 (2013), 159–170, 168; Mulheron, Reform of collective redress (fn 24) 35.

110 Mulheron (fn 24) 147.

97%[111] and in Portugal, the case *DECO v Portugal Telecom* on behalf of consumers reached almost a 100% participation rate, ie only 5 members opted out of the action.[112] These figures are exponentially higher than participation rates for opt-in actions.[113] It is especially striking that in the US, participation rates are 87% and above,[114] with opt-out rates close to zero in class actions for damages on behalf of consumers. Eisenberg and Miller found that the average opt-out rate for 39 consumer class actions was less than 0.2% in an 11-year period.[115] Corporate claimants, however, generally opt out in favour of individual proceedings.[116] It has been stated that members who opt out are generally those who are sophisticated[117] or informed,[118] whose losses are significant[119] or whose interests are divergent.[120]

It is possible to say that the reasons why consumers do not opt out are mainly practical. Opt-out actions are mostly regarded as a realistic chance to obtain redress. Members do not have the means or ability to pursue an individual claim and therefore remaining in the action seems to be the reasonable choice.[121] If group members stay passive throughout, they receive compensation in the case the action succeeds; and in the case it does not, they endure no costs.[122] If members opt out of the action, they gain nothing, irrespective of success.[123] Since group members apply for their share of compensation or receive their share after the litigation ends, they face no risk of losing the case.[124] Unlike an opt-in action, an

111 *Ibid* 153.
112 See also the two other cases brought by Deco showed a similar participation rate, *ibid* 152.
113 See *supra* section 'Opt-in actions'.
114 The data from the opt-out regime in Victoria, Australia suggests the same, Mulheron, Reform of collective redress (fn 24) ix.
115 Eisenberg and Miller, The role of opt-outs (fn 82) 1532.
116 JT Rosch, 'Designing a Private Remedies System for Antitrust Cases – Lessons Learned from the U.S. Experience' (presented at the Remarks of Federal Trade Commissioner before the 16th Annual EU Competition Law and Policy Workshop, Italy, 2011), 1–28, 14 <http://www.ftc.gov/sites/default/files/documents/public_statements/designing-private-remedies-system-antitrust-cases-lessons-learned-u.s.experience/110617roschprivateremedies.pdf> [accessed 1 July 2018]; Z Juska, 'Obstacles in European Competition Law Enforcement: A Potential Solution from Collective Redress', *European Journal of Legal Studies*, 7(1) (2014), 125–153, 144. If the number of opt-outs is considerable, then the certification decision might be overturned for not satisfying the numerosity prerequisite in the US. Mulheron, Class action (fn 90) 130.
117 Rosch (fn 116) 14.
118 Bernard and Bourjade (fn 47) 16.
119 J Bronsteen and O Fiss, 'The Class Action Rule', *Notre Dame Law Review*, 78 (2003), 1419–1453, 1442; Van den Bergh (fn 57) 22.
120 Bronsteen and Fiss (fn 119) 1442. See further *infra* section III/3.
121 Lilly (fn 76) 1036.
122 JR Macey and GP Miller, 'The Plaintiffs' Attorney's Role in Class Action and Derivative Litigation: Economic Analysis and Recommendations for Reform', *The University of Chicago Law Review*, 58(1) (1991), 1–118, 28.
123 *Ibid.*
124 Centre for European Policy Studies (CEPS), Erasmus University Rotterdam (EUR) and Luiss Guido Carli (LUISS), *Report for the European Commission 'Making*

opt-out action does not burden consumers with any active involvement in the course of litigation. The importance of this point is also proved by research in the EU that surveyed consumers in 27 Member States in order to examine their opinions towards collective redress.[125] Participants found a collective redress action desirable irrespective of the amount of loss suffered,[126] but the majority of consumers stated that if their individual damages were small,[127] they would resort to such an action provided that they were required to exert minimum time and effort and were responsible for no cost.[128]

TAKE-UP RATES

Notwithstanding their high participation rates, it has been argued that opt-out actions are no different from opt-in actions in requiring the group members, at some point within a specified timeframe, to come forward to claim their shares.[129] This is called 'opting-in later in the action'.[130] For this reason, opt-out actions have been found unsuccessful in realising a compensation objective, as, when required, relatively few claimants actually file their claims to obtain damages.[131] Indeed, there are cases where group members can only be identified by effort on their part, and thus they are required to come forward to establish their entitlements post-award in order to receive compensation,[132] this is when take-up rates become relevant. There are also situations existing whereby the group members are identified electronically, and therefore a direct refund to members is possible.[133] This being the case, take-up rates may not provide a complete picture of the number of compensated victims at the end of an opt-out action. Moreover, there is no concrete data on what proportion of group members take up their shares;[134] this is not of public record[135] and there is little research

Antitrust Damages Actions More Effective in the EU: Welfare Impact and Potential Scenarios', Final Report, 2007, 574.

125 Commission, *Consumer Redress in the European Union: Consumer Experiences, Perceptions, and Choices – Aggregated Report*, 2009 <http://ec.europa.eu/consumers/redress_cons/docs/cons_redress_EU_qual_study_report_en.pdf> [accessed 1 July 2018].

126 *Ibid* 82, 90.

127 The amount of loss is €5 and €10 per year, *ibid* 80.

128 *Ibid* 82.

129 See eg Keske (fn 12) 44.

130 Mulheron, Reform of collective redress (fn 24) 35.

131 See eg JC Coffee, 'Litigation Governance: Taking Accountability Seriously', *Columbia Law Review*, 110(2) (2010), 288–351, 334; C Hodges, 'Collective Redress: A Breakthrough or a Damp Sqibb?', *Journal of Consumer Policy*, 37(1) (2014), 67–89, 82.

132 Welfare impact report (fn 124) 568; Mulheron, Reform of collective redress (fn 24) 35.

133 See Chapter 8.

134 JP Davis and RH Lande, 'Defying Conventional Wisdom: The Case for Private Antitrust Enforcement', *Georgia Law Review*, 48(1) (2013), 1–82, 11.

135 Mulheron, Reform of collective redress (fn 24) 153.

available.[136] With this in mind, the US examples below are used to show how effective opt-out actions are in delivering compensation.

Take-up rates differ from case to case. At highest the take-up rate is 75% and at lowest 1%. It is generally below 50%.[137] Mulheron stated that in competition cases take-up rates vary between 10% and 70%, with respect to the data available in jurisdictions with opt-out actions.[138] It is worth noting that even when the take-up rate is low, the number of consumers claiming their damages is still exponentially higher than the number participating in any opt-in collective action. For instance, in the *Minolta Products* class action for competition damages, 70,000 out of 340,000 consumers received cheques for either $9 or $16,[139] a take-up rate of around 21%. In *Microsoft* in California, 620,000 of 14 million group members claimed their $5, $16 or $29 overcharge damages.[140] This claim rate is just over 4%, but it is still a substantial number of victims - more than 600,000 people - came forward for this small recovery, which would have not been possible absent the opt-out action. Similarly, in *In re Remeron End-Payor Antitrust Litigation*, the claim rate was 8%, with 65,000 consumer claims filed of 800,000 notices sent;[141] each claimant received $109.[142]

Cases where an estimate of group size is not available show a similar pattern. For instance, in a CD price-fixing case, over 3.5 million claims were filed, each to

136 G van Dijck, 'Class Membership in Class Actions: An Experimental Study', *Tilburg Law School Research Paper no 013/2011*, 2011, 1–43, 11 <http://papers.ssrn.com/sol3/papers.cfm?abstract_id=1641174> [accessed 1 July 2018].

137 Herron (fn 109) 168. Hensler's sample of ten cases –four mass tort, and six consumer class actions – found take-up rates ranging from 30% to 100%. Hensler and others (fn 95) 428–429. Pace, on the other hand, examined 29 insurance class actions, of which 10 resulted in 100% direct refund to class members. NM Pace, 'Class Actions in the United States of America: An Overview of the Process and the Empirical Literature', *RAND Institute for Civil Justice*, 2007, 1–99, 67.

138 R Mulheron, 'In a Nutshell' (presented at Rapid Response Seminar: The Consumer Rights Act 2015 – The UK Class Action: A Reaction, London, 2015).

139 S Calkins, 'An Enforcement Official's Reflections on Antitrust Class Actions', *Arizona Law Review*, 39 (1997), 413–451, 436. See the case *In re Minolta Camera Products Antitrust Litigation*, 668 F.Supp. 456 (D.Md. 1987).

140 LJ Flynn, 'Few Takers for Payments from Microsoft Settlement', *NY Times*, 2005 <http://www.nytimes.com/2005/01/05/technology/05soft.html> [accessed 1 July 2018]; C Smithka, 'From Budapest to Berlin: How Implementing Class Action Lawsuits in the European Union Would Increase Competition and Strengthen Consumer Confidence', *Wisconsin International Law Journal*, 27(1) (2009), 173–194, 178.

141 Case nos 02–2007 (FSH), 04–5126 (FSH), (D.N.J. 2005) 33 <https://casetext.com/case/in-re-remeron-end-payor-antitrust-litigation-2> [accessed 1 July 2018].

142 DA Crane, *The Institutional Structure of Antitrust Enforcement* (Oxford: Oxford University Press, 2011), 169–170. See in the US in a class action for competition damages in 1975, one out of three million affected consumers came forward and obtained damages, C Hodges, 'US Class Actions: Promise and Reality', *EUI Working Papers no Law 2015/36*, 2015, 1–36, 20–21 <http://cadmus.eui.eu/bitstream/handle/1814/36536/LAW_2015_36.pdf?sequence=1> [accessed 1 July 2018].

recover up to $20 each.[143] A huge number of consumers took an active step to submit a claim form, even for such a small amount. In an antibiotics price-fixing case, 38,000 consumers filed claims, each for approximately $434.[144] In *BuSpar*, 57,476 consumer claim forms were submitted, each to recover $647.[145] In *Relafen*, cheques were issued both to consumers who had filed a claim form and those who were identified through pharmacy records. About $1 million in cheques to the former was issued and almost $15 million in cheques were mailed to the latter, of which 80% were cashed.[146] It is therefore possible to conclude that opt-out actions are more capable of providing compensation to consumers than opt-in actions.

The proposed approach

Reflections

The foregoing suggests that the function of an opt-out action offers a realistic prospect for consumers to obtain redress. It encompasses a large group of consumers of which a great majority remain in the action and therefore *i.* the chances of providing compensation to a high number of harmed consumers are increased, and *ii.* this is an incentive for representative parties to bring an action where they would be representing many consumers with the possibility of delivering a large sum of damages.[147] Furthermore, an opt-out action achieves the economies of scale and efficiency in court proceedings as expected of a collective redress action.[148] First, it makes possible the determination of the claims of numerous individuals in a single proceeding and prevents the relitigation of the same or similar matters that would otherwise lead to high litigation costs, unnecessary delays and the risk of conflicting judgments. Secondly, it is practical as regards requiring consumers to exert minimum effort in judicial procedures and as regards not overburdening the representative party in bringing the action.

In fact, some legal systems that previously had opt-in actions in place have undergone a change to adopt opt-out actions. In the UK, the former opt-in

143 *In re Compact Disc Minimum Advertised Price Antitrust Litigation*, MDL no 1361 (D. Me. 2001), 10 <http://www.med.uscourts.gov/Opinions/Hornby/MDL/MDL1361_2003_06_13_ORDER17.pdf> [accessed 1 July 2018].
144 *State of West Virginia v Chas. Pfizer & Co.*, 314 F. Supp. 710 (S.D.N.Y. 1970) para G (5) <http://law.justia.com/cases/federal/district-courts/FSupp/314/710/1472495/> [accessed 1 July 2018].
145 JD Richards, 'What Makes an Antitrust Class Action Remedy Successful: A Tale of Two Settlements', *Tulane Law Review*, 80 (2005), 621–660, 641. See *In re Buspirone Antirust Ligation,* 185 F.Supp. 2d 363 (S.D.N.Y. 2002).
146 WH Page, 'Indirect Purchaser Suits Under the Class Action Fairness Act – Reconciling Multilayer Interests in Antitrust Litigation', in *Collective Actions: Enhancing Access to Justice and Reconciling Multilayer Interests?*, ed. by S Wrbka, S Van Uytsel and M Siems (Cambridge: Cambridge University Press, 2012), 275–298, 295, fn 98.
147 Chieu (fn 32) 150.
148 *Ibid.* See Chapter 2.

representative action was designed to be brought by consumer associations on a follow-on basis in order to seek redress for consumers affected by competition infringements.[149] The one and only case brought under this law resulted in a very low participation rate.[150] In order to remedy the situation, ie to provide redress to, *inter alia*, consumers, a reform process was begun.[151] In this context, one of the proposals was to adopt a pre-damages opt-in action, meaning plaintiffs might participate in the action before damages were awarded. This was then rejected because it had had no practice, meaning no evidence existed as to its effectiveness but also because it was not superior to an opt-out action.[152] The current regime confers on the court the discretion to choose between opt-in and opt-out actions for the case at hand.[153] As to the reason of this discretion, it has been stated that opt-in actions are more suited to cases filed by a small number of businesses all of whom are easy to identify.[154] It has been accordingly submitted that in practice consumer claims could only be brought as an opt-out action.[155] Indeed, under the UK's new collective action, there have only been two cases brought to the CAT so far and the victims in these cases were consumers, so the cases were on opt-out basis.[156]

The US class action procedure was also built and operated upon an opt-in principle between the years of 1938 and 1966. During that period, very few actions were filed.[157] It was observed that these opt-in actions did not reach many claimants and therefore left many victims uncompensated.[158] The draftsmen believed that opt-out actions would overcome the ineffectiveness and

149 *Competition Act,* 1998, sec 47B.
150 See *supra* section 'Opt-in actions'.
151 BIS, *Private Actions in Competition Law: A Consultation on Options for Reform – Government Response* (London, 2013), (Government response) para 5.12.
152 BIS, Final impact assessment (fn 21) para 180.
153 CAT rules (fn 42) para 79(3).
154 BIS, Government response (fn 151) para 5.15. CAT rules also provide that in determining whether an opt-in action is appropriate to the case at hand, the CAT would look at the claim value of the claimants. *Ibid* para 78(3)(b).
155 BIS (fn 151) para 5.12. See similarly, in Norway, the court has the discretion and must choose opt-out actions for small claims, R Gaudet, 'Turning a Blind Eye: The Commission's Rejection of Opt-out Class Actions Overlooks Swedish, Norwegian, Danish and Dutch Experience', *European Competition Law Review*, 30(3) (2009), 107–117, 112.
156 *Dorothy Gibson v Pride Mobility Products Limited* [2016] (CAT Case no 1257/7/7/16) (*Pride* case); *Walter Hugh Merricks v MasterCard Incorporated & Others* [2017] (CAT Case no 1266/7/7/16) (*MasterCard* case). None of these cases led to a damages award for different reasons. In *Pride* case, the CAT ruled that the economic expert of the representative party should quantify consumer losses caused only by the dealers that had agreed to Pride's policy restricting online discounting as found by the OFT's decision since the collective action was brought on a follow-on basis. The representative party, however, decided not to amend and refile the application in accordance with the CAT's guidance. In *MasterCard* case, the CAT did not find the claims eligible for inclusion in a collective action.
157 Russell (fn 48) 159; Jones, Foreword (fn 33) 2.
158 Bernard and Bourjade (fn 47) 13.

impracticality of opt-in actions by addressing large numbers of small claimants.[159] Indeed, the practice shows that opt-out actions have increased the attractiveness of seeking redress and operated to address small claims that are uneconomical to be pursued as an individual claim but are viable as a collective claim.[160] The opt-out regime has resulted in a significant rise in the number of actions brought,[161] in the size of group members and in the sum of damages.[162]

In the EU, the Commission wishes to introduce the opt-in action. Under the horizontal approach, the Recommendation favours adoption of opt-in actions unless it is '[d]uly justified by reasons of sound administration of justice'.[163] It does not, however, explain neither how the sound administration of justice 'justifies' an exception to the opt-in nor what form that exception takes. Given that only opt-in and opt-out actions are discussed,[164] the exception to the opt-in is necessarily an opt-out action.[165] In this respect, one can argue that the adoption of opt-out actions for consumer cases would be in accordance with the justification provided therein as opt-in actions fall short of delivering real benefits to consumers.[166] However, many stakeholders, especially businesses, are concerned by the potential for abusive litigation observed in the US.[167] At the time of the publication of the Recommendation the Justice Commissioner, similarly, emphasised that the Commission's aim with respect to collective redress mechanisms is to avoid the adoption of US-style class actions.[168]

159 *Ibid.* Similarly, AR Miller, 'Of Frankenstein Monsters and Shining Knights: Myth, Reality, and the "Class Action Problem"', *Harvard Law Review*, 92(3) (1979), 664–694, 669; Gilles and Friedman (fn 103) 110; Mullenix (fn 5) 29.
160 Miller (fn 159) 674.
161 Russell (fn 48) 159; M Gac, 'Collective Redress v. Class Actions – Convergence or Divergence Between the European and American Solutions on Group Litigation?' (presented at the Interaction of National Legal Systems: Convergence or Divergence?, Vilnius: Vilnius University Faculty of Law, 2013), 114–126, 121, fn 28 <http://www.tf.vu.lt/dokumentai/naujienos/Renginiai/tarptautine_studentu_konferencija_2013.pdf> [accessed 1 July 2018].
162 Pace (fn 137) 2.
163 Recommendation (fn 4) para V/21. It seems Slovenia is the only Member State that follows this policy in its collective redress proposal, Report on the Recommendation (fn 100) 14.
164 Communication (fn 58) para 3.4.
165 G Jones, 'Collective Redress in the European Union: Reflections from a National Judge', *Legal Issues of Economic Integration*, 41(3) (2014), 289–304, 302.
166 Similarly, J Pheasant and A Bicarregui, 'Striking the Right Balance towards a "Competition Culture" Not a "Litigation Culture"? Comment on the European Commission's White Paper on Damages Actions for Breach of EC Antitrust Rules', *Global Competition Litigation Review*, 1(2) (2008), 98–106, 99.
167 Commission, *Staff Working Document Public Consultation: Towards a Coherent European Approach to Collective Redress* (SEC(2011)173 final, 2011), para 21; Communication (fn 58) para 2.2.2, fn 26.
168 Commission, *Press Release: Commission Recommends Member States to Have Collective Redress Mechanisms in Place to Ensure Effective Access to Justice* (Strasbourg, 2013) <http://europa.eu/rapid/press-release_IP-13-524_en.htm> [accessed 1 July 2018].

The approach in competition law shows a similar pattern. The Commission implicitly suggests an opt-out mechanism for exceptional cases in the White Paper and more evidently in the withdrawn Directive,[169] and also acknowledges that an opt-out action achieves higher levels of compensation than an opt-in action.[170] However, it recommends opt-in over opt-out because *i.* an opt-out action is not compatible with European legal culture and traditions,[171] *ii.* it has certain negative effects,[172] *iii.* it gives rise to excesses when combined with other features as observed in other jurisdictions,[173] *iv.* it is a radical measure.[174] Similarly, the European Parliament states that the membership systems which do not identify group members until the judgment is given do not fit into the legal orders of Member States.[175]

It should be noted that contrary to this recommendation, opt-out actions are not foreign to the EU, and therefore not incompatible with European cultures and traditions.[176] Some Member States have them - the UK, Belgium, Portugal, Bulgaria, Spain, Denmark and the Netherlands - albeit differently designed.[177] Moreover, these alleged excesses are not experienced in Member States with existing opt-out actions,[178] so it is unclear how the Commission can justify its

169 See Chapter 3.

170 SWPWP (fn 7) para 58.

171 N Kroes, 'Reinforcing the Fight against Cartels and Developing Private Antitrust Damage Actions: Two Tools for a More Competitive Europe' (presented at the Commission/IBA Joint Conference on EC Competition Policy, Brussels, 2007), 1–6, 5 <http://europa.eu/rapid/press-release_SPEECH-07-128_en.htm?locale=fr> [accessed 1 July 2018]. See also Commission, *White Paper on Damages Actions for Breach of the EC Antitrust Rules* (COM(2008) 165 final, Brussels, 2008), para 1.2.

172 It does not explain these effects, Commission, *Staff Working Document Accompanying Document to the White Paper on Damages Actions for Breach of the EC Antitrust Rules – Impact Assessment* (SEC(2008) 405, Brussels, 2008), para 139.

173 SWPWP (fn 7) para 58.

174 Commission, *Proposal for a Directive of the European Parliament and of the Council on Certain Rules Governing Actions for Damages Under National Law for Infringements of the Competition Law Provisions of the Member States and of the European Union*, (2013/0185 (COD), COM(2013) 404 final, Strasbourg, 2013), explanatory memorandum, para 3.3.

175 European Parliament, *Motion for a European Parliament Resolution on 'Towards a Coherent European Approach to Collective Redress'* (2011/2089(INI), 2012), para 20 <http://www.europarl.europa.eu/sides/getDoc.do?type=REPORT&language=EN&reference=A7-0012/2012#title1> [accessed 1 July 2018].

176 Similarly, Nazzini and Nikpay (fn 52) 125–126.

177 See eg Communication (fn 58) para 3.4; Report on the Recommendation (fn 100) 13; G Barling, 'Collective Redress for Breach of Competition Law – A Case for Reform', *Competition Law Journal*, 2011, 5–20, 15. See Hungary has an opt-out action as well, but only the Hungarian Competition Office can bring the action, CI Nagy, 'Comparative Collective Redress from a Law and Economics Perspective: Without Risk There Is No Reward!', *Columbia Journal of European Law*, 19(3) (2013), 469–498, 490.

178 SWPWP (fn 7) para 43, fn 24; Leskinen (fn 9) 36–39; JG Delatre, 'Beyond the White Paper: Rethinking the Commission's Proposal on Private Antitrust Litigation', *Competition Law Review*, 8(1) (2011), 29–58, 35; Nagy (fn 177) 495.

rejection on this basis and regard these actions as radical measures. The Commission refers to the US regime in respect of its negative effects and excesses,[179] but it regrettably does not analyse the truth and extent of these in competition law. This would suggest that the scepticism towards opt-out actions is due to the adverse view of class action procedure, which is discussed in the next section.

Assessing the criticisms

OVERVIEW OF THE CRITICISMS

US class action procedure operates on an opt-out basis whereby a representative party, who is one of the affected group members, and her lawyer, who works under a contingency fee arrangement, brings the action on behalf of other harmed individuals. Some features of the US system, such as contingency fees, treble damages, jury trials and one-way costs-shifting, are generally unfamiliar to the legal systems in the EU. Therefore, it has been believed that class actions, mainly due to their opt-out nature, but also in combination with other features, lead to some negative consequences.[180] Those alleged consequences of class actions which have been put forward by commentators and the Commission can be gathered under three categories: they result in overcompensation or undercompensation and/or unmeritorious claims filed.

According to one view, the class action undercompensates victims.[181] It has been argued that opt-out actions are costly proceedings due to high court and lawyers' fees, high certification and damages distribution costs and principal-agent problems.[182] The argument follows that deducting these expenditures from the damages award leaves almost nothing to be recovered by group members,[183] especially by those who are indirect purchasers.[184] It has also been argued that defendants pay damages under the total worth of claim values[185] because they opt for settlements which are cheaper than the cost of a class action.[186] According to

179 SWPWP (fn 7) para 43, fn 24; Impact assessment (fn 172) para 139.
180 See Public consultation (fn 167) para 21.
181 CR Leslie, 'De Facto Detrebling: The Rush to Settlement in Antitrust Class Action Litigation', *Arizona Law Review*, 50 (2008), 1009–1052, 1016; C Hodges, 'Fast, Effective and Low Cost Redress: How Do Public and Private Enforcement and ADR Compare?', in *Competition Law Comparative Private Enforcement and Collective Redress across the EU*, ed. by BJ Rodger (The Netherlands: Kluwer Law International, 2014), 255–289, 266.
182 Welfare impact report (fn 124) 570.
183 DA Crane, 'Optimizing Private Antitrust Enforcement', *Vanderbilt Law Review*, 63 (3) (2010), 673–723, 682–683.
184 *Ibid* 682.
185 JC Coffee, 'Rescuing the Private Attorney General: Why the Model of the Lawyer as Bounty Hunter Is Not Working', *Maryland Law Review*, 42(2) (1983), 215–288, 226; R Wasserman, 'Dueling Class Actions', *Boston University Law Review*, 80(2) (2000), 461–543, 473.
186 Hodges, From class actions (fn 28) 43; KS Bernard, 'Private Antitrust Litigation in the European Union – Why Does the EC Want to Embrace What the US FTC is Trying to Avoid?', *Global Competition Litigation Review*, 3(2) (2010), 69–74, 73.

the Commission, the large number of individuals encompassed by an opt-out action leads to group members losing control over lawyers who may use this opportunity to their benefit (the principal-agent problem).[187] It has also been asserted that this is particularly likely in cases involving small claimants or indirect consumers who have little or no control over a lawyer.[188] The argument here is that lawyers take on a case in the hope of a settlement[189] and that they try to maximise their recovery by settling the case when litigation expenses are not high and not much time and effort has been devoted to it.[190] Lawyers settle for lesser amounts[191] and take large fees[192] whilst the claimants recover very little.[193] It has been posited that the opt-out nature of the action provides lawyers bargaining power over defendants that allows them to secure a settlement in their best interest.[194] Lastly, it has been claimed that, in some instances, plaintiffs' lawyer and defendant(s) collude to settle the case to the detriment of group members.[195]

However, another view maintains that the class action generates a blackmail settlement and overcompensates victims.[196] This time, contrary to the above, the payment made by the defendant(s) exceeds the total loss caused.[197] It has been stated that the defendant(s) overpay due to the pressure from the aggregation of many claims by opt-out actions that constitute a large damages

187 SWPWP (fn 7) para 58; Impact assessment (fn 172) para 119.

188 J Bronsteen, 'Class Action Settlements: An Opt-In Proposal', *University of Illinois Law Review*, 2005 (2005), 903–928, 912; EM Iacobucci, 'Cartel Class Actions and Immunity Programmes', *Journal of Antitrust Enforcement*, 1(2) (2013), 272–295, 294. It is especially the case in coupon settlements. See eg Smithka (fn 140) 178; MA Sittenreich, 'The Rocky Path for Private Directors General: Procedure, Politics, and the Uncertain Future of EU Antitrust Damages Actions', *Fordham Law Review*, 78(5) (2010), 2701–2750, 2736–2737. Note that the lawyers' fees in coupon settlements are now measured on the basis of the coupon value redeemed by the group members. *Class Action Fairness Act*, 28 USC, 2005, sec 1712.

189 Iacobucci (fn 188) 294.

190 JC Alexander, 'An Introduction to Class Action Procedure in The United States' (presented at the Debates over Group Litigation in Comparative Perspective, Geneva, Switzerland, 2000), 1–26, 17 <http://law.duke.edu/grouplit/papers/classactionalexander.pdf> [accessed 1 July 2018].

191 RA Nagareda, 'The Preexistence Principle and the Structure of the Class Action', *Columbia Law Review*, 103(2) (2003), 149–242, 163; Leslie, De facto detrebling (fn 181) 1015. This is labelled as 'sweetheart settlements', B Hay and D Rosenberg, 'Sweetheart and Blackmail Settlements in Class Actions: Reality and Remedy', *Notre Dame Law Review*, 75(4) (2000), 1377–1408, 1377.

192 RA Posner, 'Oligopoly and the Antitrust Laws: A Suggested Approach', *Stanford Law Review*, 21 (1968), 1562–1606, 1590; E Cavanagh, 'Antitrust Remedies Revisited', *Oregon Law Review*, 84 (2005), 147–225, 214.

193 Hodges, From class actions (fn 28) 42–43.

194 Russell (fn 48) 160.

195 Bernard and Bourjade (fn 47) 14.

196 C Silver, '"We Are Scared to Death": Class Certification and Blackmail', *New York University Law Review*, 78 (2003), 1357–1430, 1373; Welfare impact report (fn 124) 594; Rosch (fn 117) 11.

197 Hay and Rosenberg (fn 191) 1378.

amount,[198] or due to the threat of being liable for high cost and risk of such actions.[199] It has been asserted on the one hand that this happens irrespective of the value of the claim, and on the other, that claim size matters.[200] There are two views within the latter group, one that states small claims have this effect,[201] the other that this is true for large claims.[202]

The last argument is that class actions facilitate the filing of unmeritorious claims[203] due to principal-agent problems,[204] the opt-out mechanism[205] or the costs rules of the US system.[206] It has been contended that opt-out actions, by aggregating many claims, result in increased incentives to bring a suit along with increased risk of unmeritorious cases.[207] According to Waelbroeck and Slater, when each member receives a very low damages award, their claims should be regarded as unmeritorious.[208] In light of this, the next section examines the merits of these allegations.

THE MERITS OF THE CRITICISMS

The overcompensation argument seems weak in relation to competition cases, because it is difficult to imagine defendants, with greater financial and other resources with which to defend their interests, being in a more vulnerable position

198 HJ Friendly, *Federal Jurisdiction: A General View* (New York: Columbia University Press, 1973) 120; M Handler, 'The Shift from Substantive to Procedural Innovation in Antitrust Suits – The Twenty-Third Annual Antitrust Review', *Columbia Law Review*, 71(1) (1971), 1–36, 9; Hay and Rosenberg (fn 191) 1378. Similarly, Communication (fn 58) para 2.2.2.

199 Hay and Rosenberg (fn 191) 1378.

200 Silver (fn 196) 1361.

201 JM Landers, 'Of Legalized Blackmail and Legalized Theft: Consumer Class Actions and the Substance-Procedure Dilemma', *Southern California Law Review*, 47 (1974), 842–900, 843, 860; Page (fn 146) 277.

202 TS Ulen, 'An introduction to the law and economics of class action litigation', *European Journal of Law and Economics*, 32 (2011), 185–203, 195.

203 See eg TM Woods, 'Wielding the Sledgehammer: Legislative Solutions for Class Action Jurisdictional Reform', *New York University Law Review*, 75 (2000), 507–541, 515; Communication (fn 58) para 2.2.2.

204 F Weber, 'Assessing Existing Enforcement Mechanisms in Consumer Law – The Unavailability of an Allrounder', *Rotterdam Institute of Law and Economics (RILE) Working Paper Series no 2011/7*, 2011, 542–560, 557 <http://ssrn.com/abstract=1962665> [accessed 1 July 2018].

205 Bronsteen (fn 188) 920.

206 See eg Bernard and Bourjade (fn 47) 14.

207 H-B Schaefer, 'The Bundling of Similar Interests in Litigation. The Incentives for Class Action and Legal Actions Taken by Associations', *European Journal of Law and Economics*, 9(3) (2000), 183–213, 187; Communication (fn 58) para 2.2.2.

208 D Waelbroeck and D Slater, 'The Commission's Green Paper on Private Enforcement: "Americanization" of EC Competition Law Enforcement?', in *European Competition Law Annual 2006: Enforcement of Prohibition of Cartels*, ed. by C-D Ehlermann and I Atanasiu (Oxford and Portland, Oregon: Hart Publishing, 2006), 425–455, 441.

than consumers who tend to have limited resources.[209] Moreover, it is unlikely that defendants would pay a large amount unless they believed that the claim would be prosecuted and the class action would be successful.[210] The defendant's lawyer, generally working under an hourly fee arrangement, has an interest in continuing litigation in order to generate higher fees.[211] Defendants tend to delay litigation as a strategy to discourage the plaintiffs' lawyer who is generally working on a contingency fee and does not receive any payment until the case is won.[212] This is particularly true of actions on behalf of consumers, as, if the dispute is not solved through class action litigation, there is nearly no risk for the defendant being held liable by virtue of individual actions.[213]

This overcompensation due to blackmail settlement argument also states that the aggregation of claims in an opt-out action constitutes a larger claim value or the costs and risks of such an action forces the defendant to pay damages more than the worth of the claims. This ignores two facts. First, if an individual claim is relatively large then it would be perfectly possible to say that individual litigation creates the same effect.[214] Secondly, an opt-out action simply enables the bundling of numerous claims and makes their pursuit viable in courts. Although such an action increases the chances of obtaining redress by individuals, defendants pay compensation because the law requires them to do so, not because the procedural tool is adopted for enforcing the law.[215] If all victims were able to sue individually, the defendant would pay the same amount as damages in the EU and perhaps even more in legal costs due to separate expenditures on individual actions. Hence, it is not reasonable to say that the infringer should not be held liable if their act causes numerous small losses because of the total claim value.[216]

A pertinent question is then whether there is a possibility that opt-out actions lead to undercompensation of victims in a given case. In other words, the question here is to what extent damages awarded at the end of the litigation go to victims for their loss. The undercompensation argument is supported by the following: *i.* lawyers' fees are too high, *ii.* the litigation costs of class actions are large, *iii.* the damages or settlement award is too low to adequately compensate victims.[217] Although it is difficult to determine whether damages awards or settlement amounts correspond to the right value of the aggregate claims, the recent evidence

209 JP Davis and EL Cramer, 'Antitrust, Class Certification, and the Politics of Procedure', *George Mason Law Review*, 17(4) (2010), 969–1033, 979; Davis and Lande, Defying conventional wisdom (fn 134) 69.
210 Davis and Lande Defying conventional wisdom (fn 134) 77.
211 *Ibid* 69; JP Davis, 'Classwide Recoveries', *The George Washington Law Review*, 82 (2014), 890–950, 940.
212 See Silver (fn 196) 1392.
213 Bronsteen and Fiss (fn 119) 1443.
214 Silver (fn 196) 1367.
215 Mulheron, Class action (fn 90) 77.
216 Silver (fn 196) 1421–1422; AD Lahav, 'Symmetry and Class Action Litigation', *UCLA Law Review*, 60 (2013), 1494–1522, 1515.
217 See *supra* section 'Overview of the criticisms'.

in the US gives a different picture.[218] In their empirical studies Davis and Lande[219] analysed 60 private competition cases, of which 47 were class actions,[220] thus, their conclusions on private competition law enforcement are also mostly valid for class actions. They found that the recoveries[221] from those actions amounted to between $33.8 and $35.8 billion in cash,[222] of which two-thirds came from class actions.[223]

Following this, it has been claimed that the expenses of a class action are too high and that when they are deducted from a recovery the victims receive very little. The first expense is lawyers' fees. Davis and Lande found that the mean values of these fees were either 25.6% or 14.3% of the recovery. The percentage of fees were reduced by larger recovery.[224] In this respect, there are three earlier empirical works with similar findings regarding lawyers' fees. The first study on 71 class actions in competition law over the period 1993–2008 observed that lawyers' fees amount to 21.02% of the recovery on average.[225] The second study on class action settlements in the years of 2006 and 2007 in all areas of law found that while lawyers' fees and expenses were 13% of the settlement amount in 2006, the figure was 20% in 2007, but these were at least 33% of the amount in individual cases in those years.[226] The third study which analysed 1120 class actions in 1990 and 2002 showed that when on average 18.4% of the recovery was spent as lawyers' fees and other litigation costs, 81.6% went to plaintiffs. It also concluded that the lawyer took 40% of the damages award in an individual case.[227]

There are also expenses for the distribution of awards. According to the data collected by Davis and Lande, the mean value of this is 5.6% of the damages award for indirect purchasers and 3.2% for direct purchasers.[228] With distribution costs and lawyers' fees, this means at least 70% of the recovery is distributed as damages.[229] They also gathered information on the administrative costs associated with

218 Davis and Lande, Defying conventional wisdom (fn 134) 77.
219 RH Lande and JP Davis, 'Benefits from Private Antitrust Enforcement: An Analysis of Forty Cases', *University of San Francisco Law Review*, 42 (2008), 879–918; *ibid.*
220 RH Lande, Editorial, 'The Proposed Damages Legislation: Don't Believe the Critics', *Journal of European Competition Law and Practice* (2014), 1–2, 2.
221 Their sample excluded coupons, rebates, discounts, product recoveries or the value of injunctive relief or legal precedent. Davis and Lande Defying conventional wisdom (fn 134) 16.
222 *Ibid* 17.
223 Lande, Editorial (fn 220) 2.
224 Davis and Lande, Defying conventional wisdom (fn 134) 23.
225 T Eisenberg and GP Miller, 'Attorneys' Fees and Expenses in Class Action Settlements: 1993–2008', *Journal of Empirical Legal Studies*, 7(2) (2010), 248–281, 262.
226 BT Fitzpatrick, 'An Empirical Study of Class Action Settlements and Their Fee Awards', *Journal of Empirical Legal Studies*, 7(4) (2010), 811–846, 830.
227 SJ Logan, J Moshman and BC Moore, 'Attorney Fee Awards in Common Fund Class Actions', *Class Action Reports*, 24(2) (2003), 167–234, 169.
228 Davis and Lande, Defying conventional wisdom (fn 134) 24.
229 Indirect purchasers recovered $1.95 billion in 10 cases where direct purchasers in 43 cases received between $13 billion and $14.5 billion, but the data did not say how many of them were consumers. See for the figures, respectively, Lande and Davis,

class action settlements, these being in total between 13% and 30% of the settlements. Again, victims received 70% to 87% of the award.[230] In conclusion, the costs and the lawyers' fees are not too high to prevent victims from obtaining compensation in opt-out actions. Lastly, one can argue that the Commission's statements to the costliness of opt-out actions[231] apply equally to opt-in actions.[232] Perhaps, opt-in actions are more costly.[233] In 2006, the follow-on damages action brought by the French consumers' association against three cartel members on behalf of consumers proved how costly and time-consuming it can get. 'The association spent nearly 2,000 hours to prepare the action and incurred EUR 500,000 of legal expenses for a claim amounting overall to EUR 750,000 (roughly EUR 60 per consumer participating in the claim).'[234]

Furthermore, the evidence of blackmail is derived from securities litigation;[235] almost all of the papers refer to securities and stockholders rather than competition cases.[236] In competition law, it has been stated that the legal blackmail theory has no empirical basis[237] and that the potential for unmeritorious actions is not much concern owing to the substantive law.[238] Indeed, the outcome of a competition case is very uncertain and bringing a case is expensive due to the requirements for the resolution of the issues.[239] Additionally, before settlement, there are some steps available to the defendant in the US, which make it almost impossible for a class action for competition damages to be maintained if the claim is not meritorious. Indeed, 'Plaintiffs must survive motions to dismiss, oppositions to class certification and motions for summary judgment before they can even think about settling [...]'.[240]

Given that class actions differ from two-party actions, it is necessary for the court to involve and apply active control in some respects.[241] US courts apply the certification standards to review whether the case at hand satisfies them. Class

Benefits from private antitrust enforcement (fn 219) 899; JP Davis and RH Lande, 'Toward an Empirical and Theoretical Assessment of Private Antitrust Enforcement', *Seattle University Law Review*, 36 (2013), 1269–1335, 1286.

230 Davis and Lande, Defying conventional wisdom (fn 134) 47–48.

231 See *supra* fn 182.

232 Delatre (fn 178) 50.

233 *Ibid.*

234 Collective redress in antitrust (fn 26) 36.

235 Davis and Cramer (fn 209) 978.

236 *Ibid.* See eg C Scott and J Black, *Cranston's Consumers and the Law*, 3rd edn (London: Butterworths, 2000), 132; RG Bone and DS Evans, 'Class Certification and the Substantive Merits', *Duke Law Journal*, 51(4) (2002), 1251–1332, 1293–1294; P Spender, 'Securities Class Actions: A View from the Land of the Great White Shareholder', *Common Law World Review*, 31 (2002), 123–164, 128; Mulheron, Class action (fn 90) 73; Ulen (fn 202) 198.

237 Davis and Cramer (fn 209) 978.

238 Russell (fn 48) 164.

239 Leskinen (fn 9) 34.

240 Russell (fn 48) 164.

241 JW Burns, 'Decorative Figureheads: Eliminating Class Representatives in Class Actions', *Hastings Law Journal*, 42 (1991), 165–202, 200.

action settlements are also subject to court approval and judges determine whether they are fair and adequate.[242] Requirements for both are settled and have been used since the instigation of the class action procedure.[243] The fact that the settlement must be approved by the court to be effective is another means to protect the interests of the group members.[244] A study analysing class actions in competition law observed that the certification criteria operate increasingly effectively in terms of identifying unmeritorious claims and in this way permitting only cases suitable to class action treatment.[245] All cases in the sample in the study of Davis and Lande were also found meritorious.[246] It has further been observed that the certified class actions were settled by 73%,[247] but Silver found that the settlement rate for individual tort cases was exactly the same.[248] High settlement rate does not necessitate blackmail as they are subject to court approval, and moreover such settlements seem to be a feature of the US legal system and do not only pertain to class actions.[249]

It has therefore been submitted that the poor reputation of US class actions is based on isolated anecdotes rather than empirical information, overstated[250] and not representative of the whole system.[251] That said, it is not possible to analyse all cases and reflect the complete tendency of the whole system, but the above-mentioned studies challenge the common belief and show that this procedural tool actually leads to compensation for group members. Andreangeli's research also found that class actions are a viable means by which to address widespread losses and the Commission has no sustainable argument for outright rejection.[252]

With this in mind, the introduction of an EU-wide solution will ultimately require political support from Member States. One can thus argue that, despite the implicit opt-out suggestion and acceptance that an opt-out action is more capable of delivering redress to affected consumers than an opt-in action and despite creation of an exception for an opt-out action if the justice requires so, the Commission wishes to increase the acceptability of a collective redress action by

242 FRCP rule 23(e).
243 Silver (fn 196) 1388–1389.
244 PH Lindblom, 'Individual Litigation and Mass Justice: A Swedish Perspective and Proposal on Group Actions in Civil Procedure', *The American Journal of Comparative Law*, 45(4) (1997), 805–831, 828.
245 A Andreangeli, 'Collective Redress in EU Competition Law: An Open Question with Many Possible Solutions', *World Competition*, 35(3) (2012), 529–558, 529, 556.
246 Davis and Lande, Defying conventional wisdom (fn 134) 67.
247 Silver (fn 196) 1399.
248 *Ibid* 1401–1402.
249 Similarly, Mulheron, Class action (fn 90) 76.
250 CA Jones, 'Deterrence and Compensation in New Competition Regimes: The Role of Private Enforcement', in *New Competition Jurisdictions: Shaping Policies and Building Institutions*, ed. by R Whish and C Townley (Cheltenham UK: Edward Elgar Publishing, 2012), 167–182, 176.
251 Jones, Foreword (fn 33) 1. Similarly R Mulheron, 'Some Difficulties with Group Litigation Orders – and Why a Class Action is Superior', *Civil Justice Quarterly*, 24 (2005), 40–68, 64; Russell (fn 48) 152; Davis (fn 211) 940–941.
252 Andreangeli, Collective redress in EU competition law (fn 245) 529, 556.

suggesting an opt-in action. The rationale could be that this would be better than having none at all.

On the other hand, it is necessary to have the opt-out option available. Indeed, opt-out actions are capable of assisting numerous consumer claims in recovering compensation and the compensation objective would be better served by its adoption for consumer damages claims. It might therefore be reasonable to make available both opt-in and opt-out actions, leaving the choice to the court's discretion. The court, as the impartial and independent authority, taking into account all the circumstances, such as the amount of the loss and the number of harmed individuals, would be well able to decide which is more appropriate to the case at hand. In this way, the possibility of an EU opt-out action would not be disregarded, the application of opt-out actions to consumer cases would be made available with the court's discretion and with the availability of both a more acceptable solution would be provided for Member States. In light of this, the next section demonstrates how grouping consumer claims is suited to collective actions for the joint resolution of damages claims.

Grouping the claims

The ways in which the group is defined

All the membership systems necessitate a group definition to identify on whose behalf a collective action is brought. Once the group has been described, in an opt-in action, individuals must come forward and express their intention to join the group and in this way the members are identified.[253] Mandatory actions encompass all individuals in the defined group without requiring them to opt in and without granting them the right to exit. Opt-out actions automatically include all individuals in the defined group unless they wish to be excluded and for that reason the group is comprised of identifiable persons.

The group definition has a profound effect on the practical functioning of collective actions.[254] It determines the size of the group, who will be a member and bound by the judgment, and as a consequence, the liability of the defendant.[255] Hence it affects the number of other individual or collective actions that are or would be brought to courts.[256] The method and content of notification would also be framed in respect of the group definition.[257] Further, it shapes the formation of appropriate representation and the methods of calculation and distribution of damages.[258] In this regard, the key is to group similarly situated victims in order

253 S Van Uytsel, 'Collective Actions in a Competition Law Context – Reconciling Multilayer Interests to Enhance Access to Justice', in *Collective Actions: Enhancing Access to Justice and Reconciling Multilayer Interests?*, ed. by S Wrbka, S Van Uytsel and M Siems (Cambridge: Cambridge University Press, 2012), 57–92, 78.

254 SWPWP (fn 7) para 46.

255 Mulheron, Class action (fn 90) 321.

256 SWPWP (fn 7) para 46.

257 Mulheron, Class action (fn 90) 321.

258 SWPWP (fn 7) para 46.

to make the collective action a viable tool for the resolution of their claims in a single proceeding. Similarly situated victims can be selected via objective or subjective methods.[259]

The objective method defines the group considering objective criteria and avoiding subjective standards.[260] First, there has to be a clearly defined time frame. For instance, in a cartel, this would start when the defendants' anticompetitive conduct first caused a loss to individuals. Secondly, products affected by the anticompetitive practice should be identified, which in turn assists the identification of those harmed. Thirdly, a geographic boundary of the group should be set.[261] In this method, the group tends to be composed of all those who are likely to have a cause of action,[262] ie those with a potential claim against the defendant.[263] In the US, defendants prefer such a broad definition, because, in this way, a large number of claimants can be included and thus bound by the judgment.[264]

However, defining the group in an objective method can result in over-inclusion.[265] It has been claimed that this can prevent the formation of a clear group definition[266] and make the identification of who is and who is not a member difficult.[267] The objective method has especially been challenged in respect of collective actions for damages. It has been argued that these actions require more specificity in order to allow individuals to easily decide whether or not they are or they can be part of the proposed group.[268] Further, an objectively defined group can include some people who have not been harmed by the defendant's anticompetitive act,[269] or people who have divergent interests or positions.[270]

It has thus been suggested that definition by an objective method should be supplemented by subjective criteria.[271] These criteria would limit the group to those who have incurred injury, who can show a causal connection between the infringement and the harm,[272] or whose state of mind or merits of the action must be established for membership.[273] An example as regards the group definition in a subjective way can be that all persons who purchased the product X in the UK and

259 Mulheron, Class action (fn 90) 321; Van Uytsel (fn 253) 78.
260 It is the practice in the US, MCL (fn 86) 270. The proposed *Fairness in Class Action Litigation Act of 2017* also requires the class to be defined with reference to objective criteria. *The Fairness in Class Action Litigation Act of 2017* (FCALA), H.R. 985, § 1718 (a).
261 ABA, Section of Antitrust Law, *Antitrust Class Actions Handbook* (USA: American Bar Association, 2010), 54.
262 Mulheron, Class action (fn 90) 324.
263 Van Uytsel (fn 253) 78.
264 Mulheron, Class action (fn 90) 325.
265 See *ibid* 324.
266 Van Uytsel (fn 253) 78.
267 See ABA, Antitrust class actions (fn 261) 53.
268 See MCL (fn 86) 270.
269 Fischer (fn 40) 52.
270 MCL (fn 86) 271.
271 Mulheron, Class action (fn 90) 327; Van Uytsel (fn 253) 78.
272 Van Uytsel (fn 253) 78.
273 Mulheron, Class action (fn 90) 328–329.

France between 1 January 2013 and 31 August 2018 and who suffered loss resulting from the infringement in question. The last part, ie who suffered loss due to the infringement, distinguishes the subjective method from the objective method.

By using the subjective method, as Mulheron contends, a narrower group definition can be achieved, which may better identify the potential members and provide information as to what must be submitted to obtain relief.[274] Detractors of this method argue that the usage of these criteria entails determining the merits of the case before ascertaining the group, and thereby transform a purely procedural matter into one of a substantive law.[275] Furthermore, the use of subjective criteria undermines the resolution of common issues by giving rise to issues specific to each member,[276] which in turn diminishes the practicality and utility of the collective action. Its proponents argue that adding some subjective criteria to the group description does not alter what is essentially a procedural matter, and that no mini-trial is required to decide the merits of the case[277] merely though supplementing a group definition with loss or other subjective criteria.[278]

The tension between these group definitions is between subjective elements that may necessitate a prior and possible individual assessment, and the objective method which risks over inclusion.[279] However, ***homogeneity requirements*** would be the decisive factor in determining numerous claims brought in a single lawsuit.[280] Variance among group members has the potential to hinder the capacity of collective actions to resolve the dispute.[281] Therefore, 'Sufficient homogeneity of claims [is the key] for the court to issue a "one size fits all" decision, and for the victims to be able to adhere to the collective action'.[282]

In the US, certification of many class actions has been denied due to inadequate group definition in recent years.[283] Revisiting the certification criteria clarifies the way in which the group needs to be defined.[284] On this basis, group definition

274 *Ibid* 335–336.
275 Van Uytsel (fn 253) 79.
276 Mulheron, Class action (fn 90) 329.
277 Van Uytsel (fn 253) 79.
278 Mulheron, Class action (fn 90) 332.
279 See *ibid* 333–334.
280 See NERA Economic Consulting, 'Memo: Comments in relation to the White Paper on Damages Actions for Breach of the EC Antitrust Rules', 2008, para 15 <http://ec.europa.eu/competition/antitrust/actionsdamages/white_paper_comments/nera_en.pdf> [accessed 1 July 2018].
281 RA Nagareda, 'Class Certification in the Age of Aggregate Proof', *New York University Law Review*, 84 (2009), 84–173, 132.
282 A Cassone and GB Ramello, 'The Simple Economics of Class Action: Private Provision of Club and Public Goods', *IEL Paper in Comparative Analysis of Institutions, Economics and Law*, no 3, 2011, 1–18, 5 <http://polis.unipmn.it/pubbl/RePEc/uca/ucaiel/iel003.pdf> [accessed 1 July 2018].
283 In the period of 2008–2013, RH Klonoff, 'The Decline of Class Actions', *Washington University Law Review*, 90(3) (2013), 729–838, 762. For instance, the necessity of individual fact-finding to prove membership of the class leads to a rejection of certification, see *Carrera v Bayer Corp*, 727 F.3d 300, 305–308 (3d Cir. 2013).
284 See Chapter 2.

needs to clearly show that there are issues of fact or law common to all members and that these predominate over individual enquiries.[285] By so doing, it aims to aggregate these numerous claims that share similar factual issues which give rise to similar legal questions[286] and submit such an action is a superior procedural device compared to other available methods for the fair and efficient resolution of the dispute.[287] In conjunction with others, the typicality requirement seeks to ensure cohesiveness across the group[288] so that the members do not have divergent interests.[289]

To conclude, the aim of group definition is to arrive at a sufficient similarity across that group.[290] Hence, the group needs to be defined with attention to two necessary elements: *i.* the degree of individual assessment necessary to deal with damages claims of the group members in a collective action[291] and *ii.* the existence of any conflicting interests within the group. In light of this, the next section examines the two necessary elements when forming a group.

Two necessary elements of group definition

The first element requires that extensive individualised enquiries should not be necessary to solve the dispute at hand in a collective action.[292] Otherwise, the action risks becoming buried under individual issues, which in turn creates manageability problems.[293] In a collective action, group members need to share three common issues: *i.* the existence of infringement, *ii.* injury and causation and *iii.* calculation of damages sustained.[294] The inherent nature of competition infringements warrants the pursuit of damage claims in collective actions[295] because adducing the proof of the infringement itself and the nexus between the infringement and the harm are common to all claimants.[296] In other words, liability is generally proven on a group-wide basis.[297] However, problems arise when

285 Lahav, Symmetry and class action litigation (fn 216) 1512.
286 A Erbsen, 'From "Predominance" to "Resolvability": A New Approach to Regulating Class Actions', *Vanderbilt Law Review*, 58(4) (2005), 995–1088, 1005.
287 MCL (fn 86) 271–272.
288 A Andreangeli, *Private Enforcement of Antitrust: Regulating Corporate Behaviour through Collective Claims in the EU and US* (Cheltenham UK: Edward Elgar Publishing, 2014), 131.
289 ABA, Antitrust class actions (fn 261) 37.
290 Nagareda (fn 281) 131.
291 See J Johnson and G Leonard, 'Economics and the Rigorous Analysis of Class Certification in Antitrust Cases', *Journal of Competition Law and Economics*, 3(3) (2007), 341–356, 342.
292 Mulheron, Class action (fn 90) 260.
293 *Ibid.*
294 See Davis and Cramer (fn 209) 983.
295 Anderson and Trask (fn 84) 60; *Amchem Products., Inc.v Windsor*, 521 US 591 (1997), para 625.
296 Davis and Cramer (fn 209) 983.
297 Anderson and Trask (fn 84) 60.

damages suffered by each group member cannot be computed commonly to all group members.[298]

In the US, it is not enough that the harm sustained by members stems from the same common factual and legal grounds; damages need also to be able to be proven on a group-wide basis.[299] While some courts have held separate trials to quantify individual damages, others have embraced the view that those separate trials eliminate the benefits of handling claims collectively and therefore run counter to predominance and superiority requirements.[300] The need to address issues of individual damages assessments or proof of damages on an individual basis could still mean that an action is suitable for a class action treatment,[301] unless those issues render the action too burdensome for the court by entailing a multitude of complicated mini-litigations within the action.[302]

The second element is whether there exists any heterogeneity and resulting conflict of interest amongst group members which make a collective action unworkable.[303] It is not the case that all members need to pursue the same damages. However, the handling of their claims in a single suit may deteriorate if they have opposing interests,[304] or similarly, some members benefit from the same acts that are harmful to others.[305]

In consequence, an adequate group definition should consider avoiding both extensive individualised issues and possible controversy amongst group members in order to achieve joint resolution of their claims in a single binding proceeding. In that regard, the next section exemplifies how the type of the plaintiff and the

298 PE Areeda, H Hovenkamp, RD Blair and CP Durrance, *Antitrust Law: An Analysis of Antitrust Principles and Their Application*, 3rd edn (New York: Aspen Publishers, 2006), vol.IIA, 414–415.

299 S Rodrigue and L Plumpton, 'The Globalisation of Anti-Trust: How the Internationalisation of Collective Redress Is Changing the Game', *Class and Group Actions 2014*, 2013, 31–39, 34 <http://www.torys.com/Publications/Documents/Publication%20PDFs/CA2013-4.pdf> [accessed 1 July 2018]. See individualised questions of damages prevent class certification altogether, *Comcast Corp. v Behrend*, 569 US 27 (2013).

300 L Kruse and D Pirolo, 'Antitrust', in *A Practitioner's Guide to Class Actions*, ed. by M Greer (USA: American Bar Association, 2011), 421–424, 422.

301 Mulheron, Class action (fn 90) 261, 263.

302 *Danvers Motor Co. v Ford Motor Co.*, 543 F.3d 141 (3d Cir. 2008), para 149.

303 Y-K Che, 'Equilibrium Formation of Class Action Suits', *Journal of Public Economics*, 62 (1996), 339–361, 340. When plaintiffs do not form a homogenous group, who can represent them also becomes problematic. Conflict issue is usually assessed in the US in respect of the adequacy of the representative. See eg C Brummer, 'Sharpening the Sword: Class Certification, Appellate Review, and the Role of the Fiduciary Judge in Class Action Lawsuits', *Columbia Law Review*, 104 (2004), 1042–1071, 1069; ABA, Antitrust class actions (fn 261) 66.

304 HM Downs, 'Federal Class Actions: Due Process by Adequacy of Representation (Identity of Claims) and the Impact of General Telephone v. Falcon', *Ohio State Law Journal*, 54 (1993), 607–712, 685–686.

305 *Pickett v Iowa Beef Processors*, 209 F.3d 1276 (11th Cir. 2000), para 1280; *Valley Drug Co. v Geneva Pharmaceuticals, Inc.*, 350 F.3d 1181 (11th Cir. 2003), para 1189.

kind of loss suffered affect the satisfaction of these two elements in collective actions for damages in the field of competition law.

Towards an adequate group definition: what matters?

The type of loss

In determining the group members, the type of the loss, ie overcharge or lost profits, matters because in lost profits cases there exists the potential for conflict between group members and extensive individualised damages assessments.[306] Regarding the conflict issue, plaintiffs in lost profits cases are generally in a position to compete with each other in the same market.[307] To obtain damages for lost profits, each member needs to show that in the absence of the defendant's anticompetitive conduct, it would have held a certain share of the market, and that that market share would not have been held by other members.[308] Hence, each member has a financial interest in proving either or both that its business lost the most profits in a limited market[309] and that its profit loss resulted from the competition infringement but that other members' profit loss results from factors unrelated to the infringement.

The second reason is the individualised character of damages for lost profits.[310] The basis of a lost profits damage calculation is the decrease in the amount of business done by the firm in question or the amount of business not done due to the infringement. The operation of each business and the conditions within which it operates are specific to itself.[311] For instance, in a foreclosure case, the plaintiff relies on its own past economic performance to show profit lost due to an infringement.[312] Several factors, unique to the company, influence this past performance. Establishing a causal link is a similar process.[313] It differs from business to business, being very important in business claims to prove that lost profits are arisen from the infringement not from any other reason, such as market conditions, poor management of the company, or constraints of marketing expenses.[314] Thus, the proof and quantification of individual lost profits requires a member-by-member analysis in collective actions.[315]

306 ABA, Antitrust class actions (fn 261) 65–66.
307 US courts are more likely to certify a class action on the basis of overcharge rather than loss of profits. *Ibid* 65.
308 ABA, Antitrust class actions (fn 261) 65.
309 *Ibid.*
310 *Ibid.*
311 *Ibid* 66.
312 Areeda and others (fn 298) 337.
313 ABA, Antitrust class actions (fn 261) 66.
314 FW Bulst 'Private Antitrust Enforcement at a Roundabout', *European Business Organization Law Review*, 3 (2006), 725–746, 738.
315 Davis and Cramer (fn 209) 996; ABA (fn 261) 66.

The type of plaintiff

Overcharge cases are found amenable to collective actions[316] because in theory an infringement leading to an overcharge could affect the entire group of purchasers.[317] However, individual issues and conflicting interests within that group may still exist in those cases, which creates obstacles to grouping for collective redress purposes. In overcharge cases, all purchasers take a share from the initial overcharge as damages.[318] Overcharge generally changes along successive levels of the supply chain, meaning direct and indirect purchasers absorb a certain percentage and pass the rest on to downstream purchasers.[319] When the group involves all purchasers, this leads to not only a conflict of interest between businesses and between business and consumer plaintiffs, but also generate a need for individual damages calculations for members[320] other than consumers.

In overcharge cases, individual damages assessments are necessary when a collective action is brought on behalf of intermediaries. As a group, '[they] have sufficiently differing interests to make a vigorous and common pursuit of all of their interests impossible'.[321] Different passing-on rates at each level, and possibly for each claimant, and the operation of each business in its own economic circumstances means that measuring overcharge and lost profits damages of intermediaries require individual analysis.[322] Some of the business claimants who do not suffer overcharge harm because of full passing-on can still be in the group with other businesses who endure overcharge.[323] If some members have not been harmed, this needs to be established on an individual basis. For instance, the supply agreements of some business members can contain a price protection clause, or some of them may not have been charged on the basis of inflated prices due to having a good business relationship with infringers, or sometimes the price invoiced does not indicate discounts, rebates and allowances.[324]

316 ABA (fn 261) 64.

317 *In re Hydrogen Peroxide Antitrust Litigation*, 552 F.3d 305 (3d Cir. 2008), para 325. However, in *Windham v American Brands*, a price-fixing case, a variation in price from market to market, from day to day, and from product grade to product grade prevented maintaining class action because damages had to be determined separately and that would cause the multiplicity of mini-trials. *Windham v American Brands, Inc.*, 565 F.2d 59 (4th Cir. 1977) paras 63, 66.

318 Oxera and A Komninos, *Quantifying Antitrust Damages – Towards Non-Binding Guidance for Courts*, Study Prepared for the Commission (Luxembourg, 2009), iii.

319 RH Lande, 'New Options for State Indirect Purchaser Legislation: Protecting the Real Victims of Antitrust Violations', *Alabama Law Review*, 61(3) (2010), 447–492, 464.

320 Wardhaugh (fn 29) 11.

321 *Ibid.*

322 See Chapter 5.

323 BW Hamilton, 'Class Action in Price-Fixing Litigation When the Fixed Price is a Wage Rate: Law et Al. v. NCAA', *Antitrust Bulletin*, 48(2) (2003), 505–529, 512. If there is a full pass-on, then business plaintiffs are likely to incur lost profits damages. See further about lost profit damages assessment in *supra* section 'The type of loss'.

324 Areeda and others (fn 298) 415.

Within a group consisting of purchasers who are directly and indirectly harmed, ie businesses and consumers or businesses alone,[325] there exist opposing interests between members,[326] which may not allow resolving the damages issues of both types of claimants in the same lawsuit.[327] The extent of damages recovered by consumers depends on the amount of the overcharge passed on to them by intermediaries. The amount of overcharge damages received by businesses is related to both how much has been passed down to them and how much they passed on. This means purchasers at the lower level compete with those at a higher level in obtaining greater overcharge damages.[328] Therefore, each member, or those members claiming the bigger share, automatically contradicts the interest of the others because what one receives the other does not.[329]

In fact, this is observed in the UK *Emerald Supplies* case. Emerald sought to file an action on behalf of direct and indirect purchasers who, as a result of a price-fixing cartel that BA and other airlines formed, overpaid for air freight services.[330] One of the reasons why this representative action was struck out was that '[t]he relief sought in the action is not equally beneficial for all members of the class'.[331] The High Court submitted that there was a potential conflict of interest between the members, as the damages claims of indirect purchasers relied on the fact that direct purchasers had been passing the overcharge on to them.[332] Subsequently, the Court of Appeal held that the group members who have partly or entirely passed the overcharge along had different interests in recovering loss as a result of the competition infringement than those who have not passed on and have therefore absorbed the overcharge.[333] To this end, the new collective action regime provides that the CAT considers, *inter alia*, whether it is possible to award

325 PY Cremieux and others, 'Assessing Conflict, Impact and Common Methods of Proof in Intermediate Indirect-Purchaser Class Action Litigation', *Economics Comittee Newsletter*, 6(1) (2006), 4–10, 4.

326 S Hussain, D Garrett and V Howell, 'Economics of Class Certification in Indirect Purchaser Antitrust Cases', *Journal of the Antitrust and Unfair Competition Law Section of the State Bar of California*, 10(1) (2001), 18–52, 38; *ibid.*

327 Welfare impact report (fn 124) 299; Wardhaugh (fn 29) 11.

328 M Handler and MD Blechman, 'Antitrust and the Consumer Interest: The Fallacy of Parens Patriae and A Suggested New Approach', *Yale Law Journal*, 85(5) (1976), 626–676, 654.

329 Areeda and others (fn 298) 409. Similarly, BM Dickey and DL Rubinfield, 'Antitrust Class Certification: Towards an Economic Framework', *New York University Annual Survey of American Law*, 66 (2011), 459–486, 475.

330 *Emerald Supplies Ltd and another v British Airways plc* [2009] EWHC 741 (Ch), [2009] UKCLR 801, paras 1–2. See further CPR 1998, rule 19.6.

331 *Emerald Supplies* (fn 330) para 36.

332 *Ibid*; Brick Court Chambers, *Competition Litigation: UK Practice and Procedure*, ed. by M Brealey and N Green (Oxford: Oxford University Press, 2010), 142. In order to overcome the conflict issue, Mulheron suggests sub-groping, redefining the group, or that the passing-on issue is left to individual trials or that the group members are allowed to opt out to protect their interests. R Mulheron, 'A Missed Gem of an Opportunity for the Representative Rule', *European Business Law Review*, 23(1) (2012), 49–60, 57.

333 *Emerald Supplies Ltd v British Airways Plc* [2010] EWCA Civ 1284, paras 62, 64.

aggregate damages to the group in assessing the suitability of claims to be brought in collective actions.[334]

In the US, a group of affected businesses and consumers might be certified provided that a damages calculation can be made on a group-wide basis.[335] In *Methionine I*, for instance, a class action on behalf of all indirect purchasers including resellers and consumers was not allowed. The court expressed that it could not be ignored that some members were not harmed by the infringement because no overcharge was passed down to them or because they passed on the entire overcharge[336] and that individual trials would be required to find out whether each member incurred damages due to the infringement.[337] The court acknowledged the fact that each intermediary had an interest in claiming that it absorbed the entire overcharge but its reason for rejection was based on a lack of proof of injury on a group-wide basis.[338] Later the court certified the class action for a group that only consisted of consumers.[339] In *NASDAQ*, however, the court decided that potential conflict relating to the apportionment of damages between buyers and sellers[340] is not sufficient to deny certification at this stage until it is demonstrated that the conflict outweighs the substantial interest of every group member in the proceeding.[341] The court further submitted that quantifying individual damages can be left to a subsequent set of proceedings if the liability is determined through class action.[342]

Two approaches are applied in such cases: *i.* filing the case on behalf of a single level of the distribution chain, usually on behalf of consumers[343] or *ii.* allowing sub-grouping for each level of the distribution chain with their own representatives.[344] The latter, however, could engender extensive sub-grouping. In this event, the litigation would become complex,[345] or it might not qualify as a class

334 CAT rules (fn 42) para 79(2)(f).
335 *In re Hydrogen Peroxide* (fn 317) para 325; Davis and Cramer (fn 209) 990.
336 *In re Methionine Antitrust Litigation* MDL no 00–1311 CRB (N.D. Cal. 2001), 1–7, 6.
337 *Ibid* 7.
338 *Ibid* 6–7.
339 *In re Methionine Antitrust Litigation*, MDL no 00–1311 (N.D. Cal. 2003) 2.
340 *In re NASDAQ Market-Makers Antitrust Litigation,* 169 F.R.D. 493 (S.D.N.Y. 1996), para 513.
341 *Ibid* para 514.
342 *Ibid* para 524.
343 ABA, Section of Antitrust Law, *Indirect Purchaser Litigation Handbook* (USA: American Bar Association, 2007), 162–163.
344 L Popofsky, 'Opt Out Antitrust Class Actions – An American Perspective' (Oxford University, Centre for Competition Law and Policy, Oxford, 2014), 1–21, 4–5 <http://lawprofessors.typepad.com/files/popofsky.pdf> [accessed 1 July 2018]. See eg in Diamond class action, damages were quantified for direct and indirect purchasers under sub-groups and indirect purchasers were also divided into different sub-groups – indirect resellers and consumers, *Sullivan v DB Investments*, Case nos 04-CV-2819 (SRC), 01-CV-4463 (SRC), 04-CV-4098 (SRC), (D.N.J. 2008) <https://diamondsclassaction.com> [accessed 1 July 2018].
345 Leskinen (fn 9) 34.

action because each sub-group has to independently satisfy all the prerequisites[346] and this may not be possible, for instance, if the proposed sub-group does not comprise numerous claimants.[347] However, in both approaches, problems remain for businesses relating to the calculation of individual damages. If the number of business claimants and their damage determinations do not overburden courts, the court could proceed with their claims collectively to some degree. This suggests that such an action can be beneficial to businesses to some extent, such as when establishing liability, but causation as well as quantification of damages need to be determined on an individual basis.[348]

The proposed approach: grouping consumer claims

The issues relating to extensive individual treatment and conflicting interests within the group can simply be avoided if the group consists of only consumers. As a group they are the best suited persons whose claims can be determined in a collective action.[349] The type of consumers harmed by competition infringements influences whether their claims can be grouped for collective redress purposes. That said, the claims of direct and indirect consumers can form a group.[350] All who have purchased the overcharged product are harmed by paying more than the competitive price. Indeed, they are at the end of the distribution chain, have no choice but to endure the overcharge and suffer no lost profits. There is no question of passing-on nor conflicting interest between them, as per buyers and sellers of the product who act in different capacities.[351] Hence, their damages can be calculated for the group as a whole without requiring individual assessments.[352]

However, it is difficult to say the same for deadweight loss and umbrella consumers.[353] With respect to deadweight loss consumers, it is not possible to include them in a consumer group defined for a collective action seeking overcharge damages because they have entirely abandoned the product[354] and their damages

346 Fischer (fn 40) 53.

347 MCL (fn 86) 272.

348 See E Elhauge and D Geradin, *Global Competition Law and Economics*, 2nd edn (New York, USA: Thomson Reuters/Foundation Press, 2011) 31–32; Popofsky (fn 344) 4.

349 *Sullivan v DB Investments* (fn 344) 'Report and Recommendation of Special Master', 77–167, 94 <https://diamondsclassaction.com/pdfs/Diamonds.R&R.2.pdf> [accessed 1 July 2018].

350 Page submits, without specifically taking consumers into account, that although indirect purchaser class actions are certified as many as half of the direct purchaser ones, their certification rate is increased almost twice compared with the early period. Page (fn 146) 285, 294.

351 See *In re Cipro Cases I, II*, 121 Cal.App.4th 402 (Cal. App. 2004) paras 415–416.

352 See Chapter 8.

353 See Chapter 5 for the difficulties in proving their damages.

354 It is the practice in the US. JA Brander and TW Ross, 'Estimating Damages from Price-Fixing', *Canadian Class Action Review*, 3 (2006), 335–369, 340; CR Leslie, 'Antitrust Damages and Deadweight Loss', *Antitrust Bulletin*, 51(3) (2006), 521–567, 559.

is different from the overcharge.[355] If non-purchasers can be identified, they could form a separate group, but this does not constitute a solution to the difficulties associated with the common pursuit of their claims in a single proceeding. The non-purchasers would suffer damages due to different reasons. Some of them may have not been willing to pay the inflated price, some may have not found the product or its substitute, and others may have bought the product on a secondary market at a price higher than the initial anticompetitive price.[356] Depending on the reason for the non-purchase, they also incur different damages because their valuation of the product that they were unable to purchase varies.[357] As a result, '[n]o non-purchaser is particularly typical'.[358]

Umbrella consumers suffer similar problems when forming a group.[359] These consumers would not be included in the group that consists of direct and indirect consumers because they are not in the same vertical chain. This means not only the amount of umbrella damages but also proving the causal link between the harm and infringement is different from direct and indirect consumers. Umbrella consumers can form a sub-group that establishes the infringement has caused an umbrella effect in the market. However, umbrella damages claims are prone to individual issues due to the need for sub-grouping per substitute product and for sub-grouping per non-infringing seller. These consumers might have bought the product from different sellers, and as a consequence, when some will not have incurred any overcharge, some will,[360] perhaps in different amounts. In addition, it is possible that not all umbrella consumers paid more on account of a price umbrella created by the infringement. Some sellers might increase prices for reasons unrelated to the infringement, for instance, that their suppliers increase the prices.[361] Indeed, it needs to be proved for each seller that the price increase is originated from the umbrella effect not from any other reason.[362] Another possibility exacerbates the above problems: if umbrella purchasers are not consumers, the infringement may have given harm to a further indirect purchaser group who can be consumers to whom umbrella customers have passed on an overcharge.[363]

It is therefore difficult to attain sufficient similarity between umbrella consumers and between deadweight loss consumers. This makes the common pursuit of all their interests unlikely with respect to delivering compensation for harm in a collective action. However, if direct and indirect consumers are grouped, dispute can

355 Leslie (fn 354) 555.
356 *Ibid* 559.
357 *Ibid.*
358 *Ibid.*
359 Van Uytsel (fn 253) 81.
360 *Ibid.*
361 *Ibid.*
362 See Chapter 5.
363 M-O Mackenrodt, 'Private Incentive, Optimal Deterrence and Damage Claims for Abuses of Dominant Positions – The Interaction between the Economic Review of the Prohibition of Abuses of Dominant Positions and Private Enforcement', in *Abuse of Dominant Position: New Interpretation, New Enforcement Mechanisms?*, ed. by M-O Mackenrodt, BC Gallego and S Enchelmaier (Berlin: Springer, 2010), 165–189, 182.

be resolved for all members in a single proceeding and damages can be awarded to the group as a whole. This serves the purpose of a collective action, ie resolving a controversy for similarly situated numerous claimants in a single binding proceeding.

Concluding remarks

This chapter started formulating a collective redress action for consumer damages claims in EU competition cases and put forward its own proposals. The initial step in designing a collective redress action is to determine how to establish group membership. The formation of the group affects the way in which those harmed can be part of the group on whose behalf the action is filed. Opt-in actions require victims to clearly express their desire to be included in the action, at the latest before the judgment. It identifies group members individually and requires the submission of individual consents to the action. These requirements make such an action subject to the shortcomings of two-party litigation and not capable of providing redress to a group encompassing a large number of consumers. For large groups an opt-in action would be burdensome, costly and time-consuming. However, it ensures an individual's control over the litigation and would address the needs of small groups. A mandatory action, on the other hand, includes all those harmed by the infringement. It reaches a large group, but also removes the individuals' right to exclude themselves from the binding effect of the judgment. In collective actions on behalf of consumers, there seems no need to have recourse to such a membership system as consumers generally remain in opt-out actions.

Opt-out actions are well equipped to address the claims of a great number of consumers with small loses while preserving the right to exist the group. In these actions, victims do not need to take an affirmative step to be part of the group, unless they wish to be excluded. In comprising all those harmed, a large group of persons is included in the group and the action may in turn ask for a larger sum of claim amount. This group consists of identifiable persons who are required to do nothing to benefit from the court's decision at the end of litigation. It is easier for the representative party to bring the case on their behalf as they must only define the group.

These features of opt-out actions give rise to the concerns over the right of access to the courts. However, it is submitted that an effective notice requirement would overcome this concern, aiming to reach each member and provide them with information necessary to the collective action on their behalf and about their rights in that regard. With an effective notice requirement in place, opt-out actions would be compatible with this right while preserving its ability to deliver compensation to many consumers. This ability can also be attributed to the way in which these actions operate. Opt-out actions, like any other collective action, theoretically, diverges from traditional two-party litigation. These actions are based on representation and do not require active participation of group members for a case to be decided but provide them with rights to be heard or to exit. Consumers hardly ever opt-out of the action because, arguably, they are not worse off by staying. In practice, consumers do not pursue individual litigation. If an opt-out action is lost, they will not incur any costs, if the action is won they can receive compensation. Take-up and participation rates are considered as the indicators of how effectively opt-out actions realise the compensation objective compared with opt-in actions. They demonstrate that, at the end of an opt-out action, a large number of consumers receive compensation for their loss.

In terms of the collective redress initiative in competition law, the Commission acknowledges that opt-out actions are better at providing compensation to victims than opt-in actions. The horizontal approach provides an exception for their use if justice requires, but refrains from recommending it for the EU. An opt-out action, alone or in combination with other features of the class action procedure, is currently perceived as producing excesses and negative consequences, after the example of the US. Indeed, the US system has been regarded as abusive by the Commission and by some stakeholders. The Commission also sees opt-out actions as radical measures and as incompatible with European legal systems. In this regard, it should first be noted that some Member States already have opt-out actions in place and these do not observe any of the alleged negative results. Additionally, although it is not possible to conclude on the whole functioning of the system, empirical studies in the US challenge the common belief and suggest that fear of opt-out actions is unnecessary in the EU.

The reason that the Commission proposes the introduction of an opt-in action is to enhance the acceptability of such a proposal amongst stakeholders. In fact, an opt-in action would be effective in easily identifiable small groups. However, by the same token, it is not reasonable to discard opt-out actions when they better address consumer damages claims and are able to deliver compensation to a large number of consumers. Bearing all these in mind, the proposed solution is to leave the choice between opt-in or opt-out actions to the discretion of the courts in any given case. In this way, both opt-in and opt-out actions would be available and the court would decide which is more suitable to the case at hand. This solution would act as a means of obtaining political support from interested stakeholders for an EU-wide collective redress action and makes an opt-out action available as the option for the court to apply to consumer claims.

That said, the analysis in this chapter demonstrated that consumer damages claims are best suited to be pursued in a collective action. Indeed, the commencement of a collective action necessitates a group definition. Once the group is defined, it should be composed depending on the membership system chosen. In this respect, it is important to determine whether including all harmed individuals makes the joint resolution of their damages claims possible in a single proceeding. It is submitted that group definition needs to avoid extensive individual issues for the resolution of their claims and possible divergent and conflicting interests between the group members. Both are observed in lost profit and overcharge cases when the group comprises businesses.

In general, bundling only the damages claims of consumers in collective actions removes these problems as consumers can neither pass overcharge along nor suffer lost profits. However, the fact that consumers are harmed by competition infringements in different ways might prevent them forming a homogeneous group.

Damages claims of umbrella and deadweight loss consumers are prone to individual issues due to the way in which they are affected by an infringement. Therefore, it is submitted that a collective action provides a vigorous and prompt resolution of damage claims of many when the group is formed of direct and indirect consumers. These do not have conflicting interests in litigation nor does their damages calculation necessitate any individual assessments. Of especial importance to opt-out actions is the possibility of awarding damages to a group as a whole since all who purchased the product in question have had no choice but to absorb the consumer level overcharge. Hence, the group should consist of direct and indirect consumers. After submitting this, the next step is to decide who should be allowed to bring a collective action on their behalf and using what funding mechanism(s); these will be analysed in the next chapter.

7 Designing collective redress actions

Representative party and funding rules

Introduction

This chapter explores the possible representative parties and funding schemes for collective redress actions. The representative party files the action on behalf of group members, represents their interests in courts and endures the costs and risks of litigation. In this respect, the available funding mechanisms are an important factor that influence whether these actions are brought to courts.

The current chapter first discusses who should be entitled to bring a collective redress action on behalf consumers harmed by EU competition infringements. The representative party could be a lead plaintiff, or, alternatively, an ideological claimant. Then the chapter considers the possible funding mechanisms that should be available to representative parties when bringing a collective action on behalf affected consumers in the EU.

Determining the representative party

Lead plaintiff

A representative party pursues competition infringements,[1] bringing the action on behalf of those harmed and establishing an effective link between the lawyer and group members.[2] Collective actions can be brought by a lead plaintiff who is one of the members of the group. The lead plaintiff is almost always found by a lawyer who searches for competition infringements and their victims.[3] This is especially

1 SE Keske, *Group Litigation in European Competition Law: A Law and Economics Perspective* (Antwerp-Oxford-Portland: Intersentia, 2010) 85.
2 R Mulheron, *The Class Action in Common Law Legal Systems: A Comparative Perspective* (Oxford and Portland, Oregon: Hart Publishing, 2004) 291.
3 This is the US practice, JE Fisch, 'Class Action Reform, Qui Tam, and the Role of the Plaintiff', *Law and Contemporary Problems*, 60(4) (1997), 167–202, 171.

the case for consumers[4] and particularly because their claim value does not incentivise them to act for a group.[5]

This introduces the problem of monitoring lawyers who may seek to further their own interests, departing from those of group members[6] and who may not exert necessary effort to safeguard the interests of group members.[7] Collective actions are indeed different from individualistic two-party litigation in terms of the relationship between lawyer and client. First, in collective actions lawyers' fees are determined by the court, not by the negotiation with the lead plaintiff.[8] Secondly, lawyers have greater incentive to litigate because of having higher fees *vis-à-vis* individual damages of group members.[9] They may initiate a collective action when it is financially profitable to do so,[10] providing that they work under contingency fee arrangements. Thirdly, the lead plaintiff, ie consumer, may be unable to monitor the lawyer due to a lack of understanding of the legal issues and/or of the collective action litigation necessary for taking an active role[11] and has no motivation to do so because it requires time, effort and money.[12] A consumer, who is not a repeat player, would have no ongoing relationship with nor any leverage over the lawyer.[13] As a consequence, principal-agent problems can arise.[14]

Judicial monitoring could overcome these shortcomings.[15] The US class action procedure, which allows a lead plaintiff and her lawyer to file an action on behalf of similarly situated persons, gives a more active role to the judge to control and guide litigation.[16] Typically, lead plaintiffs do not choose or reject the lawyer, which makes lawyers non-excludable from the litigation.[17] However, it is required

4 See further Chapter 2.
5 See WB Rubenstein, 'Why Enable Litigation?: A Positive Externalities Theory of the Small Claims Class Action', *University of Missouri-Kansas City Law Review*, 74(3) (2006), 709–728, 715.
6 Keske (fn 1) 65, fn 244.
7 S Keske, A Renda and R Van den Bergh, 'Financing and Group Litigation', in *New Trends in Financing Civil Litigation in Europe: A Legal, Empirical, and Economic Analysis*, ed. by ML Tuil and L Visscher (Cheltenham UK: Edward Elgar Publishing, 2010), 57–91, 64–65.
8 Fisch (fn 3) 172.
9 JW Burns, 'Decorative Figureheads: Eliminating Class Representatives in Class Actions', *Hastings Law Journal*, 42 (1991), 165–202, 182; *ibid* 168.
10 See eg Burns (fn 9) 182; A Gidi, 'Class Actions in Brazil – A Model for Civil Law Countries', *American Journal of Comparative Law*, 51 (2013), 311–408, 369.
11 Burns (fn 9) 183.
12 See Fisch (fn 3) 173.
13 See AD Lahav, 'Fundamental Principles for Class Action Governance', *Indiana Law Review*, 37 (2004), 65–140, 80.
14 See *supra* section 'Ideological claimant'.
15 B Wardhaugh, 'Bogeymen, Lunatics and Fanatics: Collective Actions and the Private Enforcement of European Competition Law', *Legal Studies*, 34(1) (2014), 1–23, 8.
16 Burns (fn 9) 184.
17 JC Coffee, 'Rescuing the Private Attorney General: Why the Model of the Lawyer as Bounty Hunter Is Not Working', *Maryland Law Review*, 42(2) (1983), 215–288, 233.

to satisfy the adequacy requirement and serve due process objectives[18] that a lead plaintiff must fairly and adequately protect the interests of group members and hold no interests in conflict with that group. By the same token, the lawyer needs to have sufficient expertise and experience to prosecute the case for the benefit of the group.[19]

In terms of the adequacy of the representative test,[20] courts assess the competency of the lawyer and put little emphasis on the selection of the lead plaintiff.[21] The judge considers, *inter alia*, lawyers' knowledge and qualification when appointing them[22] and supervises their conduct on behalf of group members.[23] Both the settlement and the amount of lawyers' fees must be approved by the judge.[24] This plays a key role in opt-out actions where the total amount at stake is substantial and the group is large. Finally, lawyers' behaviour should not be associated only with collective actions, because in any type of litigation lawyers may be inclined to achieve the minimum acceptable quality result with the least possible effort.[25] Nonetheless, it has been argued that ideological claimants are more effective monitors of lawyers[26] and also have a genuine interest in litigation compared with lawyers.[27]

Ideological claimant

Ideological claimants are not one of those harmed but are instead interested in the subject matter of the litigation.[28] In other words, they do not have a cause of action against the defendant, their aim is to defend the interests of the group members they represent. With respect to a collective action on behalf of

18 Jones argues that as far as group members have the right to be heard and exit, the adequacy of representative is not much of a concern. C Jones, *Theory of Class Actions* (Toronto: Irwin Law, 2003), 222.
19 Federal Judicial Center, '*Manual for Complex Litigation* (fourth)' (2004), (MCL) 258 <http://www.fjc.gov/public/pdf.nsf/lookup/MCL40000.pdf/$file/MCL40000.pdf> [accessed 1 July 2018].
20 FRCP 23(g).
21 Mulheron, Class action (fn 2) 293. However, the proposed *Fairness in Class Action Litigation Act of 2017* requires courts not to certificate a class unless it is demonstrated that each class member '[s]uffered the same type and scope of injury as the named class representative or representatives'. *The Fairness in Class Action Litigation Act of 2017* (FCALA), H.R. 985, § 1716 (a).
22 MCL (fn 19) 278–279.
23 *Ibid* 278.
24 Wardhaugh (fn 15) 8.
25 *Ibid* 7.
26 Gidi (fn 10) 370. See that the possibility of third-party monitoring is briefly mentioned in Centre for European Policy Studies (CEPS), Erasmus University Rotterdam (EUR) and Luiss Guido Carli (LUISS), *Report for the European Commission 'Making Antitrust Damages Actions More Effective in the EU: Welfare Impact and Potential Scenarios', Final Report*, 2007, 282.
27 BIS, *Private Actions in Competition Law: A Consultation on Options for Reform – Government Response* (London, 2013), (Government response) para 5.30.
28 See Gidi (fn 10) 370.

consumers, consumer associations are regarded as suitable representative parties[29] as one of their core tasks is the protection of consumer interests.[30] Compared with an individual member, consumer associations have greater access to information and means to finance the action.[31] These associations are deemed successful in litigating on behalf of consumers since they have the requisite expertise identifying and acting against possible infringements that harm consumers.[32] They are generally not-for-profit organisations and are devoted to furtherance of consumer interests. They do not, therefore, value their own financial interests above those of consumers. There is therefore less concern for principal-agent problems in representative actions.[33] These associations use monetary benefits to achieve the purpose of the association, not for the purposes of profit[34] and wish to develop and sustain credibility.[35]

However, it has been stated that those associations find competition law complex.[36] Often they do not have enough sources to bring a collective action,[37]

29 See eg Commission, *Green Paper on Damages Actions for Breach of EC Antitrust Rules* (COM(2005) 672 final, Brussels, 2005), option 25; Commission, *Staff Working Paper Accompanying the White Paper on Damages Actions for Breach of the EC Antitrust Rules* (SEC(2008) 404, Brussels, 2008), para 49. See similarly A Stadler, 'Group Actions as a Remedy to Enforce Consumer Interests', in *New Frontiers of Consumer Protection: The Interplay between Private and Public Enforcement*, ed. by H-W Micklitz and F Cafaggi (Oxford-Portland: Intersentia, 2009), 305–328, 325; G Howells, 'Cy-pres for Consumers: Ensuring Class Action Reforms Deal With "Scattered Damages"' in J Steele and WH van Boom (eds) *Mass Justice Challenges of Representation and Distribution* (Edward Elgar Publishing limited Cheltenham UK 2011) 58–72, 67–68.

30 SWPWP (fn 29) para 50.

31 O Dayagi-Epstein, 'Representation of Consumer Interest by Consumer Associations – Salvation for the Masses?', *Competition Law Review*, 3(2) (2006), 209–249, 211. Similarly, *ibid.*

32 European Consumer Consultative Group (ECCG), *Opinion on Private Damages Actions*, 2010, para 2.2 <http://ec.europa.eu/dgs/health_consumer/dgs_consultations/docs/eccg/eccg_opinion_on_actions_for_damages_18112010_en.pdf> [accessed 1 July 2018].

33 F Weber, 'Assessing Existing Enforcement Mechanisms in Consumer Law – The Unavailability of an Allrounder', *Rotterdam Institute of Law and Economics (RILE) Working Paper Series no 2011/7*, 2011, 542–560, 557 <http://ssrn.com/abstract=1962665> [accessed 1 July 2018]; S Rodrigue and L Plumpton, 'The Globalisation of Anti-Trust: How the Internationalisation of Collective Redress Is Changing the Game', *Class and Group Actions 2014*, 2013, 31–39, 32.

34 Welfare impact report (fn 26) 321.

35 See M Galanter, 'Why the "Haves" Come Out Ahead: Speculations on the Limits of Legal Change', *Law and Society Review*, 9(1) (1974), 95–160, 99.

36 Commission, A Bouchagiar, *Detailed Minutes of the Public Hearing 'Towards a Coherent European Approach to Collective Redress'* (Brussels, 2011), 16 <http://ec.europa.eu/competition/consultations/2011_collective_redress/study_heidelberg_hearing_en.pdf> [accessed 1 July 2018].

37 C Hodges, 'Competition Enforcement, Regulation and Civil Justice: What is the Case?', *Common Law Market Review*, 43 (2006), 1381–1407, 1388.

which is exacerbated when they are not-for-profit. Hodges further expressed that consumer associations regard pursuing court proceedings as outwith their role.[38]

The Commission favours the standing of consumer associations[39] and regards them as one of the safeguards preventing abusive litigation.[40] According to the Commission, these associations can be qualified in advance or certified on an *ad hoc* basis.[41] In terms of the former, national laws determine the criteria by which a designated entity may file a collective action to represent their members and other affected consumers before courts.[42] The latter refers to the possibility that an entity could be formed to file such an action against a particular infringement.[43] It is sensible to grant standing to both designated and *ad hoc* certified consumer associations as either may be willing to initiate a collective action.[44]

It is also important to ensure that associations are capable of bringing a collective action and acting in the best interests of those represented.[45] The Recommendation presents two principles to determine the adequacy of designated entities as a representative. First, in addition to being not-for-profit, there should be a direct link between the primary objective of the association and the subject matter of a collective action. Secondly, the association should fully protect the interests of group members by having both enough financial and human resources and legal expertise.[46] Two further criteria has been suggested, namely, that these

38 *Ibid.*

39 Green Paper (fn 29) option 25; Commission, *White Paper on Damages Actions for Breach of the EC Antitrust Rules* (COM(2008) 165 final, Brussels, 2008), para 2.1. See in favour of ideological claimants, Commission, *Recommendation on Common Principles for Injunctive and Compensatory Collective Redress Mechanisms in the Member States Concerning Violations of Rights Granted Under Union Law* (Strasbourg, C(2013) 3539/3, 2013), para III/4.

40 J Almunia, 'Common Standards for Group Claims across the EU' (University of Valladolid, School of Law, 2010), 1–7, 6 <http://europa.eu/rapid/pressReleasesAction.do?reference=SPEECH/10/554&format=HTML&aged=0&language=EN&guiLanguage=en> [accessed 1 July 2018].

41 SWPWP (fn 29) paras 52–54; Recommendation (fn 39) para III/6.

42 SWPWP (fn 29) para 52; Recommendation (fn 39) para III/4.

43 The White Paper suggested that they can only represent identified persons. SWPWP (fn 29) paras 53–54.

44 ELI, 'Statement of the European Law Institute on Collective Redress and Competition Damages Claims', 2014, 1–81, 24 <http://www.europeanlawinstitute.eu/fileadmin/user_upload/p_eli/Projects/S-5-2014_Statement_on_Collective_Redress_and_Competition_Damages_Claims.pdf> [accessed 1 July 2018].

45 Commission, *Proposal for a Council Directive on Rules Governing Damages Actions for Infringements of Articles [101] and [102] of the Treaty*, 2009, art. 7 <http://allegati.unina.it/postlaurea/perf/Esclusiva_Juridico.pdf> [accessed 1 July 2018]. See the suggestion of using auction for selecting the representative party, eg D Rosenberg and JP Sullivan, 'Coordinating Private Class Action and Public Agency Enforcement of Antitrust Law', *Journal of Competition Law and Economics*, 2(2) (2006), 159–187; Keske (fn 1) 116–123. According to the auction procedure, a mandatory collective action is brought by the bidder on her behalf and the bid is distributed among group members who assigned their rights to the bidder. Welfare impact report (fn 26) 281. See why the assignment of rights would not work for consumer claims in Chapter 2.

46 Recommendation (fn 39) para III/4.

have existed at least two years before the collective action and have a substantial number of members.[47]

The standing of consumer associations would be a more acceptable solution because it is found compatible with the legal traditions[48] and existing rules of Member States.[49] Indeed, these already have standing to bring collective actions, mainly for injunctions, in the great majority of Member States.[50] One can argue that they have experience and expertise in this regard and do not see court proceedings as outside the scope of their tasks. Their standing can thus be extended to claiming damages in competition cases with only a slight change of law.

To conclude, consumer associations and lawyers should work together to file a collective action on behalf of affected consumers. These associations would then be more willing to initiate such actions as any lack of specialism, expertise and experience on their side can be offset by the input of lawyers.[51] With greater knowledge of the claim[52] and leverage over lawyer by being a repeat player,[53] they are also more capable of controlling the conduct of a lawyer as opposed to lead plaintiffs. Consumer associations are '[p]ublicly recognised and independent bodies [...]',[54] thus they would likely represent consumers in an adequate manner. Finally, the problem of inadequate funds of consumer associations can be overcome by means of a fee arrangement with lawyers,[55] which is, along with other possible options, discussed in the next section.

Funding

Liability for costs

The funding mechanisms available in collective actions are one of the important factors which influence the extent to which these actions are brought. Aside from the fact that costs are likely to increase if there are many individual actions rather

47 M Ioannidou, 'Enhancing the Consumers' Role in EU Private Competition Law Enforcement: A Normative and Practical Approach', *Competition Law Review*, 8(1) (2011), 59–85, 78. Indeed, in Italy, three years of existence, a threshold of individual paying members and existence in five different regions are required for a consumer association to be a representative party. Similarly, France requires one year of existence and a certain number of members. Commission, *Report from The Commission to The European Parliament, The Council and The European Economic and Social Committee on the Implementation of the Commission Recommendation of 11 June 2013 on Common Principles for Injunctive and Compensatory Collective Redress Mechanisms in the Member States Concerning Violations of Rights Granted under Union Law*, (COM (2018) 40 final, Brussels, 2018) (Report on the Recommendation), 5.
48 Ioannidou (fn 47) 76.
49 Welfare impact report (fn 26) 291.
50 See the Member States who permit consumer associations to claim damages, *ibid* 274.
51 Similarly, Dayagi-Epstein (fn 31) 238.
52 They can use in-house lawyers for that, see Keske (fn 1) 112.
53 Galanter (fn 35) 97.
54 ECCG (fn 32) para 2.2.
55 Similarly, Dayagi-Epstein (fn 31) 238.

than one single proceeding, collective actions can be costly proceedings. As one party consists of numerous individuals, issues related to litigation need to be dealt with on an aggregate basis. Costs in collective actions include the costs of notice, if applicable, of certification,[56] of experts, filing fees, court costs, lawyers' fees and, in the event of success, the costs of damages distribution.[57] Since some of these costs must be paid upfront[58] and some on an ongoing basis,[59] having appropriate mechanisms for financing is important in order for collective actions to be brought by a representative party.

Although in opt-in actions it is possible to apportion the costs between group members whose identities are known and who are limited in number, the representative party can also be responsible for the costs. In opt-out actions, on the other hand, because the group consists of numerous identifiable but not yet identified persons, it is thus sensible for the representative party to be liable for costs.[60] In any case, the burden would be put on the representative party, otherwise the situation for consumers is unlikely to change, since costs are one of the reasons for the paucity of actions for damages.[61]

Cost rules governing litigation determine how to allocate the responsibility for these costs between parties.[62] The majority of Member States follow the loser-pays principle.[63] Due to this, and to prevent abusive litigation,[64] the Commission wishes to preserve this principle for collective actions as well.[65] This means the

56 See eg Portuguese opt-out actions do not require certification, JG Delatre, 'Beyond the White Paper: Rethinking the Commission's Proposal on Private Antitrust Litigation', *Competition Law Review*, 8(1) (2011), 29–58, 50.

57 The Law Reform Commission of Hong Kong, '*Class Actions*', 2012, 1–313, 185 <http://www.hkreform.gov.hk/en/publications/rclassactions.htm> [accessed 1 July 2018]; L Craig and L Hannah, 'Collective Proceedings and Settlements before the CAT: A New Dawn', *Competition Law Journal*, 12(4) (2013), 408–415, 413.

58 Craig and Hannah (fn 57) 142–143.

59 Commission, *Communication from the Commission to the European Parliament, the Council, the European Economic and Social Committee and the Committee of the Regions 'Towards a European Horizontal Framework for Collective Redress'* (COM (2013) 401/2, Brussels, 2013), para 3.9.

60 The same can be said for mandatory actions.

61 See further Chapter 2.

62 See further Chapter 1.

63 Welfare impact report (fn 26) 626; Report on the Recommendation (fn 47) 8.

64 *Ibid* 626; Communication (fn 59) para 2.3. Similarly, E Paulis, 'Policy Issues in the Private Enforcement of EC Competition Law', in *Private Enforcement of EC Competition Law*, ed. by J Basedow (The Netherlands: Kluwer Law International, 2007), 7–16,15; M Hviid and S Peyer, 'Response to EC Consultation "Towards a Coherent European Approach to Collective Redress"', 2011, 1–7, 6 <http://ec.europa.eu/competition/consultations/2011_collective_redress/hviid_peyer_en.pdf> [accessed 1 July 2018].

65 See eg European Parliament, *Motion for a European Parliament Resolution on 'Towards a Coherent European Approach to Collective Redress'* (2011/2089(INI), 2012), para 20 <http://www.europarl.europa.eu/sides/getDoc.do?type=REPORT&language=EN&reference=A7-0012/2012#title1> [accessed 1 July 2018]; Communication (fn 59) para 3.9.3; Recommendation (fn 39) para III/13.

losing party is responsible for both parties' costs.[66] In this case, the representative party's cost burden becomes high not merely because they might pay the opponent's costs, but also because they pay the costs of bringing a collective action. In the face of this risk, a representative party, be it individual or consumer association, may abstain from filing a collective action as they are not in a financial position strong enough to bear these costs.[67] One can argue that consumer associations have a stronger financial position[68] but still this may not be enough, particularly if they are self-funded through subscription fees paid by their members. These associations usually do not have many members[69] to fund litigation after covering operational expenses.[70]

It has thus been suggested that the costs liability of consumer associations should be capped.[71] Alternatively, it has been argued that these associations should be exempted from paying the defendant's costs if they lose.[72] A similar recommendation was made by the Green Paper, that a 'cost protection order' could be available to economically weak parties.[73] One can easily argue that consumers are the economically weak parties of the litigation so that such an order could be applicable to collective actions on behalf of consumers. However, these proposals, ie a cap or one-way costs rules, might unbalance equality between litigating parties.[74] It also does not solve the problem entirely as the representative party may still not be able to undertake the upfront and ongoing costs of bringing a collective action.

No-way costs rules, according to which the defendant and the representative party would be liable for their own costs irrespective of the success or loss of the case, show a similar pattern, because collective actions still require the

66 Welfare impact report (fn 26) 626.

67 Craig and Hannah (fn 57) 412.

68 See *supra* section 'Ideological claimant'.

69 P Buccirossi and M Carpagnano, 'Is It Time for the European Union to Legislate in the Field of Collective Redress in Antitrust (and How)?', *Journal of European Competition Law and Practice*, 4(1) (2013), 3–15, 6.

70 Dayagi-Epstein (fn 31) 244.

71 Welfare impact report (fn 26) 627.

72 See eg R Mulheron, *Costs and Funding of Collective Actions: Realities and Possibilities*, A Research Paper for Submission to the European Consumers' Organisation (BEUC) (Brussels, 2011), 1–133, 16 <http://www.law.qmul.ac.uk/docs/staff/department/71112.pdf> [accessed 1 July 2018]. This rule exists in Spanish group action litigation, Civic Consulting (Lead) and Oxford Economics, *Commission – DG SANCO, Evaluation of the Effectiveness and Efficiency of Collective Redress Mechanisms in the European Union, Final Report, Part I: Main Report* (SANCO/2007/B4/004, Brussels, 2008), 97–98. Further, it has been proposed that the representative should be responsible for costs in the event of filing unmeritorious cases. See eg JC Alexander, 'An Introduction to Class Action Procedure in The United States' (presented at the Debates over Group Litigation in Comparative Perspective, Geneva, Switzerland, 2000), 1–26, 26 <http://law.duke.edu/grouplit/papers/classactionalexander.pdf> [accessed 1 July 2018].

73 Commission, *Staff Working Paper Annex to the Green Paper Damages Actions for Breach of the EC Antitrust Rules* (SEC(2005)1732, Brussels, 2005), para 220.

74 See Hodges, Competition enforcement (fn 37) 1388.

representative to make an upfront and ongoing investment in litigation. This is also unfair to the winning party who, even in the event of success, has to pay its own costs.[75] Therefore, it would appear that preserving the loser-pays rule has the advantage;[76] it renders the adoption of collective redress more likely in the EU by not necessitating any change in the existing rules of the majority of Member States and eliminates concerns over unmeritorious actions. This does, however, elevate the importance of available funding mechanisms in order to motivate the representative party to bring such action. Indeed, the limited funding to the consumer association has resulted in the limited application of the Portuguese opt-out actions.[77]

Possible options for funding

Several funding options have been discussed around collective actions. The first of these is the use of public funding. Consumer associations could attain funding through the EU budget,[78] through legal aid available in Member States[79] or under other public financing schemes. However, public funding is dependent on budgetary constraints[80] which would lead to prioritising some cases over others on the basis of public or political interest.[81] These might also be subject to restrictive eligibility conditions and not finance the entire cost of an action.[82] Further, this makes the entitlement of damages through collective actions entirely dependent upon public initiatives.[83] The Commission states that public sources should not be used for civil litigation, even if one of the parties involves numerous individuals.[84] One might argue similarly for allocation of fines for use in the collective actions,[85] which again uses the public budget for the resolution of civil disputes.

75 Mulheron, Costs and funding (fn 72) 27.

76 The recent report on the impact of the Recommendation found that the overwhelming majority of Member States apply the loser-pays rule to collective actions, Report on the Recommendation (fn 47) 8.

77 R Mulheron, *Reform of Collective Redress in England and Wales: A Perspective of Need* (CJC, 2008), 1–161, 100 <https://www.judiciary.gov.uk/wp-content/uploads/JCO/Documents/CJC/Publications/Other+papers/reform-of-collective-redress.pdf> [accessed 1 July 2018].

78 Ioannidou (fn 47) 81.

79 ELI (fn 44) 32.

80 BIS, *Private Actions in Competition Law: A Consultation on Options for Reform – Impact Assessment* (London, 2012), para 210.

81 See Welfare impact report (fn 26) 322

82 See for legal aid schemes, ELI (fn 44) 33.

83 Welfare impact report (fn 26) 321.

84 Communication (fn 59) para 3.9.2. The conclusion here can also be extended to the public bodies that use public funds.

85 Using fines for financing of collective actions was suggested during the parliamentary discussion for the Directive. Opinion of the Committee on the Internal Market and Consumer Protection, *The Proposal for a Directive of the European Parliament and of the Council on Certain Rules Governing Actions for Damages under National Law for Infringements of the Competition Law Provisions of the Member States and of the European Union* (COM(2013)0404 – C7–0170/2013–2013/0185(COD), 2014), amendment 16, Recital 41(a) <http://www.europarl.europa.eu/sides/getDoc.do?typ

Moreover, a special fund, which receives some portion of the damages award,[86] could be established to provide financing to consumer associations.[87] Lawyers' fees could be included or recovered by a separate agreement.[88] However, the creation of this kind of fund could lead to problems in the EU regarding initial funding and ownership.[89] In order to overcome these problems, public or third-party funding may be used until it becomes self-sufficient[90] and if the Commission does not wish to have responsibility for funding decisions, this could be left to a non-governmental organisation.[91] Additionally, since this fund does not provide any legal support,[92] it may need to be supplemented by other mechanisms, especially by conditional or contingency fee arrangements.

It has also been suggested that the representative party can obtain before-the-event insurance for funding a collective action.[93] However, Mulheron stated that each group member should have such insurance prior to the action in order to pool them together.[94] This then would probably not work in consumer cases. She further expressed that it would only cover the individual's own costs, therefore the representative party needs to have recourse to other funding mechanisms for its own expenses.[95] Another means open to the representative party is after-the-event (ATE) insurance. This can be purchased after deciding to bring a collective action. The insurance policy protects the representative from paying opponent's costs in the event of losing.[96] Since the premium is usually paid at the conclusion of the action,[97] it does not burden the representative at the time of filing the claim. However, this premium might be quite high due to the size and complexity of collective actions for competition damages and may not be recoverable from the losing party.[98] In any case, this option can be assessed by consumer associations

e=REPORT&reference=A7-2014-0089&format=XML&language=EN> [accessed 1 July 2018]. It has also been discussed by some scholars. See eg Dayagi-Epstein (fn 31) 244–245; A Stephan, 'Cartels', in *Handbook on European Competition Law – Substantive Aspects*, ed. by I Lianos and D Geradin (Cheltenham UK: Edward Elgar Publishing, 2013), vol.I, 217–241, 239.

86 See Chapter 8.

87 Quebec and Ontario class action regimes have this kind of funding. Dayagi-Epstein (fn 31) 239; A Riley and J Peysner, 'Damages in EC Antitrust Actions: Who Pays the Piper?', *European Law Review*, 31 (2006), 748–761, 757.

88 See some schemes include lawyers' fees, some do not. Riley and Peysner (fn 87) 756–757, fn 45.

89 Welfare impact report (fn 26) 286.

90 Riley and Peysner (fn 87) 757, 761.

91 Such as the Council of Bars and Law Societies of Europe, *ibid* 760–761.

92 *Ibid* 759.

93 ELI (fn 44) 33.

94 Mulheron, Costs and funding (fn 72) 80.

95 *Ibid.*

96 See it also covers consumer association's own disbursements, *ibid* 76.

97 *Ibid* 78.

98 See this is the case in the UK, D Lawne, 'Private Enforcement and Collective Redress: A Claimant Perspective on the Proposed BIS Reforms', *Competition Law Journal*, 2 (2013), 171–181, 179.

on a case-by-case basis by considering the amount of the defendant's costs *versus* the premium.

Further, third parties, who are not connected with the action at hand, can be allowed to fund all or part of the costs incurred by the representative party,[99] which can include lawyers' fees if they do not work on a CFA or contingent basis.[100] Third-party litigation funding (TLF)[101] refers to financing of litigation for profit by private-sector companies.[102] This provides financial but no legal help. If the case is won, third party funders receive a success fee paid out of the damages award,[103] which can be either a multiplier of the costs paid,[104] or a percentage of damages.[105] If the case is lost, they recover nothing.[106] It has, on the one hand, been argued that TLF enhances access to justice.[107] On the other, critics see it as capable of giving rise to the filing of unmeritorious cases[108] and of '[c]reating a compensation culture driven by profit-seeking financial entities trafficking in legal claims'.[109] The approach to TLF in the EU is generally sceptical on these grounds[110] but also because it is deemed unfamiliar in national laws.[111]

The availability of TLF can increase the number of cases filed, because it is preferred by those who are in need of funding to pursue litigation, or who see it as a better option. In terms of the former, it could also be regarded as allowing the pursuit of cases which would not otherwise have been brought.[112] These claims are more likely have good merits. A study on EU third-party funders finds that the risk of funding unmeritorious cases is very low as funders carefully select cases and only provide financing to those with a high probability of success.[113] It has also been observed that many Member States permit TLF, therefore it is not that unknown to the EU.[114] These would suggest that TLF can be considered as one

99 C Veljanovski, 'Third-Party Litigation Funding in Europe', *Journal of Law, Economics and Policy*, 8 (2012), 405–449, 405.
100 Mulheron, Costs and funding (fn 72) 74.
101 Third-party is either a passive investor and does not involve in the litigation or an active investor who purchases or is assigned claims. Veljanovski (fn 99) 408. See for the latter – the CDC approach – Chapter 1. This section examines passive third-party funders.
102 C Cameron and J Kalajdzic, 'Commercial Litigation Funding: Ethical, Regulatory and Comparative Perspectives', *Canadian Business Law Journal*, 55(1) (2014), 1–16, 2.
103 Veljanovski (fn 99) 423. See further Chapter 8.
104 Mulheron, Costs and funding (fn 72) 57.
105 Welfare impact report (fn 26) 321.
106 Mulheron, Costs and funding (fn 72) 57; Veljanovski (fn 99) 407.
107 Veljanovski (fn 99) 406.
108 Buccirossi and Carpagnano (fn 69) 6.
109 Veljanovski (fn 99) 408.
110 See eg Communication (fn 59) para 3.9.1.
111 European Parliament, Motion (fn 65) para 20.
112 Veljanovski (fn 99) 446.
113 *Ibid* 445.
114 *Ibid* 406. Indeed, three cases where TLF was actually used to fund collective proceedings were reported from the UK, the Netherlands and Germany, Report on the Recommendation (fn 47) 9.

of the options for funding, and that third parties might be allowed to finance part of the costs for collective actions with court approval over their remuneration. The Recommendation is also not against this option,[115] with one condition that Member States provide for a public body to monitor its use.[116]

Collective actions can also be financed by lawyers who would pay the costs of litigation out of pocket and recover costs and fees only if and when the lawsuit is won.[117] In this scenario, lawyers undertake the upfront and ongoing costs of filing a collective action and bear the risk of losing the case.[118] They also put their efforts into case preparation, evidence collection and case management.[119] In light of this, 'no win no fee' arrangements can be grouped into two categories: CFAs and contingency fee arrangements.

CFAs refer to either 'no win no fee'[120] or 'no win less fee' arrangements.[121] If it designed as 'no win no fee', in the event of unsuccessful case, as a contingency fee arrangement, the representative party does not reimburse the lawyer for litigation costs nor pay lawyers' fees. In the event of success, due to the loser-pays rule, the losing party pays for costs as well as fees, and the success fee of the lawyer can be paid either by the representative party or by the losing party. For instance, the previous system in the UK allowed the success fees or part of it to be paid by the losing party but under the current system the claimant must pay the success fee.[122] Under CFAs, there might be a cap to the fees recoverable by lawyers. In the UK, for instance, these are at most double normal fees.[123] Contingency fees are defined by the Commission as granting the lawyer a certain percentage of the damages award[124] and, therefore, with reference to the US system, have been found to encourage abusive litigation.[125] The Recommendation does not favour having these arrangements. However, if Member States adopt them exceptionally, contingency fees should be subject to certain rules that protect the rights of group members.[126]

There is a divide among the stakeholders in the EU.[127] Some believe that contingency fee arrangements provide greater access to justice.[128] In that regard, the

115 See the limitations to be imposed on TLF, Recommendation (fn 39) para III/16.
116 *Ibid* para IV/32.
117 JP Davis and EL Cramer, 'Antitrust, Class Certification, and the Politics of Procedure', *George Mason Law Review*, 17(4) (2010), 969–1033, 980.
118 C Leskinen, 'Collective Actions: Rethinking Funding and National Cost Rules', *Competition Law Review*, 8(1) (2011), 87–121, 108.
119 Communication (fn 59) para 3.9.1.
120 Mulheron, Costs and funding (fn 72) 93.
121 Keske (fn 1) 46.
122 *The Conditional Fee Agreements Order*, no 689, 2013, explanatory note.
123 *Ibid* art. 3.
124 SWPWP (fn 29) para 244. See for other types of contingency fees, Mulheron, Costs and funding (fn 72) 92–93.
125 See eg Communication (fn 59) para 2.2.2.
126 Recommendation (fn 39) para V/30.
127 SWPWP (fn 29) para 244; Communication (fn 59) para 3.9.1.
128 Communication (fn 59) para 3.9.1.

Commission has been criticised for both preserving the loser-pays rule and not allowing contingency fee arrangements, thereby discouraging collective actions.[129] On the other hand, it has been argued that contingency fee arrangements give rise to excessive fees[130] and principal-agent problems[131] and have been seen to lead to unmeritorious cases filed and have therefore been found incompatible with legal traditions of Member States.[132] The next section analyses the ways in which contingency fees operate in the US.

Contingency fees as one of the options

US competition litigation adopts the one-way costs rule[133] and contingency fee arrangements in order to finance class actions.[134] These fees are not always a percentage of damages. When a case is resolved by adjudication, in the event of success the defendant is liable for the litigation costs and reimbursing lawyers' fees calculated on the lodestar method.[135] If the case is lost, due to the 'no win no fee' arrangement, lawyers recover neither their fees nor expenses but they are not responsible for the defendant's costs or lawyers' fees.[136] In case of settlement,[137] lawyers' fees are calculated either on the basis of a percentage of the fund, or the lodestar method, or both – this is in order to cross-check whether the percentage is excessive.[138] Lawyers can also claim the litigation costs they spent independent of their fees.[139] Depending on the agreement between

129 See eg T Chieu, 'Class Actions in the European Union?: Importing Lessons Learned From the United States' Experience into European Community Competition Law', *Cardozo Journal of International and Comparative Law*, 18 (2010), 123–157, 148; MA Sittenreich, 'The Rocky Path for Private Directors General: Procedure, Politics, and the Uncertain Future of EU Antitrust Damages Actions', *Fordham Law Review*, 78(5) (2010), 2701–2750, 2746.

130 See eg the authors refer to it as a main criticism, Riley and Peysner (fn 87) 753.

131 See eg JC Coffee, 'Understanding the Plaintiff's Attorney: The Implications of Economic Theory for Private Enforcement of Law through Class and Derivative Actions', *Columbia Law Review*, 86(4) (1986), 669–727, 680.

132 G Berrisch, E Jordan and R Salvador Roldan, 'EU Competition and Private Actions for Damages', *Northwestern Journal of International Law and Business*, 24 (2004), 585–600, 598.

133 *Clayton Antitrust Act*, 15 USC, 1914, sec 4.

134 *Model Rules of Professional Conduct*, 1983, rule 1.8(e)(1).

135 See the lodestar method in Chapter 1.

136 CG Lang, 'Class Actions and the US Antitrust Laws: Prerequisities and Interdependencies of the Implementation of a Procedural Device for the Aggregation of Low-Value Claims', *World Competition*, 24(2) (2001), 285–302, 289.

137 Settlement fund has been regarded as 'common fund'. *In re Cardizem CD Antitrust Litigation*, 218 F.R.D. 508 (E.D. Mich. 2003) para 531. See further for common fund, eg Mulheron, Costs and funding (fn 72) 37.

138 T Eisenberg and GP Miller, 'Attorneys' Fees and Expenses in Class Action Settlements: 1993–2008', *Journal of Empirical Legal Studies*, 7(2) (2010), 248–281, 252; MCL (fn 19) 334–335.

139 See eg *In re Cardizem* (fn 137) paras 534–535.

parties, those costs can be paid either out of the settlement fund[140] or separately by the defendant.[141]

Both means of calculating fees are subject to judge's scrutiny. In the lodestar method, the hourly fee is multiplied by the number of hours a lawyer expended, after which the court adjusts this amount by applying a multiplier by considering several factors, such as the level of the risk involved,[142] the magnitude of damages obtained, the quality and amount of lawyer's work[143] and the complexity of the litigation.[144] The same factors are used to determine percentage.[145] In this way, courts evaluate the reasonableness of lawyers' fees.[146] In practice, the lodestar method does not lead to lower fees than the percentage method.[147]

There have been criticisms levelled at both methods. The lodestar method has been found time-consuming and burdensome as lawyers have to submit records of the hours they spent on the case with the supporting evidence.[148] This method also carries a risk of lawyers claiming unnecessary hours.[149] It has been argued that the percentage method is easier to apply and incentivises lawyers to obtain the highest possible award.[150] However, the percentage method has also been criticised as arbitrary and unreflective of the realities of the case.[151] It has also been argued that this method can result in conflict between a group and its lawyer as both the individual damages and fees are paid out of the same award.[152] Therefore, the lodestar cross-check is generally preferred to determine lawyers' fees in courts.[153]

140 See eg *ibid.*
141 MCL (fn 19) 335.
142 See eg if it is a follow-on case, their fees are lower, Coffee, Rescuing the private attorney general (fn 17) 287.
143 MCL (fn 19) 195–196. According to the FCALA, '[t]he portion of any attorneys' fee award to class counsel that is attributed to the monetary recovery shall be limited to a reasonable percentage of any payments directly distributed to and received by class members. In no event shall the attorneys' fee award exceed the total amount of money directly distributed to and received by all class members.' FCALA (fn 21) § 1718 (b)(2).
144 A Andreangeli, *Private Enforcement of Antitrust: Regulating Corporate Behaviour through Collective Claims in the EU and US* (Cheltenham UK: Edward Elgar Publishing, 2014), 168.
145 See for all the factors, MCL (fn 19) 191–192.
146 Andreangeli, Private enforcement of antitrust (fn 144) 168.
147 Lang (fn 136) 289. In the FCALA, lodestar method is unavailable to lawyers, FCALA (fn 21) § 1718 (b)(2).
148 MCL (fn 19) 194.
149 M Gilles and G Friedman, 'Exploding the Class Action Agency Costs Myth: The Social Utility of Entrepreneurial Lawyers', *University of Pennsylvania Law Review*, 155 (2006), 103–164, 143.
150 MCL (fn 19) 188.
151 *Ibid*; B Anderson and A Trask, *The Class Action Playbook* (Oxford: Oxford University Press, 2010), 239.
152 Anderson and Trask (fn 151) 239.
153 Gilles and Friedman (fn 149) 139. See eg, *In re NASDAQ Market-Makers Antitrust Litigation,* 169 F.R.D. 493 (S.D.N.Y. 1996), paras 488–489.

With these explanations in mind, one should be sceptical about fears of the contingency fee arrangement. The prospect of fees motivates lawyers[154] who are experienced in complex procedural and substantive matters[155] to provide legal and financial help for victims who would not otherwise have the means to pursue a legal action.[156] Indeed, the lawyer shapes the litigation and litigation strategy.[157] Contingency fees encourage lawyers to actively seek out infringements rather than passively waiting for clients.[158] It is reasonable to assume that the cases lawyers undertake would not be unmeritorious because, unlike lawyers working on an hourly fee, the only way to recover fees and costs under this arrangement is if the case is successful.[159] It was affirmed by empirical studies that contingency fees lead to cases of good merit, and that lawyers act as gatekeepers – they do not accept cases with a low probability of success.[160] Furthermore, lawyers' interests are congruent with the interests of group members,[161] since the judge takes the size of damages award and the number of group members who recovered damages into consideration when approving lawyers' fees that are calculated using the percentage or lodestar method.[162] It should also not be overlooked that fee awards are subject to court approval and that lawyers are bound to act according to ethical rules and have a reputation to uphold.[163]

The proposed approach

In order for collective actions to work in practice and motivate the representative party to bring an action, thereby making it possible for consumers to receive compensation, the ways in which they are financed are of fundamental importance. It is possible to conclude that if various funding options are available to the representative party, the chances of filing collective actions increase. Various sources of funding, such as TLF, legal expenses insurance, CFAs and contingency

154 Alexander (fn 72) 2.
155 See Burns (fn 9) 183, 189.
156 Coffee, Understanding the plaintiff's attorney (fn 131) 679.
157 Burns (fn 9) 189.
158 Coffee, Understanding the plaintiff's attorney (fn 131) 679.
159 M Hausfeld and others, 'The Contingency Phobia – Fear without Foundation', *Global Competition Litigation Review*, 4(1) (2011), 39–42, 39; Leskinen, Collective actions: rethinking funding (fn 118) 107.
160 HM Kritzer, 'Contingency Fee Lawyers as Gatekeepers in the Civil Justice System', *Judicature*, 81(1) (1997), 22–29, 29; E Helland and A Tabarrok, 'Contingency Fees, Settlement Delay, and Low-Quality Litigation: Empirical Evidence from Two Datasets', *Journal of Law, Economics, and Organization*, 19(2) (2003), 517–542, 540; Welfare impact report (fn 26) 204.
161 AM Polinsky and DL Rubinfield, 'A Note on Settlements under the Contingent Fee Method of Compensating Lawyers', *International Review of Law and Economics*, 22 (2) (2002), 217–225, 218; Leskinen, Collective actions: rethinking funding (fn 118) 107.
162 MCL (fn 19) 192, 195.
163 See for the latter argument, Leskinen, Collective actions: rethinking funding (fn 118) 107.

arrangements, would allow the representative party to select appropriate methods based on the case at hand. For instance, TLF and ATE insurance might be used to cover opponents' costs. Although the cost burden for the lawyer in a given case might be increased, CFAs and contingency fee agreements can also include an opponent's costs under the loser-pays principle.[164] Furthermore, the creation of a special EU fund can be considered, which might obtain funds from the donations of successful claimants[165] or take a percentage of the damages award[166] with respect to the judge's discretion.[167]

In particular, it is submitted that the availability of contingency fees for collective actions would create greater incentive for representative parties because in this way the risk of running a case, and search and litigation costs are shifted from them on to lawyers. Competition litigation involves complex analysis and collective actions are complex procedures compared with traditional two-party suits. The way in which this arrangement functions incentivises consumer associations which have nothing to lose by the lawyers working under contingency fee arrangements. In opt-out actions that give rise to large groups, and thereby large damages awards, lawyers would have incentive to agree to this arrangement.[168] As a result, both consumer associations and lawyers would be more willing to bring collective actions to courts.

In light of this, it is possible to state that both CFA[169] and contingency fee arrangements would be made available to the representative party in order to fund collective actions.[170] There has been an increase in the adoption of contingency fees in national laws[171] and providing the option either to agree a success fee, or adjusted hourly fees with lawyers, as per the lodestar or percentage methods,

164 See eg Leskinen, Collective actions: rethinking funding (fn 118) 109; I Benöhr, 'Consumer Dispute Resolution after the Lisbon Treaty: Collective Actions and Alternative Procedures', *Journal of Consumer Policy*, 36(1) (2013), 87–110, 105. See both arrangements would not cover opponent's costs, Mulheron, Costs and funding (fn 72) 93.

165 ELI (fn 44) 34.

166 Ioannidou (fn 47) 81.

167 See further Chapter 8.

168 Similarly, CJC, *Report of the Working Party on Damages Based Agreements (Contingency Fees)*, 2012, 1–11, 8 <http://www.judiciary.gov.uk/wp-content/uploads/JCO/Documents/CJC/Publications/Pre-action+protocols/contingency-fees-working-party-report1.pdf> [accessed 1 July 2018].

169 See any statutory limitation on the amount of lawyers' fees could result in a decrease in not only their willingness to pursue such action but also in the amount of damages. Hausfeld and others (fn 159) 40. See cost-capping may have a negative effect on the incentives for contingency fees in meritorious actions, Leskinen, Collective actions: rethinking funding (fn 118) 119.

170 The authors state that no-win-no-fee arrangements are the only realistic means of funding. Hviid and Peyer (fn 64) 7.

171 Leskinen, Collective actions: rethinking funding (fn 118) 115–116; Benöhr (fn 164) 105. The recent report on the impact of the Recommendation observed that there are currently nine Member States where contingency fees are available in collective actions, Report on the Recommendation (fn 47) 16.

would enhance the possibility of acceptance by Member States. Finally, if the judge were to exert authority regarding the reasonableness of lawyers' fees the negative attitude toward these arrangements may be overcome.

Thus, in addition to other funding mechanisms, availability of contingency fees in the context of opt-out actions would motivate both representative and lawyer to pursue competition infringements and might therefore give rise to the filing of not just follow-on,[172] but stand-alone cases.[173] Although additional measures might be needed for stand-alone cases, such as adopting or enhancing the scope of discovery rules, opt-out actions with the availability of contingency fees would contribute to the filing of such cases. This said, a substantial increase in follow-on cases filed would be expected[174] as these are less costly and risky[175] and have a high probability of success. The Commission and the European Parliament wish to encourage follow-on actions.[176] This is in accordance with the compensation objective whereby consumers obtain compensation for their damages after infringement is found.[177] It would also serve the need in this area because a quarter of all infringements identified by the Commission have led to a claim for damages.[178] The Directive particularly paves the way for follow-on actions in making final decisions given by other national authorities at least *prima facie* evidence for the competition law infringement in damages actions before national courts. The infringement decision of the national competition authority constitutes full proof before the court in the same Member State.[179]

172 See, from the economics perspective, the analysis of whether a follow-on or stand-alone action would better serve the deterrence aim and which one does not cause inefficiencies in terms of the usage of resources, eg Keske (fn 1) 78; Hviid and Peyer (fn 64) 4.

173 BJ Rodger, 'Why Not Court? A Study of Follow-on Actions in the UK', *Journal of Antitrust Enforcement*, 1(1) (2013), 104–131, 130; EM Iacobucci, 'Cartel Class Actions and Immunity Programmes', *Journal of Antitrust Enforcement*, 1(2) (2013), 272–295, 283–284; RH Lande, 'The Proposed Damages Directive: The Real Lessons from the United States', *CPI Antitrust Chronicle*, 2 (2014), 1–12, 11.

174 de Smijter, E, and D O'Sullivan, 'The Manfredi Judgment of the ECJ and How It Relates to the Commission's Initiative on EC Antitrust Damages Actions', *Competition Policy Newsletter*, 3 (2006), 23–26, 25; J Pheasant and A Bicarregui, 'Striking the Right Balance towards a "Competition Culture" Not a "Litigation Culture"? Comment on the European Commission's White Paper on Damages Actions for Breach of EC Antitrust Rules', *Global Competition Litigation Review*, 1(2) (2008), 98–106, 99.

175 G Monti, *EC Competition Law*, (Cambridge: Cambridge University Press, 2007), 435.

176 European Parliament, Motion (fn 65) para 21; Commission, *Frequently Asked Questions: European Commission Recommends Collective Redress Principles to Member States* (MEMO/13/530, Strasbourg, 2013), 1–4, 2.

177 HKS Schmidt, 'Private Enforcement-Is Article 82 EC Special?', in *Abuse of Dominant Position: New Interpretation, New Enforcement Mechanisms?*, ed. by M-O Mackenrodt, BC Gallego, and S Enchelmaier (Berlin: Springer, 2010), 137–163, 144.

178 See Chapter 2.

179 *Directive 2014/104/EU of the European Parliament and of the Council of 26 November 2014 on Certain Rules Governing Actions for Damages under National Law for*

In the US, when 75% of actions were brought as follow-on actions in the 1960s, recent studies have shown that half of the cases are now stand-alone cases. Accordingly, it has been stated that the follow-on experience is the necessary first step for the development of stand-alone actions.[180] Moreover, the reports from Member States have shown that whenever a collective action is launched, it has received significant media attention.[181] As a result, successful cases and the media attention that usually accompanies collective actions would raise awareness leading to an increase in the use of these actions and a change in perspective: no longer would they be seen as causes of excesses. In this way, the chances of consumers to obtain redress through collective actions would be enhanced.

Concluding remarks

This chapter presented the possible representative parties and funding schemes in collective redress actions for consumers. The representative party could be a lead plaintiff who is one of the victims of the competition infringement of case at hand, or, alternatively, an ideological claimant who has no cause of action against the defendant but has an interest in the subject matter of the case. It is submitted that consumer associations – which are generally not-for-profit and aim to value and further consumer interests – would adequately represent the interests of consumers in a collective action. These have better means by which to access information, pursue competition infringements and control the case, as compared to consumer as a lead plaintiff. In any case, they would likely need to benefit from a lawyer's experience and expertise when bringing a collective action against competition infringements. In addition to the fact that competition cases are already costly and complex, collective actions are more so.

Particularly with the not-for-profit nature of the representative party and with the preservation of the loser-pays rule, funding is of great importance when utilising a collective redress action. The representative party indeed needs funding for upfront and ongoing costs to file such actions. In that regard, it would seem reasonable to make a wide range of funding sources available to consumer associations, giving them the chance to choose or combine those most appropriate ones to the case. This would help them raise the necessary funds and therefore encourage them to bring a collective action.

Among the various funding options, fee arrangements with the lawyer would provide funding alongside legal help. Lawyers working under 'no win no fee' arrangements would fashion the claim, collect the necessary evidence, determine the litigation strategy but also undertake the risk and costs of running a collective action. Hence, the availability of contingency fees would make the representative

Infringements of the Competition Law Provisions of the Member States and of the European Union, (OJ L 349/1), 2014, art.9.

180 BJ Rodger, 'Institutions and Mechanisms to Facilitate Private Enforcement', in *Competition Law Comparative Private Enforcement and Collective Redress across the EU*, ed. by BJ Rodger (The Netherlands: Kluwer Law International, 2014), 23–71, 32–33.

181 Civic Consulting (fn 72) 97–98.

party more willing to pursue such actions. The same could be said of lawyers who have a chance to serve the interests of many consumers and obtain high fees in opt-out actions. This is ultimately beneficial to consumers who would not otherwise have a realistic opportunity to recover losses arising from competition infringements. The next chapter moves on to the other elements of the collective action and will discuss the calculation and distribution of damages awards amongst group members.

8 Calculation and distribution of damages in collective actions for consumers

Introduction

This chapter continues the design for a collective redress action for consumer damages claims in EU competition cases. In this regard, this chapter analyses how consumer damages would be calculated and distributed. To this end, the chapter starts with the discussion of the quantification of damages to a group of consumers. It first explores whether overcharge harm of group members would be assessed on an individual or aggregate basis, then the issues associated with the quantification of the damages of consumers. The section particularly deals with the passing-on issue, ie the ways in which damages of consumers who are indirect purchasers can be calculated for collective redress purposes.

The third section of the chapter turns the attention to the distribution of a damages award amongst group members. In this respect, it examines the means to identify and directly reimburse the victims to the greatest possible extent. However, irrespective of the efforts, there can still be a sum that is not distributed to some of the group members. This gives rise to the problem of undistributed damages which is one of the issues in the collective redress discussion that has created substantial controversy in the literature. The chapter lastly analyses how to approach undistributed damages and proposes a way forward for an EU-wide collective redress action for consumers.

Possible ways of awarding damages to a group

Aggregate v individual damages assessment

Two methods are discussed by which to calculate a group of consumer damages arising from competition infringements in a collective action. The first one is the aggregation of individual losses. Each member's loss is calculated on the basis of individual assessments and individual proof of damages.[1] This method, although

1 R Mulheron, *The Class Action in Common Law Legal Systems: A Comparative Perspective* (Oxford and Portland, Oregon: Hart Publishing, 2004), 407.

burdensome for the courts and the representative party,[2] could be used in opt-in actions[3] where the participation rate is limited, ie the group is small enough to make this workable. In an opt-out action, however, the group tends to encompass large numbers of harmed consumers, therefore estimating the harm on an individual basis using individual proof would be impractical and expensive.[4]

The second method is an aggregate assessment where damages are calculated for the group as a whole. The aggregate amount is either a lump sum amount payable by the defendant, or calculated based on a formulation applied to individual members' claims, but it does not require proof of individual damages at trial.[5] In collective actions for consumer damages claims, the per-unit overcharge at the consumer level multiplied by the number of products sold gives the aggregate measure of overcharge.[6] Determining the price actually paid or the number of products sold does not entail information from group members. Both can be derived from the retailers/defendants' computerised invoice records,[7] other existing records or some statistical methods.

Quantifying competition damages requires but-for analysis which compares the actual situation with that absent an infringement.[8] Because this is a hypothetical situation,[9] it is only possible to determine this counterfactual scenario by using some form of estimation based on relevant data.[10] In this respect, economic

2 See the *SAS/Maersk* case where the requirement of submitting the exact amount for each consumer made it not possible for the Danish Consumer Council to bring a collective action for damages. O Dayagi-Epstein, 'Representation of Consumer Interest by Consumer Associations – Salvation for the Masses?', *Competition Law Review*, 3 (2) (2006), 209–249, 222.

3 Similarly, Commission, *Communication from the Commission to the European Parliament, the Council, the European Economic and Social Committee and the Committee of the Regions 'Towards a European Horizontal Framework for Collective Redress'* (COM (2013) 401/2, Brussels, 2013), para 3.4.

4 RH Dreyfuss, 'Class Action Judgment Enforcement in Italy: Procedural Due Process Requirements', *Tulane Journal of International and Comparative Law*, 10 (2002), 5–36, 13.

5 Mulheron, Class action (fn 1) 407–408.

6 LJ Basso and TW Ross, 'Measuring the True Harm from Price-Fixing to Both Direct and Indirect Purchasers', *The Journal of Industrial Economics*, 58(4) (2010), 895–927, 900.

7 PE Areeda, H Hovenkamp, RD Blair and CP Durrance, *Antitrust Law: An Analysis of Antitrust Principles and Their Application*, 3rd edn (New York: Aspen Publishers, 2006), vol.IIA, 415.

8 Commission, *Staff Working Document: Practical Guide Quantifying Harm in Actions for Damages Based on Breaches of Article 101 or 102 of the Treaty on the Functioning of the European Union Accompanying the Communication from the Commission on Quantifying Harm in Actions for Damages Based on Breaches of Article 101 or 102 of the Treaty on the Functioning of the European Union* (SWD(2013) 205, Strasbourg, 2013), paras 11–12.

9 CA Jones, 'Deterrence and Compensation in New Competition Regimes: The Role of Private Enforcement', in *New Competition Jurisdictions: Shaping Policies and Building Institutions*, ed. by R Whish and C Townley (Cheltenham UK: Edward Elgar Publishing, 2012), 167–182, 181.

10 Practical guide (fn 8) para 12.

experts – who are almost always used in these cases[11] – apply straightforward, standard methodologies to compute average overcharge by drawing upon market-wide data.[12] In addition, the practical guide suggests that any documents of an infringing undertaking that discuss or implement agreed price increases, or that assess the enhancement of market position, could be used to quantify harm incurred by the victims.[13] The same applies to the number of products sold to consumers. In the *JJB case* in the UK, for instance, cartel members were aware of this number.[14]

In large groups, an aggregate damages assessment makes the calculation of damages possible and manageable and thus appears to be a feasible and reasonable method for opt-out actions.[15] This method is also found to fit well with the rationale behind the need for collective actions for consumer claims; as these actions aim to address claims that are not economically feasible to be pursued in individual suits, individualised proof of damages used in individual litigation might also be impractical or economically unfeasible.[16] Aggregate damages assessment is widely used by US courts in class actions for competition damages[17] and the new collective redress regime in the UK also provides for the court to calculate aggregate damages for a proposed group where appropriate.[18]

Aggregate damages assessment and the compensation objective

As the damage is not calculated on an individual basis, it raises the question whether this method is in accordance with the compensatory objective of collective redress actions and whether it is prejudicial to defendant(s) or group members.[19] The compensation objective aims to compensate the victims for their loss, no more, no less, thereby holding the defendant(s) liable for the harm they caused.

An aggregate assessment is comprised of two elements, *i.* the overcharge per product and *ii.* the total volume of purchases at the consumer level. As to the first element, the per-unit overcharge for the product in question, ie the difference

11 Areeda and others (fn 7) 127; AP Komninos, 'Private Enforcement in the EU with Emphasis on Damages Actions', in *Handbook on European Competition Law – Enforcement and Procedure*, ed. by I Lianos and D Geradin (Cheltenham UK: Edward Elgar Publishing, 2013), vol.II, 228–272, 255. The Green Paper also suggests the use of court-appointed experts. Commission, *Green Paper on Damages Actions for Breach of EC Antitrust Rules* (COM(2005) 672 final, Brussels, 2005), para 2.9.

12 JP Davis and EL Cramer, 'Antitrust, Class Certification, and the Politics of Procedure', *George Mason Law Review*, 17(4) (2010), 969–1033, 999.

13 Practical guide (fn 8) para 14.

14 G Jones, 'Collective Redress in the European Union: Reflections from a National Judge', *Legal Issues of Economic Integration*, 41(3) (2014), 289–304, 302.

15 Dreyfuss (fn 4) 13; B Dellavedova and R Gilsenan, 'Challenges in Cartel Class Actions', *University of New South Wales Law Journal*, 32 (2009), 1001–1021, 1021.

16 Mulheron, Class action (fn 1) 411.

17 *Ibid* 409; Davis and Cramer (fn 12) 998.

18 *Consumer Rights* Act 2015 (c.15), 2015, sch 8, sec 47C(2).

19 See Davis and Cramer (fn 12) 998.

between the actual and counterfactual price,[20] is what consumers overpaid and what the defendants have been able to overcharge by virtue of competition infringement. As to the second element, the total number of purchases corresponds to the amount sold by defendants and bought by the group of harmed consumers at an artificially high price. These figures do not change whether calculated on an individual or aggregate basis. In that regard, it is important that the distribution of aggregate damages to group members ensures that the real victims receive compensation. In addition, if there are consumers who actually paid different amounts, their damages could be calculated in sub-groups. After all, the aim is to group similar claims for collective redress purposes. In an aggregate damages assessment the responsibility of defendants tends to be equal to the harm they caused[21] to consumers and the damages award tends to be equal to the harm inflicted on the group of affected consumers as a whole.

On a relevant note, the aggregate damages assessment has been regarded as restitution[22] that aims to remove the illegal profit derived from anticompetitive conduct.[23] Subtracting defendants' counterfactual profits from actual profits amounts to the illicit profit.[24] In addition to the calculation of individual loss, restitution was also offered as a damages calculation method in the Green Paper[25] for a collective action on behalf of not precisely identified victims.[26] If all consumers were direct purchasers of infringers, in theory the illegal profit would equal the aggregate damages, ie the sum of overcharge on all units sold.[27] The aggregate assessment does not, however, estimate the infringer's profit, rather calculates the total damages to consumers.[28]

20 *Ibid.*

21 JP Davis, 'Classwide Recoveries', *The George Washington Law Review*, 82 (2014), 890–950, 894.

22 Dayagi-Epstein (fn 2) 222; JA Brander and TW Ross, 'Estimating Damages from Price-Fixing', *Canadian Class Action Review*, 3 (2006), 335–369, 337–338.

23 Oxera and A Komninos, *Quantifying Antitrust Damages – Towards Non-Binding Guidance for Courts*, Study Prepared for the Commission (Luxembourg, 2009), 98.

24 *Ibid.*

25 Green Paper (fn 11) option 25; Commission, *Staff Working Paper Accompanying the White Paper on Damages Actions for Breach of the EC Antitrust Rules* (SEC(2008) 404, Brussels, 2008), para 194. Similarly, I Gubbay, 'Which? Consultation Response – Green Paper on Damages Actions for Breach of the EC Antitrust Rules', 2006, 1–14, 7 <http://ec.europa.eu/competition/antitrust/actionsdamages/files_green_paper_comments/which.pdf> [accessed 1 July 2018]. See restitution suits competition cases, C Cauffman, 'The DCFR and the Attempts to Increase the Private Enforcement of Competition Law: Convergences and Divergences', *European Review of Private Law*, 18 (2010), 1079–1119, 1119. See restitution accords with European values, K Bernard, 'Making Victims Whole: A Restitution Approach to Cartel Damages', *Concurrences Journal*, 1-2012 (2012), 1–9, 5–6.

26 SWPWP (fn 25) para 194.

27 F Maier-Rigaud and U Schwalbe, 'Quantification of Antitrust Damages', in *Competition Damages Actions in the EU: Law and Practice*, ed. by D Ashton and D Henry (Cheltenham UK: Edward Elgar Publishing, 2013), 210–261, 226.

28 See Oxera (fn 23) 99.

As a result, the aggregate assessment of overcharge is consistent with the compensation objective of collective redress actions and practical for courts to apply to large groups. The latter is important for such actions as courts should be able to determine the damages claims of numerous consumers. In this respect, the next section sheds light on the estimation of the per-unit overcharge for consumer group members.

Calculation of damages to consumers

When all consumers in the group are direct purchasers of the infringers, the damages computation is based on the initial overcharge engineered by defendants, the same as that endured by victims. When affected consumers are indirect buyers of the overcharged product, the overcharge harm is the amount passed on to them, ie 'downstream overcharge'.[29] If the entire overcharge was passed on, then the damage calculation is no different than that of a direct consumer.[30] However, if it is partially passed on, then the downstream overcharge is not equal to the initial overcharge, which requires the calculation of the proportion endured by indirect consumers. Therefore, the challenge when estimating damages for the group as a whole lies with indirect consumers. It needs to be demonstrated in these cases that *i.* group members suffered an overcharge by reason of passing-on, ie proof issues,[31] and *ii.* the damages can be computed by a formula common to all, ie the quantification of damages issue.[32]

Although most distribution chains are not very complex,[33] satisfying these conditions might not be easy in situations where *i.* there are several stages of intermediaries before the product reaches consumers,[34] and *ii.* the product in question is incorporated to other product(s) and then sold to consumers.[35] As regards the former, it has been posited that in a long distribution chain, it is not easy to estimate the counterfactual price for consumers who are naturally at the bottom of the chain because there might be many markets to consider above

29 Basso and Ross (fn 6) 919.

30 ABA, Section of Antitrust Law, *Indirect Purchaser Litigation Handbook* (USA: American Bar Association, 2007) 168–169.

31 See the proof problems for individual indirect purchasers in the EU context, eg M Strand, 'Indirect Purchasers, Passing-On and the New Directive on Competition Law Damages', *European Competition Journal*, 10(2) (2014), 361–386, 374–375.

32 CS Coutroulis and DM Allen, 'The Pass-on Problem in Indirect Purchaser Class Litigation', *Antitrust Bulletin*, 44 (1999), 179–210, 185–186.

33 H Hovenkamp, 'Quantification of Harm in Private Antitrust Actions in the United States', *University of Iowa Legal Studies Research Paper*, 2011, 1–10,7 <http://dx.doi.org/10.2139/ssrn.1758751> [accessed 1 July 2018].

34 WH Page and JE Lopatka, 'Indirect Purchaser Suits and the Consumer Interest', *Antitrust Bulletin*, 48 (2003), 531–570, 543, 547.

35 WH Page, 'Indirect Purchaser Suits Under the Class Action Fairness Act – Reconciling Multilayer Interests in Antitrust Litigation', in *Collective Actions: Enhancing Access to Justice and Reconciling Multilayer Interests?*, ed. by S Wrbka, S Van Uytsel and M Siems (Cambridge: Cambridge University Press, 2012), 275–298, 288.

them.[36] The latter argument concerns proving overcharge harm where the overcharged product is transformed or incorporated into other products along the distribution chain.[37] In this event, there may be multiple retailers selling differentiated products in different product and geographic markets[38] at different prices.[39]

It should be noted that the Directive has submitted a rebuttable presumption in favour of indirect purchasers which would facilitate demonstration of the link between the price increase at the indirect purchaser level and an infringement. According to this presumption, in order to prove passing-on, indirect purchasers need to submit that the competition infringement raised prices above competitive levels for direct purchasers and that they have bought the overcharged product itself or any other product containing or using it.[40] Therefore, even if there is a long distribution chain, or the overcharged product is one of the components in an end product, indirect consumers benefit from this presumption and can establish that their harm is the result of the passing-on of overcharges. It therefore remains to calculate the overcharge absorbed by indirect consumers.

There are various means and techniques by which to obtain a counterfactual price.[41] This price is used to calculate the initial overcharge, which is that suffered by direct purchasers. For indirect purchasers, the practical guide states that there are two ways to calculate loss. The first is to determine the pass-on rate on each level of the distribution chain after quantifying the initial overcharge.[42] It then points out that the alternative approach is easier to apply:[43] this is to compute the overcharge only at the indirect purchaser level through comparator-based methods without making any pass-on analysis.[44]

Of comparator-based methods, the yardstick method compares the affected market with a similar but unaffected product/geographic market;[45] the before-

36 Areeda and others (fn 7) 416.

37 WH Page, 'Class Certification in the Microsoft Indirect Purchaser Litigation', *Journal of Competition Law and Economics*, 1(2) (2005), 303–338, 308.

38 See Areeda and others (fn 7) 414.

39 *Somers v Apple Inc.*, Case nos C 07–06507 JW, C 05–00037 JW (N.D. Cal. 2009), 11 <http://www.appliedantitrust.com/05_class_actions/class_actions/somers/somers_classcert_opp4_20_2009.pdf> [accessed 1 July 2018].

40 *Directive 2014/104/EU of the European Parliament and of the Council of 26 November 2014 on Certain Rules Governing Actions for Damages under National Law for Infringements of the Competition Law Provisions of the Member States and of the European Union* (OJ/L 349/1, 2014), art. 14(2).

41 A complete review of all methods for quantification of competition damages is beyond the scope of this book. See eg further Oxera (fn 23) 46, 80–86; Practical guide (fn 8) paras 32–121. See, in addition to comparator-based methods, other methods that use information from the cartelised market, eg T van Dijk and F Verboven, 'Quantification of Damages', in *Issues in Competition Law and Policy*, ed. by WD Collins (USA: American Bar Association, 2009), 2331–2348, 2336–2338.

42 Practical guide (fn 8) para 166.

43 *Ibid.*

44 *Ibid* para 167.

45 H Hovenkamp, *Federal Antitrust Policy: Law of Competition and Its Practice*, 4th edn (USA: West, 2011), 682.

and-after method compares prices during the infringement with those before and/or after the infringement.[46] In indirect purchaser cases, the latter measures how retailer prices change in the period just prior to the illegal price increase and soon after its cessation, and in this way detecting retailers that raised prices and those that did not.[47] These two methods can also be applied together, which is called 'difference-in-differences', to control differences by comparing the data obtained by each;[48] this can even lead to more robust results.[49] If other factors influence the pricing decision of retailers over the time, these might need to be included into the analysis as additional explanatory variables.[50] Overall, these methods are found easy to implement and not complex.[51] They also rely on real-life data.[52]

In the EU, national courts have limited experience with respect to the issues relating to passing-on due to the low number of actions for damages brought before them. What has been observed so far from these cases is that in the assessment of pass-on national courts and experts only use basic parameters, such as the number of firms harmed by an overcharge, and they employ simple or theoretical methods to calculate damages arising from passing-on.[53]

On the other hand, US courts have a vast experience in calculating damages in competition cases. In the US, some commentators have stated that there is no need to calculate a pass-on rate[54] and that only downstream overcharge can be estimated through comparator-based methods.[55] State courts, whose laws allow indirect standing, do not approve theoretical methods that rely on assumptions on the grounds that these methods do not consider specificities of the case in question. In indirect cases, the first assumption is that the markets are perfectly competitive and overcharges are always passed along by intermediaries to stay in the business. The alternative is the incidence analysis that assumes that '[d]istributors and retailers do not act strategically with respect to each other'.[56] State courts, however, generally approve the empirical methods[57] that are proposed by

46 Practical guide (fn 8) para 38.
47 ABA (fn 30) 171.
48 Oxera (fn 23) 59.
49 RBB Economics and Cuatrecasas, Gonçalves Pereira, *Study on the Passing-on of Overcharges*, Study Prepared for the Commission (Brussels, 2016) v.
50 *Ibid* 46. Regression can also be included in these methods, DL Rubinfield, 'Antitrust Damages', in *Research Handbook on the Economics of Antitrust Law*, ed. by E Elhauge (Cheltenham UK: Edward Elgar Publishing, 2012), 378–393, 380–384.
51 Areeda and others (fn 7) 161; Hovenkamp, Federal antitrust policy (fn 45) 682.
52 Practical guide (fn 8) para 37.
53 RBB (fn 49) ii.
54 Areeda and others (fn 7) 161; BD Richman and CR Murray, 'Rebuilding Illinois Brick: A Functionalist Approach to the Indirect Purchaser Rule', *Southern California Law Review*, 81 (2007), 69–110, 98; Hovenkamp, Federal antitrust policy (fn 45) 682.
55 Areeda and others (fn 7) 161; Hovenkamp (fn 45) 682.
56 ABA (fn 30) 141–142.
57 *Ibid.*

experts.[58] These methods involve: *i.* correlation, *ii.* regression[59] and *iii.* yardstick[60] or before-and-after analysis.[61]

A correlation analysis detects the correlation between two prices.[62] In indirect cases, it examines the correlation between an anticompetitive price increase and retail prices over time in order to determine whether those two prices have shifted together.[63] However, it has been argued that this method does not capture whether the price rise at the retailer level is a response to the initial overcharge, as market conditions unrelated to the infringement could influence the calculation.[64] A regression analysis adds to the assessment variables which are not influenced by the infringement, in order to demonstrate to what extent the price is affected by the infringement *versus* those variables.[65] In indirect cases, it attempts to show how retailer prices are affected by manufacturer price increase *versus* these variables. Appropriate variables and their application in a given case are a matter of debate.[66] It has also been argued that a single regression gives only the average effect across retailers, therefore the analysis needs to be conducted for each retailer, making it difficult to apply in collective actions.[67]

All in all, the appropriate method to measure the downstream overcharge can be chosen on a case-by-case basis, depending on the availability of the data.[68] More importantly, it seems possible to calculate the consumer level overcharge – that is, the harm suffered by group members – without estimating the pass-on rate on each level.[69] To some extent this mitigates the complexities of long distribution chains as overcharges are calculated only for one level, consumers.

However, damage quantification remains difficult if an overcharged product is used as a component of another finished good, resulting in different products sold

58 *Ibid* 141.
59 *Ibid* 171.
60 See eg in a class action for competition damages, the expert calculated the overcharge damages of indirect consumers by using the yardstick method. *Cipro Cases I and II*, Case nos J.C.C.P. 4154 and 4220 (Cal. Super. 2013), (Coordination Proceeding Special Title (Rule 1550(b)), attachment F <https://ciprosettlement.com/Portals/0/Documents/2013-10-01%20Decl%20of%20JRS%20ISO%20Final%20Approval%20w%20ex.pdf> [accessed 1 July 2018]. Lopatka remarks that the plaintiffs' experts applied the yardstick approach to estimate damages in class action on behalf of consumers against Microsoft. JE Lopatka, 'Overcharge Damages for Monopolization of New Economy Markets', *Antitrust Bulletin*, 51 (2006), 453–505, 490–491.
61 ABA (fn 30) 171, 186.
62 PA Johnson, 'The Economics of Common Impact in Antitrust Class Certification', *Antitrust Law Journal*, 77 (2011), 533–567, 559.
63 ABA (fn 30) 173.
64 *Ibid* 172.
65 Practical guide (fn 8) para 69.
66 ABA (fn 30) 145.
67 *Ibid* 173.
68 Oxera (fn 23) iv.
69 See the application of before-and-after approach to calculate consumer level overcharge in cartel cases, U Laitenberger and F Smuda, 'Estimating Consumer Damages in Cartel Cases', *ZEW Discussion Paper no 13–069*, 2013, 1–19, 6, 16–17 <http://papers.ssrn.com/sol3/papers.cfm?abstract_id=2333598> [accessed 1 July 2018].

by different retailers in different markets. In these cases, first, the complexity of damages quantification can vary from case to case. A US court has stated that, as the overcharged product sold at the consumer level is unchanged, it is easy to determine the amount absorbed by consumer group members.[70] According to another court, even if Microsoft software was included as part of a personal computer, constituting no more than 3% of the total cost of the final product, a class action on behalf of indirect purchasers might proceed because it is not unmanageable to assess how the overcharge affected the final retail price.[71] Secondly, this complexity is not unique to indirect consumers, but is also possible in direct purchaser cases.[72] For instance, in the US, in a price-fixing class action on behalf of direct purchasers, the court submitted that the fact that defendants sell five differentiated products to various customers through different distribution channels makes it difficult to employ a group-wide method to calculate damages.[73] Rejecting the analysis of the plaintiffs' expert, the court suggested that the methodology for calculating damages should be built on separate data for particular products and direct purchasers/resellers.[74] For both direct and indirect consumers, therefore, if it is identifiable that an overcharged component affects the price of the final product, the portion of overcharge absorbed could be quantified on the basis of the product and its purchasers.

It is possible to submit that estimating only consumer level overcharge by these methods is compatible with the compensation objective. In principle, the sum of overcharges at each layer of the supply chain does not exceed the initial overcharge.[75] 'Theoretically, there can be no double-counting of overcharge harm at different levels of the supply chain.'[76] Subtracting the downstream overcharge from initial overcharge gives the amount to be shared between intermediaries. It is also practical to apply; quantification would hinge upon the height to which an infringement raised prices per product at the consumer level. Indeed, all competition cases require reasoned estimation for an acceptable measure of damages.[77] The practical guide suggests that the exercise of the right to damages should not be hindered by '[o]verly demanding requirements regarding the degree of certainty and precision of a quantification of the harm suffered'.[78] In that regard, the

70 *B.W.I. Custom Kitchen v Owens-Illinois*, 235 Cal.Rptr. 228 (Cal. App. 1987) para 1352 <https://www.courtlistener.com/opinion/2119106/bwi-custom-kitchen-v-owens-illinois-inc/> [accessed 1 July 2018].

71 S Hussain, D Garrett and V Howell, 'Economics of Class Certification in Indirect Purchaser Antitrust Cases', *Journal of the Antitrust and Unfair Competition Law Section of the State Bar of California*, 10(1) (2001), 18–52, 32–33, fn 41.

72 See further SV Walle, *Private Antitrust Litigation in the European Union and Japan – A Comparative Perspective* (Antwerpen-Apeldoorn: Maklu, 2013), 271.

73 *In re Graphics Processing Units Antitrust Litigation*, 253 F.R.D. 478 (N.D. Cal. 2008), paras 480, 489.

74 *Ibid* para 493.

75 Oxera (fn 23) 120; Maier-Rigaud and Schwalbe (fn 27) 226.

76 Oxera (fn 23) 120.

77 J Brennan, dissenting, *Illinois Brick Co v Illinois* 431 US 720 (1977) para 759.

78 Practical guide (fn 8) para 8.

next section is devoted to the final important element of collective redress action, the apportionment of a damages award among group members.

Allocation of damages

At the outset, it should be noted that courts have the discretion to determine the way by which damages awards would be distributed.[79] In this respect, the court can itself distribute the award to group members, or the defendant, by the court's order, is made responsible for the distribution. Alternatively, the defendant can be asked to pay the damages awarded to a court fund or any other repository, and subsequently the court can appoint a designated party, who could be the representative party, or an administrator, or a non-party, for instance a trust company, for its distribution.[80]

In light of the primary objective of collective redress actions, the distribution of damages needs to aim to provide compensation to group members to the greatest possible extent. Hence, the section first considers the ways in which the victims are directly compensated for their loss, followed by possible approaches to undistributed damages.

Distribution of damages to group members

Distribution is reasonably less problematic for opt-in actions where the group is small and the identities of the members are known. The same cannot be said for opt-out actions. According to the Communication, an opt-out action runs counter to the compensation objective, because the group consists of identifiable but unidentified people so that the damages award could not be distributed to them.[81] There are, however, two ways by which to directly compensate group members in opt-out actions as well. Group members can be targeted to either provide them with their shares, or request them to come forward and claim their damages.[82] Regarding the first way, if the group members can be drawn from defendant's/retailers' records or any other accessible databases,[83] the distribution can be achieved using that same information and individuals would not be required to take any proactive steps or show evidence to receive a payment.[84] In this event, members can directly be compensated by virtue of available data verifying their

79 Mulheron, Class action (fn 1) 423.
80 *Ibid* 424–425.
81 Communication (fn 3) para 3.4.
82 Centre for European Policy Studies (CEPS), Erasmus University Rotterdam (EUR) and Luiss Guido Carli (LUISS), *Report for the European Commission 'Making Antitrust Damages Actions More Effective in the EU: Welfare Impact and Potential Scenarios'*, Final Report, 2007, 568.
83 See the example in fn 88, JD Richards, 'What Makes an Antitrust Class Action Remedy Successful: A Tale of Two Settlements', *Tulane Law Review*, 80 (2005), 621–660, 627.
84 Mulheron, Class action (fn 1) 425; RP Mulheron, *Reform of Collective Redress in England and Wales: A Perspective of Need* (CJC, 2008), 1–161, 35.

identities and damages.[85] For instance, in a class action settlement in the US, such a clause exists in the settlement and the notice explains that the fund will be distributed to those who submits a claim from and to those who have already been identified from the defendant's records.[86]

Finding the identities of members through defendant's/retailers' records or any other accessible databases works well in many instances; for example, in the event where consumers are registered to use a service, such as an airline company, or where firms hold data on their customers for loyalty reasons, such as a loyalty card scheme. It also works in the case of an ongoing financial arrangement,[87] such as with a bank or a continuing relationship between defendant(s) and consumers, for example where a telecommunication company or an energy supplier overcharges its consumers. Alternatively, it can work when buyer information ought to be taken and stored by other companies or liable bodies in order for them to sell the product to customers. In *Relafen* in the US, for instance, more than 900,000 affected purchasers were identified from the databases of retail pharmacies.[88] In all these cases, it is possible to find the identities of affected consumers from the defendant's or retailer's records, or from other databases and a damages award can be directly distributed to them in respect to the amount of loss they incurred in cash, by abatement, or in credit.[89]

Locating and making payments to group members through electronic methods is also cost-efficient.[90] Technological developments have made it easier to store and obtain such data. It is lately the case in US indirect purchaser class actions where aggregate purchases of consumers are detected and damages awards are matched with consumer names and addresses with a high degree of efficiency through ubiquitous computer databases in which most industries routinely maintain regularly conducted business activities.[91] Therefore, when appropriate, this approach should be preferred to reimburse injured consumers based on volume of their purchases.

If group members cannot be located from the existing records, as a second method, they can be asked to come forward and show proof of purchase in order

85 Federal Judicial Center, '*Manual for Complex Litigation* (fourth)' (2004), 332 <http://www.fjc.gov/public/pdf.nsf/lookup/MCL40000.pdf/$file/MCL40000.pdf> [accessed 1 July 2018].

86 *In re Baby Products Antitrust Litigation*, Case no WL 5996622013 (E.D. Pa 2011), (Settlement agreement, 2013), exhibit B <http://www.babyproductsantitrustsettlement.com/documents/Settlement_Agreement.pdf> [accessed 31 July 2015]; Notice, 1–9, 5 <http://www.babyproductsantitrustsettlement.com/documents/notice.pdf> [accessed 1 July 2018].

87 NM Pace, 'Class Actions In the United States of America: An Overview of the Process and the Empirical Literature', *RAND Institute for Civil Justice*, 2007, 1–99, 43.

88 Richards (fn 83) 627.

89 See Mulheron, Class action (fn 1) 425.

90 JC Kleefeld, 'Book Review', *Canadian Class Action Review*, 4(1) (2007), 203–210, 209 (reviewing R Mulheron, *The Modern Cy-Près Doctrine: Applications and Implications* (London: UCL Press, 2006)).

91 Richards (fn 83) 639.

to be entitled to compensation.[92] Presenting proof of purchase can be problematic in competition cases – perhaps a long time has elapsed between the infringement and the collective action – and victims most probably have not retained their receipts.[93] However, if a purchase is made with debit or credit card, the transaction could be traced through banks. Moreover, proof may take many forms: the overcharged product itself or its package, bottle,[94] product code or photographs, or sworn affidavits from two other people.[95] In *JJB Sports* case in the UK, for instance, the representative action was brought in 2007 against a cartel operating in 2000 and 2001 and the settlement announced in 2008. Victims were asked to show a till receipt, credit card statement or bank statement, but if they did not have these, to bring the product in question – a shirt – with the label intact.[96] The settlement provided a lesser amount – £5 – for one without the label.[97] In the *Microsoft* case in the US, consumers needed only to provide the product code or serial number unique to every software product.[98] In this respect, any reasonable proof of purchase can be accepted for compensation purposes.

In summary, the focus needs to be on distributing an award to group members to the greatest possible extent.[99] The electronic means by which product/customer information is stored by defendants, other companies or the liable bodies, and the increasing use of credit or debit cards by plaintiffs, make demonstrable proof of purchase more likely and allows a direct refund to group members. There may be cases where these means do not exist, for instance consumers do not use any credit or debit card, defendant's sales records do not (need to) show any names, or where the product or its package is not kept, such as food.[100] However, in other cases, such as collusion between car dealers, or real estate agents,[101] or travel

92 Pace (fn 87) 43; Mulheron, Reform of collective redress (fn 84) 35.
93 This happened in *JJB Sports* case in the UK. C Binham, 'Which? Action to Settle', *The Lawyer*, 2007 <http://www.thelawyer.com/which-action-to-settle/130344.article> [accessed 1 July 2018].
94 See eg a claim form, *In re Bayer Corp. Combination Aspirin Products Marketing and Sales Practices Litigation*, Case no 09-MD-2023 (BMC) (E.D.N.Y. 2013), 2.
95 *Baby Products* (fn 86) exhibit B III(1).
96 Which?, 'JJB to Pay Fans over Football Shirt Rip-off: Which? Helps Consumers to Get Cash Back' <http://www.which.co.uk/news/2008/01/jjb-to-pay-fans-over-football-shirt-rip-off-128985/> [accessed 1 July 2018].
97 M Herman, 'Everyone's a Winner in Football Shirts Settlement', *The Times*, 2008 <http://www.thetimes.co.uk/tto/law/article2210528.ece> [accessed 1 July 2018].
98 Richards (fn 83) 629. See eg Microsoft-California Class Action Settlement, 'Finding Your Proof of Purchase Identifying Numbers' <http://www.microsoftcalsettlement.com/FindIDNumbers.htm> [accessed 1 July 2018].
99 Similarly, SWPWP (fn 25) para 56. It seems the proposed *Fairness in Class Action Litigation Act of 2017* encourages direct distribution to class members as it requires attorneys' fees not to be determined or paid '[u]ntil the distribution of any monetary recovery to class members has been completed'. *The Fairness in Class Action Litigation Act of 2017* (FCALA), H.R. 985, § 1718 (b)(1).
100 A beer cartel is cited as an example by Welfare impact report (fn 82) 314.
101 *Ibid.*

companies, or energy suppliers or insurance companies, consumers have a very real chance to obtain damages through collective actions.

Possible alternatives for undistributed damages and the proposed approach

Notwithstanding the efforts to provide compensation to as many group members as possible, full distribution may not always be possible, especially in situations where claimants are required to come forward and submit documentation.[102] Opt-out actions tend to encompass a large number of consumers who neither need be identified[103] nor have to be involved in litigation until the distribution stage. In this respect, group members might not be located[104] or might be unaware of the damages award, or unable to provide any evidence of purchase, or find their loss not worth claiming.[105] The problem of undistributed damages can also be observed in opt-in actions when group members do not collect their damages, for instance, if they do not cash the cheques issued in their names.[106] This section discusses possible means by which to address an undistributed fund, which is one of the most controversial issues in collective redress.

An undistributed award can be apportioned on a pro-rata basis amongst those group members who were identified or submitted a claim form.[107] However, this raises concerns as to overcompensation because these members receive more that is proportionate to the loss they suffered. The undistributed award can also escheat to a governmental body.[108] This option is cheap to implement,[109] but neither serves nor relates to the interests of group members in litigation.

Another alternative is the cy-près doctrine. This assigns the undistributed sum to the next best use,[110] and intends to benefit group members through indirect

102 KM Forde, 'What Can a Court Do with Leftover Class Action Funds?: Almost Anything!', *The Judges' Journal*, 35(3) (1996), 1–12, 1; Pace (fn 87) 43.
103 Group members can be identified in the event of the possibility of issuing personal notices, see Chapter 6.
104 See in the US in a class action for price-fixing on baby products in 1995, $91 million was distributed to the claimants satisfying the group definition. Despite the efforts from 1995 to 2000, additional claimants were not located and that left just over $1 million as undistributed funds. *In re Infant Formula Multidistrict Litigation*, Case no 4:91-cv-00878-MP (N.D. Fla. 2005), 3–4.
105 Jones, Deterrence and compensation (fn 9) 177.
106 R Mulheron, 'Cy-Près Damages Distributions in England: A New Era for Consumer Redress', *European Business Law Review*, 20 (2009), 307–342, 326.
107 Jones, Deterrence and compensation (fn 9) 177; Davis (fn 21) 894.
108 Treasury was discussed during the UK collective action debate. BIS, *Private Actions in Competition Law: A Consultation on Options for Reform – Government Response* (London, 2013), para 5.66.
109 Mulheron, Cy-Près damages distributions in England (fn 106) 316.
110 AA Foer, 'Enhancing Competition through the Cy Pres Remedy: Suggested Best Practices', *Antitrust Magazine*, 24 (2010), 86–91, 86. See the philosophy could be 'as near as possible' but 'next best' approach should prevail because it is wider, Mulheron (fn 106) 342.

means.[111] It can be used as a distribution system or to work off residue.[112] In the White Paper, the Commission puts forward that exceptionally, in actions on behalf of identifiable persons, damages could be distributed through cy-près without identifying members.[113] In order to be compatible with the compensation objective, priority ought to be given to direct compensation of victims, after which an indirect benefit could be considered. Similarly, in the US, a recent case submitted that first direct benefit to victims should be pursued, then having recourse to cy-près that constitutes a small percentage of total fund can be considered.[114] The cy-près doctrine encompasses two types: *i.* distribution in the form of reduced charges, ie price-rollback cy-près[115] and *ii.* organisational cy-près.[116]

Price-rollback cy-près is generally used in overcharge cases[117] where consumers are repeat purchasers of the defendant's goods or services.[118] The defendant is asked to reduce prices for a specific time until the leftover sum is spent.[119] This method is practical because it requires no engagement between the defendant and the recipients of lower prices, and is economical because it entails almost no distribution cost.[120]

However, price-rollback cy-près raises serious concerns for the compensation objective because it benefits both those harmed and unharmed[121] with the latter group receiving windfall gains. It is also possible that those harmed who have already claimed or received damages can then enjoy reduced prices and thereby a double recovery.[122] Additionally, if consumers do not wish to buy the product, the value of reductions becomes meaningless and an undistributed damages situation continues.[123] There are also drawbacks from the perspective of

111 Mulheron (fn 106) 314.

112 It is applied for both purposes in the US. American Law Institute, *Principles of the Law of Aggregate Litigation* (St. Paul, Minnesota: American Law Institute, 2010), 217–218.

113 SWPWP (fn 25) paras 52 fn 30, 56.

114 *In re Baby Products Antitrust Litigation*, 708 F.3d 163 (3rd Cir. 2013) paras 173–174 <http://www2.ca3.uscourts.gov/opinarch/121165p.pdf> [accessed 1 July 2018].

115 RP Mulheron, *The Modern Cy-près Doctrine: Applications and Implications* (London: UCL Press, 2006), 218.

116 *Ibid* 217–218.

117 *Ibid* 218.

118 JC Alexander, 'An Introduction to Class Action Procedure in The United States' (presented at the Debates over Group Litigation in Comparative Perspective, Geneva, Switzerland, 2000), 1–26, 16 <http://law.duke.edu/grouplit/papers/classactionalexander.pdf> [accessed 1 July 2018]. See also two famous examples that are usually cited from the US: the yellow taxi cab overcharging its customers and Hilton Hotels overpricing incoming phone calls. Mulheron, The modern cy-près doctrine (fn 115) 220.

119 KW Dam, 'Class Actions: Efficiency, Compensation, Deterrence, and Conflict of Interest', *The Journal of Legal Studies*, 4(1) (1975), 47–73, 63.

120 Alexander (fn 118) 16.

121 See ME Wheeler, 'Antitrust Treble-Damage Actions: Do They Work?', *California Law Review*, 61(6) (1973), 1319–1352, 1342.

122 Dam (fn 119) 63; Mulheron, Class action (fn 1) 428.

123 Mulheron (fn 1) 428.

competition law. Reduced prices might have a predatory pricing effect on the market, and give competitive advantage and opportunity to sell more[124] to the defendant as the group members are induced to make purchases to recoup their damages.[125] Finally, determining whether the residue is discharged is rather speculative for the court.[126]

The alternative is organisational cy-près where the residue would be assigned to a designated entity whose aim pertains to the purpose of the litigation[127] or to preventing similar harms that have injured group members.[128] Such an organisation might use it to fund a project, research or for other related proposes that would indirectly benefit group members.[129] For instance, in the US, a class action alleging competition infringements of bundled National Football League (NFL) programming was brought on behalf of 1.8 million purchasers. The group members received $7.5 million in cash and $436,000 of undistributed fund allocated to the NFL Youth Education Town Centers.[130]

Organisational cy-près is found to be beneficial to group members due to the relation between the purpose of the action and the organisation.[131] It has, however, been noted that there are difficulties in finding an organisation appropriate to the specificities of each case.[132] It has therefore been suggested for collective actions on behalf of consumers that the representative party, ie a consumer association, could receive these funds, or that the funds could be used to establish a fund that serves consumer interests in an alternative manner.[133] It has further been argued that these do not contradict the compensation objective so long as the consumers are first given the chance to obtain damages.[134] However, a rule that automatically leaves all undistributed damages to the representative party would run counter to the main goal of distribution, to compensate as many consumers as

124 See *ibid.*
125 Dam (fn 119) 63; Mulheron, The modern cy-près doctrine (fn 115) 220.
126 Dam (fn 119) 63.
127 Kleefeld (fn 90) 208.
128 *Jones v National Distillers,* 56 F. Supp. 2d 355 (S.D.N.Y. 1999), para 358 <http://law.justia.com/cases/federal/district-courts/FSupp2/56/355/2448949/> [accessed 1 July 2018].
129 It is called 'earmarked escheat'. Mulheron, The modern cy-près doctrine (fn 115) 222. See eg in the US, the residue contributes to the financing of Loyola Institute for Consumer Antitrust Studies, A Stephan, 'Cartels', in *Handbook on European Competition Law – Substantive Aspects*, ed. by I Lianos and D Geradin (Cheltenham UK: Edward Elgar Publishing, 2013), vol.I, 217–241, 239, fn 96.
130 *Schwartz v Dallas Cowboys Football Club*, Ltd., 362 F. Supp. 2d 574 (E.D. Pa. 2005), paras 576–577 <https://casetext.com/case/schwartz-v-dallas-cowboys-football-club-2> [accessed 1 July 2018].
131 Kleefeld (fn 90) 208.
132 BIS (fn 108) para 5.64.
133 M Ioannidou, 'Enhancing the Consumers' Role in EU Private Competition Law Enforcement: A Normative and Practical Approach', *Competition Law Review*, 8(1) (2011), 59–85, 83–84. Similarly, G Wagner, 'Collective Redress – Categories of Loss and Legislative Options', *Law Quarterly Review*, 127 (2011), 55–82, 76–77.
134 Ioannidou (fn 133) 83.

possible, to which the representative party should also contribute. That a representative could gain from all undistributed award might introduce unwelcome incentives.

It should therefore be possible to allocate a certain percentage of the value of undistributed damages to the representative party and/or to a special fund that finances the costs of filing a collective claim. It should also be possible to use undistributed damages to pay TFL and the expenses of the representative party not recovered from the losing party, such as expert fees, ATE premiums and, if applicable, success fees of lawyers.[135] In each instance, the court should decide the appropriate amount by considering the particular facts of the case, including the distribution and/or take-up rates and for the allocation to the representative party, *inter alia*, its efforts in identifying and reimbursing the victims. Normally, the cy-près doctrine has been criticised for supporting only deterrence as it has been argued that the harmed group gains no compensation by allocation of the award elsewhere.[136] However, if the approach above is adopted, the amount taken from the undistributed damages would be a proportion subject to the court's discretion, but, more importantly, this amount would incentivise the representative party to contribute to the distribution of the award to as many group members as possible in the case at hand, and to bring a collective action on behalf of consumers in the future.

If any, the rest of the undistributed fund could be returned to the defendant.[137] This approach has been criticised for undermining the deterrence objective, allowing the infringer to benefit from its wrongdoing.[138] It has been also asserted that defendants may deliberately keep poor records to prevent the identification of victims in order to claim this fund.[139] Mulheron cited a case as an example of this which was in the field of employment law and decided in 1986.[140]

In this context, so long as the emphasis is upon verifying and providing redress to group members, there can be little concern for deterrence, because the higher the compensation received by consumers, the higher the level of deterrence through the compensation paid by defendants. The amount, if returned to the defendants, would also be subject to the court's decision because the court would decide the amount the organisation and the amount any special fund would receive. With respect to the poor record keeping of the defendant, *i.* in some sectors firms are obligated to keep records, and others do so for different reasons,

135 See it is the case in the UK collective action regime, *Consumer Rights Act* (fn 18) sec 47C(6). Thus, the approach suggested in this book is 'as near as possible'. See *supra* fn 110.

136 *Mirfasihi v Fleet Mortg. Corp.*, 356 F.3d 781 (7th Cir. 2004) para 784.

137 It must be returned to defendant in Ontario, *Class Proceedings Act*, 1992, sec 26(10). In Australia, the court may decide to return it to defendant, *Federal Court of Australia Act*, no 156, 1976, sec 33ZA(5). It is among the options in British Columbia, *Class Proceedings Act*, RSBC 1996, sec 34(5).

138 BIS (fn 108) para 5.66.

139 Mulheron, The modern cy-près doctrine (fn 115) 252, fn 231.

140 *Ibid.*

ii. other companies, such as intermediaries, other liable bodies or databases might also have information on purchasers, *iii.* records are easy to keep and access using technological means,[141] *iv.* this is not the only way to provide redress; group members may still come forward and present proof of purchase.

Finally, it has been argued that the problem of undistributed damages is especially observed in cases with too small losses.[142] Consumer losses can be included in that category; it is indeed the case that their losses tend to be smaller than that of a business. However, consumer losses are not always too small, for instance in *Manfredi*, the actual loss of the plaintiff consumer was €444.55,[143] and again a cartel can operate a long time – eight years on average – meaning the individual loss of a consumer increases over time.[144] Even where the loss is small, most consumers would wish to obtain damages if they have chance. It has been pointed out before that they are willing to pursue their claims when a collective redress action is available[145] even if their loss is small.[146]

Thus, it becomes important that a notice reaches victims. It has been found in a study that, rather than individual notices, the published and/or electronic notice constitutes an adequate way of informing a large number of small claimants.[147] This said, it would be less costly and more practical to establish a toll-free telephone number and/or a website specific to the case at hand to inform a large number of victims about the case and the distribution method for compensation.[148] It was done in a class action for damages in the US and ended up over 3.5 million consumers submitting their damages claims and over 5 million people visiting the website.[149]

These measures still might not constitute a solution. In such a case, no solution would be perfect to deliver compensation to the victims. Then, the court could decide to run the case on an opt-in basis in order to mitigate the undistributed amount *vis-à-vis* an opt-out action, even though an opt-in action would not be that successful in dealing with large numbers of claims.[150] Alternatively, the court

141 Richards (fn 83) 638.
142 See eg TL Russell, 'Exporting Class Actions to the European Union', *Boston University International Law Journal*, 28 (2010), 141–180, 155.
143 Sentenza del Giudice di Pace di Bitonto no 172/2003, *Manfredi Vincenzo c Lloyd Adriatico Assicurazioni*.
144 See further Chapter 5.
145 See Chapter 2.
146 See Chapter 6.
147 T Eisenberg and GP Miller, 'The Role of Opt-Outs and Objectors in Class Action Litigation: Theoretical and Empirical Issues', *Vanderbilt Law Review*, 57 (2004), 1529–1567, 1561.
148 MCL (fn 85) 288.
149 The toll-free number and the website www.musiccdsettlement.com were specifically set up for *In re Compact Disc Minimum Advertised Price Antitrust Litigation*, Case no MDL Docket 1361 (D. Me 2001) 1–52, 10 <http://www.med.uscourts.gov/Opinions/Hornby/MDL/MDL1361_2003_06_13_ORDER17.pdf> [accessed 1 July 2018].
150 See Chapter 6.

might consider an indirect benefit appropriate and approve an organisational cy-près for the part undistributed.

Concluding remarks

This chapter proposed a design framework for the elements of calculation and distribution of damages of a collective redress action. It first dealt with the calculation of damages of a group of consumers. In opt-in actions, the calculation could be achieved through individual assessment and individual proof of losses. However, individual proof and calculations are not viable in opt-out actions as these tend to encompass a large numbers of consumers.

To this end, an aggregate damages assessment could be applied in collective actions on behalf of consumers. This is the amount found by multiplying the consumer level overcharge per product by the quantity purchased by consumers. It is submitted that direct and indirect consumer damages are suited to be calculated for the group as a whole because neither the overcharge per unit nor the number of products sold require the submission of any information by consumers. Damages can be calculated without having recourse to individualised proof of damages. Therefore, the aggregate method would be practical to apply. It is also in line with the compensation objective because the aggregate damages correspond not only to the total harm suffered by consumer group members, no more and no less, but also the total harm inflicted by the defendant on consumers.

As regards aggregate assessment, the number of products sold can be found from the records of defendants, retailers or any other source. In terms of the amount of overcharge endured by consumers, the damages to direct purchasers is equal to the initial overcharge caused by the infringer, but if the entire overcharge has not been passed along, the damages to indirect purchasers requires determining the amount passed on. This is where the analysis becomes complicated. However, as the Commission suggests in its practical guide, it is possible to calculate only consumer level overcharges through comparator-based methods without making any pass-through analysis of each level in the distribution chain. It is easier to measure damages when the overcharge per product is calculated only for one layer, consumers. Subsequent to this step, consumer group members would need to receive compensation proportionate to the volume of their purchases.

Therefore, the final step is to distribute aggregate damages to group members by seeking to reimburse them directly to the greatest possible extent. In some cases, the identities of consumers and the volume of their purchases can be detected using the defendants'/retailers' records or any other accessible databases with the help of modern technological means of storing and accessing data. In this event, it would be possible for courts to award damages to group members without requiring them to submit any evidence. However, when consumers cannot be located via these sources, the alternative is to ask group members to bring evidence in order to be entitled to compensation. In this scenario, it would be possible to regard any reasonable proof of the existence of the purchase of the overcharged product as the fulfilment of evidentiary requirements.

Despite these efforts, some undistributed award may still exist. There are several ways to address this problem. At the discretion of the court, it would be possible to allocate a portion of an undistributed award to the representative party, ie a consumer association, and a portion to a special fund that finances collective actions. The representative party could use the money to fund future cases as well as the costs and expenses expended to bring the collective action at hand, especially those that are not recovered from the losing defendant. So long as it is required that efforts would be made to identify and reimburse the group members directly to the greatest possible extent, and so long as the group members are given the priority to obtain damages, this would be compatible with the compensation objective. Furthermore, awarding part of the undistributed fund to the representative party and part to a special fund would operate to increase the number of collective actions filed on consumers' behalf and thereby their chances to obtain compensation.

9 Conclusions

Concluding remarks

Competition infringement has a particular characteristic, like a few areas of tort, that is a single act by the infringer(s) causes widespread harm. Therefore, numerous persons at the different levels of the distribution chain are harmed by the infringement. To date, the studies carried out by and for the Commission as well as by external researchers demonstrate that victims of competition infringements rarely seek compensation for their loss in courts. This is especially the case for consumers, who are at the bottom of the chain, do not bring a case when affected by the infringement, in consequence do not obtain any compensation, due to, among other things, the lack of a collective redress action.

Against this backdrop, this book has structured a collective redress action for consumer damage claims in EU competition cases. It firstly described a collective redress action, the development of this procedural device, the way it operates and the purpose of its creation. It then identified the problem in the EU, ie the paucity of actions for damages in respect of the type of victims and explained how such an action can overcome the difficulties these victims face in obtaining redress. In this regard, it addressed previous efforts towards collective redress in the EU in order to provide a better understanding of the Commission's proposals in this area and reflect on the policy choice that would guide the future initiative. Subsequently, it discussed the objective(s) of compensation and deterrence pursued by collective redress actions in EU competition cases in order to satisfy the need. The significance of this discussion stems from the fact the primary objective pursued by such an action defines its final shape. Further, the book analysed the different groups of injured parties and the types of damages they suffer from competition infringements in order to identify the characteristics of consumer damages claims that fit the characteristics of the claims suited to be determined in a collective redress action. With these assessments in mind, the book finally delineated how to structure a collective redress action for consumer damages claims in EU competition cases.

This book contributed to knowledge by demonstrating that both the purpose and working principle of a collective redress action are suited to address consumer damages claims and by proposing a design for the action that provides a realistic opportunity for consumers to exercise their right to damages and obtain redress.

First, the book revealed that a collective redress action has evolved to provide a feasible and viable option to make it likely for a large group of victims whose losses are similar and small to obtain compensation. Such an action therefore provides a forum for those claims that would not otherwise be pursued on an individual or other aggregation basis. A collective action is built upon representation – a representative party files a claim on behalf of a group of people and then manages the case. By dealing with many similar claims in a single proceeding, such an action achieves economies of scale to the parties and to the judiciary and promotes consistency.

Following this, the book showed that there is a need for a collective redress action for consumers and the characteristics of their claims make them suitable to be determined in a single proceeding for damages. It drew attention to the fact that consumers in particular almost never sue when they are harmed by competition infringements. The number of harmed consumers tends to be large, but it is unlikely they seek individual redress due to the value of their individual damages, their limited resources and their lack of sufficient understanding and knowledge of competition law, the infringement and the fact that the infringement has caused loss to them. It is impractical to bring all these affected consumers to court to solve the controversy between them and the defendant(s). The existing aggregation procedures in national legal systems in the EU suffer also from the shortcomings of individual litigation and are not capable of addressing numerous claims.

The research also demonstrated that although the Commission could have taken a more consistent and clear stance in respect of its collective redress proposals, it appears to have favoured the introduction of a collective redress action in competition law. In the Green Paper the Commission acknowledged that such an action should be put in place for consumers as practicalities make it highly unlikely they bring an individual action and proposed a different design for their claims. The White Paper stated that introduction of a collective action would be beneficial to all claimants, but particularly to small claimants as the delays, costs, risks, uncertainties and burdens associated with individual damages actions discourage them from suing. All the papers in competition law, including the withdrawn Directive, provided different collective redress definitions and formulations, albeit only slightly. These papers were followed by each other in consumer law which discussed possible options but made no concrete suggestions. These initiatives in different areas were criticised by interested stakeholders for giving rise to the risk of fragmentation of the law. For this reason, the collective redress debate has shifted toward a horizontal approach aiming to comprise all areas of law. The Directive did not contain any provisions regarding collective redress and referred to its respective treatment in the Recommendation.

In this regard, it appeared that a distinctive approach to competition law is necessary as here the existence and extent of the problem is clear, and the particular characteristics of this area of the law give rise to this problem. The introduction of a horizontal approach to collective redress raises two questions. The first is whether fragmentation of the law would be created by this approach. This is especially so with the recognition by the European Parliament, the Commission and interested stakeholders that the characteristics of competition law are likely to necessitate specific provisions for collective redress and that this might be achieved in a distinctive approach attached to the horizontal document. The second question is to what extent such a horizontal approach is capable of addressing these characteristics in the formulation of collective redress. In order for a collective redress action to constitute a solution in competition law, it needs to consider the problem, how such an action would be designed to address this problem and what objective(s) it would serve.

Subsequently, the book submitted that a collective redress action should aim to advance the primary objective of compensation. The compensation objective intends to compensate the victims of competition infringements for their loss through damages paid by the defendant. It therefore entails that the amount of compensation corresponds to the harm suffered by the victims and to the harm caused by the defendant(s), no more no less. Deterrence aims to make the prospective infringers refrain from engagement in anticompetitive practices. Although there are various factors that influence an infringer's decision to breach the law, the prospect of sanctions by reducing the utility expected from an infringement may operate as a deterrent to anticompetitive conduct. The compensation objective requires a link between a victim and the infringer who caused the loss whereas deterrence is not concerned with recovery so long as defendant(s) pay for the wrong committed at the lowest possible price. Hence, choosing one objective over the other yields different formulations.

A collective redress action primarily promotes the compensation objective. Unlike individual actions and existing aggregation mechanisms, a collective action offers a realistic means for victims to seek redress who would have been otherwise unable to do so. In addition to this, a collective action is capable of assisting a great number of consumers in obtaining compensation. The greater the number of victims restored to a pre-infringement position the more the compensation objective is realised. By so doing, a collective redress action through the pursuit of primary objective of compensation makes the defendant(s) liable for the loss caused, limits their anticompetitive advantage gained through illegal profits and contributes to the restoration of the normal balance of the market and deterrence of potential infringers. If designed properly, the availability of a collective action would deter because a credible threat of paying compensation to a large number of harmed parties changes any cost-benefit assessment in the mind of the infringer. This said, the primary objective of a collective action is the same when designed to address consumer claims; need in the field of private EU competition law enforcement derives from the fact that consumers sue for damages only in the rarest instances. If the design pursued deterrence as a primary objective, then it would not take into consideration the calculation and distribution of damages awards to the victims. This would not be compatible with need; with or without such an action in place, consumers would remain uncompensated.

The book then illustrated that damages stemming from competition infringements come in the form of overcharges, loss of profits and reduction of quality, choice and innovation. However, competition litigation most frequently concentrates on compensating victims for their overcharge and lost profits damages because *i.* it is found difficult to establish the causation between loss of quality, choice, and innovation and the infringement, *ii.* the models to quantify these losses are relatively underdeveloped and *iii.* especially for loss of innovation, the fact that these innovations have never existed makes the identification of victims and the quantification of their individual damages practically impossible. To this end, the book focused on the overcharge and lost profits damages and identified the characteristics of damages claims of competitors, intermediaries and consumers. It is submitted with respect to consumers that – since they purchase for purposes that are outside trade or business – they incur damages only in the form of overcharge and cannot suffer from lost profits and so their damages tend to be less than those of businesses. In addition, there are a large number of affected consumers with similar losses because they are at the end of the distribution chain and have no choice but to endure the entire consumer level overcharge. Those characteristics make their damages claims well suited to be pursued in a collective action.

That said, consumers are harmed by competition infringements in different ways. Direct consumers who purchase the product from the defendant(s) have standing to sue and are entitled to the initial overcharge created by the infringement. Indirect consumers purchase the overcharged product from intermediate sellers and incur the overcharge that is passed on to them. Deadweight loss consumers who choose not to purchase the product due to increased price are harmed by being deprived of its benefit. However, there are difficulties in identifying these victims who might have purchased the product at a competitive price and establishing that their decision not to purchase stems from the infringement. The same can be said for quantification of damages which relates to how they value a product that they did not or were not able to buy. Umbrella consumers purchase the substitute product from sellers other than the infringer(s). These non-infringing sellers are able to increase their own product prices under a price umbrella created by infringement, which leads to consumers paying more than the price they would have absent the infringement.

In light of these explanations, the sixth and seventh chapters of the book were devoted to formulating a collective redress action for consumer damages claims arising from EU competition infringements. First, with respect to group membership, an opt-in action requires that individuals who satisfy the group definition state their wish to be part of the group within a specified timeframe, at the latest before the judgment is rendered. In so doing, it ensures an individual's control over litigation, identifies each member and entails the submission of individual consents. These requirements are burdensome and time-consuming when dealing with a large group of claimants and make litigation impractical and unfeasible. These requirements may also discourage the representative party from bringing an opt-in action because in large groups the representative might be unable to identify and communicate with each claimant and unwilling to do so at the commencement of the action. As very low opt-in rates show, consumers generally do not join a group and those actions have limited participation. Therefore, opt-in actions are successful in addressing a small group of harmed persons who are easy to identify and whose losses are of high value. A mandatory action, on the other hand, automatically includes all those harmed who satisfied the group definition without granting them the right of exit. However, there is no need to resort to such an action in the EU as consumers almost never exit the group in an opt-out action.

An opt-out action makes all claimants who satisfy the group definition part of the group, unless they wish not to participate. In order to commence the action, the representative party is asked to define the group on whose behalf the action is brought, without identifying the members individually, obtaining individual consents or specifying the exact number. In that regard, the representative party avoids exerting extensive time, resources and cost when bringing an opt-out action. Moreover, the group is formed quickly and comprises a large number of individuals. Of interest to consumers is that an opt-out action provides them with a realistic opportunity to obtain redress because such an action does not require the group members to take any active steps in order to enjoy the decision at the end of the litigation. Concerns over the right of access to the courts – arising from the fact that group members do not consent to be part of the group, nor are they parties to the litigation, but are nonetheless bound by the judgment – could be overcome by effective notice requirements that seek to reach all group members in order to give information about their rights to be heard, excluded from the group or take part in the action. It should also be noted that an opt-out action is based on representation, which can be viewed as necessary to deal with numerous similar claims in an efficient and timely manner. Participation and take-up rates in opt-out actions can be considered as two indicators that demonstrate their ability to provide compensation to larger number of consumers. These figures show that opt-out actions are more successful in this respect when compared to opt-in actions.

In the White Paper the Commission accepted that opt-out actions are considerably better at achieving compensation than opt-in actions and it made an implicit recommendation of opt-out actions for exceptional cases, and more apparent in the withdrawn Directive for representative actions. In the horizontal document the Commission recommends that, if justice requires, opt-out actions could be preferred. However, the proposition for the way forward is the introduction of opt-in actions. Opt-out actions are censored due to the alleged negative consequences seen in the US system. The Commission and interested stakeholders approach opt-out actions with fears that stem from alleged abusive litigation in the US. This seems to be the reason for avoiding the adoption of opt-out actions. This book examined these allegations by considering recent empirical data available in this jurisdiction in competition law. It concluded that, although it is not possible to conduct a comprehensive examination of the system, the analysis shows that opt-out actions usually lead to compensation to the group members, the risk of filing unmeritorious cases is low in the field of competition law and therefore the common belief should be revisited.

With this in mind, the introduction of an EU-wide solution requires acquiring political support from Member States. The Commission may view the availability of an opt-in action as an improvement upon current circumstances. However, opt-out actions provide a realistic means for consumers to obtain compensation and realise the compensation objective more effectively. It is thus necessary to have opt-out actions available. This entails a solution consisting of both opt-in and opt-out actions, giving the discretion to the court to make the choice between them with respect to the own circumstances of the case at hand. In this way, the chances of acceptance of collective redress actions by the Member States is increased, an EU opt-out action is made possible and the court has the option to run the case on an opt-out basis for consumer claims.

Due to the fact that each membership system requires a group definition to identify who needs to opt in to an action, who may opt out of that action or who is automatically part of the group, the book submitted that the group definition needs to only encompass direct and indirect consumers. Indeed, group definition needs to avoid extensive individual issues and any possible conflict of interest among group members in order to provide a joint resolution to their damages claims in a single proceeding for damages. If there are extensive individual issues, *i.* a collective action would sustain manageability problems and *ii.* such an action is not an appropriate means by which to adjudicate the dispute. If there are conflicting interests between the group members, some members might benefit from the outcome of the case at the expense of others.

When grouping businesses for collective actions for damages, the need for extensive individualised assessments for damages and the issue of conflict of interest can be readily observed. For lost profits, each member has the financial motive to assert that *i.* its business lost the most and *ii.* profits lost by other members originate from factors unrelated to the competition infringement. The quantification of lost profits damages of each business also entails individual assessments. This is also true for the overcharge damages of businesses. They may not have been affected by way of passing the entire overcharge down the distribution chain, or are less affected by way of negotiating pricing, benefiting from discounts, incurring different amounts of overcharge damages or passing on different amounts. In addition, in overcharge cases, where the group consists of all purchasers there is a conflict of interest amongst members due to passing-on. All those affected would be seeking a share of the initial overcharge inflicted by the infringement. Each layer of the supply chain incurs damages dependent on how much overcharge has been passed on to them by upstream firms and how much they passed on in turn. Each purchaser is motivated to claim that they absorbed a higher proportion of overcharge.

However, this book showed that these issues are not a problem if a group consists of direct and indirect consumers, whose damages claims are well suited for collective redress. That said, the damage claims of deadweight loss and umbrella consumers – even if they are categorised as separate sub-groups – might not have sufficient similarity to be pursued in a collective action due to the way in which they are harmed.

With respect to determination of those allowed to sue on behalf of consumers, the book submitted that consumer associations should be the representative party in collective actions on behalf of consumers. These associations are unaffected by an infringement but have a genuine interest in the subject matter of the litigation. In this respect, they may be regarded as the appropriate and adequate representatives in collective actions on behalf of consumers. These associations are repeat players, not-for profit organisations, founded to further consumer interests, and have greater means to monitor a lawyer than individual consumers. In addition, they are already allowed to bring a collective action in the majority of Member States, mainly for injunctions. In light of this, their standing to sue for damages on behalf of consumers would present an acceptable solution in the EU. However, due to the complex nature of competition claims and the need for adequate funding, these associations need to work with a lawyer not merely to bring the action but also to run the case, collect the evidence and potentially provide a source of funding, among other options.

The availability of sufficient funding to a representative party is one of the factors that allows a collective redress action to work in practice, especially with the preservation of the loser-pays rule. This book suggested that various options would be made available to a representative party to utilise according to the case. As such may be ATE insurance for opponent's costs, a special fund that obtains some portion of undistributed damages in order to provide funding for collective actions to be filed, third-party funders who finance the action for profit and CFAs and contingency fee arrangements. Under the latter arrangements lawyers not only provide legal help but also bear the risk and costs of the litigation. Contingency fees in opt-out actions would encourage the lawyer to seek competition infringements and pursue a collective action. The availability of these fees would be beneficial both to the representative party and to the consumer group members. In providing funding and legal assistance, lawyers working under contingency fee arrangements make it more likely for consumers to obtain compensation through collective redress actions. By the same token, for the representative party, the risk of running a case, and search and litigation costs are placed on lawyers, who do not recover these costs or fees in the event of losing.

With respect to the last element in the formulation of a collective redress action, this book submitted that it would be possible to make an aggregate damages assessment in collective actions on behalf of consumers without requiring submission of individual proof. Consumers as a group do not hold opposing interests and have no individual issues regarding damages calculation. In addition, aggregate damages assessment is found by multiplying the number of products sold to consumers by the overcharge per product. These figures can be obtained without the input of consumers.

Accordingly, the distribution of those damages should, as a priority, aim to compensate the group members to the largest possible extent. There are two ways to provide compensation directly to the group members. The first way is to find and reimburse victims electronically. Victims can be identified through the defendant's or retailer's sources or any other available databases. In such a case, without requiring the members to come forward and submit evidence, it is possible to compensate members in cash, abatement or by credit. This means of distribution would be less costly and practical to apply and is appropriate many cases in the internet age in the availability of contemporary technology. The second way is to require the members to show the proof of their purchases in order to obtain a share of the damages award. In such a case, it would be possible to accept any viable proof, such as receipt, credit or debit card statements, the product or its packaging, a photograph or a unique product code or serial number. It is, of course, still possible that in some cases neither means of distribution works.

The problem of undistributed damages is a highly controversial and sensitive issue. There are various views as to how to approach the problem. Among those, organisational cy-près could be chosen whereby a certain amount of the undistributed sum could be allocated to a special fund that finances collective actions, and to the representative party, ie a consumer association which can then recover the costs and expenses of the collective action, especially those not paid by the losing defendant. The court would decide the amount considering the particular characteristics of the case, and the representative party's effort in identifying group members and distributing the damages award. In this way, the representative party would not only be incentivised to contribute to the distribution. The representative party would also be incentivised to bring collective actions given that it could use the funding allocated to itself and/or obtain funding from the special fund. The rest of the undistributed sum, if any, could be returned to the defendant. This approach would be compatible with the compensation objective so long as the group members are first given the chance to obtain compensation and so long as the focus is primarily on the direct reimbursement of damages to victims.

The considerable debate and diverse opinions around collective redress actions and the different dynamics that shape their formulation make it impossible to present a perfect answer to the question of how a collective redress action should be designed. This book has nonetheless demonstrated that the current situation and the EU approach on collective redress could be significantly improved by implementing a formulation that provides a realistic opportunity for consumers to obtain compensation for the loss caused by competition infringements. In this regard, the proposed collective redress action can be stated as follows.

The book suggested to make both opt-in and opt-out collective actions available and leave the discretion to choose between them to the court and in this way aimed to make the use of opt-out actions possible for consumer claims when found appropriate by the court. After establishing the boundaries, it suggested to define the group in a way which only encompasses direct and indirect consumers. According to the book, the standing to bring actions on behalf of affected consumers should be granted to consumer associations who would work with lawyers in collective actions and various means of funding mechanisms should be made available to the representative party, including contingency fee arrangements. The book proposed aggregate damages assessment for the calculation of damages of the group of consumers and suggested ways to distribute the damages award to the group members to the greatest possible extent. Where applicable, direct reimbursement to the victims via electronic methods should be preferred, and as an alternative way, the group members could be asked to submit evidence of purchase to obtain their shares. In the event of undistributed damages, part of the sum could be allocated to the representative party who brings the collective action and part could be given to the special fund which provides financing for collective actions.

All in all, in the EU the introduction of a collective redress action is controversial as there are a lot of legal, political and practical issues and difficult questions as to its implementation. Nevertheless, a collective redress action is an important part of private enforcement, and if it is adopted it would contribute to the achievement of effective application of EU competition law.

Bibliography

Books

ABA, *Section of Antitrust Law, Indirect Purchaser Litigation Handbook* (USA: American Bar Association, 2007)

ABA, *Section of Antitrust Law, Antitrust Class Actions Handbook* (USA: American Bar Association, 2010)

Akman, P, *The Concept of Abuse in EU Competition Law: Law and Economic Approaches* (Oxford and Portland, Oregon: Hart Publishing, 2012)

American Law Institute, *Principles of the Law of Aggregate Litigation* (St. Paul, Minnesota: American Law Institute, 2010)

Anderson, B, and A Trask, *The Class Action Playbook* (Oxford: Oxford University Press, 2010)

Andreangeli, A, *Private Enforcement of Antitrust: Regulating Corporate Behaviour through Collective Claims in the EU and US* (Cheltenham UK: Edward Elgar Publishing, 2014)

Areeda, PE, H Hovenkamp, D Blair and CP Durrance, *Antitrust Law: An Analysis of Antitrust Principles and Their Application*, 3rd edn (New York: Aspen Publishers, 2006)

Brick Court Chambers, *Competition Litigation: UK Practice and Procedure*, ed. by M Brealey and N Green (Oxford: Oxford University Press, 2010)

Bucan Gutta, N, *The Enforcement of EU Competition Rules by Civil Law* (Antwerpen-Apeldoorn: Maklu, 2014)

Colino, SM, *Competition Law of the EU and UK*, 7th edn (Oxford: Oxford University Press, 2011)

Craig, P, *EU Administrative Law*, 2nd edn (Oxford: Oxford University Press, 2012)

Crane, DA, *The Institutional Structure of Antitrust Enforcement* (Oxford: Oxford University Press, 2011)

Dabbah, MM, *International and Comparative Competition Law* (Cambridge: Cambridge University Press, 2010)

Davies, K, *Understanding European Union Law*, 4th edn (Oxford: Routledge, 2011)

Dobbs, DB, PT Hayden and EM Bublick, *The Law of Torts*, 2nd edn (St. Paul, Minnesota: West Group, 2011), vol.i

Dougan, M, *National Remedies Before the Court of Justice: Issues of Harmonisation and Differentiation* (Oxford and Portland, Oregon: Hart Publishing, 2004)

Elhauge, E, and D Geradin, *Global Competition Law and Economics*, 2nd edn (New York: Thomson Reuters/Foundation Press, 2011)

Ezrachi, A, *EU Competition Law: An Analytical Guide to the Leading Cases*, 4th edn (Oxford and Portland, Oregon: Hart Publishing, 2014)

Friendly, HJ, *Federal Jurisdiction: A General View* (New York: Columbia University Press, 1973)

Goyder, J, and A Albors-Llorens, *Goyder's EC Competition Law*, 5th edn (Oxford: Oxford University Press, 2009)

HenslerDR, and others, *Class Action Dilemmas: Pursuing Public Goals for Private Gain* (Arlington: RAND, 2000)

Hodges, C, *The Reform of Class and Representative Actions in European Legal Systems: A New Framework for Collective Redress in Europe* (Oxford and Portland, Oregon: Hart Publishing, 2008)

Horsey, K, and E Rackley, *Tort Law*, 3rd edn (Oxford: Oxford University Press, 2013)

Hovenkamp, H, *Federal Antitrust Policy: Law of Competition and Its Practice*, 4th edn (USA: West, 2011)

Howells, GG, and S Weatherill, *Consumer Protection Law*, 2nd edn (England: Ashgate Publishing, Ltd., 2005)

Ioannidou, M, *Consumer Involvement in Private EU Competition Law Enforcement*, (Oxford: Oxford University Press, 2015)

Jones, A, and B Sufrin, *EU Competition Law: Text, Cases & Materials*, 5th edn (Oxford: Oxford University Press, 2014)

Jones, CA, *Private Enforcement of Antitrust Law in the EU, UK and USA* (Oxford: Oxford University Press, 1999)

Jones, C, *Theory of Class Actions* (Toronto: Irwin Law, 2003)

Keske, SE, *Group Litigation in European Competition Law: A Law and Economics Perspective* (Antwerp-Oxford-Portland: Intersentia, 2010)

Komninos, AP, *EC Private Antitrust Enforcement: Decentralised Application of EC Competition Law by National Courts* (Oxford and Portland, Oregon: Hart Publishing, 2008)

Marcus, RL, and EF Sherman, *Complex Litigation: Cases and Materials on Advanced Civil Procedure*, 1st edn (St. Paul, Minnesota: West, 1985)

Monti, G, *EC Competition Law* (Cambridge: Cambridge University Press, 2007)

Motta, M, *Competition Policy: Theory and Practice* (USA: Cambridge University Press, 2009)

Mulheron, R, *The Class Action in Common Law Legal Systems: A Comparative Perspective* (Oxford and Portland, Oregon: Hart Publishing, 2004)

Mulheron, R, *The Modern Cy-Près Doctrine: Applications and Implications* (London: UCL Press, 2006)

Milutinovic, V, *The 'Right to Damages' under EU Competition Law: From Courage v. Crehan to the White Paper and Beyond* (The Netherlands: Kluwer Law International, 2010)

Nazzini, R, *The Foundations of European Union Competition Law: The Objective and Principles of Article 102* (Oxford: Oxford University Press, 2011)

Neale, AD, and DG Goyder, *The Antitrust Laws of the United States of America: A Study of Competition Enforced by Law*, 3rd edn (Cambridge: Cambridge University Press, 1980)

O'Donoghue, R, and AJ Padilla, *The Law and Economics of Article 102 TFEU*, 2nd edn (Oxford and Portland, Oregon: Hart Publishing, 2013)

Page, WH, *Proving Antitrust Damages: Legal and Economic Issues*, 2nd edn (USA: American Bar Association, 2010)

Rodger, BJ, and A MacCulloch, *Competition Law and Policy in the EU and UK*, 5th edn (Oxford: Routledge, 2015)

Scott, C, and J Black, *Cranston's Consumers and the Law*, 3rd edn (London: Butterworths, 2000)

Tridimas, T, *The General Principles of EU Law*, 2nd edn (Oxford: Oxford University Press, 2006)

Van den Bergh, RJ, and PD Camesasca, *European Competition Law and Economics: A Comparative Perspective*, 2nd edn (London: Sweet & Maxwell, 2006)

Varuhas, JNE, *Damages and Human Rights* (Oxford and Portland, Oregon: Hart Publishing, 2016)

Walle, SV, *Private Antitrust Litigation in the European Union and Japan – A Comparative Perspective* (Antwerpen-Apeldoorn: Maklu, 2013)

Whish, R, and D Bailey, *Competition Law*, 7th edn (Oxford: Oxford University Press, 2012)

Yeazell, SC, *From Medieval Group Litigation to the Modern Class Action* (New Haven and London: Yale University Press, 1987)

Book chapters

Athanassiou, L, 'Collective Redress and Competition Policy', in *Cross-Border Class Actions: The European Way*, ed. by A Nuyts and NE Hatzimihail (Munich: Sellier European Law Publishers, 2014), 145–171

Basedow, J, 'Introduction', in *Private Enforcement of EC Competition Law*, ed. by J Basedow (The Netherlands: Kluwer Law International, 2007), 1–5

Calvani, T, 'Cartel Penalties and Damages in Ireland: Criminalization and the Case for Custodial Sentences', in *Criminalization of Competition Law Enforcement: Economic and Legal Implications for the EU Member States*, ed. by KJ Cseres, MP Schinkel and FOW Vogelaar (Cheltenham UK: Edward Elgar Publishing, 2006), 270–289

Cramer, EL, and DC Simons, 'Parties Entitled to Pursue a Claim', in *Private Enforcement of Antitrust Law in the United States: A Handbook*, ed. by AA Foer and RM Stutz (Cheltenham UK: Edward Elgar Publishing, 2012), 64–94

Cseres, KJ, 'Consumer Protection in the European Union', in *Regulation and Economics*, ed. by RJ Van Den Bergh and AM Pacces, 2nd edn (Cheltenham UK: Edward Elgar Publishing, 2012), 163–228

Danov, M, 'Collective Redress and Competititon Law Claims: Some Specific Issues', in *Collective Redress in Europe – Why and How?*, ed. by E Lein, D Fairgrieve, M Otero Crespo and V Smith (London: The British Institute of International and Comparative Law, 2015), 337–355

Dunne, N, 'The Role of Private Enforcement within EU Competition Law', in *Cambridge Yearbook of European Legal Studies*, ed. by A Albors-Llorens, KA Armstrong and MW Gehring, vol.16 (Oxford and Portland, Oregon: Hart Publishing, 2014), 143–187

Ezrachi, A, 'From Courage v Crehan to the White Paper – The Changing Landscape of European Private Enforcement and the Possible Implications for Article 82EC Litigation', in *Abuse of Dominant Position: New Interpretation, New Enforcement Mechanisms?*, ed. by M-O Mackenrodt, BC Gallego and S Enchelmaier (Berlin: Springer, 2010), 117–135

Fischer, M, 'Class Definition', in *A Practitioner's Guide to Class Actions*, ed. by M Greer (USA: American Bar Association, 2011), 47–56

Gerber, DJ, 'Private Enforcement of Competition Law: A Comparative Perspective', in *The Enforcement of Competition Law in Europe*, ed. by TMJ Möllers and A Heinemann, 1st edn (Cambridge: Cambridge University Press, 2007) 431–452

Harlow, C, 'A Common European Law of Remedies?', in *The Future of Remedies in Europe*, ed. by T Novitz, C Kilpatrick and P Skidmore (Oxford and Portland, Oregon: Hart Publishing, 2000), 69–83

Hinteregger, M, 'Reconciling Multilayer Interests in Environmental Law – Access to Justice in Environmental Matters in the European Union and the United States', in *Collective Actions: Enhancing Access to Justice and Reconciling Multilayer Interests?*, ed. by S Wrbka, S Van Uytsel, and M Siems (Cambridge: Cambridge University Press, 2012), 143–166

Hodges, C, 'Fast, Effective and Low Cost Redress: How Do Public and Private Enforcement and ADR Compare?', in *Competition Law Comparative Private Enforcement and Collective Redress across the EU*, ed. by BJ Rodger (The Netherlands: Kluwer Law International, 2014), 255–289

Howells, G, 'Cy-pres for Consumers: Ensuring Class Action Reforms Deal With "Scattered Damages"', in J Steele and WH van Boom (eds) *Mass Justice Challenges of Representation and Distribution* (Cheltenham UK: Edward Elgar Publishing, 2011) 58–72

Jolowicz, JA, 'Group Litigation, Damages, and Judicial Control by Civil Courts', in *Judicial Review in International Perspective*, ed. by M Andenas and D Fairgrieve (The Netherlands: Kluwer Law International, 2000), vol.ii, 481–491

Jones, CA, 'Deterrence and Compensation in New Competition Regimes: The Role of Private Enforcement', in *New Competition Jurisdictions: Shaping Policies and Building Institutions*, ed. by R Whish and C Townley (Cheltenham UK: Edward Elgar Publishing, 2012), 167–182

Keske, S, A Renda and R Van den Bergh, 'Financing and Group Litigation', in *New Trends in Financing Civil Litigation in Europe: A Legal, Empirical, and Economic Analysis*, ed. by ML Tuil and L Visscher (Cheltenham UK: Edward Elgar Publishing, 2010), 57–91

Kocher, E, 'Collective Rights and Collective Goods: Enforcement as Collective Interest', in *Mass Justice: Challenges of Representation and Distribution*, ed. by J Steele and WH Van Boom (Cheltenham UK: Edward Elgar Publishing, 2011), 118–135

Kodek, GE, 'Class Actions – Some Reflections from a European Perspective', in *Collective Redress in Europe – Why and How?*, ed. by E Lein, D Fairgrieve, M Otero Crespo and V Smith (London: The British Institute of International and Comparative Law, 2015), 117–132

Komninos, AP, 'Civil Antitrust Remedies between Community and National Law', in *The Outer Limits of European Union Law*, ed. by C Barnard and O Odudu (Oxford and Portland, Oregon: Hart Publishing, 2009), 363–400

Komninos, AP, 'Private Enforcement in the EU with Emphasis on Damages Actions', in *Handbook on European Competition Law – Enforcement and Procedure*, ed. by I Lianos and D Geradin (Cheltenham UK: Edward Elgar Publishing, 2013), vol.ii, 228–272

Kruse, L, and D Pirolo, 'Antitrust', in *A Practitioner's Guide to Class Actions*, ed. by M Greer (USA: American Bar Association, 2011), 421–424

Lawrence, J, 'Seeking the Perfect Balance: Some Reflections on the Commission Green Paper on Damages Actions for Breach of the EC Antitrust Rules', in *European Competition Law Annual 2006: Enforcement of Prohibition of Cartels*, ed. by CD Ehlermann and I Atanasiu (Oxford and Portland, Oregon: Hart Publishing, 2006), 457–476

Layton, A, 'Collective Redress: Policy Objectives and Practical Problems', in *Extraterritoriality and Collective Redress*, ed. by D Fairgrieve and E Lein (Oxford: Oxford University Press, 2012), 93–104

Mackenrodt, M-O, 'Private Incentive, Optimal Deterrence and Damage Claims for Abuses of Dominant Positions – The Interaction between the Economic Review of the Prohibition of Abuses of Dominant Positions and Private Enforcement', in *Abuse of Dominant Position: New Interpretation, New Enforcement Mechanisms?*, ed. by M-O Mackenrodt, BC Gallego and S Enchelmaier (Berlin: Springer, 2010), 165–189

Maier-Rigaud, F, and U Schwalbe, 'Quantification of Antitrust Damages', in *Competition Damages Actions in the EU: Law and Practice*, ed. by D Ashton and D Henry (Cheltenham UK: Edward Elgar Publishing, 2013), 210–261

Meyer, D, 'Panel Discussion – A Reformed Approach to Article 82 and the US Practice: An Overall Appreciation', in *European Competition Law Annual 2007: A Reformed Approach to Article 82EC*, ed. by C-D Ehlermann and M Marquis (Oxford and Portland, Oregon: Hart Publishing, 2008), 193–196

Michaels, R, 'European Class Actions and Applicable Law', in *Cross-Border Class Actions: The European Way*, ed. by A Nuyts and NE Hatzimihail (Munich: Sellier European Law Publishers, 2014), 111–141

Milutinovic, V, 'Private Enforcement Upcoming Issues', in *EC Competition Law: A Critical Assessment*, ed. by G Amato, C-D Ehlermann and A Komninos (Oxford and Portland, Oregon: Hart Publishing, 2007), 725–758

Møllgaard, P, 'Assessment of Damages in the District Heating Pipe Cartel', in *Cases in European Competition Policy: The Economic Analysis*, ed. by B Lyons (Cambridge: Cambridge University Press, 2009), 159–176

Page, WH, 'Indirect Purchaser Suits Under the Class Action Fairness Act – Reconciling Multilayer Interests in Antitrust Litigation', in *Collective Actions: Enhancing Access to Justice and Reconciling Multilayer Interests?*, ed. by S Wrbka, S Van Uytsel and M Siems (Cambridge: Cambridge University Press, 2012), 275–298

Paulis, E, 'Policy Issues in the Private Enforcement of EC Competition Law', in *Private Enforcement of EC Competition Law*, ed. by J Basedow (The Netherlands: Kluwer Law International, 2007), 7–16

Prechel, S, 'Protection of Rights: How Far?', in *The Coherence of EU Law: The Search for Unity in Divergent Concepts*, ed. by S Prechal and B van Roermund (Oxford: Oxford University Press, 2008), 155–182

Rodger, BJ, 'United Kingdom: A Licence to Print (Monopoly) Money? Replica Football Kit and Toys and Games, Resale Price Maintenance and the Competition Act 1998', in *Landmark Cases in Competition Law: Around the World in Fourteen Stories*, ed. by BJ Rodger (The Netherlands: Kluwer Law International, 2013), 319–343

Rodger, BJ, 'Collective Redress Mechanisms and Consumer Case-Law', in *Competition Law Comparative Private Enforcement and Collective Redress across the EU*, ed. by BJ Rodger (The Netherlands: Kluwer Law International, 2014), 157–192

Rodger, BJ, 'Institutions and Mechanisms to Facilitate Private Enforcement', in *Competition Law Comparative Private Enforcement and Collective Redress across the EU*, ed. by BJ Rodger (The Netherlands: Kluwer Law International, 2014), 23–71

Rodger, BJ, 'The Empirical Data Part 2: Provisions Relied Upon, Remedies and Success', in *Competition Law Comparative Private Enforcement and Collective Redress across the EU*, ed. by BJ Rodger (The Netherlands: Kluwer Law International, 2014), 121–156

Rubinfield, DL, 'Antitrust Damages', in *Research Handbook on the Economics of Antitrust Law*, ed. by E Elhauge (Cheltenham UK: Edward Elgar Publishing, 2012), 378–393

Schmidt, HKS, 'Private Enforcement – Is Article 82 EC Special?', in *Abuse of Dominant Position: New Interpretation, New Enforcement Mechanisms?*, ed. by M-O Mackenrodt, BC Gallego, and S Enchelmaier (Berlin: Springer, 2010), 137–163

Stadler, A, 'Collective Action as an Efficient Means for the Enforcement of European Competition Law', in *Private Enforcement of EC Competition Law*, ed. by J Basedow (The Netherlands: Kluwer Law International, 2007), 195–213

Stadler, A, 'Group Actions as a Remedy to Enforce Consumer Interests', in *New Frontiers of Consumer Protection: The Interplay between Private and Public Enforcement*, ed. by H-W Micklitz and F Cafaggi (Oxford-Portland: Intersentia, 2009), 305–328

Stephan, A, 'Cartels', in *Handbook on European Competition Law – Substantive Aspects*, ed. by I Lianos and D Geradin (Cheltenham UK: Edward Elgar Publishing, 2013), vol.i, 217–241

Van Boom, WH, 'The Law of Damages and Competition Law: Bien Étonnés de Se Trouver Ensemble?', in *Competition of Private Losses – The Evolution of Torts in European Business Law*, ed. by R Schulze (Munich: Sellier, 2011) 165–178

Van Dijk, T, and F Verboven, 'Quantification of Damages', in *Issues in Competition Law and Policy*, ed. by WD Collins (USA: American Bar Association, 2009), 2331–2348

Van Uytsel, S, 'Collective Actions in a Competition Law Context – Reconciling Multilayer Interests to Enhance Access to Justice', in *Collective Actions: Enhancing Access to Justice and Reconciling Multilayer Interests?*, ed. by S Wrbka, S Van Uytsel and M Siems (Cambridge: Cambridge University Press, 2012), 57–92

Waelbroeck, D, and D Slater, 'The Commission's Green Paper on Private Enforcement: "Americanization" of EC Competition Law Enforcement?', in *European Competition Law Annual 2006: Enforcement of Prohibition of Cartels*, ed. by C-D Ehlermann and I Atanasiu (Oxford and Portland, Oregon: Hart Publishing, 2006), 425–455

Journal articles

Akman, P, 'To Abuse, or Not to Abuse: Discrimination between Consumers', *European Law Review*, 32(4) (2007), 492–512

Akman, P, '"Consumer" versus "Customer": The Devil in the Detail', *Journal of Law and Society*, 37(2) (2010), 315–344

Akman, P, 'The European Commission's Guidance on Article 102TFEU: From Inferno to Paradiso?', *Modern Law Review*, 73(4) (2010), 605–630

Allen, DM, and CS Coutroulis, 'Back to the Future: Toward A More Rigorous Analysis of Antitrust Class Actions', *Antitrust Bulletin*, 48(2003), 463–503

Amos, L, P Collis, T Ohta, S Tuxford, M Watts, F Weedon and others, 'EU Update', *Computer Law and Security Review*, 29(2013), 616–620

Andreangeli, A, 'Collective Redress in EU Competition Law: An Open Question with Many Possible Solutions', *World Competition*, 35(3) (2012), 529–558

Andrews, N, 'Multi-Party Actions and Complex Litigation in England', *European Business Law Review*, 23(1) (2012), 1–24

Aresu, A, 'Optimal Contract Reformation as a New Approach to Private Antitrust Damages in Cartel Cases', *European Law Review*, 35(3) (2010), 349–369

Arnull, A, 'The Principle of Effective Judicial Protection in EU Law: An Unruly Horse?", *European Law Review*, 36(1) (2011), 51–70

Barling, G, 'Collective Redress for Breach of Competition Law – A Case for Reform', *Competition Law Journal* (2011), 5–20

Basset, DL, 'U.S. Class Actions Go Global: Transnational Class Actions and Personal Jurisdiction', *Fordham Law Review*, 72(1) (2003), 41–92

Basset, DL, 'Just Go Away: Representation, Due Process, and Preclusion in Class Actions', *Brigham Young University Law Review*, 2009(5) (2009), 1079–1126

Basso, LJ, and TW Ross, 'Measuring the True Harm from Price-Fixing to Both Direct and Indirect Purchasers', *The Journal of Industrial Economics*, 58(4) (2010), 895–927

Becker, R, N Bessot, and E De Smijter, 'The White Paper on Damages Actions for Breach of the EC Antitrust Rules', *Competition Policy Newsletter*, 2(2008), 4–11

Benöhr, I, 'Consumer Dispute Resolution after the Lisbon Treaty: Collective Actions and Alternative Procedures', *Journal of Consumer Policy*, 36(1) (2013), 87–110
Bernard, KS, 'Private Antitrust Litigation in the European Union – Why Does the EC Want to Embrace What the US FTC is Trying to Avoid?', *Global Competition Litigation Review*, 3(2) (2010), 69–74
Bernard, KS, 'Making Victims Whole: A Restitution Approach to Cartel Damages', *Concurrences Journal*, 1–2012 (2012), 1–9
Bernard, C, and S Bourjade, 'Economic Incentives in Class Actions: An Analysis through the US/EU Examples', *Global Competition Litigation Review*, 6(1) (2013), 12–17
Berrisch, G, E Jordan and R Salvador Roldan, 'EU Competition and Private Actions for Damages', *Northwestern Journal of International Law and Business*, 24(2004), 585–600
Blennerhassett, J, 'Is It Time to Get the Multi-Party Started? Exploring the Spectrum of Mass Harm Redress in Ireland', *Supreme Court Law Review (2d)*, 53 (2011), 347–383
Bone, RG, and DS Evans, 'Class Certification and the Substantive Merits', *Duke Law Journal*, 51(4) (2002), 1251–1332
Bourgoignie, T, 'Characteristics of Consumer Law', *Journal of Consumer Policy*, 14(3) (1991), 293–315
Bourjade, S, 'The Role of Private Litigation in Antitrust Enforcement', *Global Competition Litigation Review*, 3(3) (2010), 118–123
Brander, JA, and TW Ross, 'Estimating Damages from Price-Fixing', *Canadian Class Action Review*, 3(2006), 335–369
Bronsteen, J, 'Class Action Settlements: An Opt-In Proposal', *University of Illinois Law Review*, (2005), 903–928
Bronsteen, J, and O Fiss, 'The Class Action Rule', *Notre Dame Law Review*, 78(2003), 1419–1453
Brummer, C, 'Sharpening the Sword: Class Certification, Appellate Review, and the Role of the Fiduciary Judge in Class Action Lawsuits', *Columbia Law Review*, 104(2004), 1042–1071
Buccirossi, P, 'Quantification of Damages in Exclusionary Practice Cases', *Journal of European Competition Law and Practice*, 1(3) (2010), 252–256
Buccirossi, P, and M Carpagnano, 'Is It Time for the European Union to Legislate in the Field of Collective Redress in Antitrust (and How)?', *Journal of European Competition Law and Practice*, 4(1) (2013), 3–15
Bulst, FW, 'Private Antitrust Enforcement at a Roundabout', *European Business Organization Law Review*, 3(2006), 725–746
Burns, JW, 'Decorative Figureheads: Eliminating Class Representatives in Class Actions', *Hastings Law Journal*, 42(1991), 165–202
Calkins, S, 'An Enforcement Official's Reflections on Antitrust Class Actions', *Arizona Law Review*, 39(1997), 413–451
Cameron, C, and J Kalajdzic, 'Commercial Litigation Funding: Ethical, Regulatory and Comparative Perspectives', *Canadian Business Law Journal*, 55(1) (2014), 1–16
Campion, JA, and VA Stewart, 'Class Actions: Procedure and Strategy', *Advocates' Quarterly*, 19(1997), 20–66
Cane, P, 'Distributive Justice and Tort Law', *New Zealand Law Review*, 4(2001), 401–420
Cauffman, C, 'The DCFR and the Attempts to Increase the Private Enforcement of Competition Law: Convergences and Divergences', *European Review of Private Law*, 18 (2010), 1079–1119
Cavanagh, E, 'Antitrust Remedies Revisited', *Oregon Law Review*, 84(2005), 147–225

Cengiz, F, 'Antitrust Damages Actions: Lessons from American Indirect Purchasers' Litigation", *International and Comparative Law Quarterly*, 59(2010) 39–63
Che, Y-K, 'Equilibrium Formation of Class Action Suits', *Journal of Public Economics*, 62 (1996), 339–361
Chieu, T, 'Class Actions in the European Union?: Importing Lessons Learned From the United States' Experience into European Community Competition Law', *Cardozo Journal of International and Comparative Law*, 18(2010), 123–157
Cirace, J, 'Apportioning Damages between Direct and Indirect Purchasers in Consolidated Antitrust Suits: ARC America Unravels the Illinois Brick Rule', *Villanova Law Review*, 35(1990), 283–332
Coffee, JC, 'Rescuing the Private Attorney General: Why the Model of the Lawyer as Bounty Hunter Is Not Working', *Maryland Law Review*, 42(2) (1983), 215–288
Coffee, JC, 'Understanding the Plaintiff's Attorney: The Implications of Economic Theory for Private Enforcement of Law through Class and Derivative Actions', *Columbia Law Review*, 86(4) (1986), 669–727
Coffee, JC, 'Litigation Governance: Taking Accountability Seriously', *Columbia Law Review*, 110(2) (2010), 288–351
Combe, E, and C Monnier, 'Fines against Hard Core Cartels in Europe: The Myth of Overenforcement', *Antitrust Bulletin*, 56(2) (2011), 235–275
Connor, JM, and RH Lande, 'How High Do Cartels Raise Prices? Implications for Reform of the Antitrust Sentencing Guidelines', *Tulane Law Review*, 80(2005), 513–569
Coutroulis, CS, and DM Allen, 'The Pass-on Problem in Indirect Purchaser Class Litigation', *Antitrust Bulletin*, 44(1999), 179–210
Craig, L, and L Hannah, 'Collective Proceedings and Settlements before the CAT: A New Dawn', *Competition Law Journal*, 12(4) (2013), 408–415
Crane, DA, 'Optimizing Private Antitrust Enforcement', *Vanderbilt Law Review*, 63(3) (2010), 673–723
Cremieux, PY, A Decter, S Herscovici and R Mascola, 'Assessing Conflict, Impact and Common Methods of Proof in Intermediate Indirect-Purchaser Class Action Litigation', *Economics Comittee Newsletter*, 6(1) (2006), 4–10
Cseres, KJ, 'The Controversies of the Consumer Welfare Standard', *Competition Law Review*, 3(2) (2006), 121–173
Dam, KW, 'Class Actions: Efficiency, Compensation, Deterrence, and Conflict of Interest', *The Journal of Legal Studies*, 4(1) (1975), 47–73
Davis, JP, and EL Cramer, 'Antitrust, Class Certification, and the Politics of Procedure', *George Mason Law Review*, 17(4) (2010), 969–1033
Davis, JP, and RH Lande, 'Defying Conventional Wisdom: The Case for Private Antitrust Enforcement', *Georgia Law Review*, 48(1) (2013), 1–82
Davis, JP, and RH Lande, 'Toward an Empirical and Theoretical Assessment of Private Antitrust Enforcement', *Seattle University Law Review*, 36(2013), 1269–1335
Davis, JP, 'Classwide Recoveries', *The George Washington Law Review*, 82(2014), 890–950
Dayagi-Epstein, O, 'Representation of Consumer Interest By Consumer Associations – Salvation for the Masses?', *Competition Law Review*, 3(2) (2006), 209–249
De, O, 'Analysis of Cartel Duration: Evidence from EC Prosecuted Cartels', *International Journal of the Economics of Business*, 17(1) (2010), 33–65
Delatre, JG, 'Beyond the White Paper: Rethinking the Commission's Proposal on Private Antitrust Litigation', *Competition Law Review*, 8(1) (2011), 29–58
Dellavedova, B, and R Gilsenan, 'Challenges in Cartel Class Actions', *University of New South Wales Law Journal*, 32(2009), 1001–1021

Dewees, DN, JRS Prichard and MJ Trebilcock, 'An Economic Analysis of Cost and Fee Rules for Class Actions', *The Journal of Legal Studies*, 10(1) (1981), 155–185

Dickey, BM, and DL Rubinfield, 'Antitrust Class Certification: Towards an Economic Framework', *New York University Annual Survey of American Law*, 66(2011), 459–486

Diemer, C, 'The Green Paper on Damages Actions for Breach of the EC Antitrust Rules', *European Competition Law Review*, 27(6) (2006), 309–316

Downs, HM, 'Federal Class Actions: Due Process by Adequacy of Representation (Identity of Claims) and the Impact of General Telephone v. Falcon', *Ohio State Law Journal*, 54 (1993), 607–712

Dreyfuss, RH, 'Class Action Judgment Enforcement in Italy: Procedural Due Process Requirements', *Tulane Journal of International and Comparative Law*, 10(2002), 5–36

Duffy, MM, 'Chipping Away at the Illinois Brick Wall: Expanding Exceptions to the Indirect Purchaser Rule', *Notre Dame Law Review*, 87(2012), 1709–1748

Duron, A, 'Private Damages Actions in the Wake of a Commitment Decision: New Risks after the Judgment of the Paris Commercial Court in Eco-Emballages', *Journal of European Competition Law and Practice* (2015), 1–5

Duval, BS, 'The Class Action as an Antitrust Enforcement Device: The Chicago Experience (II)', *American Bar Foundation Research Journal*, 1(4) (1976), 1273–1358

Editorial Comments, 'A Little More Action Please! – The White Paper on Damages Actions for Breach of EC Antitrust Rules', *Common Market Law Review*, 45(3) (2008), 609–615

Eger, T, and P Weise, 'Some Limits to the Private Enforcement of Antitrust Law: A Grumbler's View on Harm and Damages in Hardcore Price Cartel Cases', *Global Competition Litigation Review*, 3(4) (2010), 152–160

Eisenberg, T, and GP Miller, 'The Role of Opt-Outs and Objectors in Class Action Litigation: Theoretical and Empirical Issues', *Vanderbilt Law Review*, 57(2004), 1529–1567

Eisenberg, T, and GP Miller, 'Attorneys' Fees and Expenses in Class Action Settlements: 1993–2008', *Journal of Empirical Legal Studies*, 7(2) (2010), 248–281

Erbsen, A, 'From "Predominance" to "Resolvability": A New Approach to Regulating Class Actions', *Vanderbilt Law Review*, 58(4) (2005), 995–1088

Ezrachi, A, and M Ioannidou, 'Public Compensation as a Complementary Mechanism to Damages Actions: From Policy Justifications to Formal Implementation', *Journal of European Competition Law and Practice*, 3(6) (2012), 536–544

Fisch, JE, 'Class Action Reform, Qui Tam, and the Role of the Plaintiff', *Law and Contemporary Problems*, 60(4) (1997), 167–202

Fitzpatrick, BT, 'An Empirical Study of Class Action Settlements and Their Fee Awards', *Journal of Empirical Legal Studies*, 7(4) (2010), 811–846

Foer, AA, 'Enhancing Competition through the Cy Pres Remedy: Suggested Best Practices', *Antitrust Magazine*, 24(2010), 86–91

Foer, AA, and EP Schultz, 'Will Two Roads Still Diverge? Private Enforcement of Antitrust Law Is Getting Harder in the United States. But Europe May Be Making It Easier', *Global Competition Litigation Review*, 3(2011), 107–112

Forde, KM, 'What Can a Court Do with Leftover Class Action Funds?: Almost Anything!', *The Judges' Journal*, 35(3) (1996), 1–12

Galanter, M, 'Why the "Haves" Come Out Ahead: Speculations on the Limits of Legal Change', *Law and Society Review*, 9(1) (1974), 95–160

Galligan, Jr, CT, 'Disaggregating More-Than-Whole Damages in Personal Injury Law: Deterrence and Punishment', *Tennessee Law Review*, 71(2003), 117–154

Gaudet, R, 'Turning a Blind Eye: The Commission's Rejection of Opt-out Class Actions Overlooks Swedish, Norwegian, Danish and Dutch Experience', *European Competition Law Review*, 30(3) (2009), 107–117

Gavil, AI, 'Antitrust Remedy Wars Episode I: Illinois Brick from Inside the Supreme Court', *St. John's Law Review*, 79(3) (2005), 553–624

Gavil, AI, 'Thinking Outside the Illinois Brick Box: A Proposal for Reform', *Antitrust Law Journal*, 76(2009), 167–203

Gidi, A, 'Class Actions in Brazil – A Model for Civil Law Countries', *American Journal of Comparative Law*, 51(2013), 311–408

Gilles, M, 'Opting Out of Liability: The Forthcoming, Near-Total Demise of the Modern Class Action', *Michigan Law Review*, 104(3) (2005), 373–430

Gilles, M, and G Friedman, 'Exploding the Class Action Agency Costs Myth: The Social Utility of Entrepreneurial Lawyers', *University of Pennsylvania Law Review*, 155(2006), 103–164

Goldring, J, 'Consumer Law and Legal Theory: Reflections of a Common Lawyer', *Journal of Consumer Policy*, 13(2) (1990), 113–132

Goyder, J, 'Cet Obscur Objet: Object Restrictions in Vertical Agreements' *Journal of European Competition Law and Practice*, 2(4) (2011), 327–339

Hamilton, A, and D Henry, 'Bricks, Beer and Shoes: Indirect Purchaser Standing in the European Union and the United States', *Global Competition Litigation Review*, 5(3) (2012), 111–117

Hamilton, BW, 'Class Action in Price-Fixing Litigation When the Fixed Price Is a Wage Rate: Law et Al. v. NCAA', *Antitrust Bulletin*, 48(2) (2003), 505–529

Handler, M, 'The Shift from Substantive to Procedural Innovation in Antitrust Suits – The Twenty-Third Annual Antitrust Review', *Columbia Law Review*, 71(1) (1971), 1–36

Handler, M, and MD Blechman, 'Antitrust and the Consumer Interest: The Fallacy of Parens Patriae and A Suggested New Approach', *Yale Law Journal*, 85(5) (1976), 626–676

Harnay, S, and A Marciano, 'Seeking Rents through Class Actions and Legislative Lobbying: A Comparison', *European Journal of Law and Economics*, 32(2) (2011), 293–304

Harris, RG, and LA Sullivan, 'Passing on the Monopoly Overcharge: A Comprehensive Policy Analysis', *University of Pennsylvania Law Review*, 128(2) (1979), 269–360

Harrison, JL, 'The Lost Profits Measure of Damages in Price Enhancement Cases', *Minnesota Law Review*, 64(1980), 751–788

Hausfeld, M, M Lehmann, S Jenkins and N Morgan, 'The Contingency Phobia – Fear without Foundation', *Global Competition Litigation Review*, 4(1) (2011), 39–42

Hay, B, and D Rosenberg, 'Sweetheart and Blackmail Settlements in Class Actions: Reality and Remedy', *Notre Dame Law Review*, 75(4) (2000), 1377–1408

Hazelhorst, M, 'Private Enforcement of EU Competition Law: Why Punitive Damages Are a Step Too Far', *European Review of Private Law*, 18(4) (2010), 757–772

Helland, E, and A Tabarrok, 'Contingency Fees, Settlement Delay, and Low-Quality Litigation: Empirical Evidence from Two Datasets', *Journal of Law, Economics, and Organization*, 19(2) (2003), 517–542

Herron, M, 'The Proposed UK Competition Law Class Action and Treatment of Unclaimed Sums: A Policy and Practical Perspective', *Competition Law Journal*, 2 (2013), 159–170

Hodges, C, 'Competition Enforcement, Regulation and Civil Justice: What Is the Case?', *Common Law Market Review*, 43(2006), 1381–1407

Hodges, C, 'From Class Actions to Collective Redress: A Revolution in Approach to Compensation', *Civil Justice Quarterly*, 28(1) (2009), 41–66

Hodges, C, 'Collective Redress in Europe: The New Model', *Civil Justice Quarterly*, 29(3) (2010), 370–395

Hodges, C, 'European Competition Enforcement Policy: Integrating Restitution and Behaviour Control an Integrated Enforcement Policy, Involving Public and Private Enforcement with ADR', *World Competition*, 34(3) (2011), 383–396

Hodges, C, 'A Market-Based Competition Enforcement Policy', *European Business Law Review*, 22(2011), 261–291

Hodges, C, 'Current Discussions on Consumer Redress: Collective Redress and ADR', *ERA Forum*, 13(2012), 11–33

Hodges, C, 'Collective Redress: A Breakthrough or a Damp Sqibb?', *Journal of Consumer Policy*, 37(1) (2014), 67–89

Homburger, A, 'Private Suits in the Public Interest in the United States of America', *Buffalo Law Review*, 23(1974), 343–410

Hoseinian, F, 'Passing-on Damages and Community Antitrust Policy – An Economic Background', *World Competition*, 28(1) (2005), 3–23

Hovenkamp, H, 'Antitrust's Protected Classes', *Michigan Law Review*, 88(1) (1989), 1–48

Hovenkamp, H, 'Book Review – The Rationalization of Antitrust', *Harvard Law Review*, 116(2003), 917–944 (reviewing RA Posner, *Antitrust Law*, 2nd edn (Chicago: The University of Chicago Press, 2001))

Hovenkamp, H, 'Restraints on Innovation', *Cardozo Law Review*, 29(1) (2007), 247–260

Hubbard, W, 'Optimal Class Size, Dukes, and the Funny Thing about Shady Grove', *DePaul Law Review*, 62(2013), 693–709

Hubert, P, and M-L Combet, 'Exploitative Abuse: The End of the Paradox?', *Concurrences Doctrines*, I(1) (2011), 44–51

Hussain, S, D Garrett and V Howell, 'Economics of Class Certification in Indirect Purchaser Antitrust Cases', *Journal of the Antitrust and Unfair Competition Law Section of the State Bar of California*, 10(1) (2001), 18–52

Iacobucci, EM, 'Cartel Class Actions and Immunity Programmes', *Journal of Antitrust Enforcement*, 1(2) (2013), 272–295

Ioannidou, M, 'Enhancing the Consumers' Role in EU Private Competition Law Enforcement: A Normative and Practical Approach', *Competition Law Review*, 8(1) (2011), 59–85

Issacharoff, S, and GP Miller, 'Will Aggregate Litigation Come to Europe?', *Vanderbilt Law Review*, 62(1) (2008), 179–210

Johnson, J, and G Leonard, 'Economics and the Rigorous Analysis of Class Certification in Antitrust Cases', *Journal of Competition Law and Economics*, 3(3) (2007), 341–356

Johnson, PA, 'The Economics of Common Impact in Antitrust Class Certification', *Antitrust Law Journal*, 77(2011), 533–567

Jones, CA, and D Beard, 'Case Comment "Co-Contractors, Damages and Article 81: ECJ Finally Speaks"', *European Competition Law Review*, 23(2002), 246–256

Jones, CA, 'Foreword – Opting-in to Opting-out: Why Collective Redress in Europe Should Adopt the Opt-out Approach to Class Actions', *Concurrences Journal*, 2(2012), 1–3

Jones, G, 'Collective Redress in the European Union: Reflections from a National Judge', *Legal Issues of Economic Integration*, 41(3) (2014), 289–304

Juska, Z, 'Obstacles in European Competition Law Enforcement: A Potential Solution from Collective Redress', *European Journal of Legal Studies*, 7(1) (2014), 125–153

Juska, Z, 'The Effectiveness of Antitrust Collective Litigation in the European Union: A Study of the Principle of Full Compensation', *International Review of Intellectual Property and Competition Law*, 49(1) (2018), 63–93

Kalajdzic, J, 'Access to a Just Result: Revisiting Settlement Standards and Cy Pres Distributions', *Canadian Class Action Review*, 6(1) (2010), 215–251

Kaplan, B, 'A Prefatory Note', *Boston College Law Review*, 10(3) (1969), 497–500

Kleefeld, JC, 'Book Review', *Canadian Class Action Review*, 4(1) (2007), 203–210 (reviewing R Mulheron, *The Modern Cy-Près Doctrine: Applications and Implications* (London: UCL Press, 2006))

Klonoff, RH, 'The Decline of Class Actions', *Washington University Law Review*, 90(3) (2013), 729–838

Kloub, J, 'White Paper on Damage Actions for Breach of the EC Antitrust Rules: Plea for a More Holistic Approach to Antitrust Enforcement', *European Competition Journal*, 5(2) (2009), 515–547

Komninos, AP, 'New Prospects for Private Enforcement of EC Competition Law: Courage v. Crehan and the Community Right to Damages', *Common Market Law Review*, 39(3) (2002), 447–487

Korenblit, CM, 'Quantifying Antitrust Damages – Convergence of Methods Recognized by U.S. Courts and the European Commission', *CPI Antitrust Chronicle*, 1(2012), 1–9

Kortmann, JS and CRA Swaak, 'The EC White Paper on Antitrust Damage Actions: Why the Member States Are (Right to Be) Less Than Enthusiastic', *European Competition Law Review*, 30(7) (2009), 340–351

Kritzer, HM, 'Contingency Fee Lawyers as Gatekeepers in the Civil Justice System', *Judicature*, 81(1) (1997), 22–29

Lahav, AD, 'Fundamental Principles for Class Action Governance', *Indiana Law Review*, 37(2004), 65–140

Lahav, AD, 'Symmetry and Class Action Litigation', *UCLA Law Review*, 60(2013), 1494–1522

Lande, RH, 'Are Antitrust "Treble" Damages Really Single Damages?', *Ohio State Law Journal*, 54(1993), 115–174

Lande, RH, 'New Options for State Indirect Purchaser Legislation: Protecting the Real Victims of Antitrust Violations', *Alabama Law Review*, 61(3) (2010), 447–492

Lande, RH, 'The Proposed Damages Directive: The Real Lessons from the United States', *CPI Antitrust Chronicle*, 2(2014), 1–12

Lande RH, Editorial, 'The Proposed Damages Legislation: Don't Believe the Critics', *Journal of European Competition Law and Practice* (2014), 1–2

Lande, RH, and NW Averitt, 'Using the Consumer Choice Approach to Antitrust Law', *Antitrust Law Journal*, 74(2007) 175–264

Lande, RH, and JP Davis, 'Benefits from Private Antitrust Enforcement: An Analysis of Forty Cases', *University of San Francisco Law Review*, 42(2008), 879–918

Landers, JM, 'Of Legalized Blackmail and Legalized Theft: Consumer Class Actions and the Substance-Procedure Dilemma', *Southern California Law Review*, 47(1974), 842–900

Landes, WM, and RA Posner, 'Should Indirect Purchasers Have Standing to Sue Under the Antitrust Laws? An Economic Analysis of the Rule of Illinois Brick', *University of Chicago Law Review*, 46(3) (1979), 602–635

Lang, CG, 'Class Actions and the US Antitrust Laws: Prerequisities and Interdependencies of the Implementation of a Procedural Device for the Aggregation of Low-Value Claims', *World Competition*, 24(2) (2001), 285–302

Lave, JM, 'Umbrella Standing: The Trade-off between Plaintiff Suit and Speculative Claims', *Antitrust Bulletin*, 48(2003), 223–269

Lawne, D, 'Private Enforcement and Collective Redress: A Claimant Perspective on the Proposed BIS Reforms', *Competition Law Journal*, 2(2013), 171–181

Leskinen, C, 'Collective Actions: Rethinking Funding and National Cost Rules', *Competition Law Review*, 8(1) (2011), 87–121
Leslie, CR, 'Antitrust Damages and Deadweight Loss', *Antitrust Bulletin*, 51(3) (2006), 521–567
Leslie, CR, 'The Significance of Silence: Collective Action Problems and Class Action Settlements', *Florida Law Review*, 59(2007), 71–134
Leslie, CR, 'De Facto Detrebling: The Rush to Settlement in Antitrust Class Action Litigation', *Arizona Law Review*, 50(2008), 1009–1052
Lilly, GC, 'Modeling Class Actions: The Representative Suit as an Analytic Tool', *Nebraska Law Review*, 81(2003), 1008–1055
Lindblom, PH, 'Individual Litigation and Mass Justice: A Swedish Perspective and Proposal on Group Actions in Civil Procedure', *The American Journal of Comparative Law*, 45 (4) (1997), 805–831
Logan, SJ, J Moshman and BC Moore, 'Attorney Fee Awards in Common Fund Class Actions', *Class Action Reports*, 24(2) (2003), 167–234
Lopatka, JE, 'Overcharge Damages for Monopolization of New Economy Markets', *Antitrust Bulletin*, 51(2006), 453–505
Macey, JR, and GP Miller, 'The Plaintiffs' Attorney's Role in Class Action and Derivative Litigation: Economic Analysis and Recommendations for Reform', *The University of Chicago Law Review*, 58(1) (1991), 1–118
Marcus, D, 'Attorneys' Fees and the Social Legitimacy of Class Actions', *University of Pennsylvania PeNNumbra*, 159(2010), 157–166
Micklitz, H-W, and A Stadler, 'The Development of Collective Legal Actions in Europe, Especially in German Civil Procedure', *European Business Law Review*, 17(5) (2006), 1473–1503
Miller, AR, 'Of Frankenstein Monsters and Shining Knights: Myth, Reality, and the "Class Action Problem"', *Harvard Law Review*, 92(3) (1979), 664–694
Mulheron, R, 'Some Difficulties with Group Litigation Orders – And Why a Class Action Is Superior', *Civil Justice Quarterly*, 24(2005), 40–68
Mulheron, R, 'The Case for an Opt-out Class Action for European Member States: A Legal and Empirical Analysis', *Columbia Journal of European Law*, 15(2009), 409–453
Mulheron, R, 'Cy-Près Damages Distributions in England: A New Era for Consumer Redress', *European Business Law Review*, 20(2009), 307–342
Mulheron, R, 'Recent Milestones in Class Actions Reform in England: A Critique and a Proposal', *Law Quarterly Review*, 127(2011), 288–315
Mulheron, R, 'A Missed Gem of an Opportunity for the Representative Rule', *European Business Law Review*, 23(1) (2012), 49–60
Nader, L, 'Disputing without the Force of Law', *Yale Law Journal*, 88(1979), 998–1021
Nagareda, RA, 'The Preexistence Principle and the Structure of the Class Action', *Columbia Law Review*, 103(2) (2003), 149–242
Nagareda, RA, 'Class Certification in the Age of Aggregate Proof', *New York University Law Review*, 84(2009), 84–173
Nagy, CI, 'Comparative Collective Redress from a Law and Economics Perspective: Without Risk There Is No Reward!', *Columbia Journal of European Law*, 19(3) (2013), 469–498
Nazzini, R, and A Nikpay, 'Private Actions in EC Competition Law', *Competition Policy International*, 4(2) (2008), 107–141

Nazzini, R, 'The Objective of Private Remedies in EU Competition Law', *Global Competition Litigation Review*, 4(2011), 131–146

Nebbia, P, '... So What Happened to Mr. Manfredi? The Italian Decision Following the Ruling of the European Court of Justice', *European Competition Law Review*, 28(11) (2007), 591–596

Nebbia, P, 'Damages Actions for the Infringement of EC Competition Law: Compensation or Deterrence?', *European Law Review*, 33(1) (2008), 23–43

Nordh, R, 'Group Actions in Sweden: Reflections on the Purpose of Civil Litigation, the Need for Reform and a Forthcoming Proposal', *Duke Journal of Comparative and International Law*, 11(2001), 381–404

Pace, NM, 'Class Actions In the United States of America: An Overview of the Process and the Empirical Literature', *RAND Institute for Civil Justice* (2007), 1–99

Page, WH, 'The Scope of Liability for Antitrust Violations', *Stanford Law Review*, 37(6) (1985), 1445–1512

Page, WH, and JE Lopatka, 'Indirect Purchaser Suits and the Consumer Interest', *Antitrust Bulletin*, 48(2003), 531–570

Page, WH, 'Class Certification in the Microsoft Indirect Purchaser Litigation', *Journal of Competition Law and Economics*, 1(2) (2005), 303–338

Pheasant, J, and A Bicarregui, 'Striking the Right Balance towards a "Competition Culture" Not a "Litigation Culture"? Comment on the European Commission's White Paper on Damages Actions for Breach of EC Antitrust Rules', *Global Competition Litigation Review*, 1(2) (2008), 98–106

Peyer, S, 'Private Antitrust Litigation in Germany from 2005 to 2007: Empirical Evidence', *Journal of Competition Law and Economics*, 8(2) (2012), 331–359

Pomerantz, AL, 'New Developments in Class Actions – Has Their Death Knell Been Sounded', *Business Lawyer*, 25(3) (1970), 1259–1266

Polinsky, AM, and S Shavell, 'The Economic Theory of Public Enforcement of Law', *Journal of Economic Literature*, 38(1) (2000), 45–76

Polinsky, AM, and DL Rubinfield, 'A Note on Settlements under the Contingent Fee Method of Compensating Lawyers', *International Review of Law and Economics*, 22(2) (2002), 217–225

Posner, RA, 'Oligopoly and the Antitrust Laws: A Suggested Approach', *Stanford Law Review*, 21(1968), 1562–1606

Richards, JD, 'What Makes an Antitrust Class Action Remedy Successful: A Tale of Two Settlements', *Tulane Law Review*, 80(2005), 621–660

Richman, BD, and CR Murray, 'Rebuilding Illinois Brick: A Functionalist Approach to the Indirect Purchaser Rule', *Southern California Law Review*, 81(2007), 69–110

Riley, A, and J Peysner, 'Damages in EC Antitrust Actions: Who Pays the Piper?', *European Law Review*, 31(2006), 748–761

Rizzuto, F, 'The Private Enforcement of European Union Competition Law: What Next?', *Global Competition Litigation Review*, 3(2) (2010), 57–68

Robertson, A, 'UK Competition Litigation: From Cinderella to Goldilocks?', *Competition Law Journal*, 9(2) (2010), 275–294

Rodger, BJ, 'Why Not Court? A Study of Follow-on Actions in the UK', *Journal of Antitrust Enforcement*, 1(1) (2013), 104–131

Rosenberg, D, 'Class Actions for Mass Torts: Doing Individual Justice by Collective Means', *Indiana Law Journal*, 62(3) (1987), 561–596

Rosenberg, D, 'Mass Tort Class Actions: What Defendants Have and Plaintiffs Don't', *Harvard Journal on Legislation*, 37(2000), 393–431

Rosenberg, D, and JP Sullivan, 'Coordinating Private Class Action and Public Agency Enforcement of Antitrust Law', *Journal of Competition Law and Economics*, 2(2) (2006), 159–187
Rubenstein, WB, 'Why Enable Litigation?: A Positive Externalities Theory of the Small Claims Class Action', *University of Missouri-Kansas City Law Review*, 74(3) (2006), 709–728
Rüggeberg, J, and MP Schinkel, 'Consolidating Antitrust Damages in Europe: A Proposal for Standing in line with Efficient Private Enforcement', *World Competition*, 29(3) (2006), 395–420
Russell, TL, 'Exporting Class Actions to the European Union', *Boston University International Law Journal*, 28(2010), 141–180
Salop, SC, and LJ White, 'Economic Analysis of Private Antitrust Litigation', *Georgetown Law Journal*, 74(1986), 1001–1064
Schaefer, H-B, 'The Bundling of Similar Interests in Litigation. The Incentives for Class Action and Legal Actions Taken by Associations', *European Journal of Law and Economics*, 9(3) (2000), 183–213
Schwartz, GT, 'Mixed Theories of Tort Law: Affirming Both Deterrence and Corrective Justice', *Texas Law Review*, 75(1997), 1801–1834
Schwartz, M, and GJ Werden, 'Illinois Brick and the Deterrence of Antitrust Violations-An Economic Analysis', *Hastings Law Journal*, 35(1984), 629–668
Shapiro, DL, 'Class Actions: The Class as Party and Client', *Notre Dame Law Review*, 73 (4) (1998), 913–961
Silver, C, '"We Are Scared to Death": Class Certification and Blackmail', *New York University Law Review*, 78 (2003), 1357–1430
Sittenreich, MA, 'The Rocky Path for Private Directors General: Procedure, Politics, and the Uncertain Future of EU Antitrust Damages Actions', *Fordham Law Review*, 78(5) (2010), 2701–2750
de Smijter, E, and D O'Sullivan, 'The Manfredi Judgment of the ECJ and How It Relates to the Commission's Initiative on EC Antitrust Damages Actions', *Competition Policy Newsletter*, 3(2006), 23–26
Smith, V, 'Publication Review', *European Law Review*, 37(3) (2012), 353–355 (reviewing SE Keske, *Group Litigation in European Competition Law: A Law and Economics Perspective* (Antwerp-Oxford-Portland: Intersentia, 2010))
Smithka, C, 'From Budapest to Berlin: How Implementing Class Action Lawsuits in the European Union Would Increase Competition and Strengthen Consumer Confidence', *Wisconsin International Law Journal*, 27(2009), 173–193
Spence, ST, 'Looking Back … In a Collective Way: A Short History of Class Action Law', *Business Law Today*, 11(6) (2002), 21–24
Spender, P, 'Securities Class Actions: A View from the Land of the Great White Shareholder', *Common Law World Review*, 31(2002), 123–164
Stiglitz, JE, 'Information and the Change in the Paradigm in Economics', *American Economic Review*, 92(3) (2002), 460–501
Strand, M, 'Indirect Purchasers, Passing-On and the New Directive on Competition Law Damages', *European Competition Journal*, 10(2) (2014), 361–386
Susman, SD, 'Prosecuting the Antitrust Class Action', *Antitrust Law Journal*, 49(1980), 1513–1527
Svetlicinii, A, and M Botta, 'Article 102 TFEU as a Tool for Market Regulation: "Excessive Enforcement" Against "Excessive Prices" in the New EU Member States and Candidate Countries', *European Competition Journal*, 8(3) (2012), 473–496

Tang, ZS, 'Consumer Collective Redress in European Private International Law', *Journal of Private International Law*, 7(1) (2011), 101–147

Tzakas, D-PL, 'Effective Collective Redress in Antitrust and Consumer Protection Matters: A Panacea or a Chimera?', *Common Market Law Review*, 48(2011), 1125–1174

Ulen, TS, 'An Introduction to the Law and Economics of Class Action Litigation', *European Journal of Law and Economics*, 32(2011), 185–203

Valdes, F, 'Procedure, Policy and Power: Class Actions and Social Justice in Historical and Comparative Perspective', *Georgia State University Law Review*, 24(3) (2007), 627–661

Van den Bergh, R, 'Private Enforcement of European Competition Law and the Persisting Collective Action Problem', *Maastricht Journal*, 1(2013), 12–34

Van Gerven, W, 'Of Rights, Remedies and Procedures', *Common Market Law Review*, 37 (2000), 501–536

Veenbrink, M, and CS Rusu, 'Case Comment – Case C-557/12 Kone AG and Others v ÖBB Infrastruktur AG', *Competition Law Review*, 10(1) (2014), 107–115

Veljanovski, C, 'Third-Party Litigation Funding in Europe', *Journal of Law, Economics and Policy*, 8(2012), 405–449

Wagner, G, 'Collective Redress – Categories of Loss and Legislative Options', *Law Quarterly Review*, 127(2011), 55–82

Wahl, N, 'Damages for Infringement of Competition Law', *Scandinavian Studies in Law*, 41(2001), 553–564

Walters, B, '"Best Notice Practicable" in the Twenty-First Century', *UCLA Journal of Law and Technology*, 7(1) (2003), 1–28

Wardhaugh, B, 'Bogeymen, Lunatics and Fanatics: Collective Actions and the Private Enforcement of European Competition Law', *Legal Studies*, 34(1) (2014), 1–23

Weinrib, EJ, 'Deterrence and Corrective Justice', *UCLA Law Review*, 50(2002), 621–640

Wheeler, ME, 'Antitrust Treble-Damage Actions: Do They Work?', *California Law Review*, 61(6) (1973), 1319–1352

Whelan, P, 'Something of a Burden: Is the Passing-On Defence Appropriate?', *Competition Law Insight*, 5(2008), 5–7

Wils, WPJ, 'Should Private Antitrust Enforcement Be Encouraged in Europe?', *World Competition*, 26(3) (2003), 1–21

Wils, WPJ, 'Optimal Antitrust Fines: Theory and Practice', *World Competition*, 29(2) (2006), 183–208

Wils, WPJ, 'The Relationship between Public Antitrust Enforcement and Private Actions for Damages', *World Competition*, 32(2009), 1–32

Woods, TM, 'Wielding the Sledgehammer: Legislative Solutions for Class Action Jurisdictional Reform', *New York University Law Review*, 75(2000), 507–541

Yeazell, SC, 'Group Litigation and Social Context: Toward A History of the Class Action', *Columbia Law Review*, 77(6) (1977), 866–896

Yeazell, SC, 'From Group Litigation to Class Action Part II: Interest, Class, and Representation', *UCLA Law Review*, 27(1980), 1067–1121

Yeazell, SC, 'The Past and Future of Defendant and Settlement Classes in Collective Litigation', *Arizona Law Review*, 39(1997), 687–704

Online articles, speeches, presentations, opinions and news

Akman, P, 'Exploitative Abuse in Article 82EC: Back to Basics?', *University of East Anglia, CCP Working Paper no 09–1*, 2008, 1–37 <http://www.uea.ac.uk/polopoly_fs/1.105848!ccp09-1.pdf> [accessed 1 July 2018]

Alexander, JC, 'An Introduction to Class Action Procedure in The United States' (presented at the Debates over Group Litigation in Comparative Perspective, Geneva, Switzerland, 2000), 1–26 <http://law.duke.edu/grouplit/papers/classactionalexander.pdf> [accessed 27 January 2018]

Almunia, J, 'Common Standards for Group Claims across the EU' (University of Valladolid, School of Law, 2010), 1–7 <http://europa.eu/rapid/pressReleasesAction.do?reference=SPEECH/10/554&format=HTML&aged=0&language=EN&guiLanguage=en> [accessed 1 July 2018]

Berk, SN, 'In the Wake of Concepcion and Dukes, Consumer Class Action Lawyers Must Soldier Forward by Leveraging Their Rich History and Taking Some Clues from the Whistleblower Bar', *The Corporate Observer – Consumer Protection*, 2012 <http://www.thecorporateobserver.com/uploads/file/120111%20Qui%20Tam%20Class%20Action%20Article_FINAL.pdf> [accessed 18 October 2013]

Biard, A, 'Collective Redress in the EU: A Rainbow Behind the Clouds?', *ERA Forum*, 2018, 1–16 <https://www.researchgate.net/publication/325207411_Collective_redress_in_the_EU_a_rainbow_behind_the_clouds> [accessed 3 July 2018]

Binham, C, 'Which? Action to Settle', *The Lawyer*, 2007 <http://www.thelawyer.com/which-action-to-settle/130344.article> [accessed 1 July 2018]

Calisti, D, and L Haasbeek,'The Proposal for a Directive on Antitrust Damages Actions: The European Commission Sets the Stage for Private Enforcement in the European Union', *CPI Antitrust Chronicle*, 2013, 1–9 <https://www.competitionpolicyinternational.com/the-proposal-for-a-directive-on-antitrust-damages-actions-the-european-commission-sets-the-stage-for-private-enforcement-in-the-european-union/> [accessed 1 July 2018]

Cassone, A, and GB Ramello,'The Simple Economics of Class Action: Private Provision of Club and Public Goods', *IEL Paper in Comparative Analysis of Institutions, Economics and Law*, no 3, 2011, 1–18 <http://polis.unipmn.it/pubbl/RePEc/uca/ucaiel/iel003.pdf> [accessed 1 July 2018]

Cauffman, C, and N Philipsen, 'Who Does What in Competition Law: Harmonizing the Rules on Damages for Infringements of the EU Competition Rules?', *Maastricht European Private Law Institute, Working Paper no 2014/19*, 2014, 1–43 <http://awards.concurrences.com/IMG/pdf/who.pdf> [accessed 1 July 2018]

CBI, 'EC Commission Green Paper on Damages Actions – CBI Response', 2006 <http://ec.europa.eu/competition/antitrust/actionsdamages/files_green_paper_comments/cbi.pdf> [accessed 1 July 2018]

CDC, 'Cases' <http://www.carteldamageclaims.com > [accessed 1 July 2018]

CDC, 'Comments on the UK Government's Proposals on Private Actions in Competition Law: A Consultation on Options for Reform Published in April 2012', 2012 <http://www.carteldamageclaims.com/CDC%20Comments_UK%20Proposals%20Private%20Actions%20in%20Competition%20Law_2012.pdf> [accessed 24 January 2013]

Cengiz, F, 'Passing-On Defence and Indirect Purchaser Standing in Actions for Damages against the Violations of Competition Law: What Can the EC Learn from the US?', *University of East Anglia, CCP Working Paper no 07–21*, 2007, 1–42 <http://competitionpolicy.ac.uk/documents/107435/107587/ccp07-21.pdf> [accessed 1 July 2018]

Connor, JM, and RH Lande, 'Optimal Cartel Deterrence: An Empirical Comparison of Sanctions to Overcharges', *American Antitrust Institute Working Paper no 11–08*, 2011, 1–62 <http://works.bepress.com/cgi/viewcontent.cgi?article=1006&context=robert_lande> [accessed 1 July 2018]

de La Serre, EB, 'Will the European Commission Reduce Use of the Commitment Procedure in Dominance Cases?', 2015 <http://www.mondaq.com/unitedstates/x/

395022/Antitrust+Competition/Will+the+European+Commission+Reduce+Use+of+the+Commitment+Procedure+in+Dominance+Cases> [accessed 1 July 2018]

Drexl, J, 'Consumer Actions After the Adoption of the EU Directive on Damage Claims for Competition Law Infringements', *Max Planck Institute for Innovation and Competition Research Paper no 15–10*, 2015, 1–34 <http://papers.ssrn.com/sol3/papers.cfm?abstract_id=2689521> [accessed 1 July 2018]

Flynn, LJ, 'Few Takers for Payments from Microsoft Settlement', *NY Times*, 2005 <http://www.nytimes.com/2005/01/05/technology/05soft.html> [accessed 1 July 2018]

Gac, M, 'Collective Redress v. Class Actions – Convergence or Divergence between the European and American Solutions on Group Litigation?' (presented at the Interaction of National Legal Systems: Convergence or Divergence?, Vilnius: Vilnius University Faculty of Law, 2013), 114–126 <http://www.tf.vu.lt/dokumentai/naujienos/Renginiai/tarptautine_studentu_konferencija_2013.pdf> [accessed 1 July 2018]

Gerard, DMB, 'Price Discrimination under Article 82(2) (C) EC: Clearing up the Ambiguities', *Global Competition Law Centre Research Paper on the Modernisation of Article 82 EC*, 2005, 1–29 <http://ssrn.com/abstract=1113354> [accessed 1 July 2018]

Gubbay, I, 'Which? Consultation Response – Green Paper on Damages Actions for Breach of the EC Antitrust Rules', 2006, 1–14 <http://ec.europa.eu/competition/antitrust/actionsdamages/files_green_paper_comments/which.pdf> [accessed 1 July 2018]

Halfmeier, A, 'The Revised German KapMuG' (presented at the Righting Private Wrongs: Competition Law, Investor Claims and Mass Litigation in the EU, London: BIICL, 2013)

Herman, M, 'Everyone's a Winner in Football Shirts Settlement', *The Times*, 2008 <http://www.thetimes.co.uk/tto/law/article2210528.ece> [accessed 1 July 2018]

Hodges, C, 'US Class Actions: Promise and Reality', *EUI Working Papers no Law 2015/36*, 2015, 1–36 <http://cadmus.eui.eu/bitstream/handle/1814/36536/LAW_2015_36.pdf?sequence=1> [accessed 1 July 2018]

Hovenkamp, H, 'Quantification of Harm in Private Antitrust Actions in the United States', *University of Iowa Legal Studies Research Paper*, 2011, 1–10 <http://dx.doi.org/10.2139/ssrn.1758751> [accessed 1 July 2018]

Hviid, M, and S Peyer, 'Response to EC Consultation "Towards a Coherent European Approach to Collective Redress"', 2011, 1–7 <http://ec.europa.eu/competition/consultations/2011_collective_redress/hviid_peyer_en.pdf> [accessed 1 July 2018]

Inderst, R, F Maier-Rigaud and U Schwalbe, 'Umbrella Effects', *IESEG School of Management Working Paper no 2013-ECO-17*, 2013, 1–22 <http://www.ieseg.fr/wp-content/uploads/2013-ECO-17_Maier-Rigaud.pdf> [1 July 2018]

Kirwan, K, 'Debunking the "Umbrella Theory" of Antitrust Standing', 2012, 1–3 <http://www.lexology.com/library/detail.aspx?g=47c9ad69-0334-4b02-a4be-6f89746a5c71> [accessed 1 July 2018]

Komninos, AP, 'Relationship between Public and Private Enforcement: Quod Dei Deo, Quod Caesaris Caesari' (presented at the 16th Annual EU Competition Law and Policy Workshop – Integrating Public and Private Enforcement of Competition Law: Implications for Courts and Agencies, Florence, 2011), 1–26 <http://ssrn.com/abstract=1870723> [accessed 1 July 2018]

Kroes, N, 'Making Consumers' Right to Damages a Reality: The Case for Collective Redress Mechanisms in Antitrust Claims' (presented at the Conference on Collective Redress for European Consumers, Lisbon, 2007), 1–5 <http://europa.eu/rapid/pressReleasesAction.do?reference=SPEECH/07/698&format=HTML&aged=0&language=EN&guiLanguage=en> [1 July 2018]

Kroes, N, 'Reinforcing the Fight against Cartels and Developing Private Antitrust Damage Actions: Two Tools for a More Competitive Europe' (presented at the Commission/ IBA Joint Conference on EC Competition Policy, Brussels, 2007), 1–6 <http://europa.eu/rapid/press-release_SPEECH-07-128_en.htm?locale=fr> [accessed 1 July 2018]

Laitenberger, U, and F Smuda, 'Estimating Consumer Damages in Cartel Cases', *ZEW Discussion Paper no 13–069*, 2013, 1–19 <http://papers.ssrn.com/sol3/papers.cfm?abstract_id=2333598> [accessed 1 July 2018]

Leczykiewicz, D, 'Enforcement or Compensation? Damages Actions in EU Law after the Draft Common Frame of Reference', *Oxford Legal Studies Research Paper no 59/2012*, 2012, 1–18 <http://papers.ssrn.com/sol3/papers.cfm?abstract_id=2159722> [accessed 1 July 2018]

Lein, E, 'Germany', *Focus on Collective Redress* <http://www.collectiveredress.org/collective-redress/reports/germany/overview> [accessed 1 July 2018]

Leskinen, C, 'Collective Antitrust Damages Actions in the EU: The Opt-in v. the Opt-out Model', *IE Law School Working Paper no 10–03*, 2010, 1–56 <http://papers.ssrn.com/sol3/papers.cfm?abstract_id=1612731> [accessed 1 July 2018]

Levenstein, MC, and VY Suslow, 'Breaking up Is Hard to Do: Determinants of Cartel Duration', *University of Michigan, Ross School of Business, Working Paper no 1150*, 2010, 1–50 <http://www-personal.umich.edu/~maggiel/Duration.pdf> [accessed 1 July 2017]

Lindblom, PH, 'National Report: Group Litigation in Sweden' (presented at the Globalisation of Class Actions, Oxford, 2007), 1–47 <http://globalclassactions.stanford.edu/sites/default/files/documents/Sweden_National_Report.pdf> [accessed 1 July 2018]

Lundgren, N, *Report on the White Paper on Damages Actions for Breach of the EC Antitrust Rules*, Debates of the European Parliament, 2009, 1–135 <http://www.europarl.europa.eu/sides/getDoc.do?pubRef=-//EP//NONSGML+CRE+20090325+SIT+DOC+PDF+V0//EN&language=EN> [accessed 1 July 2018]

Lyons, B, 'The Paradox of the Exclusion of Exploitative Abuse', *University of East Anglia, CCP Working Paper no 08–1*, 2007, 1–20 <http://competitionpolicy.ac.uk/documents/107435/107587/ccp08-1.pdf> [accessed 1 July 2018]

Maier-Rigaud, F, 'Towards a European Directive on Damages Actions', *IESEG School of Management Working Paper no 2013-ECO-16*, 2013, 1–19 <http://lem.cnrs.fr/LinkClick.aspx?fileticket=ujRpEFT6XrY%3D&tabid=1198&language=fr-FR> [accessed 1 July 2018]

Marcos, F, 'Competition Law Private Litigation in the Spanish Courts (1999–2012)', *IE Law School Working Paper no AJ8–202*, 2013, 1–111 <http://ssrn.com/abstract=2351770> [accessed 1 July 2018]

Mazurkeviciute, A, 'Determinants of the European Price-Fixing Cartels' Duration: Focus on Internal Cartel Organization' (presented at the X Workshop SIEPI, Perugia: IEL, Collegio Carlo Alberto, 2012), 1–53 <http://www.siepi.univpm.it/sites/www.siepi.univpm.it/files/siepi/SIEPI%202012/papers/MAZURKEVICIUTE.pdf> [accessed 18 July 2013]

Microsoft-California Class Action Settlement, 'Finding Your Proof of Purchase Identifying Numbers' <http://www.microsoftcalsettlement.com/FindIDNumbers.htm> [accessed 1 July 2018]

Motta, M, 'Cartels in the European Union: Economics, Law, Practice' (presented at the Fifty Years of the Treaty: Assessment and Perspectives of Competition Policy in Europe, IESE Business School, Barcelona, 2007), 1–32 <http://www.barcelonagse.eu/tmp/pdf/motta_cartelseulaw.pdf> [accessed 1 July 2018]

Mulheron, R, 'Antitrust Litigation: A White Paper Tinged with Green?', *Brussels Agenda, the Viewpoint Contribution*, 2008 <http://www.hadjimichalis.gr/keimena/Brussels_Agenda/Brussels_Agenda_2008_05.pdf> [accessed 1 July 2018]

Mulheron, R, *Reform of Collective Redress in England and Wales: A Perspective of Need* (CJC, 2008), 1–161 <https://www.judiciary.gov.uk/wp-content/uploads/JCO/Documents/CJC/Publications/Other+papers/reform-of-collective-redress.pdf> [accessed 1 July 2018]

Mulheron, R, *Costs and Funding of Collective Actions: Realities and Possibilities*, A Research Paper for Submission to the European Consumers' Organisation (BEUC) (Brussels, 2011), 1–133 <http://www.law.qmul.ac.uk/docs/staff/department/71112.pdf> [accessed 1 July 2018]

Mulheron, R, 'In a Nutshell' (presented at the Rapid Response Seminar: Consumer Rights Act 2015 – The UK Class Action: A Reaction, London, 2015)

Mullenix, LS, 'Competing Values: Preserving Litigant Autonomy in an Age of Collective Redress', *University of Texas, Public Law and Legal Theory Research Paper Series no 533*, 2014, 1–34 <http://papers.ssrn.com/sol3/papers.cfm?abstract_id=2426829> [accessed 1 July 2018]

NERA Economic Consulting, 'Memo: Comments in Relation to the White Paper on Damages Actions for Breach of the EC Antitrust Rules', 2008 <http://ec.europa.eu/competition/antitrust/actionsdamages/white_paper_comments/nera_en.pdf> [1 July 2018]

Nordh, A, 'Group Actions – The Swedish Experience' (presented at the Colloque actions collectives Cour de Cassation, France, 2005), 1–14 <http://www.courdecassation.fr/IMG/File/judge_nordh.pdf> [accessed 1 July 2018]

Peyer, S, 'Private Enforcement of Competition Law – A Case Study from Germany', *University of East Anglia, CCP Working Paper no 10–12*, 2010, 1–74 <http://competitionpolicy.ac.uk/documents/8158338/8256105/CCP+Working+Paper+10-12.pdf/fedbb885-d48d-4506-86e6-42dba23b8980> [accessed 1 July 2018]

Popofsky, L, 'Opt Out Antitrust Class Actions – An American Perspective' (Oxford University, Centre for Competition Law and Policy, Oxford, 2014), 1–21 <http://lawprofessors.typepad.com/files/popofsky.pdf> [accessed 1 July 2018]

Rodrigue, S, and L Plumpton, 'The Globalisation of Anti-Trust: How the Internationalisation of Collective Redress Is Changing the Game', *Class and Group Actions 2014*, 2013, 31–39 <http://www.torys.com/Publications/Documents/Publication%20PDFs/CA2013-4.pdf> [accessed 1 July 2018]

Rosch, JT, 'Designing a Private Remedies System for Antitrust Caes – Lessons Learned from the U.S. Experience' (presented at the Remarks of Federal Trade Commissioner before the 16th Annual EU Competition Law and Policy Workshop, Italy, 2011) 1–28 <http://www.ftc.gov/sites/default/files/documents/public_statements/designing-private-remedies-system-antitrust-cases-lessons-learned-u.s.experience/110617roschprivateremedies.pdf> [accessed 1 July 2018]

Simard, LS, 'Fees, Incentives and Deterrence: A Reply to Professor Fitzpatrick', *Suffolk University Law School Research Paper no 11–22*, 2011, 1–9 <http://ssrn.com/abstract=1832828> [accessed 1 July 2018].

Smith, V, 'European Commission Public Consultation "Towards a Coherent European Approach to Collective Redress"', 2011, 1–17 <http://ec.europa.eu/competition/consultations/2011_collective_redress/smith_vincent_en.pdf> [accessed 1 July 2018]

Tulibacka, M, 'Poland', *Focus on Collective Redress* <http://www.collectiveredress.org/collective-redress/reports/poland/generalcollectiveredressmechanisms> [accessed 1 July 2018]

Van der Woude, M, ‘The General Court: The Need and Opportunity for Reform’ (King’s College, London, 2013) <http://www.kcl.ac.uk/law/research/centres/european/KCL-Marc-van-der-Woude-GC-Reform-08-03-13.pdf> [29 January 2015]

Van Dijck, G, ‘Class Membership in Class Actions: An Experimental Study’, *Tilburg Law School Research Paper no 013/2011*, 2011, 1–43 <http://papers.ssrn.com/sol3/papers.cfm?abstract_id=1641174> [accessed 1 July 2018]

Wallis, D, ‘EU Initiatives in the Area of Collective Redress – Which Options?’ (presented at the Righting Private Wrongs: Competition Law, Investor Claims and Mass Litigation in the EU, London: BIICL, 2013)

Weber, F, ‘Assessing Existing Enforcement Mechanisms in Consumer Law – The Unavailability of an Allrounder’, *Rotterdam Institute of Law and Economics (RILE) Working Paper Series no 2011/7*, 2011, 542–560 <http://ssrn.com/abstract=1962665> [accessed 1 July 2018]

Which?, ‘JJB to Pay Fans over Football Shirt Rip-off: Which? Helps Consumers to Get Cash Back’, 9 January2008 <http://www.which.co.uk/news/2008/01/jjb-to-pay-fans-over-football-shirt-rip-off-128985/> [accessed 1 July 2018]

Zöttl, J, S Clerckx and F Amato, ‘Antitrust Alert: EU Commission Proposes New Measures to Foster Damages Litigation’, 2013 <http://m.jonesday.com/antitrust-alert–eu-commission-proposes-new-measures-to-foster-damages-litigation-06-20-2013/> [accessed 1 July 2018]

Institutional Reports, Working Papers and Commentaries

Antitrust Modernization Commission, *Report and Recommendations*, 2007, 1–449 <http://govinfo.library.unt.edu/amc/report_recommendation/amc_final_report.pdf> [accessed 1 July 2018]

BEUC, *Group Action: The Missing Tool* (Brussels, 2008), 1–26 <http://ec.europa.eu/consumers/archive/redress_cons/responses/BEUC_en.pdf> [accessed 1 July 2018]

BIS, *Private Actions in Competition Law – A Consultation on Options for Reform* (London, 2012)

BIS, *Private Actions in Competition Law: A Consultation on Options for Reform – Impact Assessment* (London, 2012)

BIS, *Private Actions in Competition Law: A Consultation on Options for Reform – Final Impact Assessment* (London, 2013)

BIS, *Private Actions in Competition Law: A Consultation on Options for Reform – Government Response* (London, 2013)

Centre for European Policy Studies (CEPS), Erasmus University Rotterdam (EUR) and Luiss Guido Carli (LUISS), *Report for the European Commission ‘Making Antitrust Damages Actions More Effective in the EU: Welfare Impact and Potential Scenarios’, Final Report*, 2007

Civic Consulting (Lead) and Oxford Economics, *Commission – DG SANCO, Evaluation of the Effectiveness and Efficiency of Collective Redress Mechanisms in the European Union, Final Report, Part I: Main Report* (SANCO/2007/B4/004, Brussels, 2008)

Civic Consulting of the Consumer Policy Evaluation Consortium, *Commission – DG SANCO, Study Regarding the Problems Faced by Consumers in Obtaining Redress for Infringements of Consumer Protection Legislation, and the Economic Consequences of Such Problems, Final Report, Part I: Main Report* (Brussels, 2008)

CJC, *Report of the Working Party on Damages Based Agreements (Contingency Fees)*, 2012, 1–11 <http://www.judiciary.gov.uk/wp-content/uploads/JCO/Documents/CJC/

Publications/Pre-action+protocols/contingency-fees-working-party-report1.pdf> [accessed 1 July 2018]

Commission, *Consumer Redress – Commission Memorandum to the Council* (COM(84) 692, Luxembourg, 1984) <http://aei.pitt.edu/1597/1/1597.pdf> [accessed 1 July 2018]

Commission, *Thirteenth Report on Competition Policy (published in Conjunction with the 'Seventeenth General Report on the Activities of the European Communities 1983'*, 1984

Commission, *Three Year Action Plan of Consumer Policy in the EEC (1990–1992)* (COM (90) 98 final, Brussels, 1990) <http://aei.pitt.edu/3712/> [accessed 1 July 2018]

Commission, *Internal Market After 1992: Meeting the Challenge (the Sutherland Report)* (SEC(92) 2044, 1992), 10–12 <http://aei.pitt.edu/1025/1/Market_post_1992_Sutherland_1.pdf> [accessed 1 July 2018]

Commission, *Action Plan on Consumer Access to Justice and the Settlement of Consumer Disputes in the Internal Market* (COM(96) 13 final, Brussels, 1996) <http://eur-lex.europa.eu/LexUriServ/LexUriServ.do?uri=COM:1996:0013:FIN:EN:PDF> [accessed 1 July 2018]

Commission, *'White Paper on Modernisation of the Rules Implementing Articles [101] and [102] of the EC Treaty' Commission Programme No 99/027* (COM(1999) 101 final, Brussels, 1999)

Commission, *Green Paper on Damages Actions for Breach of EC Antitrust Rules* (COM (2005) 672 final, Brussels, 2005)

Commission, *Staff Working Paper Annex to the Green Paper Damages actions for breach of the EC antitrust rules* (SEC(2005)1732, Brussels, 2005)

Commission – Communication from the Commission to the Council, the European Parliament and the EESC, *EU Consumer Policy Strategy 2007–2013: Empowering Consumers, Enhancing Their Welfare, Effectively Protecting Them* (COM(2007) 99 final, Brussels, 2007)

Commission, *Green Paper on Consumer Collective Redress* (COM(2008) 794 final, Brussels, 2008)

Commission, *White Paper on Damages Actions for Breach of the EC Antitrust Rules* (COM (2008) 165 final, Brussels, 2008)

Commission, *Staff Working Paper Accompanying the White Paper on Damages Actions for Breach of the EC Antitrust Rules* (SEC(2008) 404, Brussels, 2008)

Commission, *Staff Working Document Accompanying Document to the White Paper on Damages Actions for Breach of the EC Antitrust Rules – Impact Assessment* (SEC(2008) 405, Brussels, 2008)

Commission, *Communication on the Commission Legislative and Work Programme 2009: Acting Now for a Better Europe* (COM(2008) 712 final, vol.1, Brussels, 2008)

Commission, *Proposal for a Council Directive on Rules Governing Damages Actions for Infringements of Articles [101] and [102] of the Treaty*, 2009 <http://allegati.unina.it/postlaurea/perf/Exclusiva_Juridico.pdf> [1 July 2018]

Commission, *Consultation Paper for Discussion on the Follow-up to the Green Paper on Consumer Collective Redress*, 2009 <http://ec.europa.eu/consumers/redress_cons/docs/consultation_paper2009.pdf> [accessed 1 July 2018]

Commission, *Consumer Redress in the European Union: Consumer Experiences, Perceptions, and Choices – Aggregated Report*, 2009 <http://ec.europa.eu/consumers/redress_cons/docs/cons_redress_EU_qual_study_report_en.pdf> [accessed 1 July 2018]

Commission, *Communication on the Commission Work Programme 2010: Time to Act* (COM(2010) 135 final, vol.1, Brussels, 2010)

Commission, *Towards a Coherent European Approach to Collective Redress: Next Steps – Joint Information Note by Vice-President Viviane Reding, Vice-President Joaquín Almunia and Commissioner John Dalli* (SEC(2010) 1192 OJ 1932, Brussels, 2010) <http://kartellblog.de/wordpress/wp-content/uploads/Kommission-2010-information-Towards-European-Collective-Redress> [accessed 1 July 2018]

Commission, *Consumer Attitudes towards Cross-Border Trade and Consumer Protection: Analytical Report*, 2011 <http://ec.europa.eu/consumers/strategy/docs/consumer_eurobarometer_2011_en.pdf> [accessed 1 July 2018]

Commission, *Staff Working Document Public Consultation: 'Towards a Coherent European Approach to Collective Redress'* (SEC(2011)173 final, Brussels, 2011)

Commission, *Detailed Minutes of the Public Hearing 'Towards a Coherent European Approach to Collective Redress'* (Brussels, 2011) <http://ec.europa.eu/competition/consultations/2011_collective_redress/study_heidelberg_hearing_en.pdf> [accessed 1 July 2018]

Commission, *Draft Guidance Paper: Quantifying Harm in Actions for Damages Based on Breaches of Article 101 or 102 of the Treaty on the Functioning of the European Union – Public Consultation* (Brussels, 2011)

Commission, *Frequently Asked Questions: Commission Proposes Legislation to Facilitate Damage Claims by Victims of Antitrust Violations* (MEMO/13/531, Brussels, 2013), 1–4 <http://europa.eu/rapid/press-release_MEMO-13-531_en.htm> [accessed 1 July 2018]

Commission, *Frequently Asked Questions: European Commission Recommends Collective Redress Principles to Member States* (MEMO/13/530, Strasbourg, 2013)

Commission, *Communication from the Commission on Quantifying Harm in Actions for Damages Based on Breaches of Article 101 or 102 of the Treaty on the Functioning of the European Union* (OJ C 167/19, 2013)

Commission, *Executive Summary of the Impact Assessment – Damages Actions for Breach of the EU Antitrust Rules, Accompanying the Proposal for a Directive of the European Parliament and of the Council on Certain Rules Governing Actions for Damages under National Law for Infringements of the Competition Law Provisions of the Member States and of the European Union* (SWD(2013) 204 final, Strasbourg, 2013)

Commission, *Staff Working Document – Impact Assessment Report – Damages Actions for Breach of the EU Antitrust Rules Accompanying the Proposal for a Directive of the European Parliament and of the Council on Certain Rules Governing Actions for Damages under National Law for Infringements of the Competition Law Provisions of the Member States and of the European Union* (SWD(2013) 203 final, Strasbourg, 2013)

Commission, *Press Release on Antitrust: Commission Proposes Legislation to Facilitate Damage Claims by Victims of Antitrust Violations* (IP/13/525, Brussels, 2013) <http://europa.eu/rapid/press-release_IP-13-525_en.htm> [accessed 1 July 2018]

Commission, *Press Release: Commission Recommends Member States to Have Collective Redress Mechanisms in Place to Ensure Effective Access to Justice* (Strasbourg, 2013) <http://europa.eu/rapid/press-release_IP-13-524_en.htm> [accessed 1 July 2018]

Commission, *Communication from the Commission to the European Parliament, the Council, the European Economic and Social Committee and the Committee of the Regions 'Towards a European Horizontal Framework for Collective Redress'* (COM(2013) 401/2, Brussels, 2013)

Commission, *Recommendation on Common Principles for Injunctive and Compensatory Collective Redress Mechanisms in the Member States Concerning Violations of Rights Granted Under Union Law* (Strasbourg, C(2013) 3539/3, 2013)

Commission, *Proposal for a Directive of the European Parliament and of the Council on Certain Rules Governing Actions for Damages under National Law for Infringements of the Competition Law Provisions of the Member States and of the European Union* (2013/0185 (COD), COM(2013) 404 final, Strasbourg, 2013)

Commission, *Staff Working Document: Practical Guide Quantifying Harm in Actions for Damages Based on Breaches of Article 101 Or 102 of the Treaty on the Functioning of the European Union Accompanying the Communication from the Commission on Quantifying Harm in Actions for Damages Based on Breaches of Article 101 or 102 of the Treaty on the Functioning of the European Union* (SWD(2013) 205, Strasbourg, 2013)

Commission, 'Commission Work Programmes', *European Commission at Work*, 2017 <http://ec.europa.eu/atwork/key-documents/index_en.htm> [accessed 1 July 2018]

Commission, 'European Competition Network (ECN) Statistics', 2017 <http://ec.europa.eu/competition/ecn/statistics.html#3> [accessed 1 July 2018]

Commission, 'Competition: Delivering for Consumers', 2012 <http://ec.europa.eu/competition/consumers/index_en.html> [accessed 1 July 2018]

Commission, *Study on the State of Collective Redress in the EU in the Context of the Implementation of the Commission Recommendation* prepared by the British Institute of International and Comparative Law (JUST/2016/JCOO/FW/CIVI/0099, 2017)

Commission, *Press Release on Commission Work Programme 2018: An Agenda for a More United, Stronger and More Democratic Europe* (IP/17/4002, Strasbourg, 2017) <http://europa.eu/rapid/press-release_IP-17-4002_en.htm> [accessed 1 July 2018]

Commission, *Communication from the Commission to the European Parliament, The Council, The European Economic and Social Committee and the Committee of the Regions – Commission Work Programme 2018* (COM(2017) 650 final, Strasbourg, 2017)

Commission, *Inception Impact Assessment: A New Deal for Consumers – Revision of the Injunctions Directive*, (Ares (2017)5324969, 2017) <www.ec.europa.eu/info/law/better-regulation/initiatives/ares-2017-5324969_en> [accessed 3 July 2018]

Commission, *Report from The Commission to The European Parliament, The Council and The European Economic and Social Committee on the Implementation of the Commission Recommendation of 11 June 2013 on Common Principles for Injunctive and Compensatory Collective Redress Mechanisms in the Member States Concerning Violations of Rights Granted under Union Law*, (COM(2018) 40 final, Brussels, 2018)

Commission, *Proposal for a Directive of the European Parliament and of the Council amending Council Directive 93/13/EEC of 5 April 1993, Directive 98/6/EC of the European Parliament and of the Council, Directive 2005/29/EC of the European Parliament and of the Council and Directive 2011/83/EU of the European Parliament and of the Council as Regards Better Enforcement and Modernisation of EU Consumer Protection Rules* (COM(2018) 185 final, 2018/0090(COD), Brussels, 2018)

ELI, 'Statement of the European Law Institute on Collective Redress and Competition Damages Claims', 2014, 1–81 <http://www.europeanlawinstitute.eu/fileadmin/user_upload/p_eli/Projects/S-5-2014_Statement_on_Collective_Redress_and_Competition_Damages_Claims.pdf> [accessed 1 July 2018]

European Consumer Consultative Group, *Opinion on Private Damages Actions*, 2010 <http://ec.europa.eu/dgs/health_consumer/dgs_consultations/docs/eccg/eccg_opinion_on_actions_for_damages_18112010_en.pdf> [accessed 1 July 2018]

European Parliament, ECON, *Draft Report on the White Paper on Damages Actions for Breach of the EC Antitrust Rules*, (2008/2154(INI), 2008) <http://www.europarl.europa.eu/sides/getDoc.do?pubRef=-//EP//NONSGML+COMPARL+PE-412.315+01+DOC+PDF+V0//EN&language=EN> [accessed 1 July 2018]

European Parliament, reporter K-H Lehne, *Report on the White Paper on Damages Actions for Breach of the EC Antitrust Rules*, Debates of the European Parliament, 2009, 1–135 <http://www.europarl.europa.eu/sides/getDoc.do?pubRef=-//EP//NONSGML+CRE+20090325+SIT+DOC+PDF+V0//EN&language=EN> [accessed 1 July 2018]

European Parliament, *European Parliament Resolution of 26 March 2009 on the White Paper on Damages Actions for Breach of the EC Antitrust Rules* (2008/2154(INI), Strasbourg, 2009) <http://www.europarl.europa.eu/sides/getDoc.do?pubRef=-//EP//NONSGML+TA+P6-TA-2009-0187+0+DOC+PDF+V0//EN> [accessed 1 July 2018]

European Parliament, *Resolution on 'Towards a Coherent European Approach to Collective Redress'* (2011/2089(INI), 2012) <http://www.europarl.europa.eu/sides/getDoc.do?pubRef=-//EP//TEXT+TA+P7-TA-2012-0021+0+DOC+XML+V0//EN> [accessed 1 July 2018]

European Parliament, *Motion for a European Parliament Resolution on 'Towards a Coherent European Approach to Collective Redress'* (2011/2089(INI), 2012) <http://www.europarl.europa.eu/sides/getDoc.do?type=REPORT&language=EN&reference=A7-0012/2012#title1> [accessed 1 July 2018]

European Parliament, Directorate-General for Internal Policies, *Collective Redress in Antitrust* (IP/A/ECON/ST/2011–2019, 2012)

European Parliament, *Opinion of the Committee on the Internal Market and Consumer Protection for the Committee on Economic and Monetary Affairs on the Proposal for a Directive of the European Parliament and of the Council on Certain Rules Governing Actions for Damages under National Law for Infringements of the Competition Law Provisions of the Member States and of the European Union* (COM(2013)0404 – C7–0170/2013–2013/0185(COD), 2014) <http://www.europarl.europa.eu/sides/getDoc.do?type=REPORT&reference=A7-2014-0089&format=XML&language=EN#top> [accessed 1 July 2018]

Federal Judicial Center, 'Manual for Complex Litigation (fourth)' 2004 <http://www.fjc.gov/public/pdf.nsf/lookup/MCL40000.pdf/$file/MCL40000.pdf> [accessed 1 July 2018]

Federal Judicial Center, 'Judges' Class Action Notice and Claims Process Check List and Plain Language Guide', 2010 <http://www.fjc.gov/public/pdf.nsf/lookup/NotCheck.pdf/$file/NotCheck.pdf> [accessed 1 July 2018]

ICC, 'ICC Comments on the Commission's Green Paper on Damages Actions for Breach of the EC Antitrust Rules', 2006 <http://ec.europa.eu/competition/antitrust/actionsdamages/files_green_paper_comments/icc.pdf> [accessed 1 July 2018]

Ministry of Justice, *The Government's Response to the Civil Justice Council's Report: 'Improving Access to Justice through Collective Actions'*, 2009 <http://collections.europarchive.org/tna/20100208150045/http:/www.justice.gov.uk/about/docs/government-response-cjc-collective-actions.pdf> [accessed 1 July 2018]

Notes of Advisory Committee on Rules – *1966 Amendment to Rule 23(b)(3)*, 1996 <http://www.law.cornell.edu/rules/frcp/rule_23> [accessed 1 July 2018]

OECD, *Recommendation of the Council Concerning Effective Action against Hard Core Cartels* (C(98)35/FINAL, 1998), 1–4 <http://www.oecd.org/daf/competition/2350130.pdf> [accessed 1 July 2018]

OECD, *Quantification of Harm to Competition by National Courts and Competition Agencies* (DAF/COMP(2011)25, 2011) <http://www.oecd.org/daf/competition/QuantificationofHarmtoCompetition2011.pdf> [accessed 1 July 2018]

Oxera, A Komninos and others, *Quantifying Antitrust Damages – Towards Non-binding Guidance for Courts*, Study Prepared for the Commission (Luxembourg, 2009)

RBB Economics and Cuatrecasas, Gonçalves Pereira, *Study on the Passing-on of Overcharges*, Study Prepared for the Commission (Brussels, 2016)

The Law Reform Commission of Hong Kong, 'Class Actions', 2012, 1–313 <http://www.hkreform.gov.hk/en/publications/rclassactions.htm> [accessed1 July 2018]

The Law Society of England and Wales, '*Response to Towards a Coherent European Approach to Collective Redress*', 2011 <http://ec.europa.eu/competition/consultations/2011_collective_redress/law_society_of_england_and_wales_en.pdf> [accessed 1 July 2018]

Tortell, L, *Evaluation of the Effectiveness and Efficiency of Collective Redress Mechanisms in the European Union – Country Report Portugal*, 2008, 1–33 <http://ec.europa.eu/consumers/archive/redress_cons/pt-country-report-final.pdf> [accessed 1 July 2018]

UK Government, 'UK Response to EU Consultation on Collective Redress', 2011 <http://ec.europa.eu/competition/consultations/2011_collective_redress/uk_en.pdf> [accessed 1 July 2018]

Waelbroeck, D, D Slater and G Even-Shoshan, *Ashurst Study on the Conditions of Claims for Damages in Case of Infringement of EC Competition Rules, Comparative Report* (Brussels, 2004)

Index

For Product Safety Concerns and Information please contact our EU
representative GPSR@taylorandfrancis.com
Taylor & Francis Verlag GmbH, Kaufingerstraße 24, 80331 München, Germany

www.ingramcontent.com/pod-product-compliance
Ingram Content Group UK Ltd.
Pitfield, Milton Keynes, MK11 3LW, UK
UKHW022132190926
475702UK00013B/1765
* 9 7 8 1 0 3 2 2 4 1 6 7 8 *